MARKSMANSHIP IN THE U.S. ARMY

MARKSMANSHIP IN THE U.S. ARMY

A HISTORY OF MEDALS, SHOOTING PROGRAMS, AND TRAINING

BY WILLIAM K. EMERSON

UNIVERSITY OF OKLAHOMA PRESS : NORMAN

To Duncan Campbell

Other books by William K. Emerson

Chevrons: An Illustrated History (Washington, D.C., 1983)
An Encyclopedia of United States Army Insignia and Uniforms
(Norman, Okla., 1996)

Library of Congress Cataloging-in-Publication Data

Emreson, William K., 1941–
    Marksmanship in the U.S. Army: a history of
  medals, shooting programs, and training / by
  William K. Emerson.
      p.   cm.
  Includes bibliographical references and index.
  ISBN 0-8061-3575-1 (alk. paper)
    1. Shooting, Military—United States—History.
  2. Sharpshooting (Military science)—United States—
  History.   3. United States. Army—Medals, badges,
  decoration, etc.   I. Title.

  UD333.E44 2004
  355.5'47'0973—dc22

                     2004041230

The Orders and Medals Society of America endorses William K. Emerson's *Marksmanship in the U.S. Army* as a standard reference work.

Dean S. Veremakis
President OMSA

The Company of Military Historians, through its Reviewing Board, takes pride in sponsoring *Marksmanship in the U.S. Army* as a standard reference in American Military History.

Joseph M. Thatcher
President

CONTENTS

TABLES

PREFACE

MANY PEOPLE HAVE A passing interest in army artifacts—a person may be curious about a trinket that a relative earned, a collector may want to complete a grouping, or a researcher may be tracing the significance of a medal. Whatever the case, Americans count on references that help identify badges, medals, and insignia. In addition, historians study army training, hardware, and tactics in order to determine whether battle captains applied these resources properly. In this book these two general areas intersect. Its purpose is both to identify U.S. Army–related weapons badges, prizes, and trophies and to provide their origin.

The U.S. Army had a chance to begin serious marksmanship training just before the Civil War, when Captain Henry Heth published the army's new training manual on shooting. Lack of command emphasis led to situations in which some soldiers in battle loaded their weapons successive times without firing. During the early wars pitting Indians against the U.S. Army, the military usually prevailed by sheer numbers and persistence. It was after the Indians defeated George Custer that the army took shooting training seriously. Skilled marksmen came to the forefront as sportsmen in Europe, especially in Great Britain, coincidently with the American Civil War. Britain soon exported shooting contests to the American East. The New York National Guard adapted long-range firing as a training goal and instituted the first regular shooting award in the United States, although certainly other militia units had their contests and gave special prizes. The history of the many army awards for rifle and pistol proficiency has become lost over the years.

The nation's heavy artillery that guarded our coasts in the 1880s also began to recognize skills through the presentation of unique badges and insignia, continuing to do so for more than half a century. After the introduction of many new weapons during World War I, the army changed its approach and provided a set of three badges that showed skill levels and then applied this concept to virtually all weapons, from grenades to aerial bombs. The U.S. Army still uses this set of badges today.

Prizes, given by the army at special contests, logically followed from badges. These highly collectable artifacts, starting with those introduced in the nineteenth century, changed considerably over time. Perhaps because the prizes represent the highest levels of proficiency, weapons collectors in particular like to gather some of these relics. Others collect prizes because famous soldiers won them. These prizes, given at annual contests, have also come and gone without anyone's recording and publishing their history.

A wide range of organizations have sponsored trophies for military skills such as shooting, and trophies frequently come with medals to those individuals who helped win the award. Many famous trophies were given at Camp Perry, Ohio, as it became the shooting Mecca early in the twentieth century. Soldiers competed for these trophies and medals, and the National Rifle Association worked closely with the military for many years in hosting the events. Given the close relationship between national marksmanship matches and military shooting, some key trophies are included, as are less well-known and more mundane awards such as pocket patches given for tank gunnery.

I hope that this summation of weapons-proficiency awards and their history will help those interested in army history in general, as well as military collectors, weapons connois-seurs, marksmen past, present, and future, and students of tactics and training.

WILLIAM K. EMERSON
Madison, Alabama

ACKNOWLEDGMENTS

PORTIONS OF THE INFORMATION contained in this book initially appeared in the *Journal* of the Orders and Medals Society of America. The author thanks the members of the Orders and Medals Society of America for their positive comments regarding these early articles. The author also wishes to thank the following for their assistance in the preparation of this book; without their help it would not have been possible. Many collectors, researchers, competitive shooters, institutions, army units, and historians assisted in the assembly of data. They include: Alan C. Aimone; Gary Anderson; Armor School Library; Army Marksmanship Unit; Robert Aylward; Leonard Ball; William A. Barrett; John Beard; William Block; Robert Borrell; Walter Bradford; Thomas R. Buecker; Martin Callahan; Duncan Campbell; Ray P. Carter; Casemate Museum, Fort Monroe, Virginia; Center of Military History; Civilian Marksmanship Program; John W. Cook; Charles H. Cureton; Charles D. Davis; Gary Delscamp; Deputy Chief of Staff for Personnel, Department of the Army's office; Director of Civilian Marksmanship's office; Thomas C. Duclos; Colonel John Elting; Marcie S. Emerson; Phillip W. Emerson; Robert E. Emerson; George Ernhard; Marla Faulker; Ronald E. Fischer; Fort Sill Command Historian's office; David Foster; Thomas W. Fugate; Albert Garland; Master Sergeant (Ret.) Dan Gillotti; Albert Gleim; Carl-Eric Granfelt; John J. Grubar; Kenneth Hamill; Donald W. Harpold; William Henry; Hoover Institution on War, Revolution, and Peace, Stanford University; John Huffman; Huntsville, Alabama, Public Library; Infantry Museum; Infantry School Library; The Institute of Heraldry; David J. Johnson; The Kentucky Military History Museum; Nancy King, Marine Corps Museum; Fort Leavenworth Library; Library of Congress; Thomas McDougall; U.S. Marine Corps Museum; Joseph Massaro; Marsha L. Moody; National Archives; National Rifle Association; Nevada State Archives; New York State Historical Society; Ohio Historical Society; Hayes Otoupalik; Dr. Buddy Patterson; Dave Parham; Patton Museum of Cavalry and Armor; The Pennsylvania State Library; Pentagon Library; Charles Pfeiffer; Willis L. Powell; Christie Prantice; Cliff Presley; John M. Purdy; Fort Robinson, Nebraska; Rock Island Arsenal Museum; ROTC Instructor Group, University of Hawaii; James A. Sawicki; Ken Smith-Christmas; Sarah Smith; Dr. George Snook; Hubbie Snyder; John Stacy; General (Ret.) Donn Starry; Textual Reference Division, National Archives; Joseph Thatcher; Thomas N. Trevor; U.S. Military Academy Library; University of Kansas Libraries; Terry VanMeter; West Point Museum; Todd Wheatley; Richard Williams; Colonel (Ret.) David Willis; Mike Winey; S. G. Yasinitsky; Michael Yockelson.

MARKSMANSHIP IN THE U.S. ARMY

CHAPTER ONE

THE EARLY YEARS

SETTING THE STAGE

GUNPOWDER WEAPONS SYMBOLIZE the modern soldier. Muskets, rifles, and cannons, along with uniforms, represent the profound transformation in soldiering that has occurred since the mid-sixteenth to early seventeenth centuries' changes began to modify substantially the warriors of ancient and medieval times. Once breech-loading weapons and, soon thereafter, smokeless powder appeared, the pace of improvements and the lethality of soldiers' weapons grew steadily. Nevertheless, the myth that U.S. soldiers are natural marksmen, fostered even today by American outdoor life and firearms access, should have died with George Custer. As late as 1940 the chairman of the Senate Military Affairs Committee declared that "our boys learned to shoot by the time they were in knee pants" and went on to declare that at 100 yards mountaineers from North Carolina could hit a squirrel in the right eye and avoid hitting the body. The senator may have actually believed that.[1]

In the U.S. Army there was precious little marksmanship training or even interest in shooting skills until the last quarter of the nineteenth century. While a few militia units and individuals took up the cause of good marksmanship before the Civil War, these were isolated events. Three factors caused this state of affairs, which, at first glance, appears to be counterintuitive, considering that individual firearms were the primary means of dispatching one's adversary during a war. First, lack of technological advances in all of the key areas conspired against good marksmanship training; bullets, musket barrels, and powder had not yet been adequately developed, much less joined to make precision shooting possible. Second, leaders had developed battlefield tactics that compensated for this lack of

accurate shooting; once they were learned, it was difficult for many officers to comprehend other ways to accomplish closing with and destroying the enemy. Third, the U.S. Congress created budgetary straitjackets with each year's appropriations. It was tough to be innovative within the existing War Department fiscal constraints.

This is not to say that Americans were not familiar with firearms. True frontiersmen such as the early mountain men certainly were as proficient as the hardware allowed, but this was not typical. Weapons inevitably accompanied those who lead the migration sweeping across the continent, and those emigrants who did not stay on the big city seaports but went west picked up rifles, shotguns, and pistols. Such familiarity did not mean, however, that they were proficient or that the owners even treated weapons with respect. Many wagon-train members could tell their own firsthand account of at least one in their party who was accidentally killed by misuse of firearms, including such careless acts as grabbing the barrel of a loaded rifle lying in a full wagon and dragging it across the contents. Especially in the nineteenth century, familiarity with weapons led to contempt.

Marksmen's hard-earned skills, learned in the school of necessity, are not the same thing as "natural ability." A 1743 South Carolina colonial law required men to carry firearms to Sunday church services, and stories tell of marksmen firing from behind rocks and trees, Indian style, as the British withdrew to Boston after Lexington and Concord. Shooters frequently boasted that American shooters had special gifts. "Citified folks," out of ignorance, believed it. With the help of writers and politicians, sharpshooters such as Annie Oakley reinforced people's belief that virtually all

Fig. 1.1a and b. An early silver militia shooting prize ornately engraved **For The Best Shot**. The reverse is engraved **Presented by the Independent Grays to Wm. E. Conoway Target Firing Oct. 12, 1849.**

Fig. 1.2a and b. An early sterling-silver shooting prize, nearly 3 inches in diameter. The obverse is an engraving of the pre–Civil War Ohio Seal. The beautifully executed reverse bears **FIRST BRIGADE THIRTEENTH DIVISION OHIO VOLUNTEER MILITIA** near the rim, with the wording **Awarded at Camp Harrison Sept 1st 1859 to the Columbus Vedettes Brig. Gen. L. Buttles. Com.d.g.** on the shield. The Columbus Vedettes became a company in the 2d Ohio Volunteers when the Civil War began.

Americans could shoot. Although Alvin York was an exceptional shot, the Tennessee hills schooled him, not the U.S. Army.[2]

Throughout its first one hundred years, the young U.S. Army conducted only rudimentary marksmanship training. Some militia organizations conducted weapons training and gave prizes for shooting well before the Mexican War, but this was not the norm. The weapons limited the accuracy anyone could obtain, and this discouraged many unit leaders from conducting weapons training. The isolated initiatives that selected leaders did pursue never took hold nationally until a decade after the Civil War.

With or without formal training Americans, emigrants all, demonstrated no special skills except through practice. Indeed, one regimental commander with Indian War experience stated that "beyond 100 or 150 yards, all the firing of our men is pretty much a matter of chance." Obviously, a soldier's ability to use his weapon is a key factor in the sphere of military skills, and motivated soldiers respond to good training. Considering these facts, it is amazing that for decades the army had such abysmal training programs.[3]

Soldiers respond to good training, provided of course that they are motivated. The first successful American army-wide attempt to provide good marksmanship training and, simultaneously, a psychological carrot started three years after Lieutenant Colonel (Brevet Major General) Custer was buried. Surprising as it seems, Custer and his command's fate did not cause this revolutionary change.

Politics, personal pride, and technology came together in the 1870s. Various generals espoused the virtues of rifle training, while rifle teams from the newly formed National

Fig. 1.1a

Fig. 1.1b

Fig. 1.2a

Fig. 1.2b

Rifle Association (NRA) outshot those from the regular army. Various awards initially helped speed the militias and, soon behind them, the regular army towards real training. As a result of training, supported by prizes, trophies, and badges, eastern militias, especially New York's, produced proficient marksmen. These organizations, citing the superior intellect and capability of their members, quickly threw down the gauntlet, daring the "lower class" regular army to match the citizen soldier in performing this critical skill. This book concerns the use of a plethora of rewards, their history, and the ways in which they helped the U.S. Army train during the last 130 years.

William C. Church, a key person in the marksmanship movement, used his highly influential *Army and Navy Journal* as a platform from which to lobby for national marksmanship-training and weapons improvements. Church and some of his highly placed friends in the New York militia formed the NRA, one of several clubs organized by civilian shooting enthusiasts in the 1870s. He even helped institute the Nevada Trophy as a reward to the best company in the entire army, and in 1881 personally presented it to army commander General William T. Sherman.

The die was cast. Money flowed. The army created bronze, then silver badges. The U.S. Mint struck gold prizes. A dozen years after Custer's demise, shooting was a major recreational activity and an essential skill for soldiers of the U.S. Army. Yet the beginnings of the story of medals, training, and weapons started long before the Civil War, when muskets and rifles were the two common types of long arms.

The difference between muskets and rifles was common knowledge. Muzzle-loading muskets, which fired a lead ball, were the usual weapons of all the world's armies for most of the eighteenth and the first half of the nineteenth centuries. The musket, a smoothbore, long-barreled arm of limited accuracy at distances of over 50 yards, was easily manufactured and relatively quick to load with a ball in a paper cartridge.

Muzzle-loading rifles, although used in both recreation and the military before the nineteenth century, had limited usage, primarily because it was difficult to manufacture the weapon's grooved barrel. The rifle had spiral grooves cut into the inner surface of its barrel to spin the fired bullet, making it more accurate at greater distances than the musket, but only a skilled man could load it, because the ball had to be tight in the bore. Consequently, the rate of fire of the muzzle-loading rifle could never match that of a muzzle-loading musket.

The U.S. Army, while often myopic, could occasionally see the future clearly. One instance of this was the periodic use of rifle units. In 1792 General "Mad" Anthony Wayne organized the Legion of the United States, placing one battalion of riflemen in each of the four sublegions. This unit, never fully manned or equipped, was dropped four years later in 1796. In 1808 the army organized a Regiment of Riflemen; three others were added in 1814 during the War of 1812. These four regiments, combined in 1815, were abolished in 1821 when Congress severely reduced the army.[4]

In 1842 Congress redesigned the 2d Regiment of Dragoons as the Regiment of Riflemen. Besides eliminating their horses, the act replaced their carbines with rifles. The carbine allows easier handling due to a slightly shorter barrel, but the price is usually a minor decrease in accuracy. The 2d Regiment continued afoot until 1844, when Congress remounted the men and restored the unit's original designation. The remounted unit discarded the muzzle-loading rifle and adopted the breech-loading Hall rifle carbine, primarily for its ease of loading while the shooter was mounted.[5] Throughout this period of stop-and-start organization of rifle units the breech-loading rifle did not gain wide acceptance, because political and commercial rivals, holding a range of breech-loading patents, exploited breech failures of rival systems.

Secretary of War Jefferson Davis discussed the army's appropriations bill and at one hearing testified that breech-loading arms were only suitable for cavalry and not for infantry. Taking a political stance agreeable to both sides, Davis stated, "[T]he value of breech loading, so far as applies to military purposes, is confined to those cases where the man has not freedom of action to load the piece at the muzzle. The infantry-man who has space enough, and is in proper position to load his piece at the muzzle, I think is better served with a muzzle loading piece than a breech loading piece." Ironically, these events did little to change the army's attitude towards marksmanship training.[6]

Certain civilian and military leaders, however, seeing the advantages of rifles' greater

Fig. 1.3. A Model 1855 rifle musket. This weapon was just coming into use when the U.S. Army began to formulate a formal marksmanship policy. The weapon's overall length is 56 inches, and all of the metal is bright steel. The hinged rear leaf sight is graduated to an optimistic 800 yards.

Fig. 1.4. Henry Heth, who, as a captain, chaired the War Department board that wrote the 1858 book, A System of Target Practice. That volume espoused the army's formal marksmanship training policy until 1879, even though in practice much of the army ignored Heth's work. A captain in the 10th Infantry at the start of the Civil War, Heth became a Confederate general, serving under his good friend Robert E. Lee.

Fig. 1.5. A Minie ball, of the general type invented by Frenchman C. Etienne Minie in 1847. Slightly smaller than the rifle bore so that it could be easily pushed down on top of the powder charge, the hollow rear filled with propelling gasses when the rifle fired. This expanded the sides of the bullet, forcing it to conform to the rifling in the barrel, which in turn caused the bullet to spin in a stable manner.

accuracy, continued to improve them by developing more rapid loading approaches. Inventors worked to design a safer breech-loading system, to improve manufacturing processes, and to create a satisfactory cartridge for a breech-loading concept. The devil is always in the details, and two details required of cartridges for good breech-loading weapons, not solved until late in the nineteenth century, were the adoption of a solid and safe center fire primer and a sturdy and easily manufactured cartridge lip to insure reliable extraction without a jam. Early firearms were ignited by a variety of means, including a smoldering wick or a flint that struck steel, creating sparks. A percussion cap that was placed in a receptacle under the weapon's hammer replaced these initial ignition means and was the forerunner of the primer that eventually went into a modern bullet's metal case. The army mass-produced and used arms prior to these refinements, but modern weapons came after a modern metal cartridge case became universally available.

Despite several deficiencies, the potential of breech-loading rifles finally caused the army to convene a board to examine these evolving arms and practice policies. Infantry units were just beginning to use the 1855 rifle musket, and for a time, only a few men in each company received the weapon. The army initially created a very limited practice course, with ranges from 200 to 700 yards, for the weapon. The War Department picked Captain Henry Heth of the 10th Infantry as a member of the board that started to meet in August 1857. Heth, a Virginian and an 1847 graduate of the military academy, initially served in the 6th Infantry then went to the 10th in 1855. He resigned in April 1861 to join the Confederate army, rising to major general while serving the South. Heth died in 1899.[7]

Throughout this pre-1870 period, training was abysmal. Without central direction for real training, at best unit commanders only showed men simply how to load and operate the weapons. Most of the army felt it was wasteful to study marksmanship with inherently inaccurate muskets. The smoothbore flintlock musket's accuracy was such that

Fig. 1.4

Ulysses S. Grant wrote of his Mexican War experience, "At the distance of a few hundred yards a man might fire at you all day without your finding it out." This lack of accuracy was tactically overcome by the massing of troops in lines to increase fire impact.[8]

Precision marksmanship by the common soldier was made possible when French Army Captain C. Etienne Minie invented a revolutionary new bullet in 1847. His radical bullet made it possible for the first time to load rifled weapons easily. One of Minie's balls—a ball in name only—was slightly smaller than the rifle's bore, so it could be easily dropped down a grooved barrel. The U.S. version of the elongated Minie ball, refined in 1853–54 by James Burton, assistant master armorer at Harpers Ferry Arsenal, was hollow from the base to one-third of its length, so that when the weapon fired, the propelling gasses filled the hollow base, forcing the lead into the rifling and spinning the "ball" as it traveled up the barrel. This spinning made the bullet much more accurate, creating an easily loaded

weapon with great effectiveness. With the invention of the Minie ball an easily loaded long arm's accuracy significantly improved. This, in turn, allowed humble foot soldiers to shoot down their enemies at longer ranges.[9]

On March 15, 1856, the army initiated a feeble attempt

Fig. 1.3

Fig. 1.5

to coordinate service-wide marksmanship training. Since individual training was executed at the unit level, Washington sent out an Army Headquarters circular requesting officers from the field to send in their opinions and suggestions about a shooting program. The responses were underwhelming, and nothing came from the effort. Perennially, general officers thought it unnecessary to institute expensive training that burned up money on a range. After all, the United States had won the recent Mexican War with no extensive weapons training. The huge number of Mexican troops had simply been out maneuvered. When Captain Heth and others met to consider the breech-loading arms, they were exposed to the results of the feeble 1856 efforts and the prevailing superior American attitude. The officers knew that at many recruit depots, soldiers simply received a weapon and cartridges and were told to become familiar with the weapon.[10]

By early 1858 Heth finished writing *A System of Target Practice for the Use of Troops When Armed with the Musket, Rifle-Musket, Rifle, or Carbine.* Jefferson Davis, while he was secretary of war, instituted the process by which the U.S. Army's first system of organized marksmanship instruction was conceived. On March 1, 1858, his successor, John B. Floyd, ordered it published for army-wide use, but with Davis gone there was no champion.[11]

Heth's fundamentals were sound, generally encompassing points seen by marksmen to be important ever since. His course called for instruction in aiming, positions, trigger squeeze, distance estimation, and firing for the men as skirmishers and in units, although some of Heth's particulars are strange to us today. The manual prescribed fifteen distances, from 150 to 1,000 yards. Two surprising differences between then and now were the target sizes and the number of rounds used at practice. While targets varied according to distance, the 1,000-yard target was 6 feet high and 22 feet wide, and the 150- and 225-yard targets were only 22 inches wide. Men fired a paltry four rounds at each range. To encourage this modest instruction system, Heth's manual established three attractive annual prizes to be furnished by the Ordnance Department: an army prize, regimental prizes, and company prizes.

The Army Prize of 1858

A delicate silver medal, 2 inches in diameter and suspended on a neck chain, was to be awarded annually to the best shot in the service. Soldiers were to wear the prize on all full-dress occasions, on orderly duty, and when attending the pay table. After it was awarded this prize became the soldier's property, but the winner could be stripped of his reward by sentence of a general court-martial. The soldier could wear this and his regimental prize at the same time, though he had to return his company prize to his company captain once he won a higher award.

The winning soldier's grade, name, company, and regiment were to be engraved on one side of the medal; on the other side, **Army Target Prize for** and the year. A sample design is shown, but it is interesting to note that the order did not specify which design was the obverse and which was the reverse. The name of the winner, along with his company and regiment, were to be published in Headquarters of the Army orders. A copy of the order with the army prize was to be forwarded to the winner's commanding officer, to be given to the soldier on parade by the inspector general, if present, and otherwise by the commanding officer.

The army prizewinner was to be selected from the best regimental shots. If any two regimental prizewinners had equal "strings," the regimental contests were to be shot again by the two men and the results forwarded directly

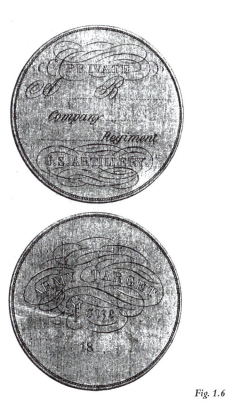

Fig. 1.6

Fig. 1.7. *One of the four 1859 silver prizes struck by Robert Lovett of Philadelphia for Captain (Brevet Major) Peter V. Hagner, commander of Frankford Arsenal. The prizes, 2 1/2 inches in diameter, were never awarded.*

Fig. 1.8. *This soldier, wearing his 1851 dress uniform and pack, also wears one of Heth's champion stadia on his right chest. The illustration is taken from* A System of Target Practice, *published in 1858.*

to Army Headquarters, which would publish the winner's name. A string was the distance from the center of the bull's-eye to each shot. A miss was noted by adding 20 inches to a competitor's string; thus a man with the shortest string had the tightest shot group around the bull's-eye and was the best shot.[12]

Heth's army prize was never awarded, and there is no evidence of its manufacture in the pattern prescribed on March 1, 1858. Even so, a second form of this medal exists in a design by Robert Lovett of Philadelphia, which is shown in figure 1.7. On the obverse are the capital block letters **ARMY TARGET** in an arc above the Old English word **Prize**, all over a stand of trophies consisting of two drums, two U.S. flags, and three stacked rifles. Frankford Arsenal, in Philadelphia, sent a lead cast of a die for the new target prize to Washington on December 7, 1858, where it was approved for manufacture upon receipt the very next day. Three of these handsome silver medals were struck for Captain (Brevet Major) Peter V. Hagner of the Frankford Arsenal in 1859. Hagner reported, "Patterns for these articles [stadia and prize medals] were prepared here, and, after adoption, enough . . . were made for the present use by the army. . . . [T]he medals [are] in Morocco boxes." One more was struck in 1870 for now unknown reasons. The War Department awarded none of them, demonstrating the army's apathy during this period.[13]

THE REGIMENTAL PRIZE OF 1858

In an inspired move Heth established a silver stadia hung from a silver chain as the award for each regimental winner. The stadia is an instrument used for estimating distances by comparing the apparent height of a standing soldier, nominally 6 feet, or a 7-foot target of a horse-mounted trooper, to predetermined measurements marked on the stadia. The instrument, cut from thin metal with an isosceles triangle removed from the center, is held horizontally at a constant distance from the eye. This distance is maintained by using a string attached to the slide, with a lead ball on the end. The ball is held between the teeth, the string stretched full length, and the slide moved to the point on the triangle where the sighted target fits within the sides formed by the slide and triangle. A reading from marks on the stadia gives the distance to the target.

Captain Henry Heth, in his groundbreaking 1858 manual, stated that the award stadia,

suspended from a short chain, would be "worn on the right or left breast, according to the arm used, musket or rifle; the lead ball passed through the button-hole, and the hook [on the end of the chain] fastened to a loop worked four inches from the row of buttons" on the chest. Presumably this meant that those stadia won with a musket were worn on the right side and those won with a rifle were worn on the left.

Fig. 1.7

Fig. 1.8

Each regimental colonel awarded a silver stadia to the best of the company marksmen and announced it in regimental orders. The prize was to be awarded by the inspector general, if present, or in his absence by the senior officer present on parade. Soldiers were to wear the prize as a badge of honor on the same basis as the army prize, but in this case it was an accountable piece held only until the next year's competition. A victor could win the prize in succeeding years and could also be stripped of the honor by sentence of a general court-martial. Regimental officers requisitioned the stadia from the Ordnance Department, and the awards were borne on the Ordnance Returns as "other property." The prizewinners were charged with loss or damage of these prizes just as they were with other issue property.

The following rules governed regimental contests:

1. The order of firing was determined by lot.
2. A circular target 3 feet in diameter, marked in the center with a black circle 8 inches in diameter on a white field, was raised from the ground at least 3 feet.
3. Each contestant fired ten shots from 200 yards.
4. After each shot the distance from the center of the ball hole was measured and recorded, and then the hole was covered with pasted paper.
5. Ricochet strikes were counted as misses.
6. Each miss counted as 20 inches on a competitor's string. The man with the shortest string was the winner.
7. Ties were settled by continuation of firing.
8. Shooters used the skirmisher standing (free-style) position.
9. Each man was required to load his piece with a full charge of powder and fire his own piece. Hang fires counted against the competitor.
10. The contest was to be completed at one session unless poor weather caused a continuation or was needed to eliminate a disadvantage to those who fired last.

Frankford Arsenal procured the first order for both silver and brass stadia from George W. Simons of Philadelphia. After they were made on September 6, 1858, two examples of each went to the Ordnance Department office in Washington for inspection and approval.

THE COMPANY PRIZE OF 1858

A similar stadia, except that it was made of brass and without decorative engraving, was authorized for each company's best marksman. It too was worn on the breast as a badge of honor, but the contest's victory was determined by firing four rounds each at fifteen distances ranging from 150 to 1,000 feet. The soldier with the greatest number of hits won. In the case of a tie the soldiers fired at a 200-yard target until the victor was decided.

Major Hagner, Frankford Arsenal commander, ordered nearly 340 brass and silver stadia as awards in 1859 and 1860. His arsenal also constructed chamois bags to hold the stadia.[14]

CIVIL WAR TO 1880

Although Heth precisely wrote out the steps for training soldiers in marksmanship, and the War Department dutifully published these instructions, the army at large took little heed. Neither soldiers nor officers recorded anything about the training, and orders from the headquarters of the army failed to mention enforcement of this fundamental soldierly task. The great and recent technological development of the Minie ball was lost on most Civil War generals, as they had matured when

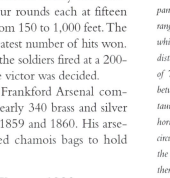

Fig. 1.9

Fig. 1.9. An 1858 brass stadia, given as the award for the best shot in a company. One side was used to estimate the range to a standing person 6 feet tall, while the other side was for judging the distance to a person on horseback, a height of 7 feet. The soldier placed one lead ball between his teeth, stretched the string taunt, and—while holding the stadia horizontal—moved the slide with the circular center until the top and bottom of the target just filled the slot. The soldier then read the range by looking at the marks on the stadia's edge.

Fig. 1.10. *A breech-loading Model 1873 .45 caliber carbine. This was the first mass-produced and widely distributed U.S. Cavalry long arm to use a metallic cartridge. The army published a sketchy marksmanship training program in 1869 that allowed soldiers to fire up to ten cartridges per man, per month.*

musketry had an effective range of about 50 yards. No doubt this affected the leaders' outlook regarding the virtue of individual weapons training.

Incredible as it seems, the war clouds of the Civil War did not signal the thorough use of Heth's *A System of Target Practice* army wide; rather, marksmanship training totally reverted to control by small unit commanders. It was ingrained in most leaders that training for firing a weapon was not necessary. One officer, later a general who commanded two different divisions during World War I, noted that his Civil War predecessors sent entire regiments into battle without any rifle practice. Some soldiers fired their muskets for the first time during battle. Generals assumed that the volume of fire was the important factor and that only by a few select sharpshooters needed to fire accurately. Even so, some evidence exists that federal troops were still being awarded the stadia prizes up to 1863. In a few cases commanders reinstituted the award about 1880.[15]

Perhaps this apathetic response was due to the fact that Henry Heth joined the forces of the South. (He was called Harry, and it is said that he was the only soldier whom Robert E. Lee addressed by this first name.) Or perhaps it was the consequence of mobilization on a huge scale, but the few progressive steps towards marksmanship training that originated at the time of Heth's work were ignored and fell into disuse. Certainly, Heth's attempt to add to the mystique of skilled shooting by providing stadia as "medals" failed.[16]

Rather than revise tactics to take advantage of muzzle loaders and Minie balls or breech-loading rifles, Civil War leaders often sought to overwhelm their opponents through massed troops. Their choice inherently ignored marksmanship. The notable exceptions, proving that they should have been used, are found in the small numbers of Confederate and Federal sharpshooters who usually shot at enemy officers and artillery men. The rattle of musketry was, unfortunately, often reserved for the battlefield and not heard on the practice range.

For a few years after the Civil War's end, target practice and marksmanship instruction

remained a matter of whim for the different department commanders. Usually, higher command offered no direction and required no target practice, much less offered incentives such as prizes for excellence in shooting. At times weapons practice evolved simply into sport. Lieutenant John Bourke of the 3d Cavalry reported that in the late 1860s at Camp Grant, Arizona, as the sun set, many troops would shoot skunks and coyotes as the animals approached the local garbage piles. This type of sport, plus hunting for food, served as the sole weapons training at many western posts. Troops "back East," without the freedom to hunt and lacking wild animals prowling around, had no such opportunity.[17]

Meanwhile, in 1865 Erskin S. Allin, the master armorer of the Springfield Armory, developed a breech-and-cartridge system suitable for converting the thousands of surplus Civil War rifled muskets to breech-loading rifles. Once his designs were perfected, quick, breech-loading, and accurate Springfield rifles were issued to the service. These are commonly called "Allin conversions." The army made various conversions and in some cases had contractors make others. Shortly afterwards, in 1869, the army published a new but very sketchy training program in response to the issue of the new Springfield breech-loading rifle.[18]

In Europe the various military powers were trying to effectively adopt the results of firearm technology that allowed a novice to fire faster than an experienced soldier with a muzzle loader. Constant threats of war from their neighbors caused continental powers to experiment continually and adopt the newest and most capable weapons, while the United States was isolated from these immediate pressures. In Europe armies were desperate for trained and accurately firing soldiers. Not so in the United States.

One is tempted to conclude that Heth's work was in vain; however, a small glow of his light remained through the Civil War. The new 1869 marksmanship program provided for general rifle practice, issue of ten cartridges per man each month for target use, and supervision and regular reports from unit commanders, though the new system did not establish standard targets, any target material, or uniform practice guidelines. Today these actions may appear miserly, but in the post–Civil War army these undertakings were great steps forward. In a regressive move, however, there was no mention of awards or medals for

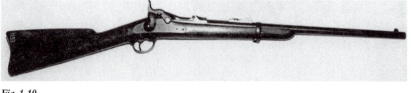

Fig. 1.10

competition or qualification. War Department directives affecting the marksmanship program between 1874 and 1877 did not correct these grievous omissions, although other details of the program were altered, primarily leaving the execution and details of the training program as a matter to be determined by individual department commanders (the equivalent of the modern-army area commander). Officers, for the most part, thought a program was totally unnecessary.[19]

A forlorn Private William Murphy, while stationed along the besieged Bozeman Trail in 1867, lamented the cost of target practice. "[T]he government charged twenty-five cents per cartridge to the men if they were short" even at target practice. And this was on top of orders not to fire at Indians unless fired upon first.[20] The 1869 program did provide that commanders on the frontier would encourage their men to hunt for large game and also directed that when available, carbine cartridges be sold at three cents and rifle cartridges at four cents for these hunts. Altered in later directives, these early programs were never successful army wide. Even so, notable exceptions in western departments did develop, such as in General Christopher C. Auger's Department of the Platte in 1867 and General E. O. C. Ord's Departments of California, Texas, and the Platte. Auger directed the firing of new weapons then coming into widespread use and the conduct of battlefield practice drills. He also stressed firing at uniform targets, although no details were provided—Auger simply pushed the concept of firing practice and left the local commanders to develop the details. Even so, Auger adamantly emphasized that commanders submit in their reports, every ten days, the name of the best shot in each company.[21]

Ord established a strong program in his commands by providing for rifle practice at each of his posts once each week, with reports to his headquarters that included distances, target sizes, number of shots by each man, and the names of the best and worst shots. Even in the winter, Ord, while commanding the Department of the Platte, directed target practice "the first day of the week on which weather may be sufficiently pleasant." He further fostered accurate shooting by awarding the best shot a day off duty, while the worst shot "was presented at company parade with a leather medal colored green." Even as late as 1877, Ord published monthly the best and worst company, the target size and distance fired, the number of hits, the average distance from the target center, and the names of the company commanders. Ord, much more than Auger, was an agitator for reform when it came to rifles and training.[22]

The crusty, outspoken Ord stated several times that he intended to publish in the *Army and Navy Journal* the regiment and companies showing the best and worst shooting averages to stimulate their men to do their best. In 1872, in a moment of public theater, he published for all to see that the cavalry had shown themselves far better marksman than the infantry. Ord wanted company commanders to reward their best shots, stating that, "The soldier is armed so that he may, in battle, hurt somebody with his rifle, and the sooner he learns to do so the better the soldier." Ord's real passion appears in Department of the Platte General Orders Number 8 of 1873, in which he authorized post commanders to direct the use of "any lumber at their posts . . . for targets. Recent campaigns against Indians, have demonstrated that it is better to expend lumber for targets than for coffins."[23]

Finally, in 1877, the Department of Texas adapted a standard set of ranges, made circular targets the norm, and established uniform scoring criteria. All firing at up to 300 yards was to be shot standing, 300–450 yards kneeling, and over 450 prone, with smaller targets, 4 x 6 feet, used for up to 300 yards (an 8-inch-diameter bull's-eye, a 26-inch-diameter "centre," and a 46-inch outer ring). In 1879 this became the NRA third class target. For 300 to 600 yards the Texas troops had a 22-inch bull's-eye, a 38-inch center ring, and a 54-inch outer ring on a 6 x 6–foot target. Initially allotted ten rounds a month, soldiers were to fire three in one week, then two in the alternate week, making the exercise familiarization rather than real training. Despite such improvements as mandatory training by Ord, it was 1879 before the War Department officially increased the number of cartridges allowed per infantryman per month to thirty, having gone from ten to twenty just two years before.[24]

Such creeping progress towards an adequate training program was none too soon. Private William Zimmer, a Civil War veteran who as a cavalry private was an active participant in the Sioux and Nez Perce campaigns throughout Montana, kept an active diary. His journal recorded as many firearm accidents as

Fig. 1.11. *Edward Otho Cresap Ord, major general of Civil War volunteers and brigadier general and brevet major general in the regular army between 1866 and 1880. Before the army instituted and enforced standards for marksmanship training in 1878–79, Ord, as commander of various geographic departments, was the primary voice that drove soldiers to proficiency with their weapons.*

Fig. 1.12. *An example of one of General Ord's publications, showing his emphasis on marksmanship. As listed at the bottom of the circular, this was read to each company under Ord's command.*

target practice sessions over the course of 1877. In one case a private on guard shot off his own fingers, and Zimmer noted that it was the third case he knew of. That summer another guard shot himself in the shoulder. Some of the 2d Cavalry units in Montana conducted mounted target practice, although occasionally the training was irrational, with practice by one troop the day after Christmas in the snow and cold of the upper Midwest, while this same unit halted practice in June, declaring the weather too hot.[25]

Company commanders in the Department of the Platte divided their shooters into two classes. The first included at least two-thirds of the company, while the second class consisted of the poorest shots. Company commanders could select ranges of 100, 200, or 300 yards for their men, but very poor marksmen had the leeway to use even shorter ranges. Beyond these brief instructions, the Department of the Platte, which had the greatest interest in marksmanship, was generally silent except to point out that Heth's *Target Practice* was to be followed. One recruit reported that in his first month with his unit he spent only one afternoon on the rifle range, while in a cavalry troop each man fired two rounds at 200 yards, and half of the rounds entirely missed the target.[26]

Brigadier General George Crook, who later fought the Apaches in Arizona, succeeded Ord as commander of the Department of the Platte. Crook injected his philosophy by having soldiers start firing at 30 yards "until perfect steadiness and a correct aim are attained" and by having practice consistently on the same day of the week. Crook, like Ord before

him, published results for all to see in his departmental general orders. But Crook took the positive approach and listed only the top two scorers in each infantry company and cavalry troop rather than the high and low scores. The next commander in the Department of the Platte was General O. O. Howard, and he even published the gallery practice and regular practice scores, listing them both by unit and by the top shooters in each unit. As successful as Ord's, Crook's, and Howard's efforts were, especially when compared to those of most other departments, the inherent lack of uniformity from command to command in target sizes and shapes, distances, scoring, and administration of ranges insured that such programs would fail on an army-wide basis.[27]

In the meantime an important development, destined to strongly influence marksmanship even to this day, was taking place in New York State. The news of this progress began to affect the army, as noted by Crook's and Howard's efforts. New stores in the middle-class civilian community offered "sportsmen's goods" that included special shooting coats, shooting hats, and cases for rifles. This civilian influence carried over to the militia's citizen soldiers.[28]

General George W. Wingate, a prominent member of the New York National Guard, knew that a carrot worked better than a stick. Wingate most enthusiastically believed training

Fig. 1.11

HEADQUARTERS DEPARTMENT OF TEXAS,
San Antonio, Texas, *February* 27, 1877.
[Circular.]

For the information of all concerned the following extracts from the reports of target practice of the Department of Texas for the month of January, 1877, showing the best and the worst shooting, is hereby announced.

Date.	Regiment.	Company.	Size of target, inches.	Distance in yards.	Number of shots.	Number of hits.	Average distance from centre, in inches	
January 15	10th Inf.	A	72-110	500	48	36	28	Ft. McKevett, Capt. Lacey.
January 8,	25th Inf.	A	72-22	200	26	4	7	Ft. Davis, Capt French.

This circular will be read to the companies at the first evening parade after receipt.

By command of Brigadier General Ord:
J. H. TAYLOR,
Assistant Adjutant General.

Official:

Aide-de-Camp.

Fig. 1.12

was essential if soldiers were to properly use rifles and that such training would succeed only when accompanied by awards. While a captain, he imported English manuals so that he could instruct his Civil War company when the majority of his volunteers proved unable to hit a barrel lid at 100 yards. Wingate's strange training actions received a universal and notably cool reception by fellow National Guard officers. All this changed in 1871 as a result of a riot in New York City. The scales fell from the eyes of many National Guard officers and politicians, and they all became instant converts, recognizing the need for troops who could deliver well-aimed fire. One must also suspect that an uprising in Paris during February–March 1871, combated by the French National Guard, was in the back of the organizers' minds. True to his form, as an added morale builder Wingate created badges for all New York troops. Every proficient and diligent soldier had a chance to earn some added plumage.[29]

Wingate introduced organized marksmanship to state National Guard organizations and presented the Soldier of Marathon Trophy as a rotating award for the most accurate shooting New York unit. He also cofounded the NRA in New York in 1871. Under his leadership the NRA established a superb target range in Queens County (now in New York City)—Creedmoor, named for Creed's farm, where it was located. To go with the facility the NRA adopted standard targets, score and range procedures, and a relatively uniform training system. Political opposition to the promotion of organized shooting from within New York State finally forced the closure of Creedmoor in 1892, and the NRA moved its matches to Sea Girt, New Jersey, after deeding Creedmoor back to the state. Wingate became inspector general of rifle practice for New York, and the state published his *Manual for Target Practice* in 1872 to help establish a standard methodology. The book, initially published as a series of articles in the *Army and Navy Journal* in 1871, was quickly adopted by the U.S. Navy and by other selected states. A few individual officers of the regular army were among the early NRA members, so several senior army officers knew of the effects of the NRA's dramatic improvements in individual marksmanship through training and practice. Even so, the War Department did not officially recognize these procedures until 1879.[30]

Creedmoor opened in 1873, and in June of that year twelve-man National Guard teams from nineteen New York and New Jersey regiments, one team from the U.S. Army's nearby battalion of the Corps of Engineers, one team of regular troops from Governor's Island (located in New York harbor), competed. With firing at 200 and 500 yards, the longer range proved too difficult for the weapons, but one of the army teams was able to place second overall. Wingate coached a U.S. team that upset a champion Irish shooting team in 1874, and that provided further notoriety. The eastern illustrated newspapers regularly reported on the many contests with England and other happenings at Creedmoor, but despite the rhetoric, regular army interest grew slowly.

Early in 1878 Major General W. S. Hancock worked with Henry Hilton to procure a magnificent trophy, to be given for competition by riflemen of the army and navy and any militia of any country. From the 1870s into the early twentieth century, one by one, many states changed the name of their militia to National Guard. Although the U.S. Army teams fared poorly at this point compared to several state militias, the competition sparked the interest of more general officers.[31]

Brevet Major General Emory Upton revised his important 1867 tactics manual in 1874, and when he did so, he felt compelled to include a section on target practice. Thus the army began to replace Heth's manual to some extent. For the first time these five pages in Upton's much-discussed manual addressed a breech-loading rifle. Senior officers noted Upton's updated manual, the initial stirrings by the NRA, and the militia shooting contests. These activities all created War Department interest. Between 1874 and 1876 the adjutant general published three orders requiring reports on target practice, but since the summaries went to the chief of ordnance, the intent of the exercise was likely accountability rather than real training.[32]

In 1879, one year before his retirement, that practioner of mandatory training General Ord severely criticized the army program in comparison to that of the militia. Ord had considerable experience. He had graduated from West Point in 1839, was promoted to general during the Civil War, and at various times commanded the Departments of Virginia, the Ohio, Arkansas, California, the Platte, Texas, and the Fourth Military District. His

Fig. 1.13. *George W. Wingate of the New York militia. A cofounder of the National Rifle Association, Wingate championed marksmanship during the Civil War and thereafter. His strong preparation was crucial in 1871, when political and business leaders in New York State decided militia members needed training in precision marksmanship. Several states and the U.S. Navy adopted Wingate's manual, which was the basis for the U.S. Army's firing manual of 1879.*

Fig. 1.14. *A gold-colored 7th Regiment team prize, given by the New York State National Guard in the early days of state shooting contests, before the famous Creedmoor Range opened. The tattered ribbon is red with two black stripes. The abbreviations on the three arms and the wording on the bars are hand engraved.*

arguments disturbed high command's inertia, and a special board convened to develop a program targeted at correcting the criticism of the existing rifle-training program. The board's task was to incorporate the best elements of the various militia and NRA efforts into an army program.[33]

Near the end of William T. Sherman's tenure as the army's commanding general, the army came further out of its comatose state. Sherman himself stated in 1882, "the men of the entire Army have improved much in precise rifle firing. This is a matter of the first importance, because one who is skilled and has confidence in his musket is worth in a fight half a dozen of 'dummies.'" Major General John Pope, while commander of the Department of the Missouri, likewise noted, "In times past it has not been unusual for a soldier to have served almost his whole term of enlistment without having once discharged his gun, either at an enemy or a target. It is inconceivable how such an essential part of a soldier's duty should have failed to receive proper attention long ago."[34]

Colonel T. T. S. Laidley, who had served in the Ordnance Department since his 1838 graduation from West Point, was named to head the board tasked with writing the real replacement for Heth's manual. Rising to colonel in 1875, he was a natural appointment, as he had received two brevet promotions for service in the Mexican War and one for meritorious service in the Civil War. With the publication of Laidley's resulting book in 1879, the army had its first complete, systematic course in rifle practice, surpassing both Heth's work and Upton's recent additions. Laidley's book, rather than a triumphant passing of Heth's torch, proved to be a source of humiliation for the army. A good portion of it was plagiarized from Wingate's manual, as Wingate soon vowed to prove in a court case.

Wingate and Laidley engaged in a very public war of words, including printed and widely distributed pamphlets concerning who copied whom. This embarrassment helped divide the U.S. Army and the militia, which had been coming together on shooting. Despite the mortification of the army's allegedly blatant copying of Wingate, the effect of Laidley's book on the army proper was to bring order and improve the shooting ability of the average soldier. In 1883 Captain Stanhope Blunt of the Ordnance Department was detailed to incorporate the lessons learned and create a

revised manual, as well as to remove the taste of the Wingate-Laidley case. He published his manual in 1885.[35]

Technology worked against the shooters, but they all had the same disadvantages. After loosing to New York's militia in 1879, the Ordnance Department modified the Springfield rifles used in the Creedmoor shooting contests. For the contests the barrels were made with six shallow grooves in place of the previous three, and the twists were increased to one turn in 19 1/2 inches rather than the older one turn in 22 inches. The butt plate, broadened and flattened, was made to form more closely to the shoulder, plus the bullets' charges were increased. These improvements finally gave the army team weapons that could accurately reach out to 500 yards and

Fig. 1.13

Fig. 1.14

more. This provided hope, and within a year shooters were consistently and successfully firing accurately at 1,000-yard targets. Seemingly minor changes allowed army shooters to reach out well beyond the previous accuracy limit of 200 yards. The essential elements of a successful shooting program were present: technology, command interest, financial support provided by Congress, and soldiers' zeal, along with competition from various state militias.[36]

With the initiation of an effective army-wide marksmanship program in the early 1880s, army awards fell into two general categories: prizes and badges. This distinction is still made today. Prizes are awarded on a very exclusive basis to those skilled enough to place at or near the pinnacle of selected competitions. In the old days the army provided only

a tightly controlled and limited number of these special forms of recognition to soldiers of great skill. Even in today's self-indulgent times of rewards for all who do merely a good job, the army gives few shooting prizes. Conversely, badges could and can still be won by any soldier who meets specified standards on set courses. As we will see, since 1880 the U.S. Army has had a checkered history regarding both badges and prizes relating to weapons training, as well as an inconsistent philosophy concerning the most effective use of rifles.

The army's on-again, off-again marksmanship program is a window through which we can see the whole of the army's training—vacillating from fervent and comprehensive commitment to mere lip service. In 1880, however, after years of neglect, the army awoke to find itself in a shooting frenzy.

Fig. 1.15. A picture of bemedaled shooters, taken at the 1884 army championship. They include Corps of Engineers Sergeant Charles Barrett, third from the left in the front row, who wears one of the stadia as a prize. Barrett's two medals are the gold prize for first place in the initial army match in 1882 and a silver prize for placing fourth in this 1884 match.

Fig. 1.15

CHAPTER TWO

SHOOTING BADGES, 1881–1921

THE SOLDIERS' INSPIRATION

IN THE FIFTEEN OR SO YEARS after the introduction of the Krag-Jorgensen rifle, shortly before the Spanish-American War, marksmen saw bullets and smokeless powder improve to the point that the resulting individual weapons would only slightly improve until near mid-century. The army rifle of 1903, modified in 1906, provided the U.S. Army with an effective sniper weapon into World War II, and even today the weapon continues as a favorite of marksmen. While these decisive hardware changes were still unseen before the frontier army of 1880, the army laid quite effective, solid groundwork for improvements in both weapons technology and the training programs that would accompany the deadly firepower improvements of the twentieth century.

General Steven Vincent Benét, the U.S. Army's chief of ordnance between 1874 and 1891 and grandfather of the famous American poet of the same name, convened a special board in 1879. The purpose was to develop a comprehensive small-arms training program. Benét noted, "great interest has sprung up within the last four years in the Army in regard to target practice," but he then stated that such zeal had "not been fostered to the extent it should have been, owing to the lack of funds . . . [and] . . . a well designed system of target practice." Colonel T. T. S. Laidley, the commanding officer of Watertown Arsenal and a shooting enthusiast, chaired the board whose task was to adapt applicable portions of the many militia programs and integrate the work of the fledgling NRA. The goal was to create an army program that would "enable the soldier to perfect himself as a marksman." The *Course of Instruction in Rifle Firing*, ostensibly written by Laidley but heavily plagiarized from George Wingate, was the army's first real attempt since Heth's pre–Civil War

effort to institute systematic target practice. Shooting was such a new field that Wingate and Laidley engaged in a court case and very public fisticuffs, complete with a book by Laidley pointing out, paragraph by paragraph, that it was Wingate who was guilty of copyright infringement.[1]

While the soldiers practiced shooting in the years after Custer, progressive officers debated how best to capitalize on weapons' technical improvements. Some foreign battle successes at long ranges prompted one group to extol the virtues of good individual training and the belief that superior long-range rifle fire and trenches would dominate the battlefield. Individual soldiers could move as required, using their marksmanship in a superior way. Some battles in the Russo-Turkish War saw the Turks slaughter the Russians, who were superior in every way but rifles, and this supported the progressive view. The opposing camp of conservatives pointed out that while the new long arms extended the killing range, this called for greater discipline on the battlefield and even a return to parade-ground formations so that officers could control the tactical firings and movements. These soldiers cited the Franco-Prussian War, which was supposedly won by better leadership and organization.[2]

While the intellectual battle raged in the journals as to how to use this new capability, the soldiers practiced on. Starting in 1884 the U.S. Army made two bronze badges in recognition of marksmanship achievements by the ordinary soldier. In the fall of 1884 the army modified the designs and started down the road of marksmanship badges that evolved in a piecemeal fashion until 1921. Prior to 1909 the War Department treated rifles and carbines the same in so far as badges were concerned, and pistols did not rate any badge. Even as these insignia started, well before the subsequent proliferation of artillery badges the 1890s, the army brass bragged about the War Department's liberality in providing so many artistic rewards that had "become a powerful and healthy stimulus," leading to the steady improvement of skillful long-arms marksmanship.[3]

The watershed year for individual shooting badges was 1921. In that year the War Department scrapped the series of soldier's awards that had evolved since 1881 and replaced them with the badges still used today. The pre-1921 badges began with rewards for rifle and carbine, progressed to pistol awards shortly after the turn of the century, and by World War I grew to include machine gun recognition.

RIFLES AND CARBINES IN THE NINETEENTH CENTURY

Colonel (later General) George W. Wingate, the general inspector of rifle practice for the National Guard, State of New York, and early president of the NRA, revised his 1872 *Manual for Rifle Practice* in 1875. In so doing, he established the first U.S. marksman insignia that an unlimited number of soldiers could earn. This was an extraordinary notion: a soldier could receive an award simply for reaching a predetermined proficiency level. The first award, given by the National Guard, State of New York, was an embroidered "badge of crossed muskets, worked in gold, surmounted by the word 'Marksman.'" It was worn on the left forearm immediately above the cuff. So entwined were the New York State firing program, George Wingate, and Wingate's NRA that until 1881 New York troops could earn a National Guard insignia at any NRA match, provided firers met the militia standards. In that year the legislature temporarily suspended funds for the purchase of shooting badges, and at the time the NRA stepped in and raised funds to enable the soldiers to continue to receive the badges.[4]

In 1876 gilded bronze medals made by Tiffany & Company replaced the 1875 embroidered devices. Through these early insignia the New York National Guard greatly began to encourage marksmanship. Early army and state manuals discussed rifle marksmanship. Slight modifications were made, however, for carbine-equipped cavalrymen, usually through reducing qualification scores. The differences between the two arms continued to be noted throughout the nineteenth century. In 1889, for example, the Department of the Platte decided that while firing the rifle, a sling could be used, but with the carbine, it could not. While there were many slightly different requirements and a minor range of standards for the two types of long arms, none were significant.[5]

Even before the Civil War some militia organizations offered medals or other prizes for shooting contests. Awarded infrequently, these were the shallow roots of today's badges. After New York State instituted shooting badges for attaining pre-set standards many other states followed suit, and within less than a half-dozen years numerous other alluring symbols hung from soldiers' chests. This change

Fig. 2.1

Fig. 2.2

Fig. 2.1. *In 1875 the National Guard of New York issued the first marksman badges, which were worn on the lower sleeve and embroidered with crossed muskets and the word* **MARKSMAN** *above. The style of medal shown here replaced the embroidered device the next year. From 1876 through 1879 New York provided bars showing a sun with rays for each year's qualification. Later bars showed the qualification year. These early New York badges had the newest bars added at the top, while the state later reversed the sequence. Later badges also have pendants held by two rings, with each bar showing the qualification year, including retroactive bars dated back to 1875. New York halted the awarding of this general design in 1893. (Till,* Military Awards of the Empire State, *40; Floyd, Johnson, and Paine,* Auction of Orders, Medals and Decorations of the World, *closing date, December 6, 1996.)*

Fig. 2.2. A silver-colored, 1 ¹/₂–inch-wide badge inscribed **Co. D 1ˢᵀ Inf'y 1881**. *This is typical of badges that militia units began to give after the early 1870s.*

was a powerful incentive to the individual, although some states, such as New Hampshire, were recalcitrant. As late as 1882 New Hampshire militia leaders were claiming that rifle firing was a safety hazard, and the state had not a single range for its three infantry regiments and two cavalry companies.[6]

Laidley's 1879 set of instructions replicated Wingate's targets. Both men described three targets with circular bull's-eyes and outer scoring rings that soon appeared as a decorative addition to early shooting badges. The targets used depended upon the range (100 through 600 yards) and the position of the firer. While circular targets are the norm today, this was not always the case, as we will see. To further support the infant shooting program, during the summer of 1879 the War Department increased the number of practice cartridges from twenty to thirty for each man per month and the departments implemented regular target sessions.[7]

Even before the War Department published standard instructions, various lower headquarters issued their own orders. The Department of the Platte, in June 1879, published a set of rules "otherwise known as the 'Creedmoor System'" for use by the department troops. This included such details as the placement of targets at the northern end of the range to avoid shadow problems; three classes of targets that varied according to ranges of 100 to 900 yards; a line of pegs from the firing point to the target to prevent firing on a wrong target; and even instructions on the paint composition to be used on iron, wood, and paper targets. For those infantrymen who scored at least twenty-five points beyond 600 yards and cavalrymen who fired carbines sufficiently well standing at 200 yards and kneeling at 300 yards, General George Crook established the title of "marksman" in 1879, ahead of the rest of the army. Upon his departure from the Department of the Platte, on his way to chase the wily Apaches, Crook noted, "The wonderful improvement in marksmanship [in the last year] . . . is gratifying proof of the interest taken in this important subject."[8]

The improved weapons developed during the 1878–80 years led the official record of the Military Service Institute to note in 1880 that soldiers could now be trained to fire with "deadly accuracy at ranges of 500, 600, and even up to 1,000 yards. It will not be denied that the other arms of the service have their sphere of usefulness greatly narrowed, and . . . there can no longer be any doubt that long range infantry fire . . . [will] influence . . . the future tactics of other branches."[9]

Keen army marksmanship did not herald the submission of the Plains Indians to the white settlers and soldiers—in fact, the reverse was true. In 1874 sixty-nine battles, actions, and engagements between Indians and soldiers occurred, while ten years later the army engaged Indians only once. The army's defeat of the Indians of the American West actually freed soldiers to engage in practice on firing ranges, and fewer Indian pursuits kept soldiers closer to army posts.[10]

On the heels of New York's and Crook's lead, Laidley created for the U.S. Army the annual classification of Marksman, given to those soldiers who attained 80 percent at 200 yards standing and 300 yards kneeling and 70 percent at 600 yards "lying down." To rate the lesser title of first class man, a shooter had to score 65 percent at 200, 300, and 500 yards; a second class man needed 50 percent at these ranges, while shooters with still lower scores were third class. The firing positions became correlated so closely with ranges that in 1881 the War Department stated it was understood that firings at 100 and 200 yards would be standing, 300 and 400 yards would be kneeling, and 500 and 600 would always be "lying down," to the point that when rendering reports on scores, only the range would be reported. In the West some organizations wrote their own requirements, so that cavalrymen with carbines could qualify for marksman by firing at 200 yards standing and 300 yards kneeling.[11]

Early shooting competitors used very innovative stances or positions. Starting in 1874 many of the competitive marksmen shot from their backs, and the practice quickly became widespread. In 1875 Wingate described and illustrated two of these prone positions with the firer's legs extending towards the target, and by 1885 Blunt described at length and illustrated seven versions of this general style. The army outlawed these many sporting "back positions" in 1897, allowing only the headfirst prone position, and this practice has remained to the present day. Other positions, including two different kneeling options, were widely used in the 1870s and 1880s, but like firing from the back, a major change in regulations in

1897 strictly specified the position for practice and match firings. The army's fundamental difference was preparation for combat rather than looking at shooting as a sport. It had taken awhile for military leaders to recognize the distinction.[12]

As part of General Benét's 1879 board, he and Laidley shamelessly took a page from New York's book and instituted the U.S. Army's first award available to all soldiers in unlimited quantities: recognition as a marksman. Benét's award was a pair of specially designed silver metal buttons "with a black circle in the centre." Worn with one button on either side of the uniform coat collar near the coat front, the square button resembled a target. The

Fig. 2.3. By 1885 firing "lying down" could be done from a wonderful variety of positions, as these illustrations—taken from the army's 1885 manual—show. Some positions had names, such as the Fulton position, top left, and the Texas grip, lower left and right.

Fig. 2.4. Two of the prescribed sitting positions, 1885.

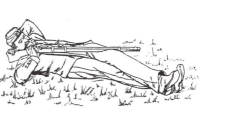

Fig. 2.3

Fig. 2.4

Fig. 2.5. This member of A Troop, 7th
Cavalry, wears one pair of marksman buttons on his uniform collar, showing that he
is currently qualified as a marksman.

Fig. 2.6. First Lieutenant Frank H.
Edmunds, West Point class of 1866.
Edmunds is wearing two pairs of first-pattern marksman buttons on his collar. The
two sets of buttons show that he qualified
as a marksman the year the photo was
taken and also the previous year. While
the year of the picture is unknown, it was
taken before 1889, as that year Edmunds
transferred out of the 1st Infantry.

Fig. 2.7. Oliver Otis Howard as a
brigadier general. Howard, a Civil War
hero, lost an arm at the battle of Fair
Oaks, Virginia, in 1862, where he
became a Medal of Honor recipient. He
also received the formal thanks of
Congress for his conduct at the Battle of
Ezra Church and during the Atlanta
campaign. As an early supporter of army
marksmanship training at the beginning of
the 1880s, this department commander
provided rewards to his soldiers who shot
well. While commanding the Department
of the Platte, each month he excused the
best shot in each company from most
duties for ten days.

army also provided the most triumphant shooters with a marksman's rifle.[13]

The introduction of rewards worked to increase soldiers' interests in shooting by providing an air of consequence. In 1881, the first year marksman buttons were available, the army issued only 454 buttons (227 pairs) to the 122 men qualifying (34 men were from the Engineer Battalion), but interest in the award grew enormously, and by 1883, 1,737 of the 22,000 soldiers earned the buttons. Again the Engineer Battalion led the army, with 163 men qualifying as marksmen. Major General John Pope, commander of the Department of the Missouri, forecast that he expected in a few years at least 50 percent of the enlisted men would be qualified as marksmen. Also by 1883, the army had established a policy that had marksmen wearing the buttons during the year in which they qualified; if any soldier failed to requalify the next year, however, he removed the buttons. The 1883 rules became such that if a man qualified in two consecutive years, he wore two pairs of buttons, but as before, only if the shooter remained qualified. This continued until 1897. Officers who qualified as marksmen could, at their option, also wear the buttons.[14]

Use of the buttons continued to grow rapidly, and in 1884 the army issued over eight thousand of the shiny silver decorations while also establishing "higher conditions" as the criteria for a marksman. Rock Island Arsenal made over fifteen thousand that year, driving the cost down from eighteen cents to a nickel. While it is easy to ascribe this growth in shooting to the buttons, commanders also continued

Fig. 2.6

to offer other rewards, as can be seen in General O. O. Howard's 1883 direction that in his department the best monthly shot in each company or troop would be excused from all daily duty except target practice, roll calls, and inspections for ten days. Certainly some soldiers took great pride in their skill, such as Private James Purvis of Fort Custer, Montana, who in 1886 wrote that "the American army has followed no old world fashions in respect to rifle practice, but adopted a genuine Yankee style of its own which has made nearly every soldier of two years service, as expert with the rifle as a backwoodsman." What a change within ten years.[15]

Fig. 2.5

Fig. 2.7

Initially, the marksman buttons were square with circular targets. Watertown Arsenal procured the first five thousand under contract. This represented Laidley's 1879 target, then known as the "Swiss" target even though the majority of misses were in the vertical plane due to minuscule flexing of the rifle barrel, variations in machining, and inconsistencies in gunpowder. Barrel flexing—caused by the bullet's passing rapidly down the barrel like a water hose that moves when high pressure is suddenly applied—resulted in some inaccuracies. Blunt thought this source of error could be eliminated only by using a heavy octagonal barrel of the style placed on the so-called "Creedmoor rifles," which added several pounds and was unsatisfactory for a service rifle.[16]

Blunt's other error sources came from the bullets themselves and from the manufacture of barrels. These problems were rooted in minor variations in the diameter of the cartridge, the diameter of the chamber of the rifle and the bore, the exact weight of the bullet, the measurement of the powder charge, and similar minor measurement problems that technology could not yet solve. *Consistency* certainly is not a word one would use today to describe nineteenth-century machine-made cartridges. Indeed, *quality* and *control* are two words joined in the twentiety century. Manufactures of the nineteenth century strived to make rounds uniform from lot to lot, and the resulting cartridge performances were similar, but the ability to achieve unvarying functioning was not attained.

Very small variations in the peak gas pressure between rounds due to these nonuniformities resulted in slight disparities in the muzzle velocities. Some rounds struck a little higher or lower than the intended point because of this anomaly. Cartridges of this era could not consistently cause a bullet to hit the same location regardless of a shooter's skill, so in 1885 Captain Stanhope Blunt adopted elongated targets. It was several more years before machines could consistently cut high-grade steel, and so the drilling of rifle bores varied slightly in their diameter. These and other slight deviations in parts further contributed to inaccuracies.[17]

Blunt, author of the army's 1885 standard marksmanship guidebook, was influential enough to become an aide to the commanding general of the army and to be promoted from captain to lieutenant colonel

in 1885. While serving as Sheridan's aide, he remained the inspector of rifle practice at army headquarters.[18]

Blunt's new bull's-eyes, like Laidley's (really Wingate's), came in three sizes depending upon the ranges fired. For 100 to 300 yards, the target had a bull's-eye 8 inches wide and 10 inches high, with the inner ring 24 inches wide and 30 inches tall and the outer ring 40 inches wide and 50 inches tall. Such an arrangement accounted for "variations incident to the arm and ammunition," and thus it would "offset the natural disbursement due to the arm and offer to the expert shot an object which he may have a reasonable expectation of hitting." His midrange target, used at 500 and 600 yards, had the bull's-eye 18 x 24 inches, the inner ring 36 x 48 inches, and the outer ring 54 x 72 inches. For those firing at 1,000 yards, the bull's-eye was 32 x 45 inches and the single ring was 51 x 72 inches. The initial suggestion for elliptical targets is reputed to have come from Colonel John Gibbon, of the 7th Infantry, in the Department of the Platte.[19]

During the 1890s through 1917 the army struggled and fought internally, trying to determine the most effective way to use riflemen. Two factions wrestled, with first one predominating, then the other. This constant flip-flop of positions was not solved until World War I. The two competing views were on the one hand that soldiers had to be given the training and freedom of action as individuals to select targets, estimate the range, set their sight, and carefully fire, or conversely—since it was too hard for everyone to learn to accurately judge battlefield distances and as the private soldier could not fairly judge critical

Fig. 2.8

Fig. 2.8. Stanhope English Blunt, West Point class of 1868. This ordnance officer was promoted to captain in 1880 and in November 1885 jumped to lieutenant colonel and aide de camp to Lieutenant General Sheridan. While serving with Sheridan, Blunt was concurrently the army's inspector of rifle practice. He authored the army's 1885 and 1888 manuals on rifle practice.

points on the battlefield—that officers had to select the most important target areas, estimate the range, and direct all fire at those points. Sometimes called "field fire," this alternative philosophy also called for more warlike targets, such as troops' silhouettes rather than bull's-eyes, since any target hit was good and a close miss was worthless. Pershing and the army's Great War experience ultimately demonstrated that neither was correct, as a squad leader became the leader who directed the fire of a handful of infantrymen, but that was two or more decades off yet.

John C. Kelton, a Civil War veteran who served in the Adjutant General's Department after the war and rose to become the army's adjutant general in 1889, was heavily involved in shooting and in expressing his views on that topic. In 1884 he published his own book, and during the 1880s he pushed for the individual rifleman who could think for himself. Kelton and other progressive officers appeared to have won the day in 1892, when emphasis shifted to the squad and the corporal squad leader and away from the captain and his company when it came to firing on the battlefield. This view was soon discounted (Kelton died in 1893), and the army turned to "field fire," in which officers estimated ranges and the men fired accordingly. This was a concept of mutual support and cooperation.[20]

As a result of reversing Kelton's training concept, in a radical change in 1897, the army adopted rectangular universal targets bearing outlines of mounted and dismounted soldiers.

Early in the twentieth century, however, circular targets officially returned, and photos show that in 1898, during the Spanish American War, many units used circular or the older oval targets. The 1897 official short-range target was a front-view silhouette of a soldier firing in the prone position, at midrange of a soldier firing in the kneeling position, at 800 yards of a soldier firing in the standing position, and at 1,000 yards the silhouette of a soldier on horseback.[21]

Scoring the many targets involved a myriad of soldiers. Immediately in front of the row of targets was a trench ("the pit"), usually over seven feet deep and running perpendicular to

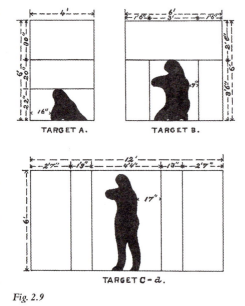

Fig. 2.9

Fig. 2.10

the bullets' paths. Soldiers stood in the pit, craning their necks upward, watching for a bullet hole to appear in the target. During normal firings, when a target hit occurred, one of the soldiers in the pit held up a large colored disk on a stick so that the disk covered the hole and showed the firer his bullet's strike. For department, division, and army competitions, however, such signaling was considered "inconvenient," and the Signal Corps furnished telephones to carry the tidings from the pits to the firing line.[22]

As a side note, it should be said that working on a rifle range was hazardous. In 1884, for example, the surgeon general reported that "accidental deaths and injuries at the rifle range has increased." While no soldier died in actual warfare that year, rifle-range accidents killed five and wounded an additional fifteen soldiers. Walter Reed, while post surgeon at Fort Robinson, Nebraska, in 1884 reported a typical accident involving a private from the 4th Infantry, who, while working in the rifle pit as a marker, was struck by a ricochet round fired 300 yards away. The soldier's right lung was penetrated and two ribs were broken, resulting in several bone fragments that caused other injuries. After twelve days the soldier finally died, and the next day, following an autopsy, Reed sent "A portion of the third and fourth ribs, showing the wound entrance, together with bullet and fragments of clothing found in the wound" to the army medical museum.[23]

A significant factor in increased injuries on firing ranges lay in the difficulties caused by the heavy, dark gun smoke, which prevented firers from seeing targets or danger flags at long range. Often, however, the pit crew simply exposed themselves carelessly, or the protective berm was penetrated after constant erosion caused by the thousands of poorly aimed balls hurled generally in the direction of the targets.[24]

Following Blunt's modification of individual targets from round to oval in 1885, Rock Island Arsenal changed marksman buttons to properly reflect the actual targets, although the 1881-style buttons lasted well beyond 1885. Both the 1881 square and the later oval buttons had welded shanks on the back so that they could be affixed to the collar like a button. Marksman buttons were fastened to soldiers' coats in several ways. A common method was to cut a small slit like a buttonhole through the collar, insert the shank, and then either sew the button in place or hold it in the hole with a split ring or other mechanical device to allow for its easy removal.

By the time of the buttons' demise in 1897, they were being issued in small, rectangular pasteboard boxes 1 13/16 x 1 inches and 11/16 inch deep, filled with pink cotton and holding two buttons. When the regular army discontinued buttons, the only insignia for marksmen became the silver marksman bar, a discussion of which follows. Rock Island Arsenal, in a political acknowledgment, continued to make marksman buttons until 1903 for selected state militia. At least one state unit continued to use buttons until 1910.[25]

Many of the state militias proudly supplied a myriad of buttons or buttonlike shooting insignia to be affixed to the collar, in imitation of the federal system. Often these rewards, either square or rectangular targets or small sharpshooter crosses, had two tines (staple like prongs) that could be inserted through the collar and then bent over. These came in a wide range of designs, including red or black enamel on German silver or even embroidered cloth "buttons," and by the time of the Spanish-American War some state marksman buttons had the qualification year or even the unit designation added.

Some men easily qualified initially and then requalified as marksmen year after year. The army provided no special recognition to those

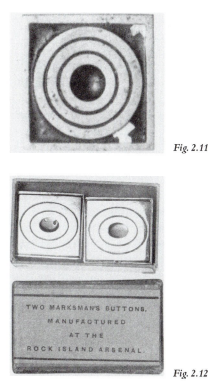

Fig. 2.11

Fig. 2.12

Fig. 2.11. The army's first-pattern marksman button, made from German silver with black added to emphasize the target design. Produced at Rock Island Arsenal, these have a heavy shank on the reverse to allow the button to be fixed to the collar. By contrast, many militia buttons made by commercial companies have prongs on the reverse.

Fig. 2.12. Second-pattern army marksman buttons, in an issue box filled with pink cotton. These were made at Rock Island Arsenal for sale to state militia organizations until 1903, even though the regular army quit using them in 1897.

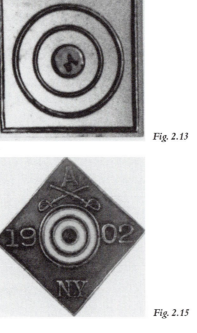

Fig. 2.13

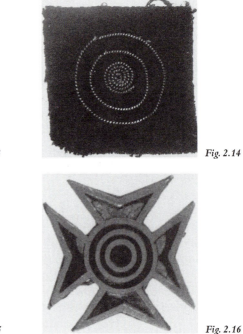

Fig. 2.14

Fig. 2.15

Fig. 2.16

Fig. 2.13. A typical, late nineteenth-century militia marksman button. Unlike the regular army's first version, the background of this button is silver rather than enamel and the reverse has two tines so that they could be inserted through the collar and bent over, securing the device to the coat.

Fig. 2.14. A cloth marksman "button" used by Michigan troops at the turn of the century.

Fig. 2.15. By the late nineteenth century some state units were adding the year of qualification to marksman buttons, and a great many versions exist. This is a very late and ornate example for New York's Cavalry Squadron A.

Fig. 2.16. Many militia organizations allowed highly qualified shooters to wear collar "buttons" in the shape of the sharp-shooter's cross. In the Massachusetts militia, for example, qualified officers could wear the crosses in black enamel, while distinguished marksmen wore these same crosses in red enamel. (McDougall and Floyd, Masrksmanship Awards of the Massachusetts Volunteer Militia, unnumbered page with fig. 12.)

who consistently shot well and those who had unusually high scores. In the Department of Dakota several 1883 company commanders took it upon themselves to change this by presenting shooting medals for competition in their companies. This and similar initiatives were neutralized by Circular Number 5 of that year, in which the War Department directed that "medals" given by company commanders "must not be worn on occasions of ceremony." This was done in part because that year the army authorized two new marksmanship awards for the common soldier, with an eye towards greater recognition and greater individual incentives. These new badges, the marksman bar and the sharpshooter cross, supplemented the silver and black marksman buttons. Despite orders for the War Department, General Alfred H. Terry, commander of the Department of Dakota in 1883, publicly published an order recommending that the decision from Washington be rescinded. Compared to their predecessors, soldiers had rewards galore.[26]

The original bronze marksman pins, while of sadly undistinguished design, have Victorian swirls top and bottom and are made from statuary bronze that long ago turned the hue of a well-aged penny. But like a new penny, the original 1884 color was impressive. Rock Island Arsenal stamped out the original 2,500

marksman pins inside one of what were then brand-new, massive three-story stone workshops. Ordnance Department presses clanked, and the grinding wheels polished the new reward symbols. It was innovative work of this type—design and then production of the badges—that helped justify the expansion of the arsenal during the late 1870s and the 1880s while it was under the command of Daniel W. Flagler.

On March 1, 1884, Chief of Ordnance Benét suggested the original 2-inch-long marksman bar in a sketch and noted that they were to be of dark bronze, with the initial order required by early July. On the reverse the catch and foundation for the hinge were cast as an integral part of the badge. The fastening pin was made from a .050-inch-diameter wire.[27]

For a while, wearing the combination of the marksman bar and marksman buttons became rather complex. The marksman bar, a permanent award at the time of introduction, showed that the wearer had qualified as a marksman in three different years. The results of the 1884 changes were that if a soldier wore one pair of buttons and a marksman's bar, it indicated that he was qualified in the current year (shown by the pair of buttons) and that he had qualified for a total of three years (shown by the marksman bar). If he only

EARLY LONG ARMS

Arquebuses, early portable long arms supported on a forked rest when firing, appeared about the end of the fifteenth century and were soon mixed into the infantry with the pikemen. By the Thirty Years War (1616–48), states formed professional standing armies. Peasants recruited from the land and led by local lords could not stand against the disciplined fire from muskets and arquebuses defended by pikemen, but use of the long and cumbersome firearms required experience. Moving a group of musketeers so that they could be efficiently deployed and then effectively used could be accomplished only with discipline and frequent drills.

It was difficult to use the individually crafted and expensive mid-seventeenth-century muzzle-loading muskets. In the early days of firearms a row of pikemen protected the musketeers while they accomplished their complex loading tasks. A line of men armed with the muskets would then advance forward of the pikemen, at which time the soldier rested his weapon on a forked stick then ignited the charge, causing the weapon to be fired. After firing, the rank would move behind the pikemen and repeat the loading process. At times as many as six or eight ranks were involved in loading and firing. Accomplishing this over and over again required precision, brought about only by many hours of practice. Slowly, weapons became more efficient and the soldiers could load more quickly, reducing the number of firing ranks. By the end of the seventeenth century the adoption of the bayonet did away with the need for pikeman and allowed all of the common soldiers to be armed in the same way. Junior leaders became essential to a smooth working organization armed with firearms, and the officers and sergeants of the day enforced training to achieve the high degree of competence required in the new professional armies.[28]

Firearms of seventeenth-century armies were heavy, handmade, and often well-decorated muskets or arquebuses, set off by a matchlock "slow match," really a smoldering wick, or by a wheel lock, a spring-wound steel wheel with a rough surface that scraped against a hard stone, thus creating a spark. Later, a spring-loaded arm, grasping a piece of flint, replaced the "slow match" or the wheel lock. In the later system the flint ignited the weapon's charge when the spring was released and the flint rotated forward, striking a piece of metal and creating a spark. This weapon was the musket, which went through many modifications and improvements during the course of the eighteenth and nineteenth centuries.

A model 1873 breech-loading rifle. This particular weapon, made in 1878, had a hinged-leaf rear sight graduated to 1,200 yards. Some units in the Spanish-American War used this style weapon.

The initial weapon used in U.S. Army marksmanship qualification was the 1873 Springfield breech-loading rifle, with its center-fire .45-70 caliber bullet and black-powder cartridge. By the summer of 1873 those infantry and cavalry units that had been equipped with Remington, Sharp's or Ward-Burton experimental arms were directed to turn them in for the Springfield breech-loading rifles.[29]

The Springfield rifle, adopted in 1873, went through so many minor changes that it took two pages to list them in the army's own *Description* book. As an example, the rear sight underwent nine minor modifications through 1898. Additionally, a special officer's model rifle was available at a cost of $27.[30] The Danish .30 caliber Krag-Jorgensen rifle replaced the Springfield starting in the mid-1890s. This lighter-weight and higher-muzzle-velocity weapon helped improve marksmanship results. During the Spanish-American War regular forces were equipped with the Krag-Jorgensen, while many volunteers used the older Springfield.[31]

Fig. 2.17

Fig. 2.19

Fig. 2.17. Daniel Webster Flagler, West Point class of 1856. As a lieutenant colonel he commanded Rock Island during the 1880s, when that army post designed and made most marksman buttons and badges. Flagler was promoted to colonel in September 1890, and four months later he became the chief of ordnance as a brigadier general. He served in that position until he died in March 1899.

Fig. 2.18. The army made 2,500 of these 2-inch-long bronze marksman badges in 1884.

Fig. 2.19. This unknown soldier wears the 1885-design silver marksman bar on his chest and a pair of marksman buttons on his collar. In the late 1880s a soldier who had qualified as a marksman for three years wore the bar. When a soldier wore a pair of buttons and a bar simultaneously, the buttons indicated that he had qualified that year.

Fig. 2.20. Private Charles W. Fox, G Troop, 8th Cavalry, during his second enlistment, which started in 1888. Fox is improperly wearing three pairs of marksman buttons.

Fig. 2.18

Fig. 2.20

had the bar, it showed that he had qualified for three years, but the lack of buttons on the collar also showed the soldier was not currently qualified. In 1888 it became illegal for a marksman to part with his marksman's bar, although no penalty was prescribed.[32]

By 1897 the silver bar inscribed **MARKSMAN** became the sole insignia for those who qualified. Men needed 64 percent hits (62 percent for cavalrymen with carbines) to earn the badge, firing from 200 to 800 yards at stationary targets and during skirmishing. (For more on skirmishing, see chapter 6.) A tangible result of the buttons and bars was that state units had excellent familiarity with weapons when they encountered Spanish forces in 1898. This war was one of the few times American forces successfully engaged the enemy early in the conflict.[33]

Beginning in 1884, once a man qualified as a marksman he could then shoot at a longer range and try for the designation of sharpshooter. But where did the concept of firing at longer ranges for a higher badge originate? While it is not certain, the truth is probably that as officers discussed the burgeoning shooting program at various army matches, the challenge of longer range firing arose. As a

result, there was a groundswell for identification of a more skillful group, and then that these soldiers have a special badge. In 1883 Brigadier General A. H. Terry, the commander of the Department of Dakota, proposed sharpshooter badges. Captain Charles Coolidge of the 7th Infantry, instructor of rifle practice in the Department of the Platte, wrote in his 1883 annual report that once men qualified as marksmen, they should fire at 600 through 1,000 yards. Coolidge suggested that his plan would result in "a new class to be designated as sharpshooters."[34]

Starting in 1883, a sharpshooter received a simple bronze cross. Successful soldiers wore

Fig. 2.21

their new badge in one of two ways. Men currently qualified wore it "at the throat" like some of the iron crosses of German foes whom their sons and grandsons would later face half a world away. No other U.S. Army award except the Medal of Honor was worn in this curious manner. Once a sharpshooter failed to requalify, he moved the bronze cross to the left chest. General Terry proposed this elaborate scheme as well as the concept of a cross to designate a sharpshooter. Rock Island Arsenal made one thousand of these crosses in the same manner as the marksman bar, with the catch-and-hinge foundation cast as part of the basic insignia.[35]

The longer ranges used by sharpshooters in 1884 were 800, 900, and 1,000 yards, compared to 200 to 600 yards required for marksmen. General Orders 97 of 1886 showed the ranges to be 200, 300, 500, 600, 800, and 1,000 yards. Sharpshooters needed to score 88 percent at the three closest ranges rather than the normal marksman's scores of 80 percent, 80 percent, and 70 percent, and then they had to fire 76 percent at the three longer ranges. In 1886, 116 sharpshooters fired 90 percent or better and had their names published to the entire army.[36]

The army continued to tighten standards. By 1888, with firings at 200, 300, 500, 600, 800, and 1,000 yards only, 109 men scored 90 percent or higher. The Ordnance Department awarded 463 sharpshooter crosses to the regular army and 10 to the militia. In 1889 the army published the names of the top eighty

men who attained sharpshooter, although a slightly lesser overall score could still earn a sharpshooter's cross and certificate. Sharpshooter was so difficult to attain that in 1889 only nine officers in the entire army qualified with a score of 90 percent, including one regimental commander, Colonel Henry Clay Merriam of the 7th Infantry. By 1893 the army reported that two men had qualified as a sharpshooter for each of the first ten years of the badge's existence: Sergeant Henry Hopkins, H Company, 14th Infantry, and First Sergeant H. Lay, A Company, 5th Infantry. The cavalry could boast of one man who had been a sharpshooter with a carbine for nine of the ten years, Sergeant Hugh Griffith, D Troop, 8th Cavalry. Both Hopkins and Griffith became early distinguished marksmen.[37]

While these men were the exceptions, in general the army of the 1880s saw a great improvement in long-range shooting. George Armes, a cavalry officer, reported that in 1866 a company commander issued his men new Spencer carbines. Firing at 100 yards, only six shots struck targets. This same officer wrote in 1882 that he fired from 600 to 1,000 yards and made an excellent score. Practice made perfect. Many officers and men became shooting hobbyists, whiling away the hours at the local range. During the hot summer months, in the middle of firing season, some units on the Great Plains arose so early as to be at the range by 4 A.M., so they could fire before the winds picked up. Just as before, frontier soldiers went hunting to provide food, encouraged

Fig. 2.22. One of the one thousand
bronze 1884 sharpshooter crosses made at
Rock Island Arsenal.

Fig. 2.23. Traveling across the United
States in 1885, Rufus Fairchild
Zogbaum noted that at many western
posts some officers' wives had become
excellent shots, and he sketched women on
the ranges. Ten years after Custer's defeat,
the army and, indeed, much of the
civilian community had taken up
shooting as a sport, making it nearly
as popular as baseball.

Fig. 2.24. A first-design marksman
certificate. Requirements for the award
are listed on the lowest two lines of the
certificate, while just above is a box
showing the actual scores obtained.
Stanhope English Blunt (see fig. 2.8)
and Alfred H. Terry, a regular-army
general from 1865 until 1886,
signed this certificate.

Fig. 2.22

Fig. 2.23

by an 1882 general order supplying ammunition
and "encourag[ing] officer and men to hunt for
game." Troop F, 6th Cavalry, fired ten thousand
rounds while hunting in the fall of 1884 and
claimed to have saved the company fund over
three hundred dollars "on bacon alone."[38]

Beginning in 1884 the adjutant general of
the army supplied special certificates to department headquarters for issue to men who qualified as sharpshooters and marksmen. At the
department headquarters clerks entered the
qualifying scores, and for many years the
department commander personally signed
each certificate as soon as it was won. Given
the small number of men who earned the
sharpshooter title, this was easily accomplished.
During 1884 the army printed new certificates reflecting the more stringent criteria for
marksmen (firing at 800, 900, and 1,000 yards).
The army issued two types of certificates that
year, using the appropriate criteria: the older
standards for those who shot early, or the
higher, long-range yardstick for later firers.
Several versions of these certificates exist,
reflecting the constantly changing criteria. In
June 1897 the army ceased issuing certificates
to marksmen. The last certificates given to
marksmen did not have any place for scores
and were signed only by the inspector of rifle
practice rather than following the earlier practice of also being countersigned by the department commander.[39]

By 1897 sharpshooters were men who
scored 70 percent of the aggregate scores
from 200 through 1,000 yards and in the skirmishing exercise. These later certificates, rather
than having scores from each range, simply
had the total scores. Various headquarters
issued remaining certificates of this type

through 1905. In that year, in response to an
inquiry, Major William Mann, president of
the army board for the revision of the small-
arms firing regulations, simply stated, "The
Firing Regulations for Small Arms, 1904, do
not contemplate the furnishing of certificates
to marksmen, sharpshooters, or expert riflemen." With this simple statement and the 1904
firing regulations, use of certificates came to an
end.[40]

In 1885 newly designed silver badges
replaced the coarse bronze sharpshooter's cross
and the ornate bronze marksman's bar. The
new silver sharpshooter badges cost slightly
over sixty-two cents each, while a marksman's
bar cost thirty-nine cents. A special operation
that involved dipping very hot, nearly finished
silver badges into 200-degree sulfuric acid
transformed the insignia finish to a tarnish-free

MARKSMAN'S CERTIFICATE, No. *142*

Headquarters Department of _____

OFFICE OF THE INSPECTOR OF RIFLE PRACTICE,

Fort Snelling, Minn. *June 9* , 188_

_____

having qualified as MARKSMAN in conformity
with requirements prescribed by *General Orders No. 13,
series of 1884, from Headquarters of the Army,* is entitled to
wear the *Marksman's Buttons* until the ____ *30*° day
of *September,* 188_.

_____

Inspector of Rifle Practice, Department of _____

APPROVED:

_____

_____ Commanding.

QUALIFYING SCORES.

200 yds.	Per cent.	300 yds.	Per cent.	600 yds.	Per cent.
26	70	24	80	17	43
30	30	26	30	13	72
22	85	29	36	19	96

MARKSMAN'S QUALIFICATIONS.—80 per cent. at 200 yards (standing) and 300 yards (kneeling);
70 per cent. at 600 yards (lying). Three scores of five shots each.

Fig. 2.24

29

SHOOTING BADGES, 1881–1921

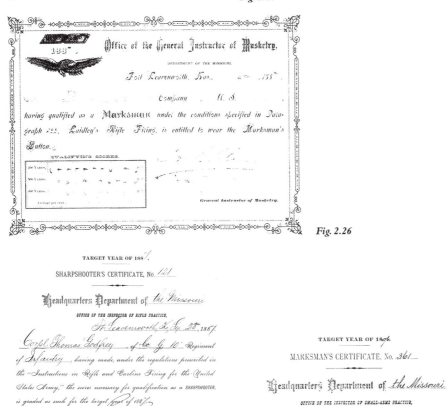

Fig. 2.25

Fig. 2.26

Fig. 2.27

Fig. 2.28

Fig. 2.29

Fig. 2.25. A 7 1/2–x–10-inch sharp-shooter certificate of the first design. Like its companion marksman certificate, it has the requirements and results at the bottom.

Fig. 2.26. A local certificate issued by the Department of the Missouri that authorized wear of a pair of marksman buttons. The certificate is 6 x 8 inches. Several departments created similar small certificates until the War Department issued its versions.

Fig. 2.27. A second-style War Department marksman certificate. The wording changed to eliminate any reference to specific requirements. Nelson Miles, who became the army commander in 1900, signed this 1885 certificate.

Fig. 2.28. A second-style sharpshooter certificate, which shows the scores for each firing at each of the six required distances and the grand total score. Since he qualified as a marksman in 1885 (fig. 2.27), Thomas Godfrey had not only sharpened his shooting skills and earned a sharpshooter's badge; he had also been promoted to corporal while remaining in G Company, 10th Infantry, at Fort Leavenworth, Kansas.

Fig. 2.29. This last style of marksman certificate was signed by Harry C. Hale, who later served on the board that wrote the 1904 Firing Regulations for Small Arms. After 1897 the army no longer authorized marksman certificates.

Fig. 2.30. *The last type of sharpshooter certificate issued by the U.S. Army. The 1904 board that revised firing regulations ended the use of certificates. The War Department never sanctioned certificates for experts.*

Fig. 2.31. *Rock Island Arsenal's Shop "C," located in Building 104 (shown here), was the manufacturing site of marksmanship badges from the late 1880s until World War I.*

Fig. 2.32. *Interior of Rock Island's manufacturing shop, which made marksman and sharpshooter badges.*

Fig. 2.33. *Between 1885 and 1921 the U.S. Army issued this style of silver bar for rifle marksmen. During 1918 and 1919 the military officially suspended issue of metal shooting badges and substituted a cloth sleeve insignia, but soldiers ignored the prohibition and wore badges made by private companies. In the early twentieth century the War Department authorized gold-colored badges for National Guard troops. Qualification requirements for the gold-colored, aluminum-bronze badges (called "bronze" at the time) were slightly less than for the silver versions.*

Fig. 2.34. *An 1885–1921 sharpshooter badge made at Rock Island Arsenal.*

Fig. 2.35. *Private Cecil Barady, Troop K, 7th Cavalry, 1909, at Fort Riley, Kansas, wearing a silver sharpshooter's badge.*

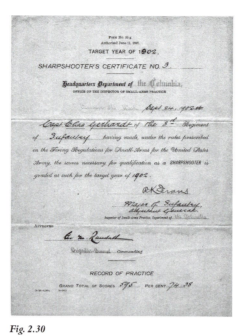

Fig. 2.30

Fig. 2.32

Fig. 2.33

Fig. 2.34

snow-white hue. These awards are familiar to many collectors and are the same ones used by the Marine Corps from the 1890s until 1921 (and revised by the marines in 1936), as well as by the U.S. Army into World War I.[41]

In the late 1880s, the War Department continued to enforce high shooting standards, including a push to have every soldier meet minimum standards. In 1889 the headquarters of the army issued an order that for all third class men (those with the lowest scores), company commanders had to submit written reports giving the reason for the poor showing. If it was attributed to a physical condition, a surgeon's certificate had to accompany the report. With several physical symbols for proficiency readily available and ammunition plentiful, the army's marksmanship program flourished.[42]

Regulations prohibited the wearing of both the marksman bar and the sharpshooter cross

Fig. 2.31

Fig. 2.35

at the same time, but some private manufacturers made a single badge incorporating both designs. Photos show that many men did frequently wear this unauthorized award, along with a scarcer combination distinguished sharpshooter badge. Numerous militia organizations, including those from states with large forces such as Illinois, New York, and Pennsylvania, gave various awards of their own, and when militia members qualified for either marksman or sharpshooter under regular army qualifications, citizen soldiers could often wear such federal recognition in addition to state badges. These requirements may account, at least in part, for initial production of the combination awards.[43]

In 1889, a year after Major General John M. Schofield became the army commander, he decided that once an officer or enlisted man qualified as a sharpshooter, if the shooter failed to requalify he could not revert to wearing the lesser marksman insignia. This changed in 1898, when the War Department stated that the sharpshooter badge became a permanent award—once earned, it could be worn thereafter. The army proved incapable of a consistent policy regarding the wearing of badges. Since their creation, staff officers had alternately decreed various badges to be worn permanently and then retracted such statements, and today the regulations are moot, leaving all that earn badges to wonder how long they may be displayed on one's uniform.[44]

A variety of factors caused the army to introduce "gallery practice" or "armory practice." These terms eventually became synonymous with indoor .22 caliber rifle firing, but until that time the army tried numerous

Fig. 2.36

Fig. 2.37

Fig. 2.38

Fig. 2.36. *Widely worn in the 1880s and early 1890s, this combination marksman-sharpshooter badge was never authorized by the army.*

Fig. 2.37. *Sergeant George J. Henry, G Troop, 2d Cavalry Regiment, who won silver prizes in head-to-head, armywide competition in both 1891 and 1892 and was named a distinguished marksman in 1892. In addition to these high prizes, he wears an unauthorized but popular combination marksman-sharpshooter badge.*

Fig. 2.38. *Similar to the popular marksman-sharpshooter badge, this distinguished sharpshooter badge was totally unauthorized, since a* **DISTINGUISHED** *bar was never contemplated by the War Department. It may be a militia award.*

schemes to reduce expenditures in powder and lead. Wingate, in his 1875 New York manual, recommended indoor "armory target practice" using reduced charges and ranges of 50, 75, and 100 feet, and he also discussed inserting a .22 caliber, 20-inch-long barrel inside the regular Remington .50 caliber rifle. This is evidently the first use of a smaller insert inside a standard service rifle.[45]

In May 1880 the headquarters of the army directed the Ordnance Department to issue to each company 125 pounds of round .45 caliber lead balls, 25 pounds of powder, 25 pounds of lubricant (beeswax and tallow), 15,000 primers, and special targets with smaller circular bull's-eyes, so that men could practice

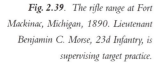

Fig. 2.39. *The rifle range at Fort Mackinac, Michigan, 1890. Lieutenant Benjamin C. Morse, 23d Infantry, is supervising target practice.*

Fig. 2.39

at reduced ranges. These "reduced targets" represented the "Creedmoor third class target" at 50, 100, and 200 yards. When fired with three grains of powder, the accuracy was satisfactory for soldiers to practice at 50 feet, and yet the system was not overly powerful. A one-inch board was about all a ball would penetrate. This system had the advantage that a soldier's own weapon could be used, rather than a .22 rifle.

Blunt, in his 1885 book, still gave the option of firing at 50, 75, or 100 feet indoors using the reduced-charge system, although the 50-foot range was the one he discussed most often. General Howard, while commanding the Department of the Platte in 1883, directed units to conduct gallery practice at 50 feet twice each week during January, February, and March, with each month devoted chronologically to "lying down," kneeling, and then standing. Clearly, the basic skills could be taught at this relatively close range. Regular army troops ended practice with reduced charges in the early 1890s with the introduction of the Krag-Jorgensen rifle and the associated modern propellants. The cost of purchasing reloading tools for use at each post caused the army to decide it was more economical to return empty cartridge cases and have all rounds "factory leaded." Nevertheless, some states continued to hand reload into the twentieth century and even prescribed how to simulate firing at ranges up to 600 yards while actually firing at 50 feet.[46]

As it was, reloading was a hazardous affair. In 1885 alone the army suffered thirty-one reloading accidents, and the next year the well-known and respected General George Crook burned off part of his famous beard and his eyelashes while reloading a shotgun shell. The potential reduced cost in soldiers' suffering was not even a factor when the army eliminated local reloading and moved exclusively to factory work.[47]

By the publication of the 1904 *Firing Regulations for Small Arms*, only 3 1/2 pages encompassed "firing at a short range with reduced charges," and when the 1913 manual was issued, only 1 1/2 pages (and those half the size of the 1904 pages) were devoted to gallery practice. These manuals encouraged informal gallery company competitions. Often, usually in the winter, the army used .22 caliber rifles indoors, but along the southern coast the "indoor period" for the coast artillery began in June and concluded at the end of September, when firing could be accomplished in the shade, escaping the oppressive sun. In June 1897 the army declared 50 feet the one and only standard range for use with .22 caliber rifles. During the Mexican border crisis of 1916, many National Guard troops called to active duty received 100 rounds of .22 caliber "gallery practice ammunition."[48]

As late as World War II some National Guard units were still awarding badges bearing **GALLERY PRACTICE**, but often by World War I such training was called small-bore marksmanship. In 1930 the regular army issued its first official awards for small-bore shooting, having previously never recognized gallery practice with any badge, despite the fact that

Fig. 2.40

the government had made a great many .22 caliber rifles, including versions of the M 1903 Springfield rifles.[49]

RIFLES AND CARBINES IN THE TWENTIETH CENTURY

By the turn of the century John Hay's "splendid little war,"[*] improved weapons, smokeless powder, and the Boer War[†] all influenced weapons practice throughout the American army. Even so, some changes came slowly. Regular and most militia units switched to round targets in 1902 and 1903, in a return to precision shooting. For the Philippine Constabulary, initially under the direction and control of the U.S. Army, old-style oval targets continued in use for carbines.[50]

During the Spanish-American War all of the volunteer and militia units, save one, were equipped with .45 caliber, black-powder, single-shot Springfield rifles. In contrast Spanish troops had magazine-fed rifles that used modern, smokeless powder. Following that war and the initial stages of the Boer War, regular army officers studied which lessons could be learned. They concluded that a modern army had to have a high-power, reduced-caliber, magazine-fed rifle with the so-called smokeless powder (made from nitrocellulose) that provided a high velocity and a flat trajectory. These studies also brought about a revolution in firearms training and a new look at use of rifles on the battlefield. Tactically, men had generally been told to fire at the base of the heavy clouds of smoke created by the traditional black powder, but with the new smokeless propellant, troop locations were hard to see. Thus the aiming at a specific target became even more important in the minds of some staff officers. All of these points jelled in 1902,

Fig. 2.41

and in that year staff officers put into motion the essential changes to modernize marksmanship. Not only did this include the introduction of a new rifle and flat trajectory bullets, but also new training.[51]

Captain J. C. Dickman, an instructor at the army's premier service school at Fort Leavenworth, stated that because of new innovations, "Renewed interest in target practice is in evidence every where. . . . Instead of the spasmodic annual effort to burn up the number of cartridges of the prescribed course great attention will be paid to instruction in field and combat firing under unfavorable conditions." This scrutiny of precision shooting was brought about by both the lapse in U.S. training during the Spanish-American War (one authority estimated that 75 percent of the men enlisted "knew practically nothing about marksmanship, or the use of the rifle") and the Boer success shown early in that African war, when individuals with keen shooting skills had been successful. It was this influence that Dickman and others felt and that breathed new life into the army's shooting program.[52]

Fig. 2.40. "Gallery practice" was a term commonly used for firing indoors with reduced charges during the 1880s and 1890s and for indoor .22 caliber shooting before World War I. This dark bronze Connecticut prize is marked **GALLERY PRACTICE** *rather than the more modern term "small bore."*

Fig. 2.41. A typical National Guard medal given for indoor .22 caliber marksmanship between the world wars. This New York medal, given by the 105th Field Artillery, has a complex design including the script cipher **WG** *(the organization was earlier known as the Washington Grays), the castle at Verdun (representing World War I service), and a Cross of St. Andrew (for Civil War service).*

★ John Hay was the secretary of war during the Spanish-American War.
† The Boer War was fought in the South African region, 1889–1902, between Great Britain and the Boers (descendants of Dutch settlers) in the Orange Free State Republic and the South African Republic (Transvaal).

Captain Harry C. Hale, an infantryman and one of the first members of the General Staff Corps, was a member of the board that rewrote the firing manual after the Spanish-American War. Hale noted the main 1902–3 changes had four focus points: (1) officers had to be able to estimate ranges accurately out to 1,000 yards (enlisted men should be able to similarly estimate); (2) disappearing targets were introduced along with various time limits, including "slow," "timed," "rapid," and "skirmish"; (3) a new, higher grade of skill was added along with pay for those who qualified; and (4) the army increased the ammunition allowance.[53]

As the army moved from the Spanish-American War and Philippine insurrection wartime footing to peace, long-arm practice resumed, stimulated by reformers in the army staff. The Department of the Missouri's sharpshooters list for 1902 totaled fifty-four men, with the best shot the first sergeant of A Troop, 10th Cavalry, followed by the 10th Cavalry's sergeant major. While standards remained high, the number of qualifying soldiers increased. For example, in the Department of the Missouri decided improvements occurred for the top qualifications between 1901 and the next year:

Table 1. Department of the Missouri Qualifications, 1901 and 1902.

Classification	1901	1902
Sharpshooters	2.1%	4.0%
Marksmen	2.2%	3.5%
First Class Men	8.9%	11.2%
Second Class Men	20.4%	20.6%
Third Class Men	66.4%	60.7%

Data taken from Department of the Missouri General Orders Number 4, 1904.

Just before 1909 the sharpshooter qualification was one of proficiency at a long range—800 and 1,000 yards—and could be fired only after attaining the marksman qualification. The army's philosophy changed again in 1909. Everyone but coast artillerymen slow fired at 200, 300, 500, and 600 yards and rapid fired at 200, 300, and 500 yards. Those who scored 202 or more points were marksmen, and those over 238 were sharpshooters. As a result of this change nearly one thousand fewer men qualified in 1910, the year the regulation took effect. After 1898 the sharpshooter's cross could be worn without a time limit once a soldier had earned the cross, but this reversed again in 1909.[54]

In the severe test of the Spanish-American War, the lack of an overall coordination staff showed. The army did not—indeed could not, due to its structure—dictate effective marksmanship training for American units sent off to war. Twenty years of lessons, crowned by annual matches, were thrown away as units descended upon Tampa, enroute to Cuba, and upon California as volunteers, militia, and regulars jostled towards the Philippines. New life had to be breathed into the twenty-year-old program that by 1903 had marksman and sharpshooter badges as the sole rewards for most shooters.

The army altered its philosophy between 1880 and 1900, vacillating between individual precision firing then unit firing, and then returning to single-soldier firing. The Spanish-American War caused the army's top marksmanship award for tactical units, the Nevada Trophy, to lapse in 1898. It was 1902 before the army even started to resume "systematic target practice" and revise the army's shooting effort, with its renewed accent on a single shooter's precision. The program's primary changes just before the war had been a shift to targets that represented troops and the introduction of the Krag-Jorgensen rifle.[55]

In 1903 the army conceived a new skill level—expert rifleman—while coincidentally starting production of the 1903 Springfield rifle and bolstering emphases by the individual soldier on precision shooting at bull's-eye targets. Cavalry officers John Guilfoyle and James Parker, both members of the board that created the expert designation, proposed that the new grade of expert would include some rapid-firing requirements to better simulate combat. After trying out their proposed concept near Washington, the board added that criterion, while also returning to circular targets. Also coupled with the 1903 change was the full resumption of rifle competition for all branches. The army institutionalized the changes in January 1904, when the War Department published a totally revised *Firing Regulations for Small Arms*.[56]

Today expert rifleman badges are found in several manufacturing variations that evolved between 1904 and World War I. By mid-1904 Rock Island was busy making the earliest style, with crossed rifles applied over the wreath. Later versions, first made in September and October 1915, had the pendant struck from one piece of metal. The army published the names of all 58 men qualifying as experts in 1903. Slowly the number of experts expanded. The Department of the Missouri published the names of 1904 experts—53 in all—along with other statistics, including the names of all sharpshooters and the best pistol shots in each battery of field artillery. The number of experts grew to 115 within the department the next year, and by 1908 nearly 2,400 soldiers qualified as experts army wide. Even so, the expert qualification remained elusive to many soldiers. In 1912, for example, an even dozen men became experts in the 2d Infantry Regiment.[57]

With the establishment of this highest award, a silver expert badge became a permanent addition to the uniform; once earned, it could be worn thereafter. Further, once a soldier earned the expert badge he could no longer wear the sharpshooter badge, even if he failed to requalify as an expert and subsequently shot at the sharpshooter level. To encourage shooters, the Ordnance Department also authorized commanders to select enlisted men, qualified as expert riflemen, to receive telescopic sights and even to have the sights carried by men at inspections.[58]

The *Provisional Small-Arms Firing Manual* of 1909 placed target practice on a footing more

Fig. 2.42

approaching battlefield conditions. By doing so it increased the difficulty for expert riflemen, requiring a score of 253 points. While 2,875 men became experts in 1909, the next year, when the 1909 manual came into effect, only 2,151 qualified.[59]

After 1885 sharpshooters who qualified three times added engraved bars, which showed the three qualification years, between the brooch and the cross. Such government-issued bars cost $.25. Different sizes and shapes of bars evolved, with the next three requalification years placed on another bar. This was extended to the expert badge in 1904. Although they represented a simple concept, requalification bars, both official and unofficial, came in two general designs—those with rounded ends and those with fishtail ends—with a further distinction between two versions insofar as dates were concerned: one-year bars and three-year bars.[60]

At first the official bars showed the three years during which a soldier qualified as an expert or sharpshooter, then in 1909 the Ordnance Department introduced bars marked for only one year. Under this 1909 scheme a man who requalified in 1909 or later would receive a bar for each year. The War Department further modified orders in 1911, so that a bar bearing a single year came to signify the last year of three years of qualification. The concept was to make the supplying of bars easier. Surviving badges and photos indicate that this 1911 provision was widely ignored, and when troopers used one-year bars, they frequently showed each year of requalification. At the end of 1916 the army officially returned to listing all three years on a single bar. When one-year and three-year bars are factored in with the wide assortment of suspension methods, it can be seen that soldiers could opt for seemingly innumerable badge and bar combinations.[61]

Ordnance staff officers must have meditated endlessly as the army toyed with requalification bars. The War Department continually redefined the criteria for these minor symbols. Today the collector must be a true connoisseur to recognize the vast multitude of requalification bars soldiers used from 1898 to 1921. The War Department's constant tweaking of such a plain device in order to simplify their supply is phenomenal. All things considered, one should not be surprised that both insignia manufacturers and soldiers ignored the fine points and were more than content to follow the general concept.

Fig. 2.42. An expert-rifle badge designed in 1903, with a requalification bar. Early badges had the crossed rifles made separately and applied to the wreath, while those made at Rock Island Arsenal after October 1915 had the entire pendant struck from one piece of metal.

Fig. 2.43

Fig. 2.43. Requalification bars appeared in 1885, although some men could order backdated bars if they had qualified earlier. This sharpshooter's badge, evidently the one earned by Captain Joseph Garrard, shows that during his initial eleven years of firing he failed to requalify only in 1890 and 1893. Garrard first qualified while he was assigned to the 1st Artillery, then transferred to the 9th Cavalry in February 1886. Promoted to captain in 1888, he remained with the black cavalry regiment until promoted to lieutenant colonel in the new 14th Cavalry in 1903. Interestingly, in 1893 Garrard failed to qualify as a sharpshooter, yet he placed third in the army's competition of distinguished marksmen. (HQA, AGO, GO 1, 1893, 18; HQA, AGO, GO 1, 1895, 18; Heitman Historical Register and Dictionary 1:447; HQA, AGO, GO 82, 1893, 9.)

Fig. 2.44. Probably a manufacturer's samples from the 1890s, the requalification bars for this unauthorized badge are of the same shape as the normal sharpshooter's brooch. The years are raised rather than being in the more common impressed or engraved style. Note that the bars are suspended by two sets of rings, as opposed to the common single set.

Fig. 2.45. Sergeant Max Simon, H Troop, 6th Cavalry. Although Simon won three division prizes and one department prize, becoming a distinguished marksman in 1887, here he wears only one prize along with his distinguished shield, marksman bar, and sharpshooter badge with requalification bars.

Fig. 2.46. Samuel Woodfill as a captain in the 60th Infantry. Before World War I Woodfill served as an enlisted man in the U.S. Army for sixteen years. He received the Medal of Honor for actions on October 12, 1918, while he was with the 5th Division. His expert rifleman's badge has two qualification bars with fishtail ends and two shorter bars with round ends.

Fig. 2.44

Fig. 2.45

bar. Soldiers in the field tended to wear what they wanted. Despite the disconcerting appearance of both fishtail and round-end bars on one badge, such mixing frequently occurred. One example is shown in figure 2.46.[62]

Besides the fishtail and round ends and the one-year and three-year variations, an assortment of suspension methods also existed. Two rings or wire loops on the top and the bottom

Officials at Rock Island Arsenal intended that the round-ended bars be used with pistol expert badges, while the fishtail style was for use with rifle expert and rifle sharpshooter badges. For a very brief time, 1908–11, the militia pistol sharpshooter badge, made in a gold color, was authorized a fishtail three-year

Fig. 2.46

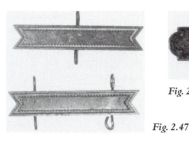

Fig. 2.48

Fig. 2.49

Fig. 2.47

were intended for expert badges, while a single ring or wire loop on the top and bottom went with the sharpshooter's badge. In addition some contractors made special bars with a single loop on the top and two on the bottom or the reverse of this, so that for sharpshooter badges, the intervening bars at least had pairs of ring suspension to keep them in place. These many types of bars provided just enough different design combinations so that during the twenty years between the Spanish-American War and the Great War, every soldier's individual tastes could be met.

Official bars had the connecting loops made by soldering one or two wires to the bar's reverse and then forming a loop at each end of the wire. Whenever a single official requalification bar was worn, the wire loop simply connected the brooch and the pendant, replacing the jump rings. When two or more qualification bars were worn, either of the top or bottom suspension-wire rings were to be twisted ninety degrees, so as to properly intersect with the mating loop. In contrast, most commercial requalification bars were made with a pierced suspension ring, with small jump links connecting the bars to the badge or to other rings.[63]

Despite these changes specified by Rock Island Arsenal and Washington, D.C., many soldiers wore whatever requalification bars they pleased. With the official reinstitution of metal

Fig. 2.50

badges in 1919 after a short official discontinuation of badges to save metal, the War Department authorized qualification bars "bearing the year of requalification."[64] Although new badges came into existence in 1921 and 1922, regulations allowed the older badges and accompanying requalifying bars to continue for those who had earned the older versions. This naturally allowed requalification bars with years beyond 1921.

By 1913 most soldiers were practicing for all grades (expert rifleman, sharpshooter, marksman, first class man, and second class man) at

Fig. 2.47. Fishtail-style blank requalification bars with single loops at the top and bottom for a sharpshooter's badge and with two loops at the top and bottom for an expert's badge. The years of qualification were stamped into these bars.

Fig. 2.48. A round-ended requalification bar, showing a single year. Officially, the round-ended styles of bars were for pistol badges and the single year signified the final of three requalification years.

Fig. 2.49. The reverse of an official requalification bar, showing the loops made from a single piece of wire. When necessary, these were twisted ninety degrees so they would interlock with another bar.

Fig. 2.50. The use of old badges continued with War Department approval for many years, allowing requalification bars well after the army quit issuing the badges in 1921.

Fig. 2.51. Fort Sill's original post-headquarters building, built in 1870. This was the home of the U.S. Army's School of Musketry between 1913 and 1917. The school actually used the original Fort Sill parade ground for machine gun training, since in 1911 the "New Post" was constructed further west, leaving the original buildings and grounds for miscellaneous operations. The musketry school moved to Fort Benning, Georgia, during World War I, becoming the Infantry School.

Fig. 2.51

Fig. 2.52. Between 1903 and 1921 only coast artillery troops could earn a Marksman A badge for firing at 200 and 300 yards. Regular army troops' badges are silver, while National Guard badges are gold colored.

200, 300, 500, and 600 yards, with further firing at 800 and 1,000 yards by those who qualified as sharpshooters and experts. For qualification itself, sharpshooters had to score at least 238 points out of 300, with five shots sitting at 300 yards, five shots kneeling at 300 yards, ten shots prone from 500 yards, and ten more prone shots at 600 yards, although at this last range soldiers used a sandbag rest to represent firing from prepared positions. Cooks and some band members were excused from firing.[65]

Coast artillery men fired rifles only in a defensive mode to protect their positions from enemy troops that might land to capture and take the big guns from the landward side. Another award created in 1903 was for Coast Artillery Corps troops who qualified at reduced ranges on a special "A" course. They fired at 200 and 300 yards only. In 1906 qualification at 200 yards was to be from the standing position, with kneeling and prone positions at 300 yards. In 1913 the A course was fired with five rounds kneeling and five rounds standing at 200 yards and five rounds prone and five rounds sitting at 300 yards. Coast Artillery Corps members could qualify only for this Marksman A award, but on the other hand, other branches could not earn it. Anyone wearing the Marksman A badge earned it while in the Coast Artillery Corps, and coast artillery men did not earn other badges except while in another branch, as was done by Lieutenant Joseph R. Davis, who garnered a sharpshooter badge while assigned to the 8th Cavalry in 1906 and again in 1907. The adjutant general concluded in 1910 that Davis, who had transferred to the Coast Artillery Corps, could continue to wear his sharpshooter's badge—a most unique award in that branch.[66] The badge, although similar to the marksman bar in that it carries the word **MARKSMAN** as the central design, also carries a letter **A** below and a single target above the inscription. This award lasted until 1921. Wearing of the special-course A badges was restricted to those who qualified for the award each year.

Fig. 2.52

A five-man board, lead by Lieutenant Colonel James Parker of the 13th Cavalry, significantly revised the small-arms firing regulations in 1903 and published it in 1904. As part of their work, the board also invented a requalification bar for the Marksman A badge. Although the board did an otherwise outstanding job, it botched this requalification symbol. Since the Marksman A bar did not have a natural way to show requalification, the 1904 regulations specified that for "the soldier who has qualified as a marksman in special course A for three years, not necessarily consecutive years, or, in the case of enlisted men, not necessarily in the same enlistment, a pin will be issued which will specify the years of qualification, and this pin will be worn above the marksman's pin so long as the soldier is entitled to wear the latter." The army never put these procedures into practice. In late 1906, when the first call came in for the three-year pin, the chief of ordnance notified the secretary of war that, "The reward for excellence in rifle shooting in the coast artillery is not great, nor does it take much skill to qualify in special course A," and went on to suggest that the requalification provision be dropped. No requalification bars were ever made for the special course A, and the provision was omitted in the 1908 firing regulations.[67]

In 1906 the army instituted the so-called "holdover classification." This assumed that if an officer or enlisted man qualified as expert, the next year the person automatically classed at least as a sharpshooter, and enlisted men could draw sharpshooter pay. To become an expert, a soldier had only to fire the expert course. Under these circumstances, even if the soldier made only a marksman's score the year after becoming an expert, the sharpshooter rating carried over. In a similar manner any sharpshooter, even if that classification was earned by holdover, automatically was rated a marksman the following year and was entitled to draw a marksman's compensation. To requalify as a sharpshooter the man had only to fire the sharpshooter course. This holdover classification also changed the pay concept. Only those men who were part of an organization normally equipped with a rifle or carbine could draw extra pay and were subject to the holdover qualification, and the Coast Artillery Corps and their Marksman A award could not draw this extra pay at all. As a result, people such as ordnance sergeants were not entitled to additional compensation, as they were not armed with a rifle or carbine. Officers who were assigned to a position not requiring them to fire could continue to wear their most recent badge. The 1906 regulations also allowed officers and men of the various staff departments, veterinarians, and post, regimental, and battalion staff (except for medical personnel and chaplains) to fire if they wanted.[68]

Fig. 2.53

With the 1913 *Small Arms Firing Manual,* the army prescribed a reduced course for National Guard members and awarded them "bronze" badges of the same design as the regular army. Actually, the so-called bronze color was made from aluminum-bronze metal, and the result was a shiny, dark-gold color. Those militiamen who fired the regular army course and met these standards received the silver badges.[69]

Prior to these special National Guard courses, in 1903 the War Department had created a vague general order that allowed the state troops to fire a "special course C." This order permitted the states to issue whatever awards they wanted, provided the militia generally followed regular army practices. In truth, the states had always created and given any awards they desired. Simply to please a select group of senior National Guard officers, James Parker, a cavalry officer and president of the 1902–3 firing board, wrote this nebulous change to the 1902 small-arms firing regulations in

one day. Parker was involved with small-arms firings all his life and had just been placed in charge of the Division of Militia Affairs in the office of the adjutant general. A political animal, Parker was going to please.[70]

Fig. 2.54

In 1915 three more badges briefly came into existence. These were for short-range rifle proficiency, and not many soldiers earned the new badges. Not as attractive as the older standard-range badges, the simple bars for all three short-range awards were all very similar to each other. With the activation of the National Guard for duty on the Mexican border and then the entry of the United States into World War I, few units ever held short-range qualification exercises. The creation of these badges was another bone thrown to the National Guard and the NRA.

Parker, while a brigadier general commanding the 1st Cavalry Brigade in Texas during 1914, recalling his time in 1903 when he headed the small-arms board, suggested that the old special course B (firing at 200 and 300 yards) be reinstituted to assist in quickly training volunteers or recruits. The War Department had terminated the original short "B Course" in 1913, but when Parker wrote the War Department from Texas, he suggested that special badges or even a civilian lapel button be authorized. The ever agreeable army staff created three short-range badges. Firing for these was only at 200 yards in the prone position, both with and without sandbag rest, and while kneeling, sitting, and standing. Although the army declared short-range badges obsolete shortly after World War I, they were listed as available in price lists until 1931.[71]

By the start of World War I most of the army's staff leaned towards the 1897 "field fire"

Fig. 2.53. By wearing a Marksman A badge, this soldier is easily identified as a member of the Coast Artillery Corps.

Fig. 2.54. Badges made at Rock Island Arsenal came in individually labeled pasteboard boxes. The frugal arsenal made even the boxes and labels.

Fig. 2.55

Fig. 2.56

Fig. 2.55. The army awarded three short-range badges (expert, sharpshooter, and marksman), all of this design, in 1915 and 1916.

Fig. 2.56. Soldiers fired for short-range badges at 200 yards prone, both with and without sandbag rest, and from kneeling, sitting, and standing positions. The army downplayed individual proficiency when it instituted short-range badges, due to the emphasis on field fire.

concept, in which men blindly followed an officer's instruction. Under this concept troops did not need to estimate the range to targets. For this reason, the NRA and the National Guard came into opposition with the regular forces. During the first days of the war regular forces pushed ahead with this philosophy, but it was reversed in September 1917, when General Pershing asserted more direct supervision over training by making it perfectly clear that he wanted soldiers who could shoot as individuals.

Pershing wanted to defeat the Germans in the open by fire and maneuver, and this required soldiers well schooled in target practice. The general had to overcome several obstacles. Rifles and machine guns were in short supply. Some men drilled with wooden weapons, and many machine gunners never even handled real weapons until they were in France. The French and British allies had given up on aimed rifle fire and depended upon artillery for long-range killing and grenades for close fighting. Pershing's staff continually had to counter the allies, who had three years of bitter trench-warfare experience. Historians may debate whether Black Jack Pershing's campaign for open warfare and the worth of

rifle marksmanship was correct, but the fact is that he had his way and shooting became a fundamental skill for members of the American Expeditionary Forces (AEF). Pressures of training the enormous army in the United States did not allow adequate emphasis on shooting, but it was a hot training topic in France. Once Pershing got his way and marksmanship training became a keystone American skill, the army continued to emphasize shooting until well after World War II.[72]

In the forty years between the introduction of long-arm badges and the Paris Peace Conference, the Ordnance Department artisans created nearly a dozen designs and produced some of them in both bronze and silver. With a square marksman button worn on the collar from the start, within a generation shooting recognition expanded to an entire family of pin-on badges. When coupled with pistol badges (which will be discussed next), these handsome forms of recognition and the extra qualification pay comprised powerful incentives available to the American soldier. Shooting in the 1880s started as an individual skill, and by the end of World War I, it again depended upon personal deftness.

U.S. ENFIELD MODEL 1917 RIFLES

In World War I most U.S. forces did not use the highly accurate and well-respected Springfield—most of the American doughboys in France carried the U.S. Enfield Model 1917, a modified British rifle. How did this strange turn of events come about?

Prior to America's entry into World War I, the British and Russian governments contracted with various U.S. companies to make rifles. The British in particular needed to build up their weapons' manufacturing capacity for many different types of arms and so arranged with three U.S. firms to make the British Enfield rifle: the Winchester Repeating Arms Company of New Haven, Connecticut; the Remington Arms–Union Metallic Cartridge Company of Ilion, New York; and the Remington Arms Company, which made them at their Eddystone, Pennsylvania, plant. All tooled their facilities to make the British rifle.

When the United States entered the war, the U.S. Ordnance Department did not have the capacity to make the millions of Springfield rifles required, so the War Department made the decision to use the available British tooling. The weapon was modified to the .30-06 round and other minor changes were made, the results becoming the U.S. Enfield Model 1917, the rifle used by most of the U.S. soldiers in the AEF.

PISTOLS

Many a poor cavalryman, armed with a pistol, could have felt neglected in the late nineteenth century, as long-arms firers shot from a multitude of ground positions and reaped shooting awards. Horseback-mounted pistol target practice languished. A document of 1875 allotted fifteen practice rounds per month for cavalry troops and allowed commanders to split the allocation between revolvers and carbines. A two-page 1882 general order described how cavalrymen should practice mounted revolver firing from 10 to 60 yards and mounted carbine firing from 30 to 210 yards, although the War Department issued no standard badges for such mounted skills. Even before the War Department invented shooting badges, the ever attentive General Ord ordered that all company commanders have their own copy of Heth's old manual and that cavalry units practice with blanks so that their horses could become accustomed to the sound of firearms. Overall though, the army avoided discussing pistol training.[73]

Blunt's 300-plus-page 1885 book is devoted to rifle and carbine firing, and only in an appendix is pistol firing discussed, limited to five short pages. Practice was to be individually at 5 and 10 yards after the men practiced in squads, using blanks to simulate combat. For those who "exhibit[ed] proficiency," firing ranges could be increased in 10 yard increments up to 60 yards. Once dismounted firing was thoroughly practiced, the men mounted and in squads started about 20 yards from a target, rode towards it, stopping to fire. When units completed such exercises, the department inspector of rifle practice completed his report on pistol firing by simply stating that such practice had been held.[74]

In field service, proficiency with pistols was no better. One second lieutenant of the 2d Cavalry, stationed in Kansas shortly after the Civil War, reported on a buffalo hunt, matter-of-factly stating, "Sergeant Miller shot his horse through the head during the excitement." This from a combat veteran of The War between the States. Lieutenant Colonel George A. Custer was no better, as he used his revolver to accidentally shoot and kill his favorite horse out from under himself in Kansas while involved in a spirited buffalo hunt, although Lieutenant David Inglis Scott, in a Minnesota buffalo hunt, dropped one pistol and then with the other accidentally shot his horse through the head.[75]

In 1889 the staff officers in Washington allowed troop commanders to eliminate revolver practice entirely for recruits, or commanders could modify it and fire that portion "they deem most advantageous." Even so, the report from the cavalry regiments for 1889 showed that most troops fired. The results were that nearly 30 percent hit targets while dismounted and 36 percent of individuals hit while mounted, and that in collective fire by platoons, 15 percent of the targets were struck. Colonel J. F. Wade, 5th Cavalry commander in 1891, stated that very little pistol firing occurred in his regiment throughout that summer, except in Troop E. Between April and July that single unit had seven days of general practice and twenty days of mounted pistol practice.[76]

The Enfield rifle, used by most U.S. soldiers in France. British in design, it was made in the United States under War Department contract because the United States did not the tooling to make enough Springfield rifles. The U.S. version was modified to include chambering for the American army's .30-06 round, with the result that the weapon became the U.S. Enfield Model 1917 rilfe.

The U.S. Model 1917 rifle sights lacked the ability to adjust for windage, a fact considered by some to be "a refinement," although windage adjustments were a key point in Springfield 1903 rifle instruction. Most importantly, the U.S. Enfield included a very large number of parts, making it hard to produce and service. In one and one-half years of U.S. participation in the war, the three contract plants made and delivered over 2 1/2 million of these rifles, while the two government plants made only slightly over 300,000 of the Springfields. While not used in many shooting contests, the U.S. Enfield Model 1917 did yeoman's duty during the Great War.

The best method for firing a pistol was not clear in the late nineteenth century. While many shooters extended their arm and locked their elbow, some fired with their elbow bent to bring the sights closer to their eyes. Others believed that with training, a shooter could do just as well by looking at the target and firing from the waist, as typified in later Western movies. It was during the 1890s that a standard dismounted position for competition shooting was refined by Chevalier Paine: an erect stance with weight evenly distributed on both feet placed about fifteen inches apart, the body and arm aligned with the target, the arm locked at the elbow. Trigger pulls of about four pounds were deemed best. These general guides are often used today.[77]

Even on the brink of the twentieth century, those fanatics who placed rifle practice next to godliness did precious little for those armed with pistols. General Orders Number 36 of 1897 revised pistol practice, and as part of the "improvement" had troopers ride an oval course firing at silhouettes of mounted cavalrymen as they passed between 5 and 25 yards. The army instituted special cavalry matches in 1889 that included revolver firing in department, division, and army competition, but while men could win opulent gold, silver, and bronze prizes in these elite contests, the army offered no badge to encourage revolver excellence by the ordinary soldier.[78]

The National Guard Association, organized during the late 1870s in St. Louis, worked to solve the plight of the pistol shooter and at the association's 1907 convention finally adopted a resolution calling on the army's chief of ordnance to create and supply bronze-color pistol expert, pistol sharpshooter, and pistol marksman badges exclusively for the National Guard. After successfully lobbying for over half of 1907 and after a distinguished committee of five men, including the U.S. Army's adjutant general and four field-grade National Guard officers selected the qualification criteria, the army then provided the badges. The four men picked to assist in lobbying included two from the District of Columbia National Guard and one from nearby Maryland. With all of that political help the army stepped forward and complied, although with a signal lack of enthusiasm at high levels.[79]

The Ordnance Department designed badges similar to those used by the regular army for rifle and carbine qualification, except for the smaller size and golden color. The awards were a bar inscribed **PISTOL MARKSMAN**, a badge consisting of a cross pendant from a small bar bearing the words **PISTOL SHARPSHOOTER**, and a badge of two crossed revolvers superimposed upon a wreath suspended from a bar inscribed **PISTOL EXPERT**. Simultaneously with the creation of these 1907 badges came the provisions for bars showing three years of qualification. The shiny bronze pistol marksman and pistol sharpshooter badges lasted until the start of 1914, and the bronze pistol expert badge survived until the end of 1915, when the latter was replaced by the silver regular-army version, which will be discussed next.[80]

Firing for National Guard marksman's and sharpshooter's badges took place dismounted at 15, 25, and 50 yards. Ten seconds were allowed to rapidly fire five shots at both 15 and 25 yards, then men had thirty seconds to fire five rounds at 25 yards. Finally shooters had one leisurely minute to fire five rounds at 50 yards. This sequence was repeated twice for a total of 200 possible points. A marksman had to score 130 points and a sharpshooter 160. Those who qualified as a sharpshooter could then fire the considerably more difficult expert course.

Pistol expert qualification required two repetitions of each of the following: five rapid-fire shots at 15 yards in eight seconds, five more rapid shots at 25 yards in eight seconds, five timed shots at 25 yards in twenty seconds, five shots at 50 yards in twenty seconds, and finally at 75 yards, five slow-fire shots with each round being fired in under twenty seconds. Those making 200 of a possible 250 points earned a gold-color pistol expert badge.[81]

The army brass never embraced revolver qualification with the passion shown for rifles and carbines. In 1909 the War Department finally adopted the National Guard's pistol expert badge design, awarding it in silver to the regulars. Army officials severely misjudged the number of officers who would deftly hone their pistol-firing skills so they could wear a badge. Cherished by officers in the field, this new silver badge was earned by 810 men in the first year, a significantly large number when one compares it to the expert rifle badge introduced in 1903. In the early years many departments, when publishing the annual firing results, included an additional column to report the number of expert revolver shots by company, troop, or battery. Many officers' primary arm was the pistol, and four years later the regular forces adopted a more extensive set of pistol courses.[82]

Fig. 2.57

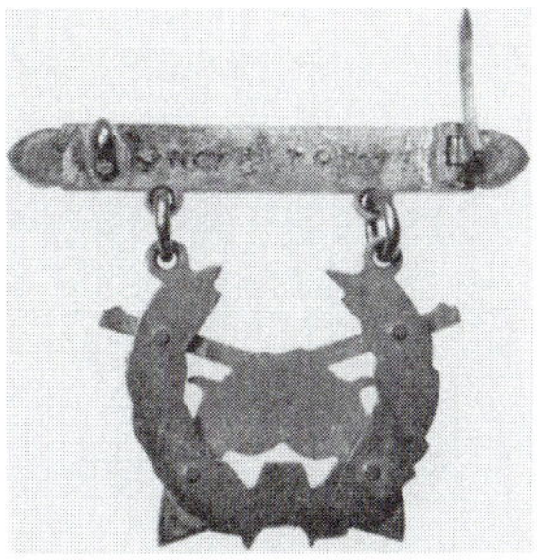

Fig. 2.58

Fig. 2.59

Fig. 2.60

ONE
MARKSMAN'S PIN
BRONZE
ROCK ISLAND ARSENAL
1915
E 729 32

Fig. 2.61

For the new 1913 course, men fired either on horseback or dismounted, depending upon their type of unit. They were rated as an expert pistol shot (dismounted: 80 percent in record course and 83 percent in expert course, or horseback: 70 percent in record course and 65 percent in expert course); a first class man (80 percent dismounted or 70 percent mounted); a second class man (70 percent dismounted or 60 percent mounted); or unqualified. With the adoption of this 1913 scheme, the army also began to issue a silver bar carrying the two lines **PISTOL SHOT FIRST CLASS**. This increase in awards, coupled with the larger army and the many other rewards, caused the U.S. Mint to assist Rock Island Arsenal in producing a machine that could make twenty-four silver strips at one time. Militia troops were authorized a first class pistol-shot bar in bright bronze color for slightly reduced standards from the regular course. After only two years the regular army ceased this militia award in late 1915. Some states also gave a similar Pistol Shot Second Class award, since men could be classed as such. National Guard bars were bronze in color and regular army bars were silver, even though the chief of ordnance was slow in updating the official drawings. (The Ordnance Department did not revise drawings to show the pistol-shot first class bar in silver until 1915—the same time the bronze pistol shot first class bar ended.)[83]

In some manuals the expert badge was called an "expert revolver shot's badge," but the 1907

National Guard badge was impressed **PISTOL EXPERT**. When the regular army gave up revolvers for the M 1911 pistol, no change was made in the expert badge. The inscription was correct, and the crossed revolvers remained for historical reasons. In the fall of 1915 the army finally switched to crossed .45 automatic pistols and simultaneously began to make the entire pendant—both wreath and crossed weapons—from one piece of material. Concurrent with this change, authorization of bronze-colored pistol expert badges ended, so National Guard pistol expert badges displaying .45 pistols were never authorized. In 1937, when the U.S. Marine Corps readopted army pre–World War I–style badges, they continued the silver crossed .45 pistols design.[84]

Fig. 2.62

Fig. 2.63

Fig. 2.57. The army established gold-colored expert pistol badges in 1907, solely for the National Guard. Later, silver versions were very popular with regular cavalry officers.

Fig. 2.58. The reverse of an expert pistol badge made by Rock Island Arsenal. The pendant, like that of the original expert rifleman badge, had the wreath struck separately from the crossed weapons, which were attached with brads.

Fig. 2.59. Slightly smaller than the rifle version of the sharpshooter's badge, this pistol variety was first made in 1907 in gold color for National Guard members.

Fig. 2.60. Only members of the National Guard could earn pistol marksman bars. While the regular army adopted pistol expert badges in 1909, it never authorized pistol marksman bars for regular troops.

Fig. 2.61. This pasteboard box does not specifically state that the badge is for National Guard troops, but it is implied by the word **BRONZE** on the label.

Fig. 2.62. Pistol-shot first class bars, first authorized in 1913. These were made in silver for federal troops and for some National Guard members and in gold color for National Guard troops making a lesser score.

Fig. 2.63. The army classified some poorer-scoring cavalry troopers as pistol shots second class but never prescribed any badge or bar for this rating. Some private companies and selected states struck bars of this design.

*Fig. 2.64. Starting in the fall of 1915,
the army switched to expert pistol
badges bearing crossed .45 caliber
automatic pistols.*

LATE NINETEENTH-CENTURY ARMY REVOLVERS

A pistol requires two actions to fire the weapon: cocking the hammer and pulling the trigger. Older pistols required the hammer to be cocked first to ready it for firing. This is called a single-action pistol—if it has not had its hammer pulled back, the weapon will not fire even if the trigger is pulled. A double-action pistol performs both actions with a long trigger pull: first cocking and then firing. Cavalrymen who fought the Plains Indians often packed their sabers away but when on campaign always carried their pistols. In the 1880s this was generally a single-action .45 caliber Colt, a weapon that was cocked with the thumb and then fired by the single action of pulling the trigger. While double-action revolvers had been used for many years, the military's opinion was that if a man was sufficiently expert to fire a single-action revolver with accuracy and rapidly, he was more accurate than with a double-action due to the effort required to pull the trigger, which in turned cocked the hammer. If the soldier was not accurate with a single-action pistol, he would not be accurate with the more difficult double-action style.

Side Elevation of Colt's Revolving Pistol.

The army issued single-action Colt .45 revolvers until 1892–93, when the chief of ordnance purchased Colt .38 caliber pistols, the so-called Army Colt that ultimately came in six models distinguished only by minor differences (and .38 Navy Colts also exist). The various .45 caliber military revolvers were proven man stoppers, but the .38 caliber pistols

A single-action Colt .45 revolver of the style issued until 1892–93. The engraving is taken from an 1898 War Department book on caliber .45 army revolvers

and other handguns showed themselves woefully inadequate in halting fanatical Moros, and so the army returned to .45 caliber pistols as a result of the Philippine insurrection. The Colt Model 1909 was briefly used until the introduction of the M 1911 semiautomatic pistol. This intimate association of revolvers with army side arms is indicated by the two revolvers shown on the pistol expert badge.

Fig. 2.64

Like rifle badges, pistol badges lingered many years after their formal demise. These obsolete insignia returned to the army Lazarus-like in about 1940 with the emergency expansion of the armed forces. By virtue of their nicer designs and the recognition that these were older badges, the pre-1921 badges provided a better splash of silver while simul-

taneously implying a whiff of experience. As a result, new soldiers often purchased these badges intended for the Marine Corps.

A final note on pistol badges, and one that also applies to the various rifle badges, relates to the pins and associated hinges and the catches. From their introduction until 1913, badges made at Rock Island Arsenal had the pin tongue hinged with a round cross bar that typically ran from the top to the bottom of the brooch. The pointed end of the pin tongue fastened into a catch made from the same diameter round wire as that forming the pin itself, the catch being made into a C shape. An example is shown in figure 2.65.

Beginning in the fall of 1913, hinges and catches changed. The hinge became a commercial style. The base was formed by a U-shaped piece soldered to the reverse of the badge. The opening of the U was left to receive the long pin tongue, which was flattened at the hinge end to fit into the U. A small wire held the pin tongue in the U-shaped base. While commercial hinges placed on badges and jewelry typically have this construction, the U-shaped base portion of the hinge also had two small lips to act as stops. These lips limited the rotation of the pin itself, since the long pin also had two small wires attached near the flattened end. An example is shown in the center of figure 2.65.

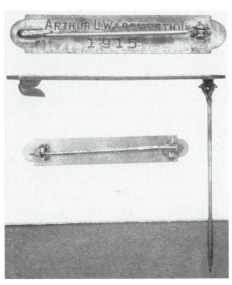

Fig. 2.65

The 1915 and later badges display still a different style catch. Officially called a George Fuller and Sons Company catch, these opened on one side only and might best be described as looking somewhat like a safety-pin catch. An example of this later catch is shown in figure 2.65. Catches of this same design, even those made by George Fuller and Sons Company, were also used on some commercially made badges, making the difference between issue and purchased badges now difficult to distinguish.[85]

Officers provided their own side arms just as they provided their own sabers, but with the introduction of the M 1911 pistol, officers could draw revolvers from units during 1912 and 1913 pending general availability of the new automatics. In 1914 the chief of ordnance stated that he tested a "method of converting the automatic pistol, caliber .45, into a gallery practice pistol" on some twenty-five weapons. But the next year, he reported that the modification was unsatisfactory, since the weight and balance were not consistent with a service pistol.[86]

MACHINE GUNS AND AUTOMATIC RIFLES

From the Civil War until the start of the twentieth century, the army experimented with both machine guns and organizations to use these weapons. Initially, artillerymen manned these weapons, and by 1897 the army allotted each machine gun one thousand rounds of ammunition for annual practice. More modern and lighter weight single-barreled weapons that used the firing recoil or portions of the propelling gases to drive the many parts of the firing cycle necessary for an automatic gun finally replaced the unwieldy and multibarreled Gatling guns. With this change the large artillery-style weapons were replaced by lighter, portable guns that easily fit into the realm of the foot soldiers who were otherwise equipped with ordinary rifles.[87]

It was 1906 when the War Department directed each cavalry squadron and infantry battalion to organize a machine gun platoon consisting of a lieutenant and one sergeant and two detachments that each included a machine gun. These provisional platoons were supposed to be equipped with M 1904 water-cooled Maxim guns, then in use in many countries, since the performance of the Gatling guns was marginal. In practice some platoons continued to be equipped with Gatling guns, while others received Maxim or Benét-Mercier guns. Despite these supposed improvements beyond the Gatling guns, the army reduced the training ammunition allocation to 500 rounds a year.

Some regimental commanders carefully nourished these special provisional units, while other colonels used the platoons for virtually any duty except firing. The 1906 ad hoc organizations became more formally sanctioned with the National Defense Act of 1916, when Congress authorized both infantry and cavalry regiments to include a machine gun company or troop as part of their organizations. This finally placed the rapid-firing weapons, including M 1895 Colt Brownings, M 1904 Vickers-Maxims, and M 1909 Benét-Merciers into the amorphous army after over a half-century of experimentation.[88]

In 1910 one of the four annual School of Musketry sessions was devoted to machine gun instruction. The commander, three non-commissioned officers, and four selected

Fig. 2.65. The top two badges have typical pins used after 1913, including a hinge end with two small stops and a safety-pin-type catch. This shielded catch was introduced in 1915. The lower badge has an older-style pin and catch, typical of badges made at Rock Island Arsenal before the 1913 and 1915 changes. Distinguishing characteristics of the earlier badges include an open catch made from round wire formed into a C and a hinge with a crossbar attached to the pin.

MACHINE GUNS

Ever since the invention of the early muskets and their predecessors, soldiers and their leaders thirsted for a multifiring weapon. Leonardo Da Vinci sketched a multibarreled set of "rifles" on large wheels like an artillery piece, and there was always a rich abundance of novel ideas for such weapons, but until the time of the American Civil War, no practical versions were available to U.S. forces. In 1862 Richard Jordan Gatling, a doctor who never practiced medicine but earned a living as an inventor of agriculture implements, created a hand-cranked, multibarrel weapon that bears his name, the Gatling gun. Gatling's weapon consisted of up to twelve rifle barrels mounted lengthwise on a spindle that passed a stationary breech that loaded and fired each barrel. Although the gun was invented during the Civil War, the federal government did not make much use of any rapid-firing weapons until after the war. The multiple-barrel Gatling gun and others like it were mounted on large wheels like contemporary field artillery. Initially, the army assigned the weapons to the artillery. During the latter half of the nineteenth century, inventors around the world worked diligently to improve rapid-firing small-caliber weapons, but it was not until a few weapons makers successfully used a single barrel that an effective and light-weight machine gun appeared, one soldiers could move easily around the battle field.

A Gatling gun from the nineteenth century. Although this multiple barrel weapon produced a lot of firepower, its mount made it too high for effective fire close to the ground and difficult to move on the battlefield with infantry troops.

Sir Hiram Maxim and John Browning both developed early self-loading weapons that used the firing recoil or a small portion of the firing gases that propelled the bullet to unlock the bolt, extract and eject the spent cartridge case, cock the weapon, and load it again, making it ready to fire. While these weapons were light and more easily handled by infantrymen in the field, the rapid heating of the barrel caused problems, as intense firing could burn out the barrel.

The only solutions were to replace the red-hot barrel quickly in combat or to cool the barrel very effectively. For the latter case, Browning invented a weapon with a heavy water jacket that allowed for more sustained firing, although it was heavy and the weapon was harder to move than an air-cooled machine gun. This water-cooled machine gun was later modified to be simply air cooled in order to give it the lighter weight necessary to move on the twentieth-century battlefield, although some water-cooled versions remained in service through the Korean War. Because of the heating problem, the ability to rapidly change barrels without any special tools became an important factor in designing these weapons. A key part of machine gun training was for the gunner to control the lengths of the bursts in order to avoid overheating the barrel while also effectively distributing the shots.

Machine guns became mounted in aircraft, tanks, and armored cars as well as on trucks and other ground vehicles and also served as anti-aircraft weapons with special ground mounts, appearing in a wide range of sizes from .30 caliber to over an inch in diameter. So pervasive was the weapon that after World War I the army classed special machine guns as

A Browning machine gun, Model 1917. Although heavy, this weapon was much lighter and more easily moved on a battlefield than the Gatling gun. The water-cooled barrel allowed more sustained fire than an air-cooled weapon.

separate weapons such as armored car weapons or anti-aircraft weapons.

privates from each machine gun platoon of all regiments serving in the Departments of California and the Columbia attended. The provisional machine gun troop (Troop D) of the 14th Cavalry was on duty at the school in early 1910 and served as the guinea pig during this training to determine the drill, organization, and best equipment for cavalry machine guns.[89]

Although the army experimented with machine guns prior to World War I, it took that conflict to drive home the weapons' value. Between 1898 and 1916 Congress annually appropriated only an average of $150,000 for procurement of machine guns. Finally in 1916 the authorization grew to $12 million, although the indecisive War Department had yet to select a weapon, and thus actual purchases were not made with the money, until 1917. At the start of World War I, the U.S. Army's total inventory of machine guns was limited to 670 Benét-Merciers, 285 Maxims, 350 Lewis guns, and 148 Colt machine guns.[90]

Weapons of war were ahead of the administration. It was June of 1917 before the U.S. Army even produced a machine gun manual, and then its title included the word *Provisional*. Targets were either 3-foot-high, 20-foot-long strips of paper bearing various markings and silhouettes or a standard "B" target, 6 feet on a side with a 20-inch-diameter bull's-eye. Only officers and men in machine gun organizations could be classified, and they were graded as expert rifleman–machine gun, sharpshooter–machine gun, marksman–machine gun, or unqualified.[91]

Despite the hyphenated titles, men wore standard rifle badges, including requalification bars. A few soldiers purchased and wore unofficial badges, one of which is shown in figure 2.66. This example was made nearly identical to the standard rifle sharpshooter badge but with the addition of two sets of the words **MACHINE GUN**, one running down the top and bottom arms and the other across the side arms, while sharing the central letter **N**. Other awards were the cloth sleeve disks introduced during World War I (discussed next), but these did not commonly see service.[92]

After the close of World War I, General John J. Pershing resolved that U.S. troops in Europe would resume marksmanship training, including a major match that took place in May 1919 and is discussed in chap-

Fig. 2.66

*Fig. 2.66. A popular but unofficial machine gun sharpshooter's badge used about the time of World War I. It is identical to the prescribed rifle sharpshooter badge except for the words **MACHINE GUN**, which run down and across the Maltese pendant.*

ter 7. The Third Army became Pershing's army of occupation. (Its insignia is a red **A** for Army, inside a white **O** for Occupation, on a blue circle.) Several divisions (units under the control of the III and IV Corps and later the VII Corps) marched into Germany starting December 1, 1918. The Third Army remained until July 2, 1920, when the War Department transferred the balance of the troops to the American Forces in Germany as a result of the treaty ending the war, which had been signed on June 28, 1920.[93]

By the end of 1919 the American Forces in Germany consisted of 842 officers and 17,986 enlisted men; by a year later the War Department had reduced the total by about 2,000. As part of the new occupation routine, in August and September 1920 the two brigades of the American Forces in Germany (AFG) held tests that allowed personnel to be "qualified as Expert Machine Gunners." On October 4 a board of three officers met at the AFG headquarters, Fortress Ehrenbreistein, opposite Coblenz, with the objective of designing a set of three machine gun badges. By October 7 the board sent a letter to the commanding general of AFG with the three designs and correspondence that were ultimately forwarded to the War Department. Someone later separated the designs from the letters, so the recommended badge concepts are now unknown.[94]

The American Forces in Germany finally issued locally made, silver-colored badges for expert machine gun qualification of the type illustrated in figure 2.67, between August 26 and September 13, 1921. The majority of the

Fig. 2.67. *An expert machine gunner badge. These were locally made for the American Forces in Germany in 1921.*

Fig. 2.68. *Champion U.S. Army shooters in Germany, 1921. The officer in the front row, center, and the enlisted men in the rear row, center and right, wear the newly awarded silver expert machine gunner badges. American Forces in Germany did not make badges for machine gun sharpshooters or marksmen.*

Fig. 2.69. *A 1919 War Department prototype machine gun marksman badge. Few of these were made and none were awarded.*

Fig. 2.70. *A post–World War I prototype machine gun sharpshooter badge.*

Fig. 2.71. *Similar to the American Forces in Germany expert machine gunner badge, this War Department sample was not made in large quantities.*

few men selected to take the AFG machine gun test qualified as experts, and no sharpshooter or marksman badges were struck in Germany. On December 15, 1921, the Provisional Machine Gun Battalion was demobilized and ordered to leave massive Fort Ehrenbreistein. Having been under intense political pressure in the United States during all of 1921 and 1922, the AFG was finally formally disbanded in early 1923. It had been reduced to a few hundred men by the end of 1922, after going to less than 6,000 men by the start of that year.[95]

While this creation of new badge designs played out on the banks of the Rhine, near the Potomac River the War Department prepared a full set of silver badges generally similar to those used for rifle and pistol qualification. In August 1919 the War Department stated that

issue of the metal rifle and pistol badges, suspended during the war to save metal, would be resumed and then went on to announce that all enlisted men could earn machine gun expert, sharpshooter, and marksman badges.[96]

The War Department struck a few prototype badges, shown in figures 2.69, 2.70, and 2.71. The Quartermaster Corps priced large quantities of these badges in bronze and silver but never issued them. The intent of the bronze badges was not to distinguish between National Guard and regular army, but to show courses. Silver was reserved for those men qualifying on the longest range, or "A" course, and anyone qualifying on the shorter rifle courses, such as the "B" rifle course, would receive the

Fig. 2.67

Fig. 2.68

Fig. 2.69

Fig. 2.70

Fig. 2.71

bronze version. Rather than implement this concept, however, in 1921 the U.S. Army brought out three badge designs of the type still used today, including a qualification bar for machine guns.[97]

During World War I the army introduced various automatic rifles, including the U.S. designed and made Browning Automatic Rifle (BAR). Men trained on the BAR, but during and immediately after the war the War Department provided that soldiers who qualified as marksman, sharpshooter, or expert would receive the same insignia (and when authorized, the same pay) "as prescribed for the magazine rifle." Even so, the army stated that only one insignia (or pay) would be recognized. The higher qualification was the "final and only qualification" recorded.[98]

CLOTH INSIGNIA, WORLD WAR I

One paradox of World War I planning was that while all soldiers received training with rifles and machine guns hopefully to do in the German Hun, the War Department removed the real training incentives. It suspended extra pay and the bright shooting badges. The First World War was America's initial war of total mobilization and state-directed sacrifices for the entire population, down to rationing and a united nationalist spirit. In an effort to save metal for the war effort, between April 1918 and August 1919 the U.S. Army prescribed cloth disks to replace the silver- and bronze-colored marksmanship badges. This resulted in sets of cloth devices, similar in size to the private first class rank insignia, 2 1/2 to 2 3/4 inches in diameter and made in both olive

drab wool and olive drab cotton. Never popular with the troops, these coarsely designed cloth insignia on the lower sleeve were worn by very few men. In a further incongruity between official policy and the supposed metal-saving effort, soldiers continued to flaunt silver-colored metal badges throughout the war.[99]

The War Department cloth designs showed a basic weapon symbol for a marksman rating, added a bar below for sharpshooter, and then added a circle around the sharpshooter design to signify expert. Symbols were a stylized five-round belt of machine gun bullets, a rifle, and—for pistol experts and first class pistol shots—a pair of crossed .45 automatics. Coast artillery marksmen who qualified on the special course A added the letter **A** below the rifle.

In the Philippine Islands, the major place where officers and men normally wore white uniforms, the island headquarters suspended wear of marksmanship badges in October 1918, probably in response to the issuance of these cloth awards. The army reinstituted shooting proficiency awards on white uniforms the next year.[100]

PAY

In 1903 Congress added an incentive for soldiers to stick to their rifle practice when legislation provided up to $12,000 for enlisted men qualifying as expert riflemen by adding one dollar of additional pay per month. Over time various bills increased incentives. In 1905 the $1.00 per month was allowed for three years, providing the soldier remained in an organization armed with a rifle or carbine, and this became the holdover classification. As

Fig. 2.72. Cloth rifle marksmanship chevrons. The War Department prescribed these unpopular and seldom worn insignia in the spring of 1918. The ring symbolized an expert, the bar a sharpshooter, and a plain rifle a marksman. The **A** indicated the Marksman A course for Coast Artillery Corps troops.

Fig. 2.73. The two bland U.S. Army cloth pistol marksmanship insignia from the latter part of World War I. Soldiers were to wear these cloth marksmanship insignia on the lower sleeve. The pistol expert had the circle added, while the first class pistol shot consisted simply of crossed .45 automatic pistols.

Fig. 2.74. Like the other cloth "badges" of 1918, these came in olive drab cotton (left) and olive drab wool (center and right). The scheme of the bar and circle was the same as that for the rifle chevrons. The belt of five rounds symbolized machine gun qualification.

Fig. 2.72

Fig. 2.73

Fig. 2.74

Fig. 2.75

Fig. 2.75. Lieutenant C. S. Murphy, 1918, wears both rifle and pistol badges in silver metal rather than the prescribed cloth sleeve marks designed to save precious metal during the world war. His ribbon represents service on the Mexican border from 1916, while the half wing shows that he was qualified as a junior military aviator—that is, a pilot who had less than three years of service. A double-wing pilot's badge officially replaced this one in late 1917, but Murphy continued to wear his older version.

one veteran of the time testified, "I qualified as an expert rifleman, and that meant an extry [*sic*] dollar a month when the eagle screamed. You'd be surprised how far an extry [*sic*] dollar went in those days."[101]

In 1905 several senior officers, including Major General Leonard Wood, commander of the Department of Mindanao; Brigadier General F. D. Grant, commander of the Department of the East; and Brigadier General W. S. McCaskey, commander of the Department of the Colorado, called for increased pay for skilled riflemen. Grant in particular noted that the shooting skills required even for marksmen were more difficult to earn than those of first class gunner, yet the extra compensation for an expert was only a dollar, while sharpshooters and marksmen received nothing. As a result, by 1908 the chief contribution from Washington, D.C., was a regulation allowing an enlisted man qualifying as expert rifleman, sharpshooter, or marksman the additional pay of $5.00, $3.00, or $2.00 a month respectively. This pay was "from the date of qualification to the end of the enlistment in which they qualify, provided that during that time they do not attain a higher classification."[102]

While regular army enlisted soldiers receiving extra marksmanship compensation were limited to cavalry, infantry, or engineers (excluding any band member), those men of the Philippine Scouts received reduced pay: expert riflemen of the scouts received $1.50 per month, sharpshooters $1.00, and marksmen $.50 per month.[103]

Late in World War I, in May 1918, the War Department suspended both the need for formal qualification and the associated proficiency pay for firing. It was well after World War I before extra pay was reinstated, although in less than three months after the war firing on courses resumed. New pay rules and new badges were about to come into being, with the badges reflecting the diversity of twentieth-century warfare.[104]

Pl. 1. One of the first eighty gold distinguished badges with oval targets that the army ordered in 1887 from New York City jeweler Jens Pedersen.

Pl. 2. The distinguished marksman badge awarded to Sergeant John B. Childers, Company H, 26th Infantry, in 1909. It has plain black, round target rings.

Pl. 3. Gerald R. Harvey's distinguished marksman badge, awarded in 1927. This badge has narrow gold edges around the black target rings.

Pl. 4. The army introduced slightly smaller distinguished pistol shot badges in 1903. Besides their size and wording, pistol badges differ from distinguished marksman badges in having rectangular targets.

Pl. 5. The army awarded thirteen gold prizes with this style of planchet to the winners of army rifle and carbine contests between 1890 and 1902. The top bar was frequently impressed ARMY. This particular striking was evidently made in about 1906 at Rock Island Arsenal to be part of a display board.

Pl. 6. This style of massive third class division prize, awarded between 1881 and 1888, is 2 inches across.

Pl. 7. A silver second class prize, 1 1/2 inches in diameter, given for department rifle competitions from 1889 through 1902.

Pl. 8. A third class carbine prize, 1 5/8 inches in diameter. The army presented this design in silver for two years and in bronze for five years.

Pl. 9. Despite the cavalry-implied design, the army awarded 316 of these bronze prizes to infantrymen for rifle competitions, making these the most common nineteenth-century prizes.

Pl. 10. A second class prize for department cavalry carbine matches, awarded in 1891.

Pl. 11. Cavalry revolver match second class prize, 1¹/₂ inches in diameter, awarded 1889–94.

Pl. 12. The United States struck twenty-two of these bronze display medals but awarded only four in gold.

Pl. 13. A second class prize given at the three division contests in 1889 and in 1890.

Pl. 14. A distinguished aerial gunner badge, given from 1926 to 1932. Lieutenant Louis Merrick received this particular award for 1926 proficency.

Pl. 15. Lieutenant George Russell, 15th Cavalry, received this army cavalry team medal for firing in 1908. The army awarded various gold team medals of similar designs between 1906 and 1923.

Pl. 16. The silver 1903 infantry prize given at the U.S. Army championship match to Engineer Corporal J. J. Gibney, 1¹/₄ inches in diameter.

Pl. 17. A 1-inch-diameter 1906 cavalry prize awarded at the division level.

Pl. 18. Corporal Neville, 26th Infantry, received this newly designed prize, 1¹/₄ inches in diameter, in 1906.

Pl. 19. The two different styles of U.S. Army marksman buttons. Soldiers first received the square version (left) in 1881. The regular army last wore rectangular-style buttons (right) in 1897, although Rock Island Arsenal continued to make them for the National Guard into the twentieth century.

Pl. 20. Rock Island Arsenal made bronze, pin-back sharpshooter crosses in 1883, replacing them with a silver version in 1885.

Pl. 21. A pistol expert badge for National Guard troops, first made in 1907. Regular army versions, in silver, appeared in 1909.

Pl. 22. A comparison of two gold pistol prizes, 1903–22 style. The later version is 1 1/8 inches in diameter, while the prize on the right, awarded in 1912, is 1 inch in diameter.

Pl. 23. A typical bronze rifle prize, 1907–20. The department's name appeared on the top bar.

Pl. 24. The American Expeditionary Forces gave this style of gold rifle prize in 1919.

Pl. 25. An Illinois shooting prize, modeled after U.S. Army prizes. More common bronze versions, with the bars bearing regimental designation, also exist.

Pl. 26. Rock Island Arsenal made boxes that held individual shooting badges.

Pl. 27. One of the 1918 pistol-marksman patches introduced to save metal.

Pl. 28. Private First Class Robert Scott won this rifle prize in 1937. The red ring containing white stars shows that Scott was a member of the Corps of Engineers team.

Pl. 29. A rifle competition artillery team prize from the 1930s. Branches represented by one color had bronze stars in the enameled ring. National Match prizes had rectangular, oak-leaf-covered bars.

Pl. 30. At the tactical corps level, match prizes had all-bronze planchets; gold, silver, or bronze crossed weapons to show placement; and top bars that indicated the awarding headquarters. Automatic rifle match winners had clasps showing crossed Browning Automatic Rifles.

Pl. 31. A VII Corps first class pistol prize, 1922–40.

Pl. 32. A 1956 prototype gold-colored prize for the fifth U.S. Army match. These were never awarded.

Pl. 33. A 1956 prototype silver second class prize intended for award at the National Natches.

Pl. 34. A medal for placing third in the National Trophy match, 1910. All National Trophy match medals at this time were bronze.

Pl. 35. A second-place team medal for the National Trophy match, 1911. Between 1911 and 1919 National Trophy match medals irregularly switched between having and not having ribbons.

Pl. 36. After World War I, medals for the National Trophy match evolved to a gold color, as exemplified in this 1953 version.

Pl. 37. The 1891 silver first class gunner badge. Most of the 500 badges were melted for scrap, so few survive today. The planchet is .85 inch in diameter.

Pl. 38. A 1903-style first class gunner's badge.

· Pl. 39. A 1904–13 field artillery first class gunner's badge.

Pl. 40. A master gunner's badge, 1903–7. Less than twenty-five soldiers received this award.

Pl. 41. An 1897 bronze heavy artillery first class gunner's badge.

Pl. 42. A planchet for an 1897 silver, full-specialist's badge. This was originally suspended from a cannon-shaped brooch in the same style as that for the 1897 bronze first class gunner's badge.

Pl. 43. A nineteenth-century militia artillery prize, engraved in silver.

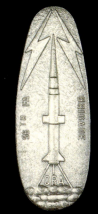

Pl. 44. A silver Senior Pershing Professional badge (intermediate-level qualification), used in the 1970s by the 56th Field Artillery Brigade while it was stationed in Europe. The badge is slightly over 2 9/10 inches high.

Pl. 45. A master badge (highest level qualification), awarded in the late 1970s by the 9th Field Artillery Missile Group, Fort Sill, Oklahoma, and by other missile organizations.

Pl. 46. The State of New York National Guard introduced the first regularly given shooting award in 1876 with this style of gilded bronze medal made by Tiffany & Company. It is .95 inch in diameter.

Pl. 47. A standard U.S. Army sharpshooter badge made in the 1930s in 14-karat gold as a special award.

Pl. 48. One of the set of brass badges the U.S. Chinese Training and Combat Command gave between 1943 and 1945.

Pl. 49. The engraved reverse of an American Expeditionary Forces table medal, awarded to winners of various 1919 shooting contests.

Pl. 50. Three versions of the President's Hundred award. These pin-back devices are intended for wear on the left upper sleeve.

Pl. 51. In 1955 the National Board for the Promotion of Rifle Practice introduced this style of badge. The badges come in various versions for rifle and for pistol. This badge was awarded in 1961.

Pl. 52. A National Guard Bureau Match bronze medal from the 1930s, given to members of a state's winning team.

Pl. 53. A post–World War II National Guard Bureau Match medal, given to members of one of six winning army area teams.

Pl. 54. A 1909 National Match souvenir given by the Hayes Brothers Company. The planchet is 1 3/10 inches high.

Pl. 55. A typical medal given at the National Matches between 1920 and the early 1950s.

Pl. 56. A medal given to members of high-placing teams that compete for the Hilton Trophy.

Pl. 57. A medal given to members of high-placing teams that compete for the Marathon Trophy. Originally presented by George Wingate, the Marathon Trophy is the oldest trophy given at the National Matches.

Pl. 58. A typical National Rifle Association medal, given in the 1920s and 1930s at the Camp Perry matches.

Pl. 59. By the 1950s National Rifle Association national-championship medals had generally changed from solid-color ribbons with narrow red, white, and blue stripes to this style of ribbon. The Wimbledon Cup was established in 1875.

Pl. 60. A medal for the Daniel Boone Trophy, given for individual rifle prowess at the National Matches.

Pl. 61. A 1958 Infantry Trophy Match medal. The National Matches introduced planchets of this design for the Infantry Trophy Match in 1923.

Pl. 62. Over time National Match medals became more gaudy, as exemplified by this 1976 version of the Infantry Trophy Match medal.

Pl. 63. Medal for the General Mellon Trophy, first presented in 1957. The trophy is given to the high National Guard team in the National Trophy pistol team match.

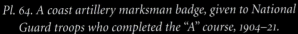

Pl. 64. A coast artillery marksman badge, given to National Guard troops who completed the "A" course, 1904–21.

Pl. 65. The army introduced bronze-colored short range badges in 1915 for National Guard troops. It did not authorize the silver versions, and neither color was widely awarded.

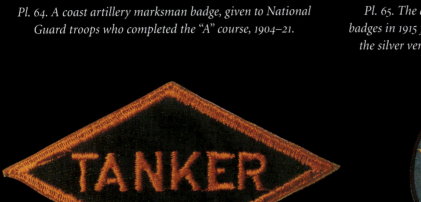

Pl. 66. A 1951 proficiency patch, worn by qualified 1st Armored Division tank crews.

Pl. 67. TCQC on this pocket patch stands for Tank Crew Qualification Course.

Pl. 68. Armor units in Germany during the late 1960s and early 1970s wore many types of colorful proficiency patches.

Pl. 69. CEV stands for Combat Engineer Vehicle, a tanklike vehicle with a 165 mm gun.

Pl. 70. Distinguished crews corresponded to expert qualification and rated a special pocket patch. Qualified crews received the same patch without the "Distinguished" banner.

Pl. 71. Some units in Germany, exemplified by this 8th Cavalry patch, had a basic patch, with the various qualifications shown by a series of tabs displaying the year and the skill.

CHAPTER THREE

THE CURRENT BADGES

NICE BUT NOT INSPIRING

IN FEBRUARY 1919 GENERAL John J. Pershing, commander of the American Expeditionary Forces, began planning for the largest marksmanship matches ever hosted by the U.S. Army. Pershing had spent several weeks of the new year inspecting troops, and he sensed the doughboys' boredom. His dual solution was both to create a series of diversions and to enforce training. Shooting contests met both goals. The matches, held in May 1919 in France, included not only traditional rifle and pistol contests, but also machine gun, automatic rifle, and platoon proficiency tests. To support these 1919 actions, the AEF even published its own small-arms training manual. Pershing's 1919 matches and manuals loudly announced to the army the future of competition in arms and training, even if America outside the military was not listening. The direction set by Pershing effectively ended the army's debate. The resulting scope of small-arms training would last through World War II.[1]

Problems loomed, however. At the end of World War I, U.S. soldiers momentarily had the world turned upside down. But as always after the end of a war, however fleetingly they had been respected and honored, in a twinkling soldiers receded into the background. By 1920 the government bureaucracy of five years before had returned with a vengeance. Economy was king, and there was no need for new weapons development or even for a significant army to keep the world free for democracy. Against this background John J. Pershing had to institute his training program.

During the world war new weapons had been created, improved, mass produced, and even rendered obsolete by still better versions at a mesmerizing pace. Artillery became a massive indirect fire weapon, while before it had been simply a large "see them and shoot them"

weapon, unchanged in direct fire techniques from the Revolution, Napoleon's time, and the Civil War. Recoil mechanisms now allowed cannons to return to their previous position. Sophisticated math and physics allowed the artillery to hit targets that gunners could not see. Chemical weapons likewise had been invented, deployed, and improved. Tanks and airplanes required new skills and the requisite measures of efficiency. Machine guns and automatic rifles dominated the infantryman's war, and these deadly devices called for revised training techniques.

The post-war training philosophy, constrained by limited funds, dictated a new scaffolding for the rewards associated with weapons proficiency. It was impractical to continue to use a large number of different badges. One for each weapon would not work. An individual soldier would look unseemly wearing too many awards, and providing a myriad of awards would cost too much. The supply system would be clogged. These factors made continuation of the pre–World War I concept of a different badge for every weapon type expensive and impractical.

Rather than continue to invent new, separate badges to recognize training with each weapon, the army's new badges recognized skill *levels*. This flexible system has withstood the test of time, and the U.S. Army still uses it today. The plain white metal badges created in the War Department were cheaper and, equally important, the scheme was simpler than the prewar versions.

In reviewing the history of current badges and the philosophy that drove them, the first step is to examine the physical aspects of the badges and qualification bars that designate the qualification weapon. The next steps are to review the proficiency pay given until 1941

Fig. 3.1. Arthur E. Dubois made these sketches in June 1921, showing his concept for three new army shooting badges. With this as the sole documentation, the army adopted his design and published his concept. The badges are still used today.

Fig. 3.2. A shiny silver expert badge, made and commonly worn between 1922 and World War II.

*Fig. 3.3. A 1921-style sharpshooter badge with a **RIFLE** bar of the type introduced in late 1924.*

for some weapons, then a few qualification requirements for various arms, followed by nonregulation badges, and finally significant developments since Vietnam.

BADGES AND BARS

War Department Circular Number 182, July 1921, announced to the army the new "badges for marksmanship and gunnery qualification" design concept that effectively reflected the new War Department's philosophy that soldiers needed to be adept with many weapons. It established three unpretentious basic badges:

• Marksman and second class gunner: "A cross patee."
• Sharpshooter and first class gunner: A cross patee, "with the representation of a target placed on the center thereof."
• Expert: A cross patee with a target placed on the center and encircled by a laurel wreath.

Arthur E. Dubois, the Quartermaster Corps's chief draftsman for heraldry and a man destined to influence U.S. Army insignia well into World War II, created the concept. In late June 1921 Dubois, always the consummate designer, sketched his preliminary notions on three 3 $\frac{1}{2}$ x 5–inch cards, each one showing a different badge. A soldier would suspend one or more bars listing his weapons of qualification below his badge. These preliminary drawings included such niceties as the old roman V in place of the letter U and different bars for field artillery and coast artillery gunnery.

Although these details did not survive, the basic concept was a brilliant break with the past in which every weapon and course had its own badge. Dubois's designs were unrivaled in simplicity. Thus informally documented, the War Department announced the new marksmanship and gunnery badges simply by describing them in the establishing circular. It was nearly a year later, in April 1922, however, before the army actually made these emblems. The designs live today, although with some color change.[2]

After forty years of marksmanship badges, the American soldiers wanted continued recognition for their proficiency with specific weapons. Those soldiers who had mastered several weapons also desired some way to show their complete skills at arms. To recognize this second need, Dubois and the insightful staff planners in Washington supplemented the

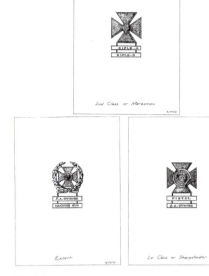

Fig. 3.1

Fig. 3.2

Fig. 3.3

Fig. 3.4

GUNNER, and **F.A. GUNNER** were never made—the official drawings show **COAST ARTY**, **MINES**, and **FIELD ARTY** as the actual product.

While the initial list was rather short, within a few years an ever-increasing number of different bars became available. By 1926 the War Department expanded the authorization to seventeen different bars. The army indulged in the modernization process by listing new weapons, and these reflected the skills deemed essential for proficiency in the "new" post–Great War army. As the army introduced new weapons and withdrew obsolete ones at a dizzying rate, qualification bars changed. Under the impulse of weapons introduction, during World War II the army issued twenty-nine different bars, and a great many insignia manufacturers produced numerous additional unauthorized versions.

Fig. 3.4. A 1921-style marksman badge, officially described as a cross patee, with the bar for field artillery qualification. Like the issue badges, many of the privately purchased early awards came in boxes, as in this example.

three new badges with a list of bars showing the particular weapons on which qualifications could be earned. One historical holdover was the four rifle courses, each of which led to different bars: **RIFLE-A**, **RIFLE-B**, **RIFLE-C**, and **RIFLE-D**, indicating the various courses. Including these four, the July 1921 founding circular resulted in only eleven qualification bars. In actuality the bars originally listed as **C. A. GUNNER**, **MINE**

MODEL 1903 SPRINGFIELD RIFLES

An M 1903A1 rifle, commonly called a 1903 Springfield.

The U.S. Army's workhorse from the early twentieth century to World War II was the Springfield rifle, Model 1903. Early twentieth-century senior army officers believed that the U.S. Army was among the best-armed military powers in the world, thanks to the M 1903 Springfield. The eight-and-one-half-pound rifle came with various stocks and sights and in many variations. It was used through World War II, although after 1941 it was primarily a sniper's weapon. Commonly known as a "Springfield" rifle, it was made at the Springfield, Massachusetts, armory. Starting in 1904 it replaced the short-lived Krag-Jorgensen rifle and in turn was replaced by the M-1 Garand rifle at the start of World War II.

In 1904 the army started to replace the Krag-Jorgensen with the new 1903 Springfield bolt-action rifle. The weapon had its roots in various experimental weapons made and tested in 1900, 1901, and 1902. The Springfield was generally a copy of a clip-fed Mauser rifle. The U.S. weapons were designed in part by William Crozier, a captain in the Ordnance Department who in 1902 was catapulted from captain to brigadier general and chief of Ordnance. The corps of cadets at West Point initially received the new rifles, but since the cartridge was different from the Krag, the weapons were not further distributed except in Alaska, China, and the Philippines until 1906 and 1907. The U.S. Army used Crozier's outstanding weapon as the standard service arm until World War II, and it was fired by marksmen in competitions for over half a century. The original cartridge design had a heavy round-nosed projectile, but in 1906 the bullet underwent vitally important changes when it was reduced in weight, given a sharper point, and its propellant was increased to forty-nine grains. The resulting muzzle velocity was 2,700 feet per second.[3]

The Springfield was not widely used during World War I, as only two government arsenals were making the weapon and it was determined that manufacturing of the tooling would take too long. While the army had over 600,000 of the Springfields in storage for emergency, it made only another 300,000 during the war. With the stocks on hand in the active forces, by war's end only about one million of the rifles existed, which helped support the army of the 1920s and 1930s.

One question that often arises is, "When were the various bars authorized?" The answer depends upon the criterion that determines "authorization." For example, until November 1941 uniform and insignia regulations provided for the **SWORD** bar, which showed expert qualification with the cavalry weapon. The training regulation that formed the authorization for award of the **SWORD** bar was withdrawn in 1938, yet in November 1940 the War Department issued Training Circular Number 9, stating that training with sabers was suspended "during the present emergency." Even so, horse-mounted cavalry units existed into 1942 and 1943, and some of these units undoubtedly continued sword testing and awarding the **SWORD** bar well after the army withdrew the training authorization. Similar examples can be made for many of the qualification bars, as such disparities grew worse with time.[4]

After the Vietnam War, for example, uniform regulations enumerated bars that represented weapons on which the army no longer trained nor even had in stock for over a decade. In the 1970s badge regulations still listed the **CARBINE** bar although the U.S. forces did not issue the weapon. In the 1990s ranger forces began to use the M-4 carbine widely, so the slowness in withdrawing the qualification bar intended for the M-1 carbine allowed it to be used for the M-4.

Army schools that prescribed courses for **AA ARTILLERY**, **MISSILE**, and **FLAME THROWER** dropped all qualification criteria, yet uniform regulations in the post-Vietnam period retained the bars. Staff officers failed to coordinate details, so the regulations persisted in listing these bars that were unobtainable—except, perhaps, by foreign troops being trained on obsolete U.S. weapons. Flame throwers were perhaps the most fearsome weapon developed during World War I, a war that particularly stands out for inventions of destructive machines, but by the end of the Vietnam War, technological advances in the enormous research and development community allowed fielding of one-shot, disposable flame weapons that were simply munitions. Extensive qualification courses were deemed unnecessary, as soldiers simply fired the M-202 flame munition that was similar to the 66 mm light antitank weapon and other plentiful and easy-to-use disposable weapons.[5]

A summary of the prescribed bars is shown in table 2. Given the uncertainties cited, the "authorized" dates listed are based on uniform and insignia regulations or modifications to these regulations rather than on training documents or other paper.

Initially, the badges and bars were "of white metal," as already noted. These bright silver insignia, the same color as the previous regular army awards, continued until World War II,

Table 2. Prescribed Qualification Bars, 1921–2001

Bar Inscription	Dates of Authorization (Per Uniform Regulations)	Notes
A A ARTILLERY	September 1951–Present	
AERIAL GUNNER	December 1926–April 1948	
AERO WEAPONS	June 1974–Present	
AERO BOMBER	December 1926–April 1948	
ARMORED CAR WEAPON	November 1931– November 1941	Never appears on price lists.
AUTO RIFLE	July 1921–Present	July 1923 circular states all enlisted men qualifying with automatic rifle will receive the **RIFLE** bar. Current criteria not clear.
BAYONET	November 1924–Present	On price list, June 1924.
CARBINE	June 1942–Present	First appears on August 1943 price list.
COAST ARTY	July 1921–February 1958	Coast Artillery dissolved, 1950.
C W S WEAPONS	November 1924–April 1948	CWS = Chemical Warfare Service. On price list, June 1924.
FIELD ARTY	July 1921–Present	
FLAME THROWER	April 1948–Present	M–1 Flamethrower introduced in 1941.
GRENADE	July 1928–Present	Not on price list until 1930.
INF HOWITZER	July 1921–June 1942	Still on August 1943 price list.
MACHINE GUN	July 1921–Present	
MACHINE RIFLE	November 1924–April 1948	On price list, June 1924.
MINES	July 1921–September 1951	Intended for Coast Artillery.

Bar Inscription	Dates of Authorization (Per Uniform Regulations)	Notes
MISSILE	February 1958–Present	
MORTAR	April 1948–Present	
PISTOL	July 1921–September 1922 and April 1948–Present	Between these two dates, **PISTOL–D** and **PISTOL–M** authorized.
PISTOL–D	September 1922–April 1948	For dismounted qualification.
PISTOL–M	September 1922–April 1948	For horseback (mounted) qualification.
RECOILLESS RIFLE	April 1948–Present	Training initially prescribed, 1945.
RIFLE	November 1924–Present	Initially on price list, June 1924.
RIFLE-A	July 1921–November 1924	
RIFLE-B	July 1921–November 1924	
RIFLE-C	July 1921–November 1924	
RIFLE-D	July 1921–November 1924	
ROCKET LAUNCHER	April 1948–Present	Training initially prescribed, 1942.
SMALL BORE	June 1930–August 1933	Starting in 1926, cavalry and infantry recruits were required to fire for qualification with small bore rifle.★
SMALL BORE MG	November 1941–April 1948	★
SMALL BORE PISTOL	August 1933–Present	★
SMALL BORE RIFLE	August 1933–Present	★
SUBMACHINE GUN	November 1931–Present	Not on price list until June 1935, when a note appeared that the price would be determined once the bars were purchased. Actual price not listed until 1940.
SUBMARINE MINES	September 1951–February 1958	
SWORD	April 1922–November 1940	Starting in 1935, price lists have note, "until exhausted." August 1943 price list shows note, "Price to be determined when manufactured."
TANK WEAPONS	November 1924–Present	On price list, June 1924.
T D 37 M M	June 1942–April 1948	TD = Tank Destroyer.
T D 57 M M	June 1942–April 1948	
T D 75 M M	June 1942–April 1948	
T D 76 M M	June 1942–April 1948	Not on 1943 price list.
T D 90 M M	June 1942–April 1948	
T D 3 INCH	June 1942–April 1948	
60 M M MORTAR	June 1942–April 1948	
81 M M MORTAR	June 1942–April 1948	

★Annual price list issued in May 1934 states small bore bar to be issued "until exhausted," but new bars (small bore MG, small bore pistol, and small bore rifle) do not appear on price lists until June 1935. Price lists for 1936 and 1937 show small bore bar to be issued in place of small bore rifle until exhausted. "Small bore" reappears on August 1942 price list, and August 1942 and later price lists do not list small bore rifle. Small bore MG, small bore rifle, and small bore pistol added to official drawing in 1934.

Data summarized from uniform regulations, training regulations, and price lists.

though this was not Dubois's original intent. His initial concept was to make the badge from silver, oxidize the surface to turn it dark, and then buff the raised areas to a lustrous finish. This use of contrasting colors allowed the details of the badges and the wording of the bars to be readily seen. Despite such official call out on drawings and specifications supplied to manufacturers, the pre–World War II badges were usually brightly silver colored and normally were not sterling. "White metal" prevailed.[6]

Given the practice in the quartermaster general's office at the time—namely, to complete the official drawing of an insignia after striking the first device to insure the docu-

mentation was accurate—it appears that the War Department had the initial sample badges made about December 1922 or the following month. Nevertheless, supply officials did not order large quantities for the troops until the spring of 1923.[7]

During the 1920s and 1930s badges were commonly made from a range of metals, and sometimes these were further coated. A common 1930s and World War II technique was to use a base metal and then either silver plate or chromium plate the badges. As a part of the overall home-front effort, the United States made a determined effort to conserve metal. One consequence was to make many insignia out of sterling silver, saving more durable metals for other war needs. This caused even more badges to be made from the proper silver. Despite such apparently minuscule efforts as officially making badges only from silver, several manufacturers produced badges and bars from a copious array of materials. Many inferior metals also saw use during this time, and some shopkeepers apparently believed that virtually any insignia, no matter how poorly made, would sell.[8]

The official badges, however, finally fell into line with the original color scheme. By World War II Dubois was the senior Quartermaster Corps civilian handling insignia. When the Philadelphia Quartermaster Depot made new specifications and produced badges early in the war, he insisted that the contrast provision be enforced. This color scheme remained in effect until April 1991, when the army officially introduced bright finish for the first time—which, of course, allowed a return to the actual concept used during the 1920s and 1930s.[9]

But Arthur E. Dubois was a Quartermaster Corps man, and before World War I the Ordnance Department had responsibility for shooting: weapons, ammunition, and targets as well as badges and prizes. Something happened during World War I that caused this responsibility change. Bureaucrats' commitment to total war in 1917 and 1918 resulted in massive confusion and inefficiencies in the purchasing and movement of war supplies. The Ordnance Department competed with the Quartermaster Corps and the U.S. Navy to buy raw materials and make war goods. Even train traffic came to a virtual standstill, as the various agencies wrestled to buy and move

Fig. 3.6

Fig. 3.7

Fig. 3.5

their products. It was every office for itself. To straighten out the mess, the War Department created several successive and related organizations, one of which was the Clothing and Equipment Division, Office of the Director of Purchase. This office streamlined procurements and ultimately purchased clothing, shoes, uniform trimmings, and all insignia, including shooting awards, both for issue to enlisted men and for sale to officers. When staff duties realigned immediately after World War I, the Quartermaster Corps just swept up the shooting awards with the responsibility for other insignia.[10]

It could hardly be expected that the vast changes introduced by the army during the switch to the 1921 badges would completely eliminate all the vestiges of the "old army" badges. While some measure of consistency might have been anticipated, the military authorities could not bring themselves to surrender completely the idea of showing annual requalification. The army, weighed down by its history, decreed that a weapons' bar (suspended from the appropriate badge) be issued for the first (original) qualification and that after three years of qualification, another identical bar be issued. Under this scheme a single bar stood for the first, second, and third qualifications and a second bar indicated the fourth, fifth, and sixth qualifications. For each intervening qualification without a new bar (the second and third, fifth and sixth, eighth, ninth, and so forth), the month and year would be engraved on the back of the latest bar. As an example, the date of the first and second requalification (second and third annual qualification) were to be engraved on the back of the original qualification bar; for the fifth and sixth qualification, the dates were to go on the back of the second bar, issued for the fourth annual qualification. Soldiers in the continental United States were to send their badge and bars to the Philadelphia Quartermaster Depot for engraving, while quartermaster offices in the Philippines, Hawaii, and the Panama Canal had them engraved locally.[11]

Soldiers usually did not adhere to two of the minor features allowed with the new 1921 badges. Viewed from Washington, engraving a bar on the back was logical, but this was impractical in the field. No one looked at the back of a soldier's shooting badge. Original examples of these bars engraved on the reverse are infrequent, and few men followed the fine point of noting the requalification dates. The regulations also permitted a soldier the option of removing the lower set of rings from the bottom bar. This made for a neater looking award, but as was the case with the engraving on the reverse, most soldiers did not take advantage of this provision. The nonremoval of the rings was probably due in part to the fact that if a soldier earned an additional bar, it was simply easier to add the newest bar to the bottom of the ladder rather than to break

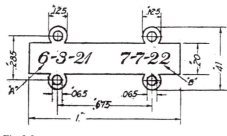

Fig. 3.8

into the ladder and then tightly close four suspension rings.

Target practice also served the very practical functions of both using up old ammunition and creating a need for new rounds. Ammunition that the army required for war reserve deteriorated during many years of storage. With the stockpile of 1918 and 1919 ammunition constituting the initial war reserve, the scheme was to expend the old ammunition through target practice and then put new bullets into storage as part of the war stocks.[12]

PAY

Annual weapons qualification was important to the individual soldier not only because of the bauble he could wear, but also because of simple economics. Qualification became so important that Congress and the War Department came together in 1903 to reward soldiers financially. This "reward for marksmen" had been suggested for at least the ten years prior, but like many good ideas, it took time to germinate. In 1910, when a private received $15 a month and a promotion to corporal increased his pay to $21, the additional money given to an expert was significant. Before and during World War I, therefore, a plethora of skills gained recognition through extra remuneration at the pay table. Compensation for enlisted men who qualified with weapons restarted in a promising way after World War I, when the secretary of war and Congress paid marksmen, sharpshooters, and experts not only for rifle or pistol qualification but also for the BAR. The army's hopes for additional pay for the machine gun and the 37 mm guns were not allowed until 1922, despite strong attempts by the general staff to obtain such remuneration in 1920 and 1921.[13]

In 1922 a new law reformed the additional pay system. Special compensation for telegraphers, coxswains, gun pointers, casemate electricians, and many others ended. In its place Congress established a flexible system that allowed the president to vary the amount of

Fig. 3.8. During the 1920s and 1930s requalification was to be shown by engraving the requalification dates on the reverse of the appropriate bar. After three qualifications (the original and two requalifications), soldiers added a new bar. The illustration is from the official 1922 War Department drawing.

additional pay a soldier could receive for weapons expertise, taking into account the appropriations passed each year. The extra pay varied over time, but throughout the lean days of the 1930s, proficiency with a weapon generally landed a skilled enlisted man extra pay. Experts earned an additional $5 a month during most of this time.[14]

In June 1922 Congress provided that as a result of a soldier's annual firings with his primary weapon, he would be classed as first, second, third, or fourth and extra pay would be given according to that classification. Men could, under some circumstances, qualify with other than their primary weapon and wear the appropriate bar on their badge, but they could not draw any proficiency pay for these other weapons.[15]

Slowly, Uncle Sam's purse contracted. In 1923 first class men received $5.00 each month, second class received $3.00, third class $2.00, and fourth class, $1.00. By 1927 the fourth class disappeared. In 1932 the third class was not funded and, in the colonial spirit of the time, Congress allowed expert and sharp-shooting Philippine Scouts natives to receive only $2.50 and $1.50 respectively—half the pay of regular soldiers. New weapons and the congressionally mandated pay ceiling worked against each other as the depression continued. The BAR became a principal arms for qualification in 1937, and even the military police in Panama and the Canal Zone received pistol-expert pay in that same year. New weapons meant more soldiers might qualify, yet the limited pay curtailed the money available. By 1940 only experts in tactical units could draw additional pay ($5.00 for the regulars and $2.50 for the Philippine Scouts).[16]

To save ammunition during the Great Depression, anyone who qualified as an expert with a particular weapon could not fire a record course for that weapon during the next two target seasons, although the soldiers could wear the expert badge during those two years. Instructors and technically skilled support troops stationed at Edgewood Arsenal, Maryland, home of the Army Chemical Center, could earn expert pay as gunners, but much to the chagrin of local soldiers, since for that station all of the soldiers were ranked by score on a single list. With the War Department's limited funds the paymaster went down the list in order, and when funds were exhausted the extra pay stopped, regardless of qualification rating. The lure of a few extra dollars was hard to resist, and many long-time khaki-clad soldiers toiled to earn the bonus. One can read official passages that encourage ammunition savings, but when it came to a few more silver dollars on payday, cash won. Every soldier wanted to be an expert.

After several false stops the army finally terminated additional marksmanship pay in 1941. Once such pay was in abeyance, then the army suspended the prohibition against soldiers' being coached during weapons qualification in the interest of increasing a soldier's skill. This was one of the waves of change that swept over the army, which never reinstituted small-arms qualification pay. While the army devoted considerable lip service to weapons training, never again did it provide a real incentive to the individual soldier on a recurring basis.[17]

As has been mentioned, during the 1920s men earned additional pay for qualification with the soldier's primary weapon: rifle, machine gun, or pistol. He might also perform with an appropriate artillery weapon and become a "gunner" (expert gunner, first class gunner, or second class gunner). In some cases the title of gunner included proficiency in artillery, machine guns, trench mortars, submarine mines, or even searchlights. In 1933 the army added aerial machine guns and aerial bombs to the list of weapons that rated extra pay for enlisted men. It was mainly officers who qualified for these two bars, but of course they could not draw additional pay. The few enlisted pilots who qualified could earn their pay through aerial qualification. Coincidentally, the "annual" qualification could last up to "one year and 4 months if no opportunity for requalification [was] . . . presented."[18]

QUALIFICATION

On the whole, training regulations and army regulations spelled out one or more courses for each weapon and then usually established the minimum scores for each of the three badges. In the case of bayonets and aerial bombing between the world wars, however, one became qualified as an expert or was not qualified at all. There were no standards for a marksman or sharpshooter badge for these two weapons. It is instructive to survey a few qualification requirements, starting with these two weapons and then progressing to other arms.[19]

During the American Revolution and before, the bayonet played a key part in battles.

Armies maneuvered and fired volleys with the objective of closing with the enemy, bayonets gleaming. An alternative use of the bayonet was to protect against cavalry charges. One way or another, cold steel drove the enemy from the field. The weapon worked two ways: through psychological shock and physical, pointed thrusts.

After the Civil War the army considered abandoning the bayonet due to "the introduction of breech-loading arms of long range" but then went on to conclude that the bayonet was still a useful weapon "in broken country, entrenched works and in timber." Thus began the lessening of the spirit of the bayonet, and although the bayonet was less important in twentieth-century battles, bayonet training continued as part of traditional infantry rigors. In the 1920s the training regulation on bayonets emphasized both "the spirit of the bayonet" and the skill of using this as an offensive weapon.[20]

Between the world wars, men qualified by running a 100 yard course that included fifteen targets (thirteen for the bayonet and two for the butt stroke). During the run the aspirants had to jump three trenches and navigate three shells holes. Men had to complete the course within forty-five seconds, with only one practice or trial run before the annual qualification. Each individual attack was allotted only one thrust, jab, or stroke, and there was only one effort at a withdrawal. Any soldier who scored eighty-two of the one hundred points became qualified as an expert. Officers who were no longer assigned to an infantry company did not have to run the course and could wear the insignia of their last qualification. After the Vietnam War the army went so far as to drop the bayonet and hand-to-hand combat from basic training, although bayonet training returned in the late 1980s. At this time only bayonet familiarization, not bayonet qualification, exists.[21]

Aerial gunners qualified as expert, marksman, or sharpshooter, but bombardiers could only become experts. Pilots assigned to attack and observation units and pilots and gunners belonging to pursuit and bombardment units all fired various aerial courses to earn their levels of aerial gunnery qualification.

Bombing was initially done from 5,000 and 8,000 feet with sixteen bombs from each altitude, but in the 1930s the Air Corps changed this to the higher altitude with only ten bombs. In 1935 those pilots who completed the ten-drop bomber course made two runs each at a ground target under five circumstances: upwind, downwind, 45 degrees into wind, 45 degrees with wind, and 90 degrees across wind. The award of aerial gunner and bombardier badges and bars ended after World War II with the formation of the air force.[22]

After giving up its aircraft to the U.S. Air Force in 1947, the army slowly returned to aviation, first with small fixed-wing aircraft, then with helicopters that really came into their own in 1964 with the 11th Air Assault Division. In 1965 this became the 1st Cavalry Division (Airmobile), which soon deployed to Vietnam. In May 1972 the commander of the Armor School at Fort Knox, Kentucky, wrote to the commanding general of the U.S. Continental Army Command requesting creation of an **AEROWEAPONS** bar for use by individual crewmen who qualified on an air-cavalry attack helicopter course. By September the Krew Company, under a contract from the Institute of Heraldry, created prototypes of the bar, and the successor to the aerial gunner bar came into being.[23]

As previously noted, after World War I the army provided for four rifle courses, uninspiringly called courses A, B, C, and D. Each had its own qualification bar. The most stringent was course A, requiring 180 practice rounds and 70 qualification rounds with ranges varying from 200 to 600 yards. Infantrymen in rifle companies and cavalrymen armed with rifles in cavalry troops were required to fire this course, although other units could fire the full sequence as an option. The B course was similar, but with ranges stopping at 500 yards and authorization of only 120 practice and 50 qualification rounds. The C course, even more condensed, had only 90 practice rounds from 200 and 300 yards, and qualification was nearly identical. All three of these courses had soldiers firing for qualification from prone (with and without a sandbag rest), sitting, kneeling, and standing, and rapid firing from various positions starting from standing.

The last course, D, was severely reduced, with only 80 practice rounds and 50 rounds for qualification, all fired from 200 yards—a practice reminiscent of the pre–World War I Coast Artillery Corps marksman A course. In 1928 the army further reduced rounds for each of the courses. In 1940 it eliminated additional rifle courses, including a 1930s 50-foot E version; modified the rounds fired and ranges on the older courses; then required riflemen to fire the B course and others armed with the rifle, the C course. All of this reinforced the wisdom of awarding a single bar for rifle qualification regardless of the course fired, a practice that was instituted in 1924. Throughout World War II the army changed firing standards and the number of rounds and distances. Documentation on these numerous changes runs on and on.[24]

After World War II combat veterans wanted to revise the army's shooting philosophy. Trainers came to see known-distance firing as having become a sterile and somewhat worthless activity with little relation to combat. Instinct firing, or "snap firing," became the focus of marksmanship at Fort Benning, with the emphasis on hand-eye coordination. Some men practiced with BB guns and then fired rifles starting at 50 yards. This post–World War II phase resembled the period immediately before the Spanish-American War, when army staff officers debated the best way to use rifle fire on the battlefield. In part the post-1945 debate grew from the writings of S. L. A. Marshall, who supposedly interviewed soldiers after selected fights and concluded that the majority of riflemen did not fire their weapons in combat.

In the early 1950s the army made the most radical change in its rifle marksmanship training philosophy since Pershing had headed the AEF. Howard C. Sarvis, a hunting-camp operator from New Meadows, Idaho, wrote President Eisenhower in 1953, suggesting that the army modify its training program to one that would develop specific muscular and mental conditioning for soldiers. Out of this grew the Trainfire system. Sarvis's straightforward logic rested on the simple belief that training should emulate combat, even during the early stages of elementary schooling. He wanted pop-up targets that would appear inside 350 yards but at ranges not known to the shooter and that would fall down immediately upon being hit. Scoring would be only "hit or miss" and would simulate combat. This was amazingly similar to the once discounted 1897 approach. When the system was finally adopted, the army had soldiers fire many rounds from a foxhole with sandbag supports, just as in combat. Later in the Trainfire course, soldiers encountered other pop-up targets while walking down a wooded trail. Scoring for qualification was simply determined by the number of targets knocked down.[25]

Whether Sarvis knew of the debate that had been ongoing since 1949 at Fort Benning, home of the Infantry School, is not clear, but his letter to Eisenhower reopened a controversy that had just closed. The great marksmanship debate at Fort Benning revolved around whether to use rigid training techniques such as known-distance firing from the "correct," prone position (with a sling and with the elbow, rather unnaturally, directly under the rifle) or to use means more amenable to combat, such as "Kentucky windage," targets shaped like human silhouettes, as well as whether to have firers use combatlike positions, such as tree stumps, piles of bricks, or other artificial supports when shooting. Perhaps the adoption of the Trainfire course in the 1950s, with its lack of emphasis on competitive-style shooting, ultimately caused the decline in popularity of the army's shooting badges after Vietnam.[26]

Trainfire changed over the years. It became known as the Quick Kill course, and by the end of the Vietnam War qualification consisted of a night course and two daytime firings, one conducted in the morning of the first day and one in the afternoon of the second day to equalize light conditions. Maximum scoring consisted of seventy points for daylight aimed fire, ten points for daylight quick fire (unaimed), and twenty points for night fire that involved universal E pop-up silhouette targets with four-inch reflective squares added. This last consideration—firing at night—had been advocated by Pershing when he was a brigadier general commanding the Department of Mindanao in the Philippine Islands in 1910. Pershing's radical recommendation was "the introduction . . . of five minutes' firing at some imaginary enemy prepared during the night. The firing would take place at the first 'crack of dawn.'"[27]

Public opposition to the Vietnam War killed the draft—the major rank-and-file filler for the U.S. Army since just before World War II—so that a generation after Pearl Harbor the "all volunteer army" became the norm. To help fill the potential acute personnel shortage, women became much more heavily recruited, although the army prohibited them from participating in combat roles. In the summer of 1975 the wider use of women in the army caused the question of women's rifle qualification to arise. The army required all women, except conscientious objectors, to undergo individual weapons training, but such firing was solely for defensive purposes. Accordingly, the deputy chief of staff for personnel investigated the possibility of awarding the women who fired such courses a bar reading **RIFLE-D**, with the **D** referring to the defense nature of the training. Ultimately, such a scheme did not come to pass, but the reintroduction of the old D-course bar was a near thing.[28]

For the pistol, only the cavalry could fire the mounted (horseback) course in the years after World War I; for all others, the dismounted course applied. Qualification in 1924 mounted called for firing thirty rounds evenly spread over two runs. During each run the horseman fired five rounds to the left, five to the right, three to the front, and, after passing through the target line and charging again, two to the rear. Experts had to hit 80 percent of the targets, sharpshooter 70 percent, and marksman 60 percent.[29]

The early dismounted-pistol course ranges were 25 and 50 yards. In 1927 this changed to 15 and 25 yards, although for competitions at which prizes were awarded, ranges remained at 25 and 50 yards except, for a few years, slow-fire competition at 75 yards. In 1941 the army pressed the .45 caliber revolver into service and made some adjustments in qualification time.[30]

Pistol courses after World War II remained generally the same known-distance circular target affairs as they had been throughout the century, although the shooter fired from the prone, kneeling, and standing positions. By 1960 sixteen hours were allotted for pistol training for new soldiers who were to be armed with the .45 automatic. The course of instruction included four hours for disassembly, function, malfunction, and safety; four hours for dry firing; four hours for preliminary practice; and four hours for record shooting on tables I, II, and III. Qualification table I consisted of ten shots each at 15 and 25 meters, slow fire. Table II was rapid fire, five shots in twelve seconds at 25 meters at a bobbing E-target from the prone and kneeling positions. Table III was a nod to combat since the table was quick fire, again at a bobbing E-target, with four shots in fifteen seconds, standing to prone, four more shots but standing to kneeling, and then two shots in six seconds fired from the crouch position. To be classified expert required thirty-five of the forty possible hits.[31]

Combat realism received greater emphasis with the 1971 manual on pistols and revolvers. Preliminary instruction was reduced to six hours. Firing was more attuned to combat, although many posts did not have the full facilities required. Even if the complete range was not available, the general concept of "walking down a combat trail" was used. This late Vietnam War course required two magazines, and shooters had to change the magazines during an eight-second delay. In total the standards dictated forty rounds to fire at thirty targets. Both single and multiple targets were exposed from two to five seconds depending upon the range. After firing at twenty targets with up to twenty-six rounds from the standing position over four tables, the firer walked a trail. On the course that exposed ten targets, the shooter started with a magazine containing a single round, which was followed by one magazine of seven rounds, then one magazine of five rounds. Of the 300 possible points (a hit was 10 points), 260 points scored expert, 210 sharpshooter, and 160 marksman.[32]

The army issued new lightweight carbines to some unit leaders during World War II and established appropriate qualification courses. Standard ranges were 100 and 200 yards, but at some posts with limited ranges qualification could be accomplished on the 1,000 inch range. When the army introduced the M-14 and M-16 rifles in the late 1950s and 1960s, it gave up the World War II and Korean War carbine. In the 1990s some light troops such as rangers and special forces began to use the M-4 carbine, which was somewhat similar to the M-16 rifle but lighter and shorter. For this weapon the army used the same scoring system as for the M-16 rifle.[33]

Between the world wars the army equipped howitzer companies in infantry regiments and some howitzer platoons in selected headquarters companies with 37 mm guns and 3-inch trench mortars. At first all men in these units took a gunner's test that consisted of laying the 37 mm gun for both direct and indirect fire and laying the 3-inch trench mortar. Men who scored at least 90 percent became first class gunners (sharpshooter badge), and those scoring less than that but at least 70 percent became second class gunners (marksman badge). Soldiers classed as first class gunners could then take an expert-gunner test, consisting of actually firing both weapons, making range cards, and computing firing data.

Chemical warfare gunners followed a similar two-step process involving the 4.2 inch chemical mortar, but with other weapons added. Requirements for tank weapons and armored-car weapons, providing further examples of complex qualifications, are discussed in chapter 5.[34]

As World War II loomed on the horizon, the army started to replace the light 60 mm mortar used by the cavalry with the 81 mm mortar, but both weapons remained in the inventory for a while. Training in these two mortars caused the establishment of two additional bars in 1942, one for the 60 mm mortar and one for the larger 81 mm mortar that remained for several years. In 1948 a single **MORTAR** bar replaced these two.[35]

Soldiers initially qualified with ground machine guns during the 1920s at a relatively close range—1,000 inches—then they fired at 600, 700, 800, and 1,000 yards. One suspects that if the longer ranges were not available, the 1,000-inch range was used liberally. The army standardized to 1,000 inches (approximately 28 yards) for short-range courses, and many posts could support infantry qualification at these distances. The 1926 training regulation called for ground machine-gun qualification at various ranges with several types of fire, including fixed, traversing (moving the gun right and left, freehand), searching (moving the gun vertically, freehand), adjustment (using a mechanical device to control gun movement), and a combination of fixed, searching, and traversing.[36]

Men in antiaircraft machine-gun units qualified by firing at 1,000 inches on a ground range, then by firing at a five-foot wood airplane model sliding down a twenty-three-degree wire (to represent a diving aircraft), and finally (for half of the qualifying score) by shooting at meteorological balloons released and allowed to travel to 300, 500, and 800 yards before opening fire. When firing at the close range, a 15 x 23–inch panel hung under the scale aircraft. Only hits on the rectangle counted. This taught the soldiers the value of proper leads when firing at a moving target. Later qualifications eliminated this diving aircraft requirement.[37]

A bar that draws some queries today is the one embossed **MACHINE RIFLE**. In the 1920s and 1930s the machine rifle was an automatic weapon like the Browning Automatic Rifle (BAR), but with a special cooling device allowing it to fire for longer periods than a standard automatic rifle. Although the army classed the World War I Lewis gun and the Model 1909 Benét-Mercier automatic machine rifle as such weapons, only the Model 1922 BAR, a cavalry weapon, was issued and recognized as a machine rifle between the world wars.[38]

Until 1928 the cavalry used a tentative qualification course based on the infantry BAR, since until then many cavalry units had only the infantry version. The machine rifle had a bipod, an adjustable stock rest, and a heavy ribbed barrel that allowed sustained fire. The 1928 course included both slow and rapid firing at 500 yards and slow firing at 600 yards, all from the prone position to emphasize that normal machine-rifle cavalry firing required accuracy.[39]

With the issuance of formal machine-rifle training regulations by the chief of cavalry in 1929, all troopers fired with a bipod from the prone position, at 200 and 300 yards on three different courses. To become an expert a cavalryman had to score at least 70 percent on all three courses, while the sharpshooter level required 60 percent and the marksman 50 percent.[40]

Soldiers qualifying with the Browning Automatic Rifle earned a bar marked **AUTO RIFLE**. All firing was done at silhouettes with the weapons in the semiautomatic mode at 200, 300, 500, and 600 yards. While any officer or enlisted man in a unit equipped with a BAR could earn a qualification insignia, initially only enlisted men in infantry and engineer units (and cavalry units until issue of the machine rifle) could earn the extra BAR pay. Within two weeks of completing the regular-rifle practice period, commanders started the automatic-rifle practice, and this period was defined, by regulations, as "not less than two weeks."[41]

By 1930 the older titles of marksman, sharpshooter, and expert were still used for rifles, pistols, machine rifles, and automatic rifles, but for most other weapons such as howitzers, chemical mortars, machine guns, and aerial gunners, the army titled the men second class gunners, first class gunners, and expert gunners. This distinction remained through the end of World War II.[42]

NONREGULATION BADGES

After World War I the army found itself with large stocks of the old-style badges. Rather than scrap this generous surplus of instant relics in the interest of uniformity, the War Department allowed—and at times even directed— the issue of these awards until they were exhausted. In addition the older badges could continue to be worn by those soldiers who had won them. This provided a loophole through which soldiers were wearing the pre-1921 badges as late as World War II. These older badges certainly looked more impressive, and for new men who earned the basic rifle award, the original metal badge presented a richer appearance than the newer versions. Soldiers simply bought the older type to be stylish.

From 1921 to 1937, when the older badges were supposedly in the wear-out period, private companies made and sold the obsolete badges, including the 1916 pistol badge with the crossed .45 automatics. One popular maker listed them in its 1932 catalog under the title "Marksmanship badges, old regulation," complete with requalification bars. This manufacturer even listed miniature marksmanship badges of the older style for expert rifleman, pistol expert, and rifle sharpshooter in silver plate, silver, and chromium plating; however, there were no miniatures in the 1920 pattern.[43]

When the Marine Corps abandoned the army badges in 1937 and returned to the earlier set of rifle and pistol badges, these older-style awards were readily available both to marines who legally wore them and to

Fig. 3.10

soldiers who pushed the envelope regarding uniforms and insignia. Photos show that the use of the 1885-style sharpshooter badges and 1903 expert awards was rather common between 1938 and 1942, although as late as 1950 a few "old-timers" still wore the 1903 expert badge, thirty years after it had theoretically become obsolete.

In the Philippine Islands native troops in the U.S. Army assigned to the Philippine Scouts wore army uniforms and marksmanship insignia and, as has been discussed, received reduced marksmanship pay. The quasi-military organization that functioned as a national police force on the island was the Philippine Constabulary, a different force from the Philippine Scouts. Initially, the constabulary was officered by men from the U.S. Army, but over time natives came into the organization as officers, and by World War I the transition to a pure Filipino organization was complete, although the islands remained under U.S. control. The badges worn by the constabulary personnel were similar to the regular army silver-colored pre-1920 badges, although above the top bar there was a raised area that carried the **PC** monogram. Badge brooches were embossed with **RIFLE EXPERT** (although most men carried and fired carbines), **PISTOL EXPERT**, and, for a while, even **BAYONET EXPERT**. In 1914 the top marksman in each district was entitled to wear a gold medal, and the best shot in each company earned a "best shot medal."[44]

Fig. 3.9

Fig. 3.9. Colonel Evan H. Humphrey in the 1930s, wearing one of the expert rifle badges that became obsolete in 1921. Humphrey retired as a brigadier general in 1939.

Fig. 3.10. Private First Class Harry Hadley, 30th Infantry, about 1937. In addition to the Soldier's Medal he won for saving a young girl after she was struck by a train and thrown into a river, Hadley wears one of the pre-1921 rifle expert badges with four qualification bars for the post-1921-style badge.

Fig. 3.11

Fig. 3.12

Fig. 3.11. An expert badge for rifle or carbine, issued by the Philippine Constabulary during the 1930s.

Fig. 3.12. Typical unauthorized qualification bars used with the 1921-design shooting badges. Rather than **REVOLVER**, *the bar should have* **PISTOL**. *Neither the* **M-14** *(a type of rifle) nor the* **EXPERT** *was ever authorized. The army never prescribed a bar for the pistol C course.*

A reality of World War II and later was the great diversity of unauthorized qualification bars that appeared. The army-and-navy-store community did a brisk business in these ersatz awards, as merchants exploited soldiers by offering nonstandard additions. Such bars expressed a particular weapon, such as **M-1 RIFLE** rather than the proper **RIFLE** or such totally unauthorized expressions as **EXPERT**. Table 3 lists a sample of this varied array of unofficial bars. While some came from military schools, most were intended for regular forces.

With the permanent peacetime expansion of the U.S. forces and their stationing around the world during the cold war, qualification bars were made globally—in Germany, Austria, Japan, Korea, and elsewhere. Bars available to "PX commandos" are legion. The **BAJONET** bar, with the German style of writing having a large serif on top of the J, would hardly be believable in fiction. Accounting for various misspellings, some truly improbable bars are known and more undoubtedly will be discovered. Other improbable bars are yet to be made.

Table 3. *Unauthorized Bars for Qualification Badges, 1921–1990s*

AAA ARTILLERY	FIELD ARTY D	RIFLE GRENADE	TRENCH MORTAR
ANTI AIR	GUNNERY	RIFLE E	22 CAL.
ANTI-AIRCRAFT	HAND GRENADE	RIFLE M	22 CALIBRE
ARMORY	HOWITZER	RIFLE N	30 CALIBRE
ART. AIRCRAFT	INF. TANK	ROCKET	37 MM
AUTO-TANK	M-1	SABRE	38 CALIBRE
B. A. R.	M 1 RIFLE	SHARPSHOOTER	45
BAJONET	M-14	SMOKE	45 CALIBER
BAZOOKA	M 14	GENERATOR	50 CALIBRE
CANNONIER	M 16	SUB MACH GUN	60 MM
CAVALRY	M 79	SUB MACHINE	75 MM
CHEM. WARFARE	M-203	SUB MACHINE	75 MM MORTAR
CNS WEAPON	MARKSMAN	GUN	75 RECOILLESS
COAST	M I	T. S. M.	RIFLE
ARTILLERY	PISTOL A	T.S.M.G.	81 MM
COAST ART'Y A.A.	PISTOL B	TANK	106 RR
C.V.S.	PISTOL C	TANK B	151 MM GUN
EXPERT	PISTOL EXPERT	TANK EXPERT	155 MM
FIELD ARTILLERY D	REVOLVER	TOMMY GUN	

The Vietnam War and
Later Philosophy

Although badges changed colors and bars, frequently men wore the late nineteenth–century-style badges into the 1940s and even for several years after World War II. Soldiers proudly wore their shooting badges well into the early 1960s. Field wear, never sanctioned by regulations, occurred after World War II, especially overseas where the conquering American army remained. During the late 1960s and the 1970s, however, the prominence of badges changed greatly. Between 1973 and 1990 significant shifts occurred not only in badges, but also in the underlying philosophy towards individual weapons training.[45]

By the 1980s soldiers with many years of service, both NCOs and officers, more often than not, did not wear their badges, and many treated the shooting awards with disdain. By 1988 this phenomenon was so prevalent that the Department of the Army conducted a study to determine whether the marksmanship qualification badges should be revised or even discarded. The study listed several reasons for this apparent lack of pride and reduced wear. During World War II a number of new badges and medals came into being, and soldiers generally received many more awards than they had just a few years before. The creation and wear of numerous ribbons, badges, and other devices of visual splendor grew enormously between 1943 and 1988. In these forty-five years, over five times more "rewards" were created than had been devised throughout the entire previous history of the U.S. Army.[46]

Questions that arose included the following: When would qualification badges be worn? (All the time? When official photos were taken?) What should be the instrument for awarding badges (letters, unit orders, or other), since official files no longer contained training records? What should be the terminating authority (if any) for qualification badges? Many generals of World War II, with service back to World War I and earlier, had only two or three rows of ribbons. Most were entitled to no badges other than those for weapons qualification. By the 1980s soldiers completing a first enlistment earned three to five ribbons, and soldiers with twenty years of experience often had an infantry badge, a parachute badge, a driver's badge, and more exotic ornaments

Fig. 3.13

Fig. 3.13. This photograph, taken in about 1950 in Germany, shows the wear of an expert badge on a field uniform.

such as pathfinders and explosive ordnance disposal badges. Ordinary shooting badges lost their significance, and soldiers treated them with contempt.[47]

Ultimately, the Department of the Army made no real changes in the regulations that limited soldiers to only three marksmanship badges from among the three authorized distinguished badges, two levels of excellence in competition badges (bronze and silver), and three qualification badges. The study did cause the added limitation that no more than three clasps (bars) would be authorized for suspension under any qualification badge. Any commander in the grade of lieutenant colonel could make an award, but the means of recording such qualification was not noted.

To what do we attribute the demise of average individual marksmanship? The real answers have to do with Vietnam tactics, adopted for the major war that NATO never fought in Europe, and with unsophisticated enemies in places like Somalia, who virtually closed to the immediate killing range of ancient gladiatorial events, where shooting skill is not needed—just brute force.[48]

In reality a good deal changed during the latter half of the cold war. In Vietnam many U.S. casualties resulted from mines and booby traps when the enemy was not directly present and from close-range small-arms fire delivered by the North Vietnamese and the Vietcong. In response to this latter assault the United States developed the tactic that, whenever possible,

American forces pulled back a short distance and called in heavy firepower delivered by artillery and from aircraft, either army helicopters or air force fighters. Thus infantry small-arms fire frequently became delivered only at short ranges as an emergency and temporary defensive measure. Initially espoused by 1st Division commander Major General William E. DePuy, later a four-star commander who significantly revised U.S. Army tactics, this concept played down the need for accurate small-arms fire at long ranges, leaving the long-range killing to this heavy firepower. This thought process carried over to the army on guard in Europe, ready to fight the huge Warsaw Pact armies.

The army of the 1970s and 1980s trained to fight the enormous Soviet combined-arms armies, with their multitude of tracked vehicles and extensive artillery. Vehicle crew training and unit training and maneuver, from platoon through Army Corps, became the primary peacetime effort. A national training center, where opposing forces maneuvered and helicopters, tanks, and long-range mechanized infantry "fired" at the opposite team, came to dominate the thinking of commanders. Heavy firepower was seen as the only way to stop these steamroller tactics, and accurate rifle fire was of secondary importance at best. Only select light forces soldiers—such as special forces, airborne and long-range reconnaissance soldiers, and rangers—remained dependent upon well-handled small arms. In the late twentieth century community/crew drills were seen as the key to success on the battlefield, and it was thought that there was generally no need for well-placed rifle shots. Ranger and other light forces practiced firing weapons at 10 meters and less range solely as a defensive measure.[49]

One historian has characterized the 1973–90 period as the time of the army's training revolution. It all started when General William E. DePuy, a serious military figure, took command of the new Training and Doctrine Command. With his practiced eye DePuy recognized that the old mobilization and training concept of using a small cadre of professional soldiers to grow a large draft army in wartime would not work. The emphasis became placed on unit training, and the major standards became the Army Training and Evaluation Program (ARTEP) for units up to battalion level and the Skill Qualification Test (SQT) for individual soldiers. The SQT was initially a written test and later a hands-on proficiency test administered with real equipment in the immediate garrison area. This test precluded actual firing of any type.[50]

In the early 1980s the army instituted Army Training 1990, a program that trained soldiers for warfare anticipated in the 1990s. This focused on three goals: train unit leaders, train units, and train the soldier. With the heavy push on the first two goals, time was squeezed out of individual training to meet the time demands of unit training. Again, marksmanship suffered. The army continued to accentuate officer and leader training. If one reads reports from that time, the emphasis is on the army school system and on officer training.

Overlaying this was the philosophy that training had to be carried to unit leaders so that they would know how to organize and fight. This philosophy came under various names as the tactics and views evolved: Army 86 organization, AirLand Battle, complete integration of reserve and National Guard units with active forces, and other "fancy named" programs. While laymen may greet these details today with a yawn, at the time many army officers considered them excitingly creative.[51]

Highlighted by the 1991 Gulf War—where individual rifle marksmanship played a minor role—well-placed, carefully aimed small-arms fire lapsed into a condition not unlike that of Custer's day. The unit as a whole and the commander's ability to maneuver the organization were viewed as the important keys to battlefield dominance. Crew and squad training were important. A high volume of fire, made possible by a huge logistical tail, was more important than the individually aimed fire of a single rifleman. As a result, marksmanship—which previously had been pushed into the backseat—was completely put out of the car.

It followed logically that in the 1990s the army continued to limit qualification badges to the green, white, and blue uniforms. Camouflaged combat clothing, called battle dress uniforms (BDU), became the common and very popular clothing of soldiers; even senior officers routinely wore BDUs to many conferences and in garrison offices. Soldiers in BDUs could be seen in major airports, changing planes along with the multitude of civilians in business dress. If the leaders did not think much of their marksmanship training and badges, how could they get their troops to take a real interest in any marksmanship program? Leaders appeared complacent about shooting.

In the late 1990s some senior NCOs began again to wear shooting badges on their green uniforms, but field grade and general officers generally ignored their shooting badges. In a time when the army was willing to indulge the modern soldiers' every whim, these were about the only awards not worn. The army showers current soldiers, unlike their ancestors, with an extensive array of badges and ribbons. Today's worth of weapons qualification for enlisted personnel is primarily in promotion points. Out of eight hundred possible points on a promotion worksheet, a perfect score with an individual weapon provides fifty. Crew served weapons are worth nothing, although the M249 machine gun counts as an individual weapon of promotion points.[52] In contrast the U.S. Marine Corps, from pre–World War I days to the present, has preached and practiced that every member is a marksman. The marines' unwavering allegiance to the known-distance ranges and to this creed, and their ostentatious display of shooting awards, stands in stark contrast to the army's recent actions.

In today's army virtually all badges can be worn on combat clothing, but an individual's shooting skills cannot be shown—a complete reversal from the introduction of badges over one hundred years ago. Now the method of wear of basic marksmanship badges on green uniforms varies widely depending upon other insignia worn and upon individual preferences. Men and women wear the badges slightly differently, as shown in illustrations from official regulations (figs. 3.14–3.16).

With the fall of the iron curtain the United States became heavily involved in peace-keeping operations such as those in Panama, Haiti, Somalia, and the former Yugoslavia. In these conflicts, especially in the various flare-ups in the Balkans, antagonists have demonstrated the worth of long-range, accurate rifle fire. Some military analysts believe that these involvements call for the U.S. Army to return to skillful, old-fashioned marksmanship to counter snipers and small armed groups while minimizing risks to noncombatants. So far the army's reward system lags behind this belief. Given the army's general neglect of individual-weapons training during the 1980s and 1990s and the intoxicating blend of ribbons and other badges that was created, it is astonishing that the seventy-five-year-old expert, sharpshooter, and marksman badges survive at all. This is in contrast to the spirit that pre-

vailed when the army introduced current-style badges. In 1923 it was reported that the 7th Cavalry (a unit not noted for its marksmanship in 1876) qualified over 98 percent of its soldiers. It is doubtful that a similar-sized unit today could make such a claim.[53]

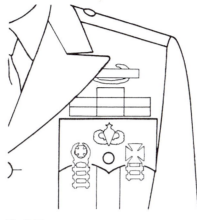

Fig. 3.14

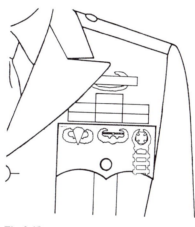

Fig. 3.15

Fig. 3.16

Fig. 3.14. In the 1990s badges on the green uniforms could be worn in a variety of ways. This example, taken from army regulations, shows shooting badges lower than the parachute badge.

Fig. 3.15. Soldiers could wear up to three badges (marksmanship or special skills) in a row on the green uniform pocket flap in the 1990s.

Fig. 3.16. An example of the up to three badges allowed in the 1990s on women's uniforms.

Fig. 3.17. *This first sergeant from the 1920s stands in stark contrast to today's soldiers. The veteran's awards are only his World War I Victory Medal ribbon and an expert badge with four bars.*

In the early twenty-first century, the United States Army invaded Afghanistan and then Iraq. Few conventional forces stood in the way in Afghanistan. American concern was overcoming irregular forces that had earlier battled the Soviet Union to a standstill. To win the Afghanistan War, often the United States employed Special Forces and militias loyal to various war lords, while at other junctures soldiers depended upon smart weapons. In many instances, however, the rifleman's skill again became important in tracking down and defeating resistance fighters. The need for a basic rifleman's skill returned in the fights on the rocky hills of eastern Afghanistan. In some cases U.S. soldiers depended upon smart weapons and sheer volume of firepower, but other engagements were similar to soldiers fighting American Indians in the nineteenth century. Individual weapon proficiency was what counted.

Generally the army used heavy mechanized forces designed to fight the Soviets in Europe to invade Iraq in 2003. But while technology was the foundation of that victory, intercity fighting and guerrilla warfare made it apparent that despite technology, all soldiers, regardless of their individual jobs, had to be able to effectively perform basic military skills. Everyone might be called upon to become a combat trooper in a moment's notice. As a result, in October of that year the new army chief of staff declared that every soldier needed to be a rifleman. The army ordered that from then on, individual weapons qualification was needed twice a year. One publication stated the new senior general was "tearing a page from the

Fig. 3.17

Marine Corps play book." Everyone would again be a rifleman.[54]

Today's focus in small arms themselves is on technology. Designers strive for weapons that overmatch any threat in a conventional battle, yet provide nontraditional solutions. Increased magazine capacity, improved ammunition lethality through features like bursting munitions, special sighting devices that provide twenty-four-hour tactical capability, as well as the traditional search for lighter weight armament are all part of the twenty-first-century search. Even laser weapons or other "ray guns," the staple of science fiction, may be supplied to the soldier. It remains to be seen whether individual skill is critical for success with these golden weapons.

CHAPTER FOUR

ARTILLERY AND
SWORDMAN'S BADGES

ARTILLERY BADGES BEFORE
THE GREAT WAR

Colonel John Hamilton, new commander of the 5th Artillery, waxed enthusiastic about his regiment's cannon target practice of 1884. His glowing report was so infectious that General Benét, chief of ordnance, included twenty pages about Colonel Hamilton's thoughts in the ordinarily dull and bureaucratic "Annual Report of the Chief of Ordnance to the Secretary of War." It was as if Colonel Hamilton had heard a siren's song. Despite the difficulties of holding live target practice at the 5th Artillery's station above the Narrows by New York City and the problems with the swift current, which dragged the anchors affixed to the floating targets, Hamilton bubbled with confidence. One can imagine the local citizenry's reaction to the rumble of artillery fire in New York Harbor and the dangerous potential for commercial ships to get in the way. This mattered not. Doing soldierly tasks obviously improved the morale and efficiency of his troops. Hamilton concluded, "Interest in the work may possibly be stimulated by an annual competition of gun detachments from each post, the place of competition alternating." This sort of wide-eyed enthusiasm by a high-ranking officer was the precursor to the artillery proficiency badges that the War Department introduced just seven years later.[1]

In 1879 the army published a *Manual of Heavy Artillery Service for the Use of the Army and Militia of the United States* by Major John C. Tidball. The author had served as aide to General Sherman from January 1881 until February 1884, received several brevet promotions for Civil War action, and retired in January 1889, so that by 1890 the title page of his book could proclaim that Tidball was

"Brevet Brigadier General, Colonel Retired, . . . Late Colonel First Regiment of Artillery and Commandant United States Artillery School." The manual was regularly published for over twenty years, the fifth edition appearing in 1898. Tidball's handy and compact book, approximately 5 x 7 inches and an inch thick, had only slightly more than eight scant pages devoted to target practice plus one information-packed drawing (plate 15) in the back. Only three pages of text (and Tidball's illustration) are devoted to seacoast gunnery practice. As one 1884 author put it, "During the Civil war [*sic*] the whole subject of the proper handling of heavy artillery was in an unsettled state." Tidball's effort was the first real manual for artillery handling and tactics. Evidently the 5th Artillery's Colonel Hamilton, for his own reasons, chose to ignore target construction details and other information in Tidball's treatise, although—given Tidball's scant emphasis on practice—it is little wonder.[2]

One key to effective seacoast artillery target practice was a floating target. Tidball's "best and most readily constructed target" for heavy coastal guns consisted of a three-sided pyramid, 12 feet on a side, with the large structure placed on a raft so as to stay stable "in the roughest seas." A diminutive red flag capped the pyramidal target, which had a 4-foot-diameter hole on each side to serve as a bull's-eye. This massive device, weighted with a 200-pound shot and accompanied by two anchors to hold it in place, is neatly captured on several of the early artillery awards as the essence of artillery expertise (fig. 4.1).[3]

Heavy artillery changed over the time between the introduction of Tidball's manual of 1879 and 1888, when the headquarters of the army published General Orders Number 108 in December 1888 on improving artillery

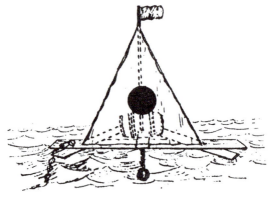

Fig. 4.1.

Fig. 4.1. The floating target for heavy coastal artillery, as shown in Colonel John C. Tidball's Manual of Heavy Artillery Service, *published in the 1880s and 1890s. This became the much-used artillery symbol at the turn of the century. The enormous triangular target was 12 feet on a side, and the entire raft-mounted device required two anchors, each weighing at least two hundred pounds, to hold it in place.*

batteries that supported cavalry and infantry in the field. At this time the heavy batteries of the regiments were generally distributed so the 1st Artillery was in and around San Francisco and the Columbia River, the 2d spread from New Orleans to St. Augustine, the 3d in Baltimore (Fort McHenry) and Washington, D.C., the 4th from New London to Portland, Maine, and the 5th around New York City, with each regiment having a heavy battery at Fort Monroe. With the regiments spread around the coastline, in time of war many decisions to fire on the enemy would be made by battery commanders. Training and testing was really accomplished at the battery level. In this environment regimental actions were usually administrative, not tactical.[5]

General Orders Number 132 of November 18, 1890, established the test for heavy-artillery gunners and described three types of artillery competitions: battery, regimental, and general. The battery test became the foundation for heavy artillery's revised training and served as the basic examination for selected gunners and for the award of new, distinctive badges. Only men designated by the battery commander could compete in the next level, the regimental test, which a board of three regimental officers administered. An extract of the order, shown in table 4, illustrates the composition of that test.

instruction. In these nine years vast improvements in gunpowder, communications, foundry techniques, and related areas of artillery technology made it obvious that the army needed new training material and routines in the heavy artillery, or coast artillery as it was later called. Again in 1889, "in anticipation of more complete equipment of artillery camps for target practice," another order detailed signals, torches, flags, vessel tracking, and similar subjects. Finally, the publication of War Department General Orders Number 132 in 1890 prescribed a complete new training and testing program for heavy artillery.[4]

From 1882 into the 1890s an artillery regiment consisted of ten heavy batteries for coastal defense and two light (horse-drawn)

Table 4. 1891 Gunnery Test

	Minimum Qualifications	Maximum Figure of Merit
1.	Setting and reading quadrants. Setting and reading on angle measuring instruments suitable for determining range. Use of plotting board.	8
2.	Service of all pieces of siege and sea-coast armament that have been available for instruction during the year, or of such of them as the examining board may designate.	8
3.	Judging distance of stationary objects.	10
4.	Judging distance of moving objects.	14
5.	Judging speed of vessels.	8
6.	Judging velocity of wind.	7
7.	Laying guns accurately as to elevation and direction.	20
8.	Cordage, block and tackle—their use in such mechanical maneuvers as may have been executed during the year which, as far as practical, will include all that the available facilities have permitted.	5
	Subtotal	80
	In addition to the foregoing, the examining board will take into consideration, in the case of each competitor, general soldierly character (the figure of merit under this head to be determined solely by the battery commander.)	20
	General aggregate	100

Data and wording from information contained in General Orders Number 132, 1890.

Once each battery contest had been held, the board classified the competitors who received 75 percent or more into one of three categories: first class gunners (the five men receiving the highest scores); second class gunners (the ten men receiving the next highest scores); and third class men (those remaining who made at least 75 percent in the battery examination). The establishing order also provided that the first and second class gunners were to wear, on the dress coat, the blouse (service coat), and the overcoat, "suitable insignia distinctive of the class in such a manner and of such device" as was to be designated. General Orders 132 also required that the classification had to be won each year, a point of no small significance, since any noncommissioned officer serving with the batteries who failed to make either first or second class gunner after 1892 was regarded as not qualified to hold an NCO's warrant.[6]

Major General John M. Schofield, commanding general of the U.S. Army, 1888–95, began the process of ordering the first badges on the basis of a staff memorandum prepared by aide-de-camp Tasker H. Bliss. Bliss pointed out that 250 first class and 500 second class badges would be needed for the entire heavy artillery, but only half that number of men were likely to qualify during the first year, 1891. He also submitted proposed designs for the two gunner badges that were simple bars, to be made at a "probable cost of a few cents each" with a pin on the back and with the front inscribed **FIRST CLASS GUNNER** and **SECOND CLASS GUNNER**, respectively. Bliss suggested that one badge be stamped from aluminum-bronze and the other from aluminum and that the metal presenting the more handsome appearance be used for the first class version.[7]

General Schofield sent Bliss's memo, with a cover letter requesting funding information, to the chief of ordnance for comment on April 15, 1891. Brigadier General Daniel W. Flagler, chief of ordnance, 1891–99, responded the next day by stating he would be glad to make the badges and to finance them from the Army contingency fund, as had been "the case of medals and insignia for small arms marksmanship until Congress authorizes their procurement." Flagler also carefully pointed out that since the infantry badges cost $.50 each, he believed the artillery badges should be of at least similar size and silver content.[8]

Fig. 4.2

Fig. 4.2. A Boston Light Artillery medal given to George W. Booth for proficiency. The reverse is dated 1857.

On April 24, 1891, the acting secretary of war approved the manufacture of gunner badges. He specified that they be made from silver and of a design prepared by the Ordnance Department. Captain Marcus W. Lyon, who commanded Rock Island Arsenal for a number of years, submitted several designs to the chief of ordnance on August 20, 1891. He sent designs for the first and second class badges and an unsolicited drawing for a third class button in case "one at any time is desired." Lyon's designs, exactly the size and weight of the sharpshooter badge and marksman bar given to the infantry and cavalry, caused him to note that these new badges would cost the same to manufacture as those given for rifle proficiency.[9]

Rock Island proceeded with the manufacture of the first class badges and second class bars of the arsenal's design. By October 20, 1891, Captain Lyon reported to General Flagler that fifty of the first class badges were ready for issue. These 1891 badges are shown in figures 4.3 and 4.4.[10]

Rock Island Arsenal made and issued second class gunners' badges between 1891 and 1896. These silver bars were the heavy artillery's counterpart of the infantry and cavalry marksman bars, down to the small targets at each end.

The chief of ordnance, at the bidding of Schofield, informed the Departments of the

Fig. 4.3

Fig. 4.3. One of the few surviving silver 1891 heavy-artillery first class gunner badges. Rock Island Arsenal made these from sheet silver between 1891 and 1896. When the army introduced a new series of badges in 1897, the remaining older awards should have been turned in for the reclaimed silver.

Fig. 4.4

Fig. 4.4. An 1891–96 heavy artillery second class gunner's silver badge, made at Rock Island Arsenal and modeled after the marksman bars then issued to the infantry and cavalry. Small floating targets on each end mirror the rifle and carbine marksman bar.

Fig. 4.5. The suggested design for a "gunner collar button" submitted to the chief of ordnance by Rock Island Arsenal commander Captain M. W. Lyon in 1891. The never-adopted button was to have been made of nickel and was to have measured 1 inch square, similar to the rifle-marksman button then in use. The design, based upon Tidball's floating target, did later serve as the pattern for the center of the 1903 Coast Artillery badge.

Fig. 4.5

East, California, and the Columbia on October 26, 1891, that as Rock Island completed badges, they would be forwarded to each heavy-artillery battery commander, who would then account for them on his ordnance returns. Each battery would receive the maximum number that could be awarded, that is, five first class and ten second class badges. In an extra burst of cost-savings zeal Flagler also specified that when a man who had previously held one of the badges failed to requalify, the badge would be returned to the battery for reissue. This made the 1891 artillery badge unique, for unlike most other badges and prizes they were initially not subject to droppage and remained an item of accountability even after issue.[11]

In the first year of issue the Department of the East's qualifications numbered 154 first class gunners, 163 second class gunners, and 27 third class gunners. No figures have been found for the other departments, but issue of the full order was probably completed by January 1892.

New tests and badges adopted in 1896 rendered the 1891 first class badges and second class bars surplus, and the Ordnance Department directed that all excess pieces be returned at year's end. Regrettably, their fate must be recorded in one of Rock Island's proud annual reports of savings. The badges returned after 1896 were melted as scrap silver for reuse.[12]

The 1896 publication of new heavy-artillery training and testing procedures also established the second series of patterns of gunner badges. This new order eliminated any badge for second class gunners, although the artillery kept the classification. The directive also altered many details of the gunners' tests, introduced new gunnery specialists' tests, established a new first class insignia, altered the badge to be awarded to first class gunners, and provided for specialists' badges.[13]

The new examination for gunnery resulted from the introduction of the modern rifled, breech-loading cannons, caused by the so-called Endicott Board that significantly changed the weapons defending the United States. The new long-range cannons required about four to five times as many men per weapon as the previous system, and the number of enlisted men serving each gun grew considerably. Revised gunnery requirements, shown in table 5, eliminated the battery commander's considerable leeway in awarding points, while the test also became more comprehensive. The manner of classifying gunners in each battery changed so that those who scored 70 to 80 percent on the test were classified as third class gunners, those who received more than 80 percent but not more than 90 percent became second class gunners, and those receiving over 90 percent became first class gunners. Requirements continued to evolve, and by 1904 the War Department even required first class gunners to display knowledge of general features of war ships.[14]

The number of new 1896 first class gunner badges became limited to not more than 25 percent of each battery's strength, although the Quartermaster's Department now provided an insignia for wear on the coat sleeve for *all* first class gunners. For the first time in

Table 5. *1896 Gunnery Test*

Minimum Qualifications	Maximum Figure of Merit
1. Use of angle measuring instruments.	15
2. Use of plotting board.	15
3. Service of the piece, including service of all B. L. siege pieces, of the 8-inch C.R., the 10-inch and 15-inch S.B. guns, and all B.L. sea coast pieces that have been available for instruction during the year (or such of them as the examining board may designate), including nomenclature, weights, charges, projectiles, and the preparation of fuzes and ammunition.	15
4. Judging distance of stationary objects.	2.5
5. Judging distance of moving objects.	2.5
6. Judging speed of vessels.	2.5
7. Judging velocity of wind.	2.5
8. Laying guns including allowances for wind, drift, and speed of the target.	20
9. Use of range tables.	15
10. Cordage. Block and tackle—including their use in such mechanical maneuvers as may have been executed during the year which will include all that the available facilities have permitted. No time limit to be required under this head.	10
Total	100

Data and wording from information contained in General Orders 41, 1896.

the U.S. Army's history, the army prescribed a sleeve insignia to show an earned qualification. The army adopted "a piece of scarlet cloth neatly piped and stitched on the outside of the right sleeve halfway between the shoulder and the elbow, below the chevron in the case of a noncommissioned officer, the shape of the insignia to be that of an elongated cannon projectile one and one half inches long and three-quarters of an inch wide, point up," to distinguish all first class gunners.[15]

One must clearly distinguish between various gunner's *badges*, which were metal pins worn on the chest and issued by the Ordnance department, and gunner's *insignia*, which soldiers worn on the sleeve and were issued by the Quartermaster's Department, especially since the 1896 limitation was on badges but not on insignia. Throughout the period between 1896 and 1913, the army used the words *insignia*, or later *chevron*, to designate cloth sleeve devices. As shall been seen, the artillery badges disappeared before World War I, but various insignia and chevrons worn exclusively by artillerymen continued until 1941, although these sleeve devices later changed a great deal. These are discussed in the following section on artillery insignia.[16]

The new 1896 tests also provided for a new category of men: gunnery specialists. Becoming a specialist required that the soldier first pass the gunner's test and then that he pass an examination either in communications or in meteorological instruments and range-table work. Details of these skill tests are listed in table 6.

A contender could qualify under either or both of the specialist categories. To pass the communications test a gunner had to score 90 percent total and 100 percent under subheading "a." Passage of the meteorological test required 90 percent overall and perfect scores on subheadings "a," "b," and "c." If a man had the ability and could pass both specialist tests, his endeavors were rewarded with the full specialist badge, whose design was a combination of the other two.

Unfortunately, although the artillery carefully laid out the tests in the 1896 order, the Ordnance Department did not have the new badges ready for issue. Under the 1896 order the 1891 first class gunner badges continued to be "used as a gunner's badge" until the new design became available. This lapse, which ran into 1897, may account for the fact that a few of the 1891 badges escaped the melter's pot

Fig. 4.6. *An 1897 heavy-artillery first class gunner's badge, struck in bronze at Rock Island Arsenal. The central design is a gunner's quadrant, used to measure a gun's elevation. The reverse is blank.*

Table 6. *1896 Gunnery Specialist Test*

Communications	Maximum Figure of Merit
a. Telegraphy and signaling. To include both the sending and receiving messages by the telegraphic sounder, or by relay and sounder; and by flag and torch. Competitors to be able to send and receive by flag and torch at the rate of five words per minute; by telegraph at the rate of ten words per minute, every five letters of the message to be counted as a word.	50
b. The practical care and maintenance of the simple batteries required in telegraphy; erection, care, and maintenance of telegraph lines; and the adjustment and care of ordinary telegraph instruments.	50
Total	100

Use of Meteorological Instruments and Range Table Work	Maximum Figure of Merit
a. The erection, care, and use of the anemometer and its appurtenances.	20
b. The use of the barometer, both mercurial and aneroid.	20
c. The use of the thermometer.	10
d. The extended use of range tables, including the application of all corrections for changes in atmospheric conditions, wind drift, weight of shot, and initial velocity, so as to furnish accurate data to the gun.	50
Total	100

Data from information contained in General Orders 41, 1896.

and are around today. The badges for gunnery specialists, "of approved design and in three forms," were to be furnished "as soon as prepared."

Seven months after publishing the 1896 order, the chief of ordnance began to receive inquiries as to when the new badges would be issued. They were still not ready in June, but on July 24, 1897, Circular 15 finally described the long-awaited new rewards. The War Department provided that the specialists' badges— Class A (for communications), Class B (for meteorological), and Full Gunnery—would be silver and that the new first class gunner's badge would be bronze. All four would be of the same size and would have similar brooches: the top view of a cannon.[17]

The four 1897 badges have pendants all approximately 1.2 inches in diameter, with the upper portion near the edge bearing **U.S. ARTILLERY.** in the top semicircle, while the lower portion carries thirteen six-point stars completing the lower half of the circular edge design. The Class A badge center displays a telegraph key and batteries, the Class B bears wind-cups and an anemometer, while the full specialist's badge bears a combined design showing the key, batteries, cups, and dial. The reverse of each is blank. The brooch, 1 ^{11}/16 inches long, is hollow on

Fig. 4.6

the reverse and is affixed with a fastening pin. The three silver specialist badges cost $1.20 each, while a bronze first class gunner's badge cost $.75. One of the quirks of the War Department order establishing the 1897 specialist badges was that men who earned one of the badges and were assigned to the artillery school at Fort Monroe could not wear their badge unless wear was approved by the school's commandant.[18]

The revolution in artillery technology that had started at the end of the 1880s continued right through the 1896 regulations. In March 1898 the War Department modified the army's practice of awarding badges, so that henceforth all first class gunners could wear a gunner's badge, rather than the previous 25 percent maximum. Three months after the March change and a few weeks after the start of the war with Spain, another general order

Fig. 4.7. The design of the silver 1897 heavy-artillery specialists' Class A badge. The communications-related badge shows a telegraph key and batteries. One of the quirks of the War Department order establishing the 1897 specialists badges was that men who had won one of the badges and were assigned to the artillery school at Fort Monroe could not wear the badge unless the school's commandant approved wear.

Fig. 4.8. Wind cups and an anemometer form the central design for the specialist Class B badge. Made of silver, its reverse is blank, like that of all the other 1897 specialists' badges.

Fig. 4.9. The silver "full specialist" 1897 badge combined the designs of both the "A" and "B" versions and was worn by soldiers who passed both the A and B tests.

Fig. 4.10. Coast Artillery Corporal Robert Dye, stationed at the Baltimore Harbor area, wears one of the bronze 1897–1903 first class gunner badges. The photograph was taken in July 1898.

Fig. 4.7

Fig. 4.8

Fig. 4.9

Fig. 4.10

allowed soldiers to retain the gunner's insignia and badge after qualification in five successive annual competitions.[19]

From experience gained in the Spanish-American War, the War Department determined that the army should place more emphasis on development and training of both harbor mining and field artillery, although the commanding general of the army had recommended, as early as 1889, "a system for target practice for field artillery." As an outgrowth of this belief, the army published new training and testing orders in 1901 and subsequent years. Each order altered artillery-training or gunnery-qualification requirements in some manner that reflected changes based on technical advances then being made, as in the use of electricity and optics.[20]

In February 1901 Congress created the Artillery Corps by dividing all artillery into the coast artillery and the field artillery, under a common chief. As a result of the act, based on experiences in the war with Spain, the coast artillery organized several different types of companies: gun companies, mortar companies, and torpedo companies, the latter of which controlled electrically detonated mines placed in harbors. While all coast artillery companies were numbered without regard to the type of unit, unit numbers were duplicated between the coast and field artillery. This parallel numbering required the individual field artillery units to use the name "battery" in contrast to the coast artillery's use of "company." Thus the 5th Artillery Company was a coast artillery unit and the 5th Artillery Battery was field. New diversity of skills in separate organizations called for revised tests that measured artillerymen's ability to capitalize on the new equipment.

General Orders Number 152 of November 1901 provided separate tests for gunners in three different types of units: gun and mortar coast artillery companies, torpedo (mine) coast artillery companies, and field artillery batteries. All tests were still to be administered at the company/battery level, except for the specialist (master gunner) test for coast artillerymen, which was given only at Fort Monroe. Before taking the first class gunner's test, all men were still required to pass the second class test, but unlike the earlier practices, a classification once earned now lasted three years rather than one.

The initial field artillery gunners' test was detailed in 1901. It provided for display of skills in five general areas, as shown in table 7. This and the next field artillery test required a score of 65 percent to qualify as a second class gunner and 85 percent as a first class gunner.[21] The December 1902 field artillerymen's test, replacing the first version, better portrayed a gunner's overall ability but was still equally vague.[22]

As might be expected, the tests for coast artillery mine companies became suitably specialized, and the army instituted separate, sequential tests, one for second class and one for first class. Each of the torpedo company tests required a passing score of 75 percent. If the soldier failed to obtain at least 65 percent on any category during the examination, the test was terminated even though the entire examination might not have been completed. Unit commanders "generally" selected NCOs from the ranks of gunners under these new regulations, but the classification was not mandatory for a warrant as had been the case under the 1890 general orders. Even so, the examination was "to ascertain in each company the qualified gunners." The test requirements for mine companies are shown in table 9. Only a few of these companies ever existed, and when the first 130 companies were formed, only the 54th Company, stationed in the New York City area, was a torpedo unit. In 1904 the 54th Company became the torpedo depot company, and the War Department designated four other companies as "torpedo" (mine) companies: the 57th in New York, the 58th in Boston, the 60th in San Francisco, and the 120th in Boston.[23]

In 1902 Headquarters of the Army Circular Number 51, dated June 18, established a single class of coast artillery specialists to replace the three classes created in 1896. These new specialists were to be chosen on a highly selective basis. The circular allowed commanders from each of the nineteen continental artillery districts, Puerto Rico, and Hawaii to choose one enlisted first class gunner to attend a technical course at Fort Monroe each year. At the conclusion of this unique course those men who passed a comprehensive test became rated as "specialists." The following year the War Department changed the title to "master gunners." This new, single class of elite artillerymen identified the most skillful cannoneers.

Table 7. *1901 Field Artillery Gunnery Test*

Task	%
a. Laying of piece.	40
b. Adjusting fuzes.	20
c. Use of authorized range finder.	15
d. Drill of gun detachment.	15
e. Military bearing and efficiency.	10
Total	100

Data and wording from information contained in General Orders 152, 1901.

Table 8. *1902 Field Artillery Gunnery Test*

Task	%
a. Laying of piece.	40
b. Adjusting fuzes.	15
c. Use of authorized range finder.	15
d. Drill of gun detachment.	15
e. Firing with subcaliber device.	15
Total	100

Data and wording from information contained in General Orders 126, 1902.

Table 9. *1904 Mine Company Gunnery Tests*

Second-Class Test	Maximum Figure of Merit
a. Ammunition, nomenclature, and service of gun assigned to company.	15
b. Manual of duties in loading room.	30
c. Manual for and duties on the water.	30
d. Knots.	5
e. Care and preservation of material.	10
f. Handling high explosives.	10
Total	100

First-Class Test	Maximum Figure of Merit
a. Knowledge and use of azimuth instruments.	10
b. Knowledge and use of plotting board.	10
c. Batteries, generators, and searchlights assigned to company.	10
d. Apparatus and operation of casemate switchboard and care and use of telephones.	10
e. Care and preservation of material and handling high explosives.	10
f. Material of and duties in loading room.	25
g. Material for and duties on the water.	25
Total	100

Data extracted from information contained in General Orders 108, 1904.

Fig. 4.11. *The scarce 1903–9 master*
gunner badge that replaced the three
specialist badges first made in 1897. This
design was based on the Fort Monroe
artillery-school insignia.

To the despair of artillerymen, another badge saw the light of day. A new 1903 master gunner badge eliminated the three different specialist badges that the army had so recently introduced, which were more attainable by common soldiers. Master gunners became qualified at "the highest standard." During the course of instruction the soldiers studied:

Surveying and triangulation.
Orienting guns and determining the height of gun trunnions and position finders above mean low tide.
Construction of various harbor charts.
Construction of plotting boards.
Construction of topographical maps.
Use of photos and blue prints.[24]

During this time ranges became greater and targets became more realistic, as the fruits of ever-increasing technology descended upon the coast artillery. By 1909 target ranges were 4 miles and targets became a rectangular screen, 60 feet long and 30 feet high, attached to a raft.[25]

Fig. 4.11

School until September 1860, when the Civil War forced closure of the post. Reopened by General Grant a couple of years after the end of the Civil War, the institution became The Artillery School of the United States Army until mid-1907, when the name changed to The Coast Artillery School, a title that survived until shortly after World War II.

Other artillery schools have come and gone, and some of these institutions, such as the Air Defense Artillery School, still exist today. Even so, Fort Monroe was the lyceum that influenced the heavy artillery, and after 1911 Fort Sill was the home of the U.S. Field Artillery.[26]

Fort Monroe, shown in a nineteenth-century engraving, is located at the entrance to the Chesapeake Bay in southern Virginia.

Production figures for the 1903 master gunner badges are lacking, but the 1902 circular establishing the specialist school at Fort Monroe limited the badge so that not more than forty-two men wore it at any one time. As an example, in 1907 the entire roster of master gunners army wide numbered only thirty-one. The army limited the annual course to twenty-one students. Success with the challenging and difficult curriculum resulted in the student receiving his new designation and badge, but also a month's furlough, exemption from guard or fatigue duty except in times of emergency, and a new sleeve insignia.[27]

When Congress reorganized the artillery in 1907 and split the Coast Artillery Corps away from the "mobile army," it allocated all forty-two master-gunner spaces to the corps. At the same time the legislative branch created the grade (rank) of master gunner. The army kept the qualification requirements for this rank the same as those used when the title of master gunner designated a man entitled to wear the oval badge. The master gunner's grade insignia became the same as the special sleeve insignia adopted in 1903, with the addition of a star above the shell. Men who ranked as master gunners continued to wear the master gunner badges until February 1909, when the War Department decreed that the badges would "no longer be issued, and the wearing of such badges will be discontinued."[28]

Financially, it was quite meaningful to be a master gunner. In 1907 a master gunner on his first enlistment received $40 per month, a

Fig. 4.12. A 1903 first class gunner's badge. This was the most widely made gunner's badge.

Fig. 4.13. A coast artilleryman, circa 1908, wearing the 1903-pattern first class gunner's badge. The secretary of war directed that the Coast Artillery Corps wear out the remaining stocks of pre-1902 uniforms. The result was a confused mixture, with the large 1872-pattern chevrons being worn point up by some coast artillerymen, as in this case.

Fig. 4.14. Rock Island Arsenal marked the 1903 first class gunner's badges on the brooch's reverse. The top row carried the unit designation, while the lower row bore the owner's company number.

rather handsome sum for the time. On the other hand artillery first class gunners received 1901 incentive payments of $2 per month, with second class gunners receiving $1 above their base pay. In 1908 these rates grew to $3 and $2 respectively. Master gunners survived as a class into World War II, and the school at Fort Monroe continued to graduate soldiers who, after 1920, were staff sergeants.[29]

While the army introduced the master gunner's badge by means of General Orders Number 94 on June 26, 1903, the same order also created the most common and widely worn first class gunner's badge. In addition the order allowed winners of the award to retain their badges. The new 1903 first class gunner's badge displayed two shiny yellow-metal cannons crossed at 90 degrees, each weapon slightly over 1.9 inches long, with a silver-colored center square .65 inches on a side. This square bore a floating target remarkably similar to Captain Lyon's never used 1891 gunner's button. The entire badge was suspended from a black-edged brass rectangle. One sample is shown in figure 4.12.

Production numbers on this popular badge are not clear, but the initial order placed in 1903 was for 1,700 badges. By 1906 Rock Island Arsenal reported a remaining inventory of 525 Coast Artillery Corps badges, and no evidence has been found that a reorder was made, although—given their popularity—the army probably needed additional badges. For example, in May 1908 twenty-one men of the 10th Company earned this style badge.

Fig. 4.13

The group included three sergeants, seven corporals, two mechanics, a cook, and eight privates. Before issue, Rock Island Arsenal stamped all coast artillery badges on the reverse of the rectangular brooch with the unit's name, for example, **10 CO COAST ART**, on one line and the owner's company number on the second line. A soldier's company number was the means of identification of his web gear and leather items and was unique to his company.[30]

Fig. 4.12

Fig. 4.14

Some unmarked badges are found. These are awards purchased from commercial sources, as some artillerymen wanted an additional badge for wear on a second coat. While the design for the unmarked commercial badges appears to be identical to that of the issue badges, close examination of the small German silver-and-black square will show a different wave pattern, often most noticeably in the lower right corner. Like the master gunner badge, the 1903 coast artillery badge ended with General Orders Number 25, 1909.

Because General Orders Number 94, 1903, was drawn in somewhat ambiguous terms, it caused complaints. The order made no mention of the field artillery, and so some members of this new branch believed that the gunner badge would be awarded only to coastal-artillery soldiers. To eliminate this apparent problem the army published Circular Number 1, January 8, 1904, stating that Order 94 applied to batteries of field artillery as well as to companies of the coast. The 1904 field-artillery issues

of the gunner's badge were appropriately marked on the reverse with "field artillery" in abbreviated form, rather than with "coast artillery." In truth, for nearly a year these "coast artillery" badges were issued to some field artillerymen, and these were marked on the top line with the unit designation and on the lower line with the man's company number, for example, **8 CO FIELD ART** and **No 10**.[31]

In the fall of 1904 the Field Artillery Board proposed a design appropriate to their branch. Chief of Artillery, Brigadier General John P. Story, accepted the design on October 15, 1904, and Rock Island Arsenal soon had these distinctive field artillery badges in production at a cost of $.65, compared to the $.60 for the coast artillery design. Rock Island made at least five hundred of these badges.[32]

As it had the counterpart badge, the Ordnance Department back marked the field artillery version with the unit and man's battery number. The field artillery returned to regimental organization in 1907, while the coast

Fig. 4.15. A commercial 1903-pattern artillery badge that is unmarked on the reverse. Note that the wave pattern is different from that on the issue badge shown in figure 4.12. The easiest-seen distinguishing waves extend from the lower right edge of the pyramid target to the corner of the center square.

Fig. 4.16. A coast artillery crew in action about 1910.

Fig. 4.17. After clarification in January 1904, field artillery men began to earn the 1903-style first class gunner badges that carried the floating coast artillery target. Rock Island Arsenal marked the back to show the field artillery unit by impressing it with **CO FIELD ART** rather than **CO COAST ART**. It would have been more accurate to mark the field artillery badges with some abbreviation for battery, since field artillery organizations were called by that name, while coast units were called "companies."

Fig. 4.18. Dissatisfaction in the field artillery with having to wear the coast-artillery-style first class gunner's badge prompted Rock Island Arsenal to make this distinctive field artillery first class gunner's badge in the fall of 1904.

Fig. 4.15

Fig. 4.17

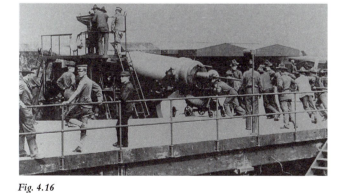

Fig. 4.16

Fig. 4.18

Fig. 4.19

Fig. 4.20

Fig. 4.19. From 1904 through 1907 the backs of field artillery first class badges were marked in this style, listing the battery of field artillery (which were numbered 1 through 30), followed by the man's battery number.

Fig. 4.20. Between 1907 and 1913, the backs of field artillery first class badges were marked with both the battery letter and the regimental number, followed by the man's number. This change reflected the reorganization of the field artillery into regiments in 1907.

artillery retained their separately numbered companies. This caused two types of back marks on the badges that bear a side view of a field gun on a rectangle carrying the words **1st CLASS GUNNER**. An example of the 1904–7 back markings is **29 BATTERY** on the first line and **FIELD ARTILLERY No 107** (the man's number) on the second line. After 1907 badges bore regimental designations, such as **B BATTERY** on the top line and **3 FIELD ART No 6** below.

In the Great War artillery became an indirect-fire weapon under the exigencies of the times. The French developed a 75 mm gun that was the most famous of the several high-velocity, rapid-firing field pieces deployed in Europe that killed hundreds of thousands of people at long range. But without a hint of these changes that were soon to unfold, the U.S. Army continued direct fire of shrapnel as the primary means for artillery support. Targets for the light artillery at the start of the century were silhouettes of a soldier on horseback, various dismounted soldiers, and artillery targets, including limbers and caisson and a gun and carriage. Even with the new 1902 three-inch gun, artillery's goal remained to "sprinkle with a hail of bullets all hostile troops exposing themselves, forcing them to deploy at long ranges, and prevent them from firing effectively upon our own troops." This no doubt came from the recent history of the U.S. Army. Commanders in the West often took the Hotchkiss "mountain gun" with them when chasing Indians, and this light weapon, mounted on a wheeled carriage, could go most places cavalry ventured. The Hotchkiss gun provided a two-pound shell that could reach out to 4,000 yards.[33]

The field artillery adopted new target drills "To secure conditions more closely simulating those of war" and introduced "new types of targets" in 1909. Accompanied by a flash, these innovative targets popped up and remained exposed for only a few moments. This sort of training, a logical extension of practices little changed from Grant's and Lee's days, dominated artillery thinking up to the entry of the United States into the Great War. As late as April 1917 War Department field artillery drill regulations called for gun crews to dismount and quickly swing the gun by the trails and then aim directly at the targets.[34]

The longer-range indirect-fire techniques adopted on the European fronts in 1914–15 was not used by the United States until it saw forces going overseas. In 1916 the U.S. Army listed the effective range of the rifle as out to 1,200 yards and the effective range of field artillery only out to 3,500 yards. By contrast Germany and the other warring countries soon perfected the ability to fire accurately on targets not seen by the gunners. The U.S. artillerymen were astonished in 1917 to discover that the French accounted for the curved surface of the earth ("every projectile fired in the northern hemisphere will drift south") and that they also accounted for the motion of the earth while the shell was in flight in two different ways.[35]

Awarding of the 1904-style field artillery badges continued without interruptions through mid-1913. In June of that year Rock Island Arsenal requested permission to stop marking the backs of the field artillery badges. The arsenal believed that theft was not a major problem, since these badges were bronze and of less value than the silver rifle badges, which were issued without markings. In addition Rock Island argued that in a later enlistment the marking would likely not be correct and that retention of marking requirements complicated manufacture, as each badge was marked by hand. In response the chief of ordnance, William Crozier, passed the request to the Field Artillery Board meeting at Fort Riley, Kansas, for their recommendation.[36]

Fig. 4.21

as was the case with the gunner's insignia, soldiers wore the master gunner's insignia on the right sleeve just below the rank chevron. In 1908 master gunner became the title of an enlisted rank. As has been noted, for that grade NCOs wore a shell in a wreath with a star above.[37]

Fig. 4.22

Fig. 4.23

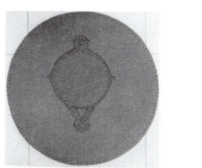

Fig. 4.24

Fig. 4.25

Fig. 4.21. Corporal Jason Laskey, stationed at Fort Riley, Kansas, wears one of the 1904-style field artillery gunner's badges.

Fig. 4.22. The first design of the cloth first class gunner's insignia, 1896–1907. The projectile is red with white stitching.

Fig. 4.23. An olive drab 1903–7 master gunner cloth insignia for the winter service uniform. This sleeve insignia replaced the original cloth first class gunner insignia used by senior gunners. For dress uniforms the red projectile was stitched in white, with a yellow silk hand-embroidered wreath.

Fig. 4.24. In 1907 the artillery made several changes to gunners' cloth sleeve insignia. First class gunners added a small bar below the insignia, while second class gunners used only the basic insignia: an outline of a sea mine for mine company gunners (shown) or a projectile for coast and field artillery gunners. Red replaced the previously used white stitching for dress insignia.

Fig. 4.25. A chevron for the grade of master gunner, introduced in 1908 and used into 1920.

The board commented that the sleeve insignia sufficiently indicated the class of gunnery and that the badge, which was only for a test, was more conspicuous than the new campaign medals first created in 1905, which represented months in combat. They recommended that the badge be dropped. The question then passed to the War College Division, where the General Staff reached a similar conclusion. Major General Leonard Wood, army chief of staff, approved the recommendation, and the War Department issued General Orders Number 49, August 1, 1913, ending the issue of official, distinctive artillery badges.

ARTILLERY INSIGNIA

The initial gunner's insignia with a red projectile stitched in white, used from 1896 until 1907, was available to all artillerymen who qualified as first class gunners, although not all could wear the first class badge. In 1907–8 the lone red shell (now minus the red stitching) became the insignia for a new skill level, second class gunners, while first class gunners' insignia added a red bar below the projectile. In coast artillery mine (torpedo) companies, first and second class gunners wore a red cloth silhouette of a sea-mine case in place of the projectile, with the higher grade also recognized by the addition of a bar under the mine. These four insignia remained in use until 1921.

The 1903 master gunner sleeve insignia consisted of the red shell stitched in white for the first class gunner, but with the addition of a yellow silk hand-embroidered wreath below and partly enclosing the projectile. Until 1908,

Fig. 4.26. *The so-called "Badge for Excellence in Target Practice," used by the Coast Artillery Corps, 1910–23, to recognize the company that scored the highest with their type of weapon, such as 12-inch mortars or 8-inch guns. This cloth insignia went on the lower right coat cuff of each artilleryman in the company who made the highest annual score with a type of weapon.*

Fig. 4.27. *The 1923–47 "Badge for Excellence in Coast Artillery Target Practice." The E (for Excellence) was red, as was the earlier 1.*

Cloth insignia, worn on the lower right sleeve of dress uniforms by all men in the best coast artillery companies, was a red embroidered **1** on a cloth circle. The War Department initially made this most unusual insignia only for the dress-blue uniform; however, troops in Hawaii, the Philippines, and the Panama Canal Zone wore only service uniforms, and for these troops, the background became olive drab or khaki in 1916. As use of the insignia increased, the design changed to a block **E** in 1923. Still worn on the coat cuff, this new **E** device, called the Excellence in Coast Artillery Target Practice chevron, lasted until 1947.

In addition to the above insignia and chevrons, the coast artillery had many more cloth devices that men could sew onto uniform sleeves. Most of these, known as ratings, came about during the 1907 artillery reorganization, some of the soldiers receiving additional pay by virtue of their positions of responsibility. Many wore the insignia for serving as plotters, mine planters, gun commanders, gun pointers, coxswains, loaders, and the like. Some of these rating insignia lasted until the start of World War II.

Fig. 4.26

Fig. 4.27

SWORDSMAN'S BADGES

With the infantryman's sharpshooting and the artilleryman's cannon proficiency recognized by War Department badges, could a reward for the cavalryman's saber be far behind? As early as 1882 the army inspector general reported that while there was a need for more marksmanship training, the saber exercise in the cavalry was totally ignored. This practice, or lack thereof, continued for many years. Early in 1907 Lieutenant Colonel Edward J. McClernand, commander of the 1st Cavalry Regiment, then stationed at Fort Sam Houston, Texas, wrote through military channels to suggest that cavalrymen be required to participate in monthly training exercises with the saber and that each regimental champion receive either a cash prize or a trophy. After dutiful circulation within the War Department staff, Colonel McClernand's suggestion, along with internal General Staff recommendations, ended up on the desk of J. Franklin Bell, the army's chief of staff. The staff recommendation, subsequently published as a general order, was to hold monthly saber and bayonet exercise contests at posts "on the same day as the field or athletic exercises are held, or on the day following."[38]

The order made no mention of rewards other than the bland statement that "Whenever practicable post commanders will be present at the contests and will do all in their power to contribute to the interest thereof by extending extra privileges to the successful contestants." This was hardly a ringing endorsement from the chief of staff, but if McClernand's initial suggestion had been acted upon as proposed, it would have been a logical extension of the War Department's current practice of increasing interest in various weapons through recognition by various badges.

Rewards for saber practice lingered in this state until February 1913, when a board that had been convened to "observe and study European cavalry" recommended that "to awaken the spirit of emulation and to encourage efforts to attain a high state of training, insignia denoting excellence in swordsmanship should be provided as is done for excellence in rifle firing." Leonard Wood, chief of staff between April 1910 and April 1914, was a graduate of the Harvard Medical School who as a surgeon received the Medal of Honor as a result of actions in the Geronimo campaign, gained fame as the colonel of the Rough Riders, and became a general of the regular army line in 1901. In 1913 Major General Wood accepted the board's recommendation to establish a swordsmanship badge. The cavalry owed its new badge to a Harvard medical doctor. As a result of Wood's decision and, as will be seen shortly, young George Patton's influence, the Ordnance Department ultimately designed an attractive swordsman's badge, which is shown in figure 4.28. Five hundred of these badges were ordered in February 1914, and the next month War Department General Orders 16 announced the particulars to the army: "A badge for excellence in swordsmanship. . . . will be issued by the Ordnance Department, at the rate of two badges for each troop and one badge for the noncommissioned staff of each regiment of Cavalry, to the best swordsman in each organization as determined by the regimental commander by actual test once in each calendar year."[39]

This lack of uniform tests between regiments caused the master of the sword at the Mounted Service School, Second Lieutenant George S. Patton, to develop a standard army-wide test. Patton, who was to gain fame as an armored-force general during World War II, excelled in fencing while he was a cadet at West Point. He won a place on the U.S. Olympic team in the summer of 1912, representing America at Stockholm's games, the Olympic competition that finally established the games as the premier athletic meet, held every four years. Patton represented the United States in the modern military pentathlon, a contest that consisted of five events: horseback riding, pistol shooting, fencing, swimming, and cross-country running, an event that represented all the skills necessary to carry a message through hostile territory.[40]

Although Patton was good enough to place fifth in the Olympics, he still wanted to further improve his skills, and accordingly in the summer of 1913 he paid his own way to the French cavalry school at Saumur, where he studied swordsmanship for three months under the French fencing champion. Ordered to report to the Mounted Service School at Fort Riley, Kansas, by October 1913, he became

the first person to hold the impressive title of Master of the Sword.[41]

In 1913 the chief of staff wrote in his annual report that "for the purpose of improving swordsmanship . . . a course has been established at the Mounted Service School. It is believed that rewards for swordsmanship should be commensurate with those for shooting." It was with this background that the War Department wrote Lieutenant Patton and asked him to establish a standard course for swordsmen. In December 1914 the War Department published Patton's standard course, unmodified from his draft. The course remained unchanged until 1922 and was based on three major points:

1. Organizational commanders were to hold tryouts to select the best five men from each troop and the two best members of the noncommissioned staff.

2. Contestants covered the approximately 275-yard course at a gallop, attacking target dummies.

3. Each contestant started with 100 points, and judges deducted points for excessive time, for poor form, and for missing targets.[42]

Given the Mexican border troubles between 1910 and 1916 and the subsequent world war, it is likely that most organizations awarded the swordsman's badge only in 1914 and perhaps 1915, when it was new. The army deployed many cavalry regiments along the southern border in 1914–15 and sent others to various domestic trouble spots, so some of the regiments probably did not hold contests during those years. At least three different dies are known for this badge; no doubt private firms made some for sale directly to soldiers.[43]

Two men per troop could earn the award, so a brief foray into the world of cavalry organization is in order to examine a U.S. troop, the cavalry combat unit commanded by a captain. Such a unit varied in size but generally remained between 60 and 110 men until well into the twentieth century, with a troop being 100 enlisted men in 1898, 65 in 1904, and 70 in 1916. Initially, all units commanded by captains were known as companies, but during the Civil War some cavalry units began to use the term *troop,* and the transition from company to troop occurred during the next twenty years. In this transition time it was not unusual for some cavalry units to call themselves *companies,* while others in the same regiment used the word *troop.* Various official papers use the

Fig. 4.28. *The 1914 old-gold-colored swordsman's badge with silver sword.*

Fig. 4.28

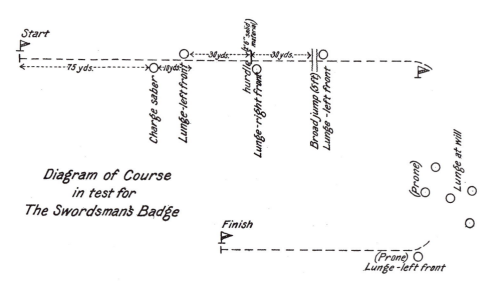

Fig. 4.29

Fig. 4.29. The swordsman's badge qualification course as established by the army's first master of the sword, Lieutenant George S. Patton, and published in a 1914 War Department general order.

words *troop* and *company* in the same document, even when referring to the same unit. By 1883 the metamorphosis was complete, and the U.S. Army officially began to call all company-sized cavalry units "troops." During World War II and later the army dismounted the cavalry units in the 1st Cavalry Division and formed them into infantry while retaining the historic cavalry designations. Well after World War II the army deliberately reorganized many cavalry units as infantry yet continued to keep the cavalry title for historical purposes. In these later units the word *company* shows an infantry intent and mission (after the 1970s possibly meaning a tank organization), while *troop* continued to show the traditional cavalry function.[44]

The history of the swordsman's badge after 1915 is vague. It is not mentioned in revised insignia and uniform regulations of 1917 and later. While the War Department replaced the metal marksmanship badges with cloth versions in 1918 and 1919 in an effort to save precious resources, it failed to mention the swordsman's badge. Perhaps the lack of opportunity to use the sword in the European trenches accounts for this oversight.

When the War Department finally published regulations on new badges in 1921, it included only awards for marksmanship and gunnery. Changes 3 to AR 600-35, dated April 20, 1922, wedged in paragraph 39 $1/2$, which was all of four words long, by stating that the swordsman's badge was authorized "As per approved design." This resurrection of the 1914 badge was thwarted five months later, when changes 5 to the same regulation

rescinded paragraph 39 $1/2$. Despite this short "revision," price lists continued to carry the swordsman badge until 1931. There are known examples of the badge's being given in the early 1920s in regular army cavalry units.[45]

Army trainers also recognized skill with a sword in the same September 1922 change by authorizing a qualification bar with the word **SWORD**. The army further corrected various oversights in 1924, when it titled a new regulation section "Badges for Marksmanship, Gunnery, and Swordsmanship Qualification." Old Dobbin, with his rider's accompanying saber, was further put out to pasture in 1928 when the title became "Badges for Marksmanship, Gunnery, Bombing, etc." Thus the successor to the short-lived yet unique, attractive, and colorful brass and silver swordsman's badge was slowly buried under the inglorious category of "et cetera."[46]

The 1914 swordsman's badge is an old-gold-colored bar bearing the raised word **SWORDSMAN**, with a silver representation of the cavalry sword, Model 1913, superimposed and running the length of the letters. This attractive design not only identified the wearer's accomplishment by noting his recognition as a swordsman, but also showed the new weapon with which he accomplished the feat. Following the 1913 cavalry board, Brigadier General James Parker, commander of the 1st Cavalry Brigade and board member, sketched on the back of one of his calling cards a proposed design for a swordsman's badge that became the basis for awards made by Rock Island Arsenal.[47]

The word *sword* refers to the whole group of edged weapons in which the blade is substantially longer than the handle. A subset of this group is the saber, which is a single-edged sword designed primarily for cutting, usually with some curve towards the point. The cavalry saber, while the primary cavalry weapon during and after the Revolution, started to be displaced by the revolver during the Civil War. By the latter half of the Civil War many cavalry engagements consisted of an exchange of revolver fire, and when these weapons were empty, one or both sides would charge with sabers, although by mid-1864 the Federal cavalry was officially stating, "As opportunities for using sabers are rare, this arm could be dispensed with altogether." The wars of the American West, pitting the U.S. Army against the Indians, reinforced the army's general tendency towards using the revolver, since the Indians, understandably, usually refused to stand and fight on the soldiers' terms. Often it was all the soldiers could do to get off a few rounds at fleeing Indians. Many cavalry units left their sabers behind during the western campaigns, although some commanders had units practice with the weapons for traditional battles.[48]

One troop commander stationed in Texas reported in 1879 that "in the past few weeks" he had held mounted saber drill in addition to target practice. Rather than comment on the quality of training, however, the captain noted that spectators found the practice interesting: "I fixed a number of posts with straw heads, where I practiced some men with their sabers in riding and knocking them off the posts, which is very interesting for the spectators who assemble afternoons when I drill."[49]

The actions in the Civil War and in the American West were consistent with the general attitude of the American cavalry. Some U.S. cavalry was actually light cavalry, used for reconnaissance and screening, but throughout the history of the U.S. Army most were truly dragoons, trained for fighting on foot and on horseback. The use of carbines and revolvers on horseback and afoot, which could result in marksmanship awards, and the limited use of a badge for the sword, mirrored the overall arms actually used by the American cavalry. Even so, commanders continued to have the troops train occasionally with the saber. Orlando S. Goff, who made his living taking photographs in the western United States between 1884 and 1900, recorded a photograph of L

Troop, 1st Cavalry, at saber practice in 1891. The irony of such practice is that at the time the troop consisted entirely of Crow Indians.[50]

From 1872 through the start of World War I the Ordnance Department issued various wooden practice swords and sabers. These broke easily and were never very popular, being used primarily in fencing drills. The lack of emphasis on development of a satisfactory model practice saber and cavalry single stick reflects the lack of enthusiasm officers and men had for dismounted saber use.[51]

At the start of the twentieth century, the army struggled to identify a proper cavalry sword. It designed several experimental models and issued a few of these, so that by 1913 the Ordnance Department had studied experimental cavalry sabers for several years.[52]

George S. Patton designed the 1913 cavalry sword shown on the swordsman's badge. It was the only army sword used by enlisted men that was manufactured in large quantities at a federal arsenal, the other swords having been made under contract or purchased overseas. While romantics may believe that Patton designed the sword resembling himself, "straight, to the point, and direct," the truth is that he wrote several articles while he was in Washington in 1912 and 1913, and by that course became friends with Secretary of War Henry L. Stimson and Army Chief of Staff Leonard Wood. Patton even acted as aide to Wood on many occasions. Through his articles and his friends, Patton influenced Wood to order the chief of ordnance to make twenty thousand of the swords Patton had designed.[53]

The U.S. Army board that examined European cavalry closed its work in 1913 and influenced Patton. He based his sword design on the British and French theory that the point of the saber was of greatest use in a cavalry action. This was opposed to the American practice at the time that emphasized cuts with the edge. The British and French practice called for a straight, tapered blade with a double edge. The result was the 1913 cavalry sword, with its distinctive guard made from a single heavy sheet of steel shaped into a full basket.[54]

Compared to many nineteenth-century blades, this sword—with its long, heavy, deep checked metal grip and thumb indentation on the top—simply reeked of twentieth-century high-quality manufacturing efficiency. It was a sign of things to come: heavy, metallic, mass-produced weapons of war. Gone was

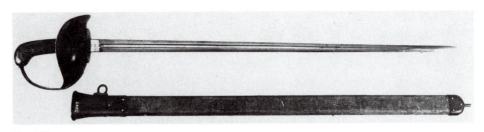

Fig. 4.30

Fig. 4.30. The 1913 enlisted cavalry sword. The scabbard is made of khaki webbing, with a blackened steel tip and throat. The ricasso (the area on the blade immediately below the grip) is marked U.S. followed the serial number, while the reverse shows the manufacturer (the letters SA for Springfield Arsenal for example), a flaming bomb for the Ordnance Department, and the year of manufacture. Soldiers never wore the weapon but used the scabbard rings on each side to affix the weapon to their saddles.

Fig. 4.31. A 1922–38 expert badge with SWORD bar, which replaced the 1914 swordsman's badge.

the American image that had lasted from the Revolution, through the Civil War and later, of a slashing cavalryman on horseback wielding a curved saber. The truth was that the pistol had become the cavalryman's personal weapon; Patton's Model 1913 sword was never used in combat.

Despite the differences between a sword and a saber, training regulations of the 1920s and 1930s were titled "Saber Exercise." These regulations started by describing the élan of cavalry: "The saber is solely a weapon of offense to be used by the trooper mounted. Accordingly, in all attacks with the saber the trooper must be taught to charge with great spirit, to disregard an opposing weapon, and to lunge at the right moment directly at his adversary's body." The army introduced a new course in 1922, varying considerably from the 1913 Patton version. With twenty-five targets the new run included four ditches or hurdles, and it was much more difficult. Training started with dismounted instruction, during which time the men placed their feet well apart, as if riding, and learned the different positions, unhampered by their mounts. Combining this with riding instruction, the men, both individually and in a unit, finally mastered mounted saber drills. Attacks culminated in charging dummies, first at a walk, then at a gallop, and finally, for 100 yards, at full speed. During qualification men initially had one and one-half minutes to complete the course, including the initial charge, but no additional points were given for completing the run in less time. In 1929 the scoring and timing changed, with troopers given forty-five seconds after striking the first dummy, and two points were deducted for each second after that time.[55]

The army graded all officers and enlisted men who were required or authorized to demonstrate proficiency with the sword into four categories: expert swordsman, excellent swordsman, swordsman, and unqualified. The first three grades correspond to the expert,

sharpshooter, and marksman badges. Officers who became exempt from requalification with the sword could wear the insignia of their last qualification, while the army allowed those who attained the grade of expert swordsman to wear the badge "thereafter." Those who qualified as expert or excellent swordsmen could earn requalification bars with dates engraved on the back, as described in chapter 3. A swordsman (marksman) could earn that level of badge but once and could wear it for only a year.[56]

In 1906, on Luzon Island in the Philippines, the U.S. Army executed its last major conventional cavalry charge. It was the final instance of the mass use of the sword by U.S. troops in combat, but that historical footnote was not written for many years, and the U.S. Army continued to practice for the great horse-mounted sword charges. In fact, as time moved on one platoon of the 26th Cav-

Fig. 4.31

alry (Philippine Scouts) performed the final—although small—U.S. Army cavalry charge on January 16, 1942, using firearms. The unit suffered only three casualties.[57]

Through 1942 the army trained for horse-mounted cavalry actions and awarded associated qualification badges. While the Poles, Russians, Germans, Japanese, and other World War II belligerents employed horses on the battlefield, the United States did not. Cavalry became a mission and a state of mind. Today's army cavalrymen qualify with aeroweapons, tanks, Bradley fighting vehicles, and other modern weapons.

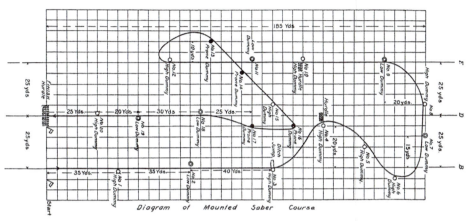

Fig. 4.32. The 1922 swordsman's course as shown in period training regulations. The course was much more difficult than Patton's original version.

Fig. 4.32

CHAPTER FIVE

UNOFFICIAL AWARDS

WHAT SOME SOLDIERS WORE

Fig. 5.1. A typical unit shooting badge given to U.S. soldiers between the world wars. The 7th Infantry badge is 1 ¹/₄ inches wide and bears the regiment's insignia in relief. This particular award is engraved on the reverse, **CLASS II** and **MG** (for Machine Gun) **Pvt. W. J. Reed**.

Fig. 5.2. A gold-colored 1 ¹/₂–inch-wide machine gun badge given by the 174th Infantry Regiment (74th New York) in the 1930s. The regiment's insignia is enameled on the brooch, and the 1936 bar shows the year of a requalification. The various lines and dots in the upper corners of the planchet represent symbols that were used on contemporary scorecards.

BOTH SOME MILITIA AND REGULAR units, and in the 1870s even General E. O. C. Ord, issued a plethora of badges and insignia that the War Department did not recognize. Prized by the recipients, the use of such devices increased after World War I and further expanded as morale boosters during the resource-strapped depression. In the 1920s and 1930s many regiments provided medals and badges. The best of these awards are often embellished with the unit's insignia and today are sought by military collectors. The sheer number of units prohibits even an attempt to list the awards.

By the end of World War II commanders showered soldiers with metal badges denoting various levels of proficiency, while cloth insignia and similar qualification doodads skyrocketed. This chapter considers only a sample of these insignia and their rationalizations;

mainly of awards given at the national level. Many others, such as the initial two examples described here, exist to the consternation of curators and regulation enforcers, while these same decorations are often cherished by collectors and by the faux warrior.

ARTILLERY

Between the world wars the Massachusetts branch of the Society of the Sons of the Revolution awarded various Knox Trophy recognitions to top artillery performers. The ambitious scheme provided rotating trophies and permanent plaques for units, and medals to individuals. Recognition went to field artillery

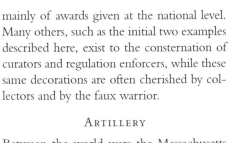

Fig. 5.1

Fig. 5.2

batteries, field artillery noncommissioned officers, coast artillery noncommissioned officers, Massachusetts National Guard field artillery batteries, Massachusetts Coast Artillery National Guard companies, Massachusetts noncommissioned officers, and, starting in 1927, regular army coast artillery companies. Although the recognitions were given by a private organization, the War Department fully cooperated, and the chief of field artillery promulgated some test criteria in the 1930s. The adjutant general of the army announced awards in an annual special letter, and regulations provided extra ammunition for the test. In addition the U.S. Navy and the Society of the Sons of the Revolution presented a Knox Trophy to the best-firing battleship.[1]

The obverse of the various Knox Trophy medals are all identical, including those given to the navy: The 1 3/8-inch-long top bar was issued blank for the inscription of the winner's name and unit. From this brooch a 1 3/8-inch-wide dark-blue ribbon edged in gold suspends a 1 3/8-inch-diameter medal bearing the profile of Henry Knox, the first secretary of war and Revolutionary War artillery commander. Around the edge of the dark bronze disk is the inscription **1750–1806** and **HENRY KNOX**. On the reverse various designs appear, identifying the award. For the army field artillery the reverse design includes crossed cannons and an eagle over a laurel wreath. Around the edge is the inscription **SOCIETY • OF • THE • SONS • OF • THE • REVOLUTION • IN • THE COMMONWEALTH • OF • MASSACHUSETTS**, and just inside that, the wording in the upper portion, **EXCELLENCE • LIGHT • ARTILLERY • U • S • ARMY**. For the regular army field artillery, the Knox Medal was awarded to the enlisted man making the highest grades at the field artillery school.[2]

The Society of the Sons of the Revolution in Massachusetts also presented unit awards in the name of Henry Knox. They gave a unit trophy to the regular army battery "attaining the highest rating in firing efficiency." New 1924 rules provided that the trophy be given to the best all-around battery, based on a test devised by the chief of field artillery to measure firing efficiency, tactical mobility, proficiency in the use of field artillery communications, and interior economy. Regional contests and regimental tests resulted in the selection of sixteen batteries that vied for the award. Minor details of the test changed annually,

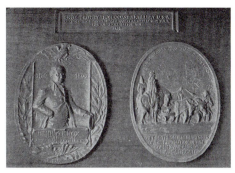

Fig. 5.3

Fig. 5.3. A Knox Trophy plaque as presented between the world wars to the best artillery units.

and units worked hard over several years in attempts to be the best in the U.S. Artillery.[3]

The winning battery commander received the trophy on January 17th each year at a special banquet honoring Ben Franklin's birthday. The trophy, first given in 1924 and last presented in 1939, was the most coveted award in the field artillery during its use. Coast artillery units of all types competed for their version of the Knox Trophy, including antiaircraft, railway artillery, and harbor defense recognitions, while the field artillery pack-mule units competed against more conventional units. The Knox Trophy itself consisted of two side-by-side plaques, framed in mahogany. The plaque on the left bears a three-quarter bas-relief portrait of General Knox, modeled from the portrait by Gilbert Stuart, while the plaque on the right shows General Knox and a staff officer, mounted, watching the progress of a yoke of oxen dragging a snow sledge, which illustrates the method of transporting the artillery from Fort Ticonderoga during the winter of 1775–76.[4]

Between 1943 and 1945 the U.S. Chinese Training and Combat Command prepared Chinese troops by teaching the use of infantry and artillery weapons. Like the Chinese soldiers, U.S. training instructors evidently also wore the attractive gold-colored badges of the style shown in figures 5.4 and 5.5. While the general design of the brooches is similar to that of the infantry China badges shown at the end of this chapter, the title **GUNNER FIRST CLASS** and the crossed cannons or the brooch marked **EXPERT GUNNER** set them apart as artillery awards. The mortar expert badge discussed at the end of the chapter might be considered by some to be an "artillery" award, however, despite the fact that the mortar is an infantry weapon.[5]

Fig. 5.4. *Thousands were probably made, yet few of these yellow-metal badges made it to America. The U.S. Chinese Training and Combat Command gave them between 1943 and 1945 to soldiers who qualified as first class gunners with field artillery cannons. These cheaply made badges have a simple pin and catch.*

Fig. 5.5. *The highest artillery-gunner award given by the U.S. Chinese Training and Combat Command during the latter half of World War II.*

Fig. 5.6. *A nickel-colored field artillery badge made between the world wars. It is not known whether these were for ROTC cadets, National Guard members, or regular troops.*

Fig. 5.7. *Similar to the badge shown in figure 5.6, this crack squad badge may represent third place in local competition.*

Fig. 5.4

Fig. 5.5

During the lean years of the 1920s and the Great Depression, various manufacturers produced a range of qualification badges, for use either in army units or in ROTC organizations. Three such examples are shown, all having similar designs. Aside from what can be gleaned from the obvious appearance, little is known of these artillery awards. They are silver-colored awards with top bar and wreath similar to those elements used on expert rifle and pistol badges before World War I. One style has the top bar bearing the wording **CRACK**

SQUAD, which may reflect the fact that an entire gun crew qualified in that unit—the one step beyond the individual qualification and earning a **FIELD ARTILLERY** bar for the expert-marksmanship badge. The number above the cannons may reflect the unit, as badges bearing a 1 and a 3 are both known, but the numbers may also indicate placement in a contest that the ROTC or other units might have conducted.

Another badge has the top bar with **CRACK BATTERY** and, above the cannons intersection, the letter P rather than a number. The letter either could represent a competition in the Philippine Islands or it could have been given by a school that had that initial, such as Pittsburgh, Purdue, or a similar institution. Still another badge of this same general design is identical to the one just described except that the top is inscribed **DIS-TINGUISHED SQUAD.** While the lineage of these artillery badges is murky, they show that there was a general interest in artillery proficiency.

Other units of the depression-era army gave individual badges of standard designs except that the awards were in 14-karat gold. The

Fig. 5.6

Fig. 5.7

Fig. 5.8

reverse of one of these gold badges, shown in figure 5.9, is identical in design and size to a standard sharpshooter's badge with a **GUN-NER** bar. The most interesting aspect of this award is that the badge is for a sharpshooter and not an expert. The sharpshooter's badge was awarded to gunners for proficiency in the preliminary gunner's examination, while actual firing was required for expert qualification. This gold badge may have been given to the soldier who had the best score on the preliminary gunner's examination (see page 61).

In 1964, as part of the plans for the unthinkable war, the army loudly deployed Pershing missiles—the latest means of delivering a tactical nuclear response in Europe. Developed between 1958 and 1964 by the Martin Marietta Corporation, the system replaced the

Fig. 5.9

Redstone and other missiles. Three versions of the Pershing missile saw service. The Pershing I system, the first to be fielded, was mounted on tracked vehicles; an erector-launcher with a missile was a second vehicle for the missile warhead, and a third tracked vehicle was for the programmer test station and a 45 kilowatt generator and communications vehicle.

In August 1967 Martin Marietta received the contract to produce the second Pershing version, the Ia, with three wheeled vehicles replacing the four tracked vehicles listed above. The training battalion at Fort Sill, Oklahoma, (2d Battalion, 44th Artillery) received these initial missiles in May 1969, with all units receiving them by July 1970. The massive Pershing II missile was fully deployed with the initial battalion in Europe in June 1984, and the switch over within Europe was completed by December 1985.[6]

The initial version of the deadly missile itself was over 34 $^{1}/_{2}$ feet long and 40 inches in diameter, with a weight in excess of five tons. Transporting, erecting, targeting, and launching the system was a complex operation that required a large number of soldiers and precise coordination. Selected units were on call twenty-four hours a day, and demands were great. The overall unit controlling the Pershing systems in Europe, the 56th Field Artillery Brigade, issued a set of pocket badges to show qualification and achievement with the Pershing missile system.

The badges come in three degrees: gold, silver, and bronze. The metal insignia show a missile being launched, the legend **56TH FA BRIGADE** (some scarcer design variations have **56 ARTILLERY BRIGADE**, and the earliest badges have **56 ARTILLERY GROUP**); and the letters **QRA** at the bottom. These elongated, egg-shaped badges, one inch wide and three inches long, are illustrated in figures 5.10, 5.11, and 5.12. The first badge, used by the 56th Artillery Group, is not common, as the Pershing missile was used in that group only between May 1969 and September 1970, after which the personnel and missiles were transferred to the 56th Field Artillery Brigade. Although the unit numbers are the same and the designations similar, the lineages of the two units are separate.[7]

When Pershing systems deployed in Europe, various crews manned them with atomic warheads. Troops assigned to tactical units spent several consecutive weeks "on station" with

Fig. 5.8. *This silver-colored badge was clearly for a company-sized unit, since the title includes the word **BATTERY**. The **P** at the cannons' intersection may indicate a college starting with the letter P. There are badges of the same design but having **DISTINGUISHED SQUAD** on the top bar.*

Fig. 5.9. *The reverse of a sharpshooter's badge, made in 14-karat gold, with a gold bar impressed on the front reading **FIELD ARTY** (artillery). The mystery is why the "best gunner" would have the middle (sharpshooter) badge rather than the expert award, unless it was given for a preliminary gunner's examination in which actual firing was not done.*

Fig. 5.10. A 1 x 3–inch metal badge used by soldiers initially deployed to Europe with the Pershing missile, who were members of the 56th Missile Group, between May 1969 and September 1970.

Fig. 5.11. In mid-1970 the 56th Missile Group became the 56th Missile Brigade, and their badges changed accordingly. These badges came in gold, silver, and bronze depending upon the qualification level. To earn a gold-colored badge a soldier had to participate in the actual firing of a Pershing missile. These badges exist in both thin and thick metal.

Fig. 5.12. Variations of the 56th Missile Brigade badge were also made with the inscriptions solely at the edges and with two lightning bolts at the top.

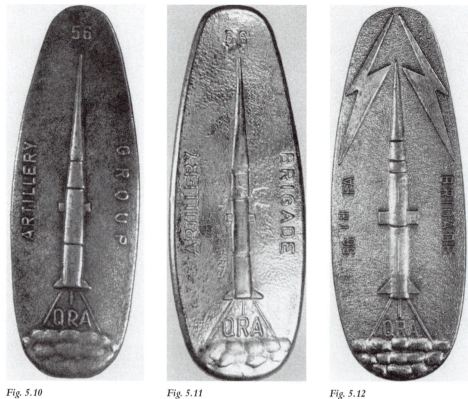

Fig. 5.10   Fig. 5.11   Fig. 5.12

these missiles. This was accomplished by each of the three missile battalions having a firing battery in the field on a permanent basis, with the field batteries rotating once a month. The units not in the field were at their home station doing maintenance and training. Initially, the Pershing Professional Badge, in bronze, was given to any soldiers recognized by a battalion commander as outstanding.[8] This soon changed to a set of three badges. Bronze and silver badges were awarded in recognition of various times spent on station, although the exact requirements are already lost to history. A silver badge was more difficult to earn and a smaller number of soldiers wore these badges than wore the bronze.

Annually selected crews participated in the launching of missiles in the United States, usually in the western part of the country, although some were launched in Florida, from Cape Canaveral at the central training facility, during the transition from the Pershing Ia to the Pershing II. The 1968 firing was typical. Members of D Battery, 1st Battalion, 81st Artillery and D Battery, 4th Battalion, 41st Artillery were airlifted with their equipment from Germany to Hill Air Force Base, Utah, starting on 27 October. The sister unit, 2d

Battalion, 44th Artillery, from Fort Sill, Oklahoma, supplied some additional equipment, and on 5 November each battery launched a Pershing that hit its target in White Sands, New Mexico.[9]

Soldiers who actually launched these missiles earned gold-colored badges. Certificates for the Pershing Professional Badge (the bronze badge) and the Senior Pershing Professional Badge (the silver badge) were issued and signed by the battalion commanders, but only the 56th Brigade headquarters issued the Master Pershing Professional Badge, the commanding general signing the certificate.

Units in the 56th Field Artillery Brigade varied over time. The first unit deployed with the new Pershing system in June 1964 was the 4th Missile Battalion, 41st Artillery. The brigade won a superior unit award for the period November 1983–December 1985, the assigned units at that time being Headquarters and Headquarters Battery, 56th Brigade; 1st Battalion, 41st Artillery; 1st Battalion, 81st Artillery; 3d Battalion, 84th Artillery; 2d Battalion, 4th Infantry (who helped guard the deployed units); 55th Maintenance Battalion; and the 266th Chemical Detachment. The 56th Field Artillery Brigade was redesignated the 56th Field Artillery Command on January 17, 1986, although the cloth badges then in use continued to carry the word **BRIGADE**.[10]

In late 1979 the U.S. Army in Europe halted the use of the colored metal badges on green uniforms, following which those soldiers who had won any of the awards could wear only a subdued cloth version (fig. 5.13) on their field uniforms. The distinctions among the various degrees became lost when this occurred, since the Department of the Army and the U.S. Army Europe began strictly to enforce the requirement that insignia worn on field uniforms be subdued.[11]

Embossed at the base of the badges was **QRA**. Officially, the secretary of defense assigned the Pershing weapon system to a quick-reaction-alert role after a Department of Defense study showed that the missile would be superior to tactical aircraft for this mission. The men in the units, however, created part of the brigade's lore by insisting that these letters stood for the weapons' attributes—quick, reliable, and accurate—and this was spelled out on the certificates.

While part of the long-range punch of the field artillery was the Pershing missile, other modern weapons such as the Lance missile took the place of the shorter-range Honest John and other more complex missiles such as the Corporal and Sergeant. In 1962 the army

Fig. 5.13

Fig. 5.13. A black-embroidered version of the 56th Brigade badge, worn on fatigue or battle-dress uniforms after 1979.

Fig. 5.14. With the 56th Brigade badges came certificates. These displayed minor differences over time.

THE "PERSHING PROFESSIONAL" CERTIFICATE
FIRST ORDER OF MERIT
is awarded to

PRIVATE FIRST CLASS RALPH HARTLEY

In recognition of outstanding achievement, QUICK, RELIABLE, ACCURATE performance, and devotion to duty while assigned as a member of this command. He has established himself as truly deserving of this coveted award and has exhibited the proper traits of a
PERSHING PROFESSIONAL, TO WIT:

Having demonstrated the required proficiency and experience as a member of the firing crew of Battery D, 3d Battalion, 84th Field Artillery.....
Having participated in the successful live firing of Artillery Ordnance Shoot 121 from White Sands Missile Range, New Mexico, on 19 June 1973.....
Having thus fully demonstrated by singular, exemplary performance that the United States Pershing force in Europe is capable of meeting its priority QRA mission for NATO.....

And therefore, by meeting the above requirements, he has fully qualified himself as a

MASTER PERSHING PROFESSIONAL

Given over our hand and seal this __6th__ day of __August__ in the year of our Lord, One Thousand, Nine Hundred, and Seventy __Three__ and in the year of the United States Artillery One Hundred and Ninety __Seven__

GEORGE E. McCLINTOCK
Major, FA
Adjutant

MILTON E. KEY
Brigadier General, USA
Commanding

Fig. 5.14

Fig. 5.15. An unofficial field artillery qualification badge used in the United States and by American troops in Germany. Starting in late 1976, the 9th Field Artillery Group at Fort Sill, Oklahoma, awarded soldiers red enamel badges with silver missiles to show field artillery missile proficiency. Later, soldiers who had earned the 56th Brigade badges could wear the red-and-silver-style badges while they were at Fort Sill. Some units in Germany also used this set of badges.

Fig. 5.16. A senior version of the 9th Group badge, the equivalent of the silver 56th Brigade badge.

Fig. 5.17. Missile men at Fort Sill who were members of the 9th Group or who taught missile gunnery at the Field Artillery School and who fired an actual Pershing missile earned the master-missile-man badge. On occasion these were also given as honorary awards to general officers.

Fig. 5.18. A wool version of the "Fort Sill" badge embroidered in Germany.

formed the 9th Field Artillery Missile Group at Fort Sill, Oklahoma. Over the years the 9th Group underwent considerable internal reorganization, but its mission was to include those missile units that supported the field artillery school. At various times units included Pershing missile battalions, Honest John battalions, Sergeant missile battalions, and separate support units such as the 17th Ordnance Company, the 225th Heavy Equipment Maintenance Company, the 226th Light Maintenance Company, the 593d Engineer Company (Construction), and later, the 82d and 85th Missile Detachments. In 1972 the 9th Group included a 9th Provisional Battalion that included all of the various support units, the 3d Battalion, 9th Field Artillery (Pershing) (prior to September 1, 1972, the 2d Battalion, 44th Artillery), and the 3d Battalion, 38th Field Artillery (Sergeant). By 1976 the group included the 3d Battalion, 9th Field Artillery; the 1st Battalion (Lance), 12th Field Artillery; the 3d Battalion, 33d Field Artillery; and a unique Field Artillery Missile System Evaluation Group.[12]

Beginning in December 1976 the 9th Group awarded soldiers silver-and-red enamel badges to show field artillery missile proficiency, although individual units such at the 1st Battalion, 12th Field Artillery, were using it in 1975. These silver-and-red rectangular badges (called the Field Artillery Missileman's Badge) bear a vertical missile with the words **US ARMY**, as shown in figures 5.15–5.17.[13]

Badges come in three versions: basic, senior (with a star on the badge top), and master (a wreath surrounds the star). To earn the basic badge a soldier had to demonstrate "professional skill and proficiency" and had to have been in the missile field for at least one year. For the senior version, additional requirements were three years of service in the missile field and participation in a minimum of three successful missile firings, while the master required at least five years and five firings. In at least one instance the design was used on a colored cloth example made in Germany, as shown in figure 5.18. The use of metal badges for the Pershing was adopted from this use of a badge by Lance and other missile units.[14]

As a result of the Intermediate Range Nuclear Force Treaty signed on December 8, 1987, and ratified by the Senate May 27, 1988, the United States began to destroy Pershing and other missiles. The last Pershing II was destroyed in May 1991 at the Longhorn Army Ammunition Plant, marking the first

Fig. 5.15

Fig. 5.16

Fig. 5.17

Fig. 5.18

time an entire class of nuclear weapons had been eliminated. The resulting drawdown of missiles caused the army to deactivate the 56th Field Artillery Command that same month. With this deactivation, even the subdued cloth 56th Field Artillery Brigade/Command badge and the red-and-silver "Ft. Sill" badges became obsolete.

ARMOR FORCES PATCHES

Benjamin Holt, an innovative American, produced a Caterpillar tractor, providing the basis of the war machine that would ultimately defy the machine gun of World War I. By act of Congress in 1950 armor became the official continuation of cavalry. The thirty-some years between World War I and 1950, however, were rocky in terms of the relations between the new, mechanized monsters and the historic hay burners. In an effort to modernize the army, Congress passed the National Defense Act of 1920. The fledgling tank units formed during World War I became casualties within the political arena. To establish the Air Service and the Chemical Warfare Service and make other branch changes, the many factions battling over the form of the new army reached a compromise. Congress abolished the temporary Tank Corps of World War I and assigned tanks to the infantry, although later Congress and General Douglas MacArthur, while he was chief of staff, allowed the cavalry to form armored car units. This state remained until the eve of World War II, when the War Department organized the armored force. With the 1950 congressional action, the metamorphosis of the cavalry to armor was complete.

Before looking at unofficial awards, it is necessary to examine official qualification requirements, since patches used by armor troops were usually based on army-wide standards. The infantry published training standards and through this means described a proficiency course for "tank marksmanship" in mimeograph form in 1927, finally printing a test in mid-1929.[15]

The test was divided into three parts, and soldiers had to pass two parts, depending upon their assignment. All crew members had to take the machine gun test, then men in light tank units proved their worth on the 37 mm gun in part two of the test, while members of heavy tank units qualified on the 6-pounder gun in part three of the test. Each test included firing the appropriate weapon on one or more courses. Machine gun firing was initially at 1,000 inches (83 $1/3$ feet) and progressed to 500 yards. The establishing training regulation lays out the firing distances, time limits, number of rounds, and other constraints by means of various tables that accompany the regulation's text. From such administrative trivia a heritage has grown. Various tank courses are to this day known as "tank tables," derived from the tables that simply describe each course and target. Soldiers earned the **TANK WEAPONS** bar for their expert, sharpshooter, or marksman badge by achieving minimum scores on the two machine gun courses and on one of the two main gun courses. Over the years the requirements have changed, but the same type of qualification bar is still awarded.[16]

In September 1931 the chief of cavalry finally published regulations that elucidated training standards for the cavalry's "tanks," the armored cars. Like the men seeking qualification in the infantry tank-weapons course, cavalrymen first had to pass a preliminary gunner's test, which was a mechanical skills test. For actual qualification on the armored-car weapons, soldiers had to fire and in some cases qualify on several weapons. Everyone had to qualify with both the .30 caliber tank machine gun and the .45 caliber Thompson submachine gun. In addition, for those cars equipped with a .50 caliber air-cooled machine gun, crewmembers had to fire (but not qualify) with that weapon. Those who could pass this strenuous 1930s test received the qualification bar embossed **ARMORED CAR WEAPON**. Qualifying men were second-class armored-car gunners, first-class armored-car gunners, and expert armored-car gunners.[17]

Fig. 5.19. An authorized expert badge, circa 1940, showing the two prescribed qualification bars related to early armored-force units.

Fig. 5.19

Fig. 5.20

Fig. 5.20. Select members of the 10th Armored Division wore this green oval, 2 1/2 x 1 3/4 inches, on the lower-right coat sleeve to show tank-crew qualification and overall proficiency. Awarded only in 1943, it continued to be worn by members after the unit transferred to Camp Gordon, Georgia, and then overseas. The tank silhouette is black, and the tiger—the nickname of the 10th Armored Division—is yellow and black.

Fig. 5.21. A certificate given with the cuff patch shown in figure 5.20.

The cavalry "light machine gun car course" of 1935 called for all firing to be done while the vehicle was stationary, with positions at 200, 300, 500, and 600 yards. Troopers who qualified were known as expert car gunners, first class car gunners, or second class car gunners.[18]

By 1940 U.S. armored forces started forming in earnest, based upon the late 1930s experiments involving the 13th Cavalry (Mechanized) and other units based in Fort Knox, Kentucky. Both the infantry troops belonging to tank units and the cavalrymen assigned to scouts cars, combat cars, and armored cars could be directed to qualify on the "several types of weapons mounted in a combat vehicle" in order to received their additional marksmanship compensation. Such 1940 requirements included qualification with each type of weapon mounted in or on the combat vehicle. A soldier so qualified could be issued orders listing him as an expert combat-vehicle gunner, a first class combat-vehicle gunner, or a second class combat-vehicle gunner, titles slightly changed from the 1930 "car gunner" names. This was the last official use of the **ARMORED CAR WEAPON** bar.[19]

The War Department created an armored force as a separate arm in July 1940, although special branch insignia were not provided until 1942. While the armored-car weapon bars disappeared early in World War II and the tank weapons bar has survived to the present day, these mechanized crew members lived with their weapons constantly, and the men wanted a means of showing their expertise on their

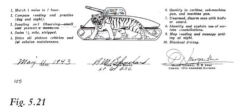

Fig. 5.21

work uniforms. The result was the invention of cloth qualification patches for field clothing.

The rapid buildup of forces for World War II resulted in a perceived lack of proficiency awards. Wheeled-vehicle mechanics received a War Department–approved a silver badge and bars similar to shooting badges, and Army Air Force mechanics and technical personnel were given a silver badge and an accompanying long list of clasps. Some armored crewmen felt that they should have an award for activities other than just weapons use.

This need was soon met. The 10th Armored Division issued the first award during World War II. Instituted in early 1943 while the unit was at Fort Benning, Georgia, the 10th Armored Division awarded a small green, black, and yellow oval patch slightly less than 2 1/2 inches x 1 3/4 inches, bearing a tiger superimposed over a black tank silhouette, for crew qualification and overall proficiency with the tank. When the unit transferred to Camp Gordon, Georgia, in September 1943 the patch, worn on the right cuff, became obsolete, but even so the winners prized their "tigers," which were eloquent testimony to the battery of skills learned and demonstrated by the recently drafted soldiers.[20]

WORLD WAR II–INSTITUTED BADGES

During World War II the U.S. Army instituted several new badges to help raise soldiers' morale and esprit de corps. The blue-and-silver combat and expert infantry badges, the all-silver glider, parachute, and combat medical badges, as well as many new three-inch-long aviation badges came into being. Most of these survived the war, as did the sleeve patch for pathfinders, although the set of five "distinctive sleeve patches" for the Army Air Force technical specialists disappeared in 1947.

Most interesting of the badges born in World War II are the drivers' and the Army Air Force technicians' badges, as they included qualification bars, which were somewhat similar to the three shooting badges designed in 1921. In January 1943 a regulation change announced the silver AAF technician badge ("a gear wheel, encircled by a wreath, surmounted by a 4-blade propeller"), showing it to be slightly over an inch wide, and then listed twenty-four different bars, although others later came into being. With the separation of the air force from the army in 1947, this badge and its many bars disappeared after having been made in many versions by private manufacturers.

Fig. 5.22. Major General Bruce C. Clarke, 1951 commander of the 1st Armored Division, instituted this green-and-yellow patch for wear above the upper pocket of the herringbone-twill overalls. To earn the award, tank crew members had to have a good maintenance record and had to qualify their vehicle on the firing range.

An Army Air Force technician's badge, used from 1943 to 1947, and a locally made, wallet-sized authorization card. Bars are of a similar size to those given with marksmanship badges.

Just prior to the introduction of the technicians' badge, the army wooed drivers and mechanics by creating a badge for qualified enlisted personnel—a design clearly taken from the sharpshooter's badge, since it shows a wheel on a cross patee and has coloring identical to that of the marksmanship badges. This badge came with just a few bars, the only hard-to-decipher factors being the letter that follows the position name. **DRIVER-A** was for amphibious vehicles, **M** for motorcycles, **T** for tracked vehicles, and **W** for wheels. The **OPERATOR-S** bar was for special operators, who handled generators and other unique equipment. This badge survives today, and for a while in the 1960s the army indulged aviation crew chiefs by showing their specialty with a bar in the shape of a propeller.

A U.S. Army driver and mechanic badge, designed in September 1942, with various bars. The **DRIVER-M**, dating from World War II, indicates a motorcycle driver; **OPERATOR-S** signifies an operator of special equipment; and the propeller bar was used in the 1960s by aviation crew chiefs.

Major General Bruce C. Clarke, while commanding the 1st Armored Division in 1951, instituted a green diamond-shaped patch with a yellow edge and **TANKER** in block letters across the center. This patch was worn above the upper pocket on the one-piece herringbone-twill work overalls. Although very short lived, it is well known to insignia collectors and was once relatively common. Similar in spirit to the 10th Armored Division tiger sleeve patch, requirements for the patch included "a good maintenance record" as well as formal qualification on the tank firing range.[21]

By the early 1960s units stationed in Germany were issuing various pocket patches to

show tank-crew qualification, as earned on Table VIII, the final table or course used by a single tank crew. This time, mechanized-force pocket patches became an instant fixture. No group of U.S. awards has engendered more

Fig. 5.22

Fig. 5.23. *Starting in the early 1960s, for twenty years many mechanized units awarded a wide range of qualification patches that soldiers wore on field jacket pockets. During the 1960s in particular, these came in a huge variety of configurations and colors. This style of dark-green patch with yellow-and-black design was given to tank crews in the 8th Infantry Division who attained sufficient score on tank Table VIII to become "qualified."*

Fig. 5.24. *The **TCQC** on this green, yellow, and black 3 3/4–inch-diameter pocket patch stands for Tank Crew Qualification Course.*

Fig. 5.25. *The 8th Infantry Division embroidered their distinguished recognition into the basic pocket patch design, which was similar to the design of the pocket patch shown in figure 5.23.*

varied insignia than the pocket qualification patch. Within a very few years of the rise of pocket qualification patches in Germany, a flurry of copycat patches proliferated in a wide range of units and weapons, such as mechanized mortars and even hand-held air-defense missiles. The design variations grew exponentially on their own, without common guidelines. Several examples are shown (see pls. 66–71 and figs. 5.23–5.27), but a complete listing is impossible not only due to the sheer number of designs, but also because units created and issued their own patches without consulting higher headquarters. No complete catalog of these patches exists, although one collector's publication lists over 620 different designs.[22]

These patches, commonly called TCQC (Tank Crew Qualification Course) patches, became widespread as a result of General Creighton Abrams, who ultimately became army chief of staff. Abrams had been an assistant division commander for the 3d Armored Division when he left in 1959, and as a major general he returned to command the division in 1961. During Abram's absence a difference of opinion had developed as to whether tank battalion commanders should or should not ride in their tanks and whether, as a tank commander, the battalion commander should attempt to qualify with his tank on tank Table VIII, the formal qualification course. Firing took considerable practice and valuable time away from other command tasks.

General Abrams let it be known his strong preference was that not only should battalion commanders fire their vehicles, but that a commander's tank (regardless of whether the unit was a battalion, company, or even platoon) should be the first of a unit to go downrange. As a result, it became a matter of pride that tank crews qualified during annual gunnery.

As a consequence of Abrams's position, the division staff created a special patch, worn on the field jacket. By 1964 many TCQC patches existed, and for over twenty years armored-crew members proudly wore a plethora of these insignia on the chest pocket of field jackets as well as on tankers' jackets. The practice of giving different qualification patches spread at an unrivaled rate to the United States and wherever U.S. armored forces served. Each unit soon had its own design. The heyday of the highly prized and locally issued armored-crew qualification patches lasted until the early 1980s, when the army cracked down on

these never-authorized awards and took strong actions to ban them.[23]

TCQC patches initially aligned with standard marksmanship badges in that "distinguished" patches went to the crews earning expert badges, while "qualified" patches were equated with sharpshooter and marksman badges. Unqualified crews did not earn either patches or badges. By the time the army eliminated the TCQC patches, the three levels of crew qualification had become entrenched. Crews were used to being designated as distinguished, qualified, and unqualified, and this was the case even twenty years later. Old habits die hard, however, and even into the 21st century, army units continued to provide a wide range of badges, patches, and similar local awards that can be worn on the uniform.[24]

Fig. 5.23

Fig. 5.24

Fig. 5.25

Fig. 5.26

Fig. 5.27

INFANTRY AND MILITIA BUREAU

The chief of infantry, whose position was created in 1920 as a result of the National Defense Act, took charge of training and doctrine of the modern infantry after World War I. Major General Charles S. Farnsworth became the first chief of infantry, early on showing great interest in the creation of squad live-fire exercises. At an NRA meeting in the winter of 1921–22, Farnsworth stated that the infantry would supply a trophy and medals if the NRA added a live-fire exercise at the annual Camp Perry, Ohio, matches. For the next two years the *Infantry Journal* dutifully reported on the funds raised by subscription, with the goal of $1 from officers and $.10 or $.15 from enlisted personnel. The Infantry Match Trophy was purchased from these funds. This trophy and the companion medals are described on pages 211–13.[25]

Modeled after recent World War I fire and maneuver experience, the exercise required that a rifle squad start 400 yards away from olive drab silhouette targets representing enemy soldiers. Each of seven riflemen had twenty rounds of ammunition, and the eighth soldier, equipped with a Browning Automatic Rifle, had eighty rounds. The targets—"F" silhouettes—were held on a pole by soldiers in a pit, and every fifteen seconds a target was replaced by another. The removed target was quickly examined, and if it contained at least twelve hits, half of the squad was allowed to advance towards the target during the next fifteen seconds, while the base portion of the squad continued to fire at the exposed silhouette. This process continued until the squad was out of ammunition. A final score was determined by considering such factors as the total number of rounds fired and the number of yards the rearmost portion of the squad had advanced.[26]

In order to support preparation for the national matches, infantry regiments held an annual competition to identify the best squad, which would be known as the regiment's Chief of Infantry's Combat Team. Though the team was never sanctioned in army-wide regulations, nevertheless each winning squad received a plaque and each member wore a rectangular patch on the cuff, reflecting their victory in the chief of infantry's competition. In one description of a winning squad, when several squads were firing and advancing at once against 150 prone silhouette targets, Corporal Lewis T. Dowdle's squad from C Company, 29th Infantry, had targets

most of which were concealed from view. [The squad] . . . was assigned a sector on the general line, which included twenty-one targets. In this sector none of the targets could be seen, but targets could be seen on the right and left, thus making it more difficult for the squad leader to keep the fire of his squad directed on the target assigned. In his sector of twenty-one targets, Corporal Dowdle's squad registered twenty-one hits on fourteen targets. The range from the initial position was 590 yards. [27]

In the case of small posts where an entire regiment was not colocated, the chief of infantry recognized the best squad at each post. A 1931 example of this was the 4th Infantry Regiment, scattered across the northern prairie. The 4th Infantry's combat-team squads were Corporal W. B. Webster's squad, Company K, at Fort Lincoln; Corporal Earl Armacost's squad, Company F, at Fort George Wright; and Corporal J. A. Cole's squad, Company C, Ft. Missoula. Even the 15th Infantry in China held these competitions.[28]

Fig. 5.26. This $2\,^3/4$–inch-diameter yellow patch has black stitching. The tab shows that the crew performed to the highest (expert) standards.

Fig. 5.27. In the 1970s units switched to black designs on olive drab to match the other subdued insignia that had come into use during the Vietnam War. The divisional cavalry squadron stationed at Fort Carson, Colorado, in 1976 used this award pocket patch.

Fig. 5.28. The Chief of Infantry's Combat Team award. This patch, worn on the lower-left coat sleeve, designated the wearer as a member of an infantry regiment's best squad in the chief of infantry's live-fire squad competition held each year during the 1930s. The background is green and light blue to represent grass and sky, with a black silhouette target. The two white stars represent the chief of infantry.

Fig. 5.29. A medal given in the 1930s by the chief of the National Guard Bureau for indoor rifle matches. The reverse of medals awarded between 1930 and 1933 states that they came from the Militia Bureau, while those given in 1934 and later are marked as being from the National Guard Bureau. Ribbons for this set are dark blue with red edges.

The patch, evidently first made in 1924, is a vertical rectangle with a gray-blue or olive drab border. In the central rectangle the top half is sky blue and the lower half bright green. In the center is a short gray-blue silhouette target. The entire design represents a prone rifleman on grass. The target is a model-1913 "F" target that was actually 26 inches wide x 19 inches high. In the upper corners of the "sky" are two white stars, representing the chief of infantry's major-general stars. With the start of World War II this competition, like numerous other interwar soldierly skill events, was discontinued.[29]

Each team member wore the "Chief of Infantry's Combat Team" patch on the left sleeve of the coat "immediately above the position authorized for the war service chevron," which was one inch above the sleeve cuff. Soldiers could also display these patches on the olive drab flannel shirt when it was worn as an outside garment. Members continued to wear the patches until the winning squad was announced the next year. Starting in 1931 National Guard infantry regiments also began to compete in the chief of infantry's competition, with the winning squad members receiving patches like those in the regular army.[30]

In 1934 the newspaper magnate William Randolph Hearst presented a large plaque to the National Guard Bureau, which was to be used as an annual award to the National Guard infantry regiment that place highest in the musketry competition. For the National Guard, Hearst provided a set of bronze medals to members of each state's winning team, and for the team winning the national plaque, he provided a set of gold medals plus the promise that Hearst's newspapers would print a full account of the competition each year. Company E, 164th Infantry of the North Dakota National Guard, won the initial competition in 1935.[31]

Congress established the Bureau of Militia Affairs in 1911 and then retitled the organization the Militia Bureau in 1916. The army renamed the organization the National Guard Bureau in 1933.[32]

In addition to the chief of infantry's competition, the National Guard Bureau issued other awards. One example, shown in figure 5.29, is a medal that was not prescribed in the uniform regulations and could not be worn on a regular basis. Established in 1930, these medals were awarded for matches conducted by the NRA, called the Chief of the National Guard Bureau's Indoor Rifle Matches. Teams consisted of ten members firing .22 caliber rifles at 50 feet, ten shots each in prone,

Fig. 5.28

Fig. 5.29

standing, kneeling, and sitting positions, with each state allowed to enter its best team in the national event. The winning national team also received a plaque. High national-team members each received a silver medal, while each state-championship team member received a bronze medal.[33]

After World War II these matches were revived, and the National Guard Bureau awarded similar medals. The post–World War II medals were awarded in three categories: a unit-team match for company and similar-sized units, a battalion or air group match, and an individual match. In each .22 caliber match the NRA and the National Guard Bureau both awarded medals. Silver medals went to the winning national team and bronze to each state's winning team in these matches, just as before the Second World War. As gold was expensive, the individual-match national champion received a gold medal from 1949 through 1951 only. After that the top individual award became silver—the same award given to the second-place finisher throughout this

time—and to the highest scorers in each army area. Bronze medals went to the third through tenth national finishers, to the second and third finishers in each army area, and to the top scorer in each state and territory. Although space was provided on the reverse of the medal for engraving a recipient's name, this was not usually done except for those winning gold and silver medals. After the Vietnam War, awards given for the Chief of the National Guard Bureau Championships became large circular gold-colored belt buckles. These lasted until 1980 when the large buckles became rectangular with an enameled design.[34]

In the 1943–45 period the U.S. Chinese Training and Combat Command awarded

Fig. 5.31

Fig. 5.30

Fig. 5.32

Fig. 5.30. *After World War II the chief of the National Guard Bureau again awarded shooting medals for the annual match, but the use of bars on the ribbons increased. This particular award is silver colored.*

Fig. 5.31. *One of the 2 1/2–inch-diameter belt buckles given as shooting prizes in the chief of the National Guard Bureau contests and designed for wear on the pistol belt. These replaced the original historic medals shown in figures 5.29 and 5.30.*

Fig. 5.32. *One of the many brass awards provided by the U.S. Chinese Training and Combat Command between 1943 and 1945 for proficiency with a British submachine gun.*

infantry weapons-qualification badges, besides those artillery versions shown in figures 5.4 and 5.5. One example (fig. 5.32) is especially unusual, since it shows qualification with a British weapon, the Bren gun, which was an effective light machine gun with both a pistol grip and a bipod. This plain, gold-colored brass badge displays a twelve-pointed "sun" with pebbled center. The identical design was used for another China badge, with the

top arc embossed **MORTAR EXPERT** (the mortar is an infantry weapon, not used in the artillery), while still another badge in this set had the top arc **USA ★ CHINA** and **RIFLE MARKSMAN** on the straight lower bar, with crossed rifles as a pendant. All of the badges in the set are cheaply made from yellow metal, with crude pin backs. All were apparently also made with Chinese rather than English characters, as shown in figure 5.35.

Fig. 5.33. U.S. Army trainers awarded brass mortar-expert badges of this design to qualified Chinese troops.

Fig. 5.34. This 1943–45 badge is unusual, since the brooch is slightly different from others in the set of Chinese Training and Combat Command awards.

Fig. 5.35. A version of the award shown in figure 5.34, bearing Chinese writing. Apparently the Chinese Training and Combat Command struck all of their awards with Chinese characters as well as with English lettering.

Fig. 5.33

Fig. 5.35

Fig. 5.34

CHAPTER SIX

NINETEENTH-CENTURY PRIZES

THE HIGH POINT OF MAGNIFICENCE

LIEUTENANT GENERAL PHILIP H. SHERIDAN, hero of the Civil War and one of the handful of nineteenth-century generals to wear three stars, took an active interest in marksmanship in early 1879, after the army had been defeated for several consecutive years during the newly formed NRA's annual matches at Creedmoor, Long Island. As the commander of the Division of the Missouri, Sheridan, half a continent away from the NRA's range, directed each of his four subordinate department commanders to send his best six marksmen to Fort Leavenworth, Kansas, to prepare for the 1879 Creedmoor competition. Each regimental commander submitted the name, rank, and company of the two best marksmen in his unit. From this Sheridan selected a potential team. The assembled expert riflemen shot vigorously for three weeks, and then the sixteen best proceeded to the NRA's facility near New York City for an additional two weeks of practice under the hot summer sun. Out of this elite group, the twelve best men fired as the Division of the Missouri team. Although the army team did well, it did not dominate the competition as Sheridan had wanted, but this special dedication and repeated honing of skills paid dividends and achieved his goal when the next year, in 1880, the army placed the top three teams against all of the various militia organizations.[1]

To support the effort, several sets of special marksman rifles were supplied to teams. Modifications included sights, grooved triggers, pistol grips, and front sight covers, and some weapons also had special twists in the rifling. To overwhelm the various state militias and prove the superiority of the regular army, Sheridan counted on the Ordnance Department's performing some magic. The department worked during the winter of 1779–80

to develop a special rifle with six grooves, special sights, and improved ammunition. These were tested at Sandy Hook, New Jersey, by Captain John Edwin Greer during the first half of 1880 and proved successful, although Greer continued ammunition tests the next year.[2]

Having developed a special arsenal, the 1880 army teams used its special arms and ammunition advantages to maul all challengers. New York had won more often than not, but this time the army swept away the puny New York militia team that had previously mastered the competition. The final six teams consisted of the U.S. Army's Missouri team, followed by the Atlantic, the Pacific, and militia teams from New Jersey, Connecticut, and Pennsylvania. The 1880 first-place team won the Hilton Shield, an enormous bronze relief plaque depicting North American Plains Indians engaged in a buffalo drive. Having conquered the citizen soldiers in 1880 after the militia's several years of championships, Sheridan smugly refused to shoot at Creedmoor except for one other match, in 1885—the year Sheridan accepted the presidency of the NRA. After Sheridan died army teams no longer participated in NRA matches during the nineteenth century.[3]

Begging a paucity of funds ("No team from the Army participated . . . owing to the limited appropriations"), the army had an alibi and did not shoot in the NRA's 1881 national championship, leaving New York's militia team to carry off the prize. In truth the army was also stung by the court challenge in which New York militia general George Wingate alleged that U.S. Army Colonel Laidley, commander of the Watertown Arsenal, had copied portions of Wingate's manual and published it as his own. As a result of this infringement

Fig. 6.1. *Philip H. Sheridan as a lieutenant general, from an 1888 engraving. Sheridan, while commander of the Division of the Missouri, started the army on its march towards competitive marksmanship.*

charge and the envy of the NRA, the army struck out on its own. It instituted an alternative to the NRA matches by establishing a separate set of military competitions.[4]

After 1885 Sheridan stood foursquare against any army team firing in NRA matches, even though he accepted the presidency of the NRA that very year. Thus the army created the somewhat unlikely concept of elaborate and ornate mammoth gold and silver prize medals whose descendants are still treasured by shooters today. The army's set of extravagant individual awards provided one way that Sherman and Sheridan could thumb their noses at the NRA.

These wonderfully varied and exotic prizes from the 1880s, largely forgotten today, were among the very few recognitions worn on nineteenth-century army uniforms. In 1879 the only decorations worn by soldiers were the Medal of Honor, instituted during the Civil War; Civil War Corps badges; and, in a few isolated instances, the old stadia instituted by Heth. The impact of the army's revised 1880 marksmanship program and its awards is hard to overstate. The everyday soldier received virtually no tangible rewards except for the marksman buttons and the marksman and sharpshooter badges introduced between 1879 and 1884. By 1881 the potential list of wearable awards a soldier might receive not only included the Medal of Honor for risking life and limb; there was also the intoxicating possibility that, simply by training, he might earn dazzling gold and silver shooting prizes and special trophy rifles.

Sheridan's grand vision for shooting competition included artistically attractive tributes and special award rifles. Implementation of his farsighted concept gave marksmanship such a boost that contests became fierce. During the 1880s target shooting became the rage, to such an extent that by 1890 some men complained about the excessive practice and long hours on the range that occurred several times a week. The heavy recoil of the massive contemporary weapons took their toll. In 1887 7th Cavalryman Clarence H. Allen described how his shoulder became black and blue from the continual recoil when firing for score. Some men even padded the butts of the rifles with several socks to help absorb the shock of firing. The weapons were certainly capable of hitting a silhouette the size of a man at 500 yards, but only if the shooter was used to the recoil and not suffering too much punishment from the rifle's kick. The army of 1876 had no

Fig. 6.1

marksmanship policy or training strategy. Sheridan and his staff superbly and quickly solved this problem. Within eight years the sudden growth of awards made shooting a training success. Most soldiers wanted to fire, and they could do so accurately. In some instances the troops were even wearied by the heavy demands of zealous officers.[5]

Weapons technology had been creeping forward since the introduction of hand-held firearms in the late fifteenth century. By the mid-nineteenth century the previous glacial enhancements placed rifles in a spot where rapid improvements could be made. Metallic cartridges could be mass produced, eliminating the need for muzzle loading. Consistent powder could be made in great quantities, and by 1890 several armies had smokeless powder. Modern breech-loading rifles with long firing pins (which gave the Prussian Dreyse rifle its famous name, the "needle gun") allowed more complex mechanisms. These and other improvements allowed soldiers to fire more rapidly than had been possible with the muzzle-loading Minie ball. The introduction of bolt-action rifles and other advancements supported the great groundswell of range shooting by the U.S. Army and throughout the world. While the Palma Trophy, the Leech Cup, the Wimbledon Cup, and other prizes came from across the ocean to be given in America, these emblems of shooting prowess were all signs pointing towards late nineteenth- and early twentieth-century technological improvements that provided the basis for World War II weapons.

The eruption of artistic creativity that accompanied army matches has no parallel in

U.S. Army awards. The series of shooting prizes presented by the army is arguably the most artistic and attractive set of military awards in the world and certainly the best presented by the U.S. government. The army issued magnificent prizes starting in 1881 but inadvertently ended the practice in 1898 due to the Spanish-American War, although the infantry awarded a few of these large prizes for rifle competitions during 1902. Having invested so much over twenty years in marksman training, it is striking how quickly, in 1898, the army reverted to its old ways when war really came, doing away with its richly developed and soundly based training programs and shooting contests.

Overall, the army awarded one set of massive prizes between 1881 and 1888, then instituted another group that coincidentally further expanded to include cavalry (carbine) and pistol competition, nominally ending in 1897. Independent of these two groups of prizes, the army interspersed large skirmishing awards as well as munificent gold and silver prizes for competition among distinguished marksmen. These skirmishing and distinguished marksmen prizes, besides being equal to the largest medals ever used by the army, tend to obscure the demarcation between the two basic sets of substantial prizes. Two additional confounding factors are (1) the close similarity of some later prize designs to earlier vignettes (one is actually identical and thus really a continuation of an earlier prize), and (2) the abolishment of divisions—the intermediate level above departments and below the army—that previously provided some of the prizes.

For a coherent understanding of these 1880s prizes and contests, one must be aware of the War Department point of view. Department matches, the lowest of the army competitions, provided the best shot with a gold prize but offered no other awards. Post commanders could select only enlisted men to compete in these department matches, but departmental commanders were empowered to select two commissioned officers from each regiment to join the contests. Each August department commanders assembled these selected marksmen, and out of three days of intensive firing, picked the twelve best shooters, who then comprised the Department team and went on to fire in the division competition. Divisions similarly held three-day tournaments. In late October 1881, for example, the Division of the Missouri held its rifle contest at St. Paul, where twelve men each for the Dakota, Missouri, Texas, and Platte Departments gathered.[6]

The first-place soldiers at both division and army received large gold wearable prizes. The War Department recognized second- and third-place men in the annual division and semiannual army contests with smaller gold Second Class Prizes. Large silver medals, known as Third Class Prizes, were given to those placing fourth through sixth in division and army competition. The ratio of first, second, and third class prizes changed as the 1890s started, but the general concept remained that these lesser awards were *classes* and not *places*.

Prizes of 1881–88 are of only two diameters: 2 inches and $1\,^3/4$ inches. Prize sizes and the metals used tell the place and the level of competition. Both army and division competition awarded 2-inch gold prizes for first place, $1\,^3/4$–inch gold prizes for second class prizes, and 2-inch silver as third class prizes. Army competitions started in 1882, although the first division competitions began in 1881. Initial department competitions, also first conducted in 1881, resulted in no tangible rewards that year.

Beginning in 1889 and lasting through 1902, the army used a different system of sizes and metals. Overall, prizes from this second period are smaller than those from the first, at the suggestion of then Captain Blunt. Generally, the later first prize medals for each competition were larger than the second and third class prizes. These later awards varied in physical size, but due to rising costs, the army had them struck from gold, silver, or bronze, with the schemes progressing towards using the inexpensive metals for the lesser awards as the twentieth century approached. At the outset both the army and division competitions had gold prizes for first place and for second class prizes (it should be noted that divisions disappeared in 1891), and by 1897 only the first and second class army prizes and the first place department prizes remained gold. During the 1891–97 period the mint changed many gold medals to silver and many silver medals to bronze. Sizes included $1\,^3/4$ inches, $1\,^5/8$ inches, and $1\,^1/2$ inches. Fortunately, this cheapening of prizes, both in terms of smaller gold and silver planchets and in the number of awards struck in precious metals, did nothing to lessen the soldiers' interest in them.[7]

After the 1894 competitions matches dwindled, despite soldiers' interests. The secretary

Fig. 6.2. This maroon ribbon, 2 ¹/₂ inches wide and embroidered in yellow with a black-and-white cloth marksman button, may have been worn by a member of the first department team in 1881.

of war temporarily suspended matches until the total army had Krag rifles and Krag carbines and the troops became familiar with them. The first unit equipped with Krags, in October 1894, was the 4th Infantry Regiment, but it took three years to complete distribution. The army again started department- and army-level matches in 1897, but it then suspended them for the next several years due to the Spanish-American War and the Philippine campaign. New 1897 War Department guidelines stated that beginning in 1898 competitions would have two categories—competition for enlisted men and a separate competition for officers, with discrete prizes given in each category. The new prizes for officers only were never implemented, however. Utter silence came from the War Department between 1898 and 1901 regarding shooting contests, then matches made a strong comeback. The infantry held a contest in 1902, and army competitions fully resumed in 1903 with the Philippines in relative calm and the army staff's interest renewed. Coincidentally, new prizes came into being.[8]

All prizes for competition among distinguished marksmen (1887–94) and among skirmishers (1884–88) were 2 inches in diameter. First-place distinguished men received gold medals, while second-place distinguished shooters earned silver. The champion army skirmisher won a gold medal, while division and department winners garnered silver prizes.

The 1881 army competition system had the best rifle shots from each troop, company, and battery meet annually for department championships. As America grew and military threats changed, the department designation and boundaries followed suit. Jurisdictional conferees decreed the 1881 departments to be Arizona, California, Columbia, Dakota, East, Missouri, Platte, South, and Texas. On May 15, 1882, the army announced the prizes that it ultimately used through 1888, by prescribing only rifle contests—a situation that would not change until after 1888. The army established three grades of competition: the department, which typically included several states (the United States was divided into the above nine departments); the division, ideally a conglomeration of two or more departments; and the total army itself. By 1883 only eight departments existed, as a result of the elimination of the Department of the South. The last troops on Reconstruction duty were transferred to other activities in early 1877. While

the Department of the South continued for several years after Rutherford B. Hayes's election (Hayes ended the occupation of the South as a result of his disputed election), that department was very small and hardly rated the name. Departmental changes continued for many years and influenced shooting prizes until World War I.[9]

Immediately prior to the start of the formal 1881 army system of matches, some other contests were in the works, including those that prepared soldiers for the Creedmoor contests of 1879 and 1880. Colonel John C. Kelton, adjutant general for the Division of the Pacific, ordered and received four rifles with special sights for marksmanship training. General Alfred H. Terry, Department of Dakota commander, received sixteen rifles for his team, as did others. Some commanders gave weapons away as prizes in these 1879–80 contests. A typical example is a Springfield Model 1879, .45-70 caliber with an engraved union-style shield on the weapon's butt. The history of many of these early long arms given as prizes is now quite vague, and the definitive history is still hidden in National Archives records.[10]

Fig. 6.2

Table 10. *1880–1902 Army Marksmanship Prizes*

Design Number	Years of Use	Prize Use	Design
1	1881–88	First Prize, Department	Federal shield, crossed rifles and flags, target, target, US, star, wreath. Wording is **ARMY DEPARTMENT MARKSMANSHIP**.
2	1881–88	First Prize, Division	Horse-mounted rifleman. Captain includes **DIVISION**.
3	1881–88	Second Class Prize, Division	Standing soldier, rifle at waist. Caption includes **ARMY**.
4	1881–88	Third Class Prize, Division	Pallas Athena head in wreath.
5	1881–88	First Prize, Army	Eagle, outstretched wings, holding wreath and rifle. Star below each wing tip.
6	1881–1902	Second Class Prize, Army	Mars's helmeted head, looking left.
7	1881–88	Third Class Prize, Army	Kneeling soldier, firing. Tents in background.
8	1884–88	First Prize, Department Skirmishing	Rifleman standing behind tree, firing.
9	1884–88	First Prize, Division Skirmishing	Cavalryman, kneeling and firing. Mountains in background.
10	1884–88	First Prize, Army Skirmishing	Prone rifleman.
11	1887–94	First Prize, Distinguished Marksmen	Indian hunting bison.
12	1887–94	Second Class Prize, Distinguished Marksmen	Plains Indians' encampment.
13	1889–1902	First Prize, Department	Federal shield, crossed rifles and flags, target, US, star, wreath. Wording is **FIRST PRIZE DEPARTMENT MARKSMANSHIP**.
14	1889–1902	Second Class Prize, Department	U.S. monogram over stacked arms and dress helmet.
15	1889–1902	Third Class Prize, Department	Shield, pistol above, crossed sabers.
16	1889–90	First Prize, Division	Prone rifleman.
17	1889–90	Second Class prize, Division	Standing soldier, rifle at waist. Wording does not include "army."
18	1889–90	Third Class Prize, Division	Kneeling infantryman firing, tents in background.
19	1889–97	First Prize, Cavalry	Mounted cavalryman firing rifle. Wording includes **CAVALRY**.
20	1889–97	Second Class Prize, Cavalry	Kneeling cavalryman, firing. Mountains in background.
21	1889–97	Third Class Prize, Cavalry	Cavalryman, standing behind tree, firing.
22	1889–94	First Prize, Revolver	Line of four horsemen.
23	1889–94	Second Class Prize, Revolver	Cavalryman, astride rearing horse, and Indian.
24	1889–94	Third Class Prize, Revolver	Standing cavalryman, holding horse by reins and firing pistol.
25	1890–1902	First Prize, Army	Eagle, outstretched wings, holding wreath and rifle. No stars below eagle's wing tips.
26	1890–1902	Third Class Prize, Army	Pallas Athena head, no wreath.

A May 1881 general order proudly announced that the three division contest winners would receive gold medals worth $100. Soldiers placing second, third, and fourth would receive rifles, and those in fifth through twelfth place would earn "a silver medal of the value of five dollars" (eight medals per division, for a total twenty-four throughout the army). The prize medals were far from completed. Army officials did not realize how long it would take for the mint to design the prizes, sink the dies, and then strike the prizes, so the awards were not ready until the first part of 1882. Once available, the division

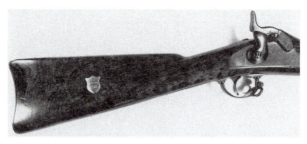

Fig. 6.3a

Fig. 6.3b

Fig. 6.3a and b. The use of rifles as prizes was an ongoing tradition before the War Department instituted the giving of special marksman rifles as a part of division contests in 1881. Prize rifles usually had a special plaque inset into the butt. This example was awarded as the first prize at an 1880 Montana shooting contest.

Fig. 6.4. General William Tecumseh Sherman, commander of the U.S. Army from March 1869 to November 1883. Under Sherman the army created marksmanship badges for qualification and prizes for contests, a tradition that survives to this day.

headquarters had to engrave and distribute the awards to the winners, but a monumental task remained. The mint still had to produce the three types of army prizes, the department prizes, and the newly added second class division prizes that replaced the marksman rifle with the inscription on the butt.[11]

Departments and divisions held matches each year, while the army hosted its championships in even-numbered years, 1882–88. An 1882 order publicized prizes of three grades and modified the previous year's system in which special rifles went to second-, third-, and fourth-place entrants.[12]

The red-haired, bewhiskered general in chief and conqueror of Atlanta and Savannah, William T. Sherman, directed that the first army-wide marksmanship tournament be held at Fort Leavenworth, Kansas, commencing October 25, 1882. For the first of the alternate-year shooting events Sherman summoned two soldiers from the Division of the Atlantic, three from the Division of the Pacific, six from the Division of the Missouri, and one from the Corps of Engineer Battalion, along with an alternate who was also from the Corps of Engineers.[13]

In formal competitions firings commenced at 200 yards with men alternating, so the odd-numbered then the even-numbered soldiers fired. This helped insure that each person fired only on his target. Similar firing continued at 300 and 600 yards. Sherman personally attended the three-day event and congratulated the first-place winner, who was the lone shooter from the Battalion of Engineers, Sergeant Charles Barrett. Barrett had the decided advantage of being stationed at Willits Point (New York City), so he had access to the NRA's range at Creedmoor on Long Island and could practice frequently.[14]

Fig. 6.4

From the Thirty Years' War through the start of the nineteenth century, armies imposed harsh discipline upon soldiers, especially in combat, so that officers could effectively maneuver units on a battlefield. Commanders discharged muskets in volleys at murderous ranges, decimating many ranks within a second or two. Soldiers stood shoulder to shoulder, giving and taking mass firings simply because the weapons required decisive engagements in such a manner.

During the Civil War many units advanced in two ranks, with the goal of expelling the enemy through the sheer volume of fire and the bayonet. The army's 1855 tactics manual, by William J. Hardee, spelled out the details of how commanders should maneuver their troops in this way. Emory Upton, a Civil War veteran, West Point graduate, and professional soldier, improved upon the existing tactics and took the next step towards today's battle-field. Upton introduced his tactics in 1867 with the approval of Ulysses S. Grant. In his new work Upton emphasized pushing skirmishers forward and placing more control in the hands of leaders below the regimental level.[15]

Upton directed that a company be thrown out in advance of the larger body. Individual skirmishers carried their pieces in the manner most convenient to them, with muzzles elevated. Officers and noncommissioned officers, while providing commands, also were to "impress each man with the idea of his individuality." These soldiers, deployed in advance of the main force, firing when the local leader wanted them to and using the terrain for cover, disrupted the enemy formations. This type of vanguard is the forerunner of the modern soldier who in battle is a fleeting target, dressed in camouflage, and is individually motivated to advance and fire. In the late 1800s, though, a debate raged between leaders who were certain that strict parade-field discipline was essential to use firearms at long ranges and progressives who believed that a soldier could be trained to fire effectively by himself. Upton's new, controversial approach eventually resulted in skirmish competitions.[16]

"As a further means of cultivating the individuality of marksmen," the army awarded prizes for skirmishing matches between 1884 and 1888. In standard rifle matches the shooters knew the precise range from the firing line to the target, but skirmishing simulated advancing towards an enemy in combat, and thus these marksmen did not know the exact ranges to their targets. When Colonel Wingate wrote his book on rifle practice, he parenthetically called skirmishing "firing at an unknown distance." To further simulate combat the officer controlling the skirmish contestants would halt the line of shooters at irregular intervals for an unspecified time so that the men could fire. As the hardheaded taskmaster General Sheridan noted in 1886, this was a natural sequence to the known distance firing and possessed great practical advantages. It "perfected fire discipline and the ability of officers to control a unit's fire, both in direction and intensity, and also presented to the eye of the soldier, an object which bore a fair resemblance to the appearance of an enemy in battle." In a normal firing season, one cavalry troop reported in 1891 that it had twenty-one days of carbine firing at known distances

and twenty-one days of individual skirmish firings, plus two days of troop skirmish firings.[17]

If Upton's pocket-sized treatise illustrated skirmish actions and thus championed these tactics that depended upon the individual soldier, General Philip H. Sheridan was the real father of skirmishing tournaments. During his tenure as the army's commanding general Sheridan noted that although the introduction of skirmishing into contests had occurred, "[There] was no direct advantage to the masses. . . . I therefore introduced skirmish firing into the general practice of the company." He later added, "I intend to require increased attention to this company skirmish firing, and to advance it to its proper position as the most practical and appropriate exercise for the company in rifle firing." Sheridan continually fretted that the lack of proper ground at some posts inhibited satisfactory practice. The results of Sheridan's efforts were that skirmish shooting became integrated into normal target practice and was one of the normally expected soldierly skills. In practice men fired as skirmishers both as individuals (really part of small squads) and as part of company-sized units. Directives cautioned officers not to place skirmish targets too close to permanent targets and not to have the firers stop at positions near regular firing points. Although skirmish shooting continued for years, it is probably not coincidental that the last year the army provided separate skirmishing prizes was 1888, the same year that Sheridan died.[18]

When competing for prizes, the late nineteenth-century skirmishing marksmen started at 600 yards, advanced to 200 yards, then retired back to the 600-yard position while stopping and firing when directed by the range officer, who was accompanied by a trumpeter to signal the shooters. This contest was an adaptation of combat firing. Rules allowed no more than three shots by each man during any one halt and allocated a total of twenty rounds per contestant, although the men did not know in advance the number of stops that would be made when advancing and retiring.[19]

As noted, skirmishing matches were phenomena of the 1880s, being first prescribed in army-wide contests for 1882 (with no prize awarded) and having the last prize awarded in 1888. The army first awarded skirmish prizes in 1884. Some units conducted this very popular practice once a week. One soldier wrote that skirmishing created a new

Fig. 6.5. *The best marksmen in the army, 1887. These twelve enlisted men assembled for the first competition of distinguished marksmen, held at Bellevue, Nebraska, in September 1887. The winner was Sergeant E. H. Stevens, G Company, 7th Infantry, seated in the center of the first row. Sergeant Hugh Griffith, D Troop, 8th Cavalry (front row right) won second place, and Sergeant G. N. King, F Company, 20th Infantry (front row left) placed third and won the last prize given. Aliases were common in the army at this time, and Sergeant King changed his name to William N. Puckett in 1893. All of these shooters had won at least three large gold, silver, or bronze prizes and a gold distinguished shield, although not all are worn in this photograph. The Medal of Honor, worn by the somber Sergeant John Nihill, Battery B, 5th Artillery (back row center), is almost unnoticed among all of the awards against the sea of blue.*

practice, resulting in "no small amount of rivalry among the men and tested their skill and judgment." He then went on to describe twenty-four targets in the shapes of men, made of iron frames and covered with target paper, the targets being placed in different natural positions for an enemy—standing, lying, or kneeling—about five yards apart. "The bugle sounded 'Advance,' 'Retreat,' until each trooper had fired 10 shots. Then the markers counted the holes in the figures. . . . B Troop, 1st Cavalry, made the highest score last year: 258 hits out of a possible 300."[20]

The army required soldiers to fire service rifles when competing for prizes, but for the additional skirmishing matches—shot at ranges out to 800, 900, and even 1,000 yards—men fired using any ammunition and special long-range Springfield rifles. A skirmisher could fire from any position, including lying on his back with his feet pointing downrange, but the quickest position, and the one used most often, was the prone position with the head downrange. Firing lines maneuvered as a unit, downrange and back, with each line composed of an equal number of members from competing teams, the successive firing groups maneuvering and shooting until all had shot.[21]

Although the army initially held skirmishing matches in 1882 during division and department matches, winners received no prize. Chief of Ordnance Benét corrected this in 1884, when he obtained prizes for department, division, and army skirmish competitions. The three first-place prizes were the only skirmishing awards made, so second and lower-place skirmish shooters went unrewarded. Like the other first prizes awarded at this time, these were 2 inches in diameter, but in a change, only the army-level medal was struck in gold, while the department and division prizes were made in silver—the metal previously used only in third class prizes.

Describing skirmish targets is one thing; making them is another. Captain Blunt sketched silhouette targets of soldiers firing prone, kneeling, and standing and left it at that. Lieutenant Colonel Flagler, Rock Island commander, had to solve the problem of making six thousand reusable skirmish targets for the army. Flagler started by having two of his captains make the target shapes out of steel rods, the thick rods having a sharp edge that faced the firer. Due to the rod thickness and the angle on the edge, this split any bullet striking the frame.

Braces made for similar steel hooked the target centers on one end, while the other pointed end was set firmly into the ground to prevent the target from being blown over. Rivet-sized holes were punched in the metal rods every six to eight inches before they were heated and bent into the proper shapes. This allowed cotton target cloth to be tied into the frames with strings, the cloth having been cut into the proper shape at Rock Island Arsenal and prepunched with holes that matched those in the steel frames. In some cases the arsenal supplied special dark-blue, nonglare paper that fit into the frames in place of the cloth.[22]

The overall popularity of shooting sowed the eventual seeds that led to the end of the

Fig. 6.5

skirmishers' prizes. The increased demands for ammunition caused problems with the army's meager appropriations. Pistol competition also started, further straining the army's ammunition account. The military responded by slowly reducing the length of the practice season. General Schofield, who became the commander of the army in 1888 upon the death of Philip Sheridan, reported in his first year as the senior general that the "season for range firing, . . . [has] been gradually diminished," and then fulfilled his statement by further shrinking the season from three months to two. To additionally save ammunition most units began to omit or severely reduce the unit firings in 1887 and 1888. The army's promising training program contracted.[23]

Under Schofield's influence, in 1889 the cavalry started pistol and carbine competition. With the increased cavalry matches more medals became available to soldiers, compensating for the loss of the skirmishing prizes. The end of the prizes did not end skirmishing, however. Skirmishing live-fire training continued, and General Order 36, 1897, modified the firing to more fully simulate combat conditions. Standard squads fired at sets of silhouette targets representing opposing troops arranged in groups of three: a kneeling target, a standing target, and a prone target. These three outlines were spread over 2 to 3 yards, and several of these groups were placed downrange, with each firing soldier directed to shoot at a particular target set. Volley firing followed this squad firing.[24]

By 1897 rigidly controlled group firings known as "collective fire" or "field fire," both in volley and at will at 600, 800, and 1,000 yards, became the doctrine. An entire company practiced at one time, each man separated by one pace, with officers announcing both the ranges to be set on the sights and when to fire, so that the unit would discharge rifles nearly simultaneously. The next year, firing regulations directed that "Company Field Practice" be conducted by firing a single company volley from 800 yards, two volleys at 700 yards, and two more volleys from 600 yards. No awards crowned the best shots. This collective fire was a temporary step back from skirmishing and precision shooting on the battlefield. The tug-of-war continued throughout the few years at the edge of the centuries, influenced in part by the fact that the respected German army relied upon highly controlled volley fire.[25]

The Spanish-American War and the Boer War reversed this trend. The U.S. Army resumed the march toward today's battlefields, although the regulations published just before the affair in Cuba did have advancing soldiers at the last, when they were "about 200 yards from the targets," fire rapidly and independently and had the line of troops rush forward with the goal of firing five cartridges within 175 yards of the target.[26]

The War Department first announced distinguished marksmen in the spring of 1884. These men of great ability had won at least three of the large prizes and, as a result of these wins, generally could not further compete in the standard department, division, and army contests. Blunt's 1885 *Instructions in Rifle and Carbine Firing* established that distinguished marksmen who had not been on an army team might be selected for that team once, but not twice. The army was feeling its way through the issue of how to let these distinguished shooters continue to compete without hindering marksmen who were not designated as distinguished. In June 1887 General Sheridan appointed Guy V. Henry, a white major in the black 9th Cavalry, to conduct a competition of distinguished marksmen at Bellevue, Nebraska, in mid-September. Department commanders selected the best shot from their distinguished marksmen to meet in this special match: three from the Department of the Platte, two each from the Department of the East and the Department of Texas, and one from the Departments of Dakota, the Missouri, the Columbia, California, and Arizona. These twelve shooters were the first to compete for special prizes given only to distinguished marksmen.[27]

Initially, the army planned to hold these distinguished marksmen matches every other year to provide an army-wide competition at times when the normal army level matches were not held. The army gave one gold and two silver prizes. This grand scheme lasted only for the first match, however. In 1889 Schofield divided the matches into separate contests for rifle and for carbine, with one gold and two silver prizes given in each contest, but the concept of a match every other year persisted. The War Department changed the frequency of competitions at the end of 1890, so from 1891 through 1894 the army held distinguished marksmen matches each year. In 1895 and again in 1896 Daniel S.

Lamont, the secretary of war, suspended contests due to a weapons change—the introduction of the Krag rifle. During this lapse between 1894 and the resumption of matches in 1897, the War Department rewrote the firing regulations. Part of the study effort that supported the rewrite included examining all matches and their rules. The staff officers ultimately eliminated the competition of distinguished marksmen.

SHOOTERS' CLOTHING AND EQUIPMENT

Starting with the 1882 *General Rules for Competitors*, shooters had to wear "the prescribed fatigue uniform, with belt, of their grade in the Army." This general requirement remained for many years, and a number of the books from the late nineteenth and early twentieth centuries show soldiers firing in field uniforms complete with army caps or hats and either cartridge belts or cartridge boxes. In addition to the field uniform for firing, soldiers had to be ready for any uniform contingency. Even in the summer, the Department of the Platte required competitive shooters to take not only dress uniforms and fatigue uniforms, field cartridge belts, and bed sacks, but even their overcoats to matches.[28]

During the twentieth century competitive shooters began to wear special jackets with shoulder and elbow padding as well as placing bullets in special wood blocks, drilled with a predetermined number of holes slightly larger than a bullet, to help keep count of rounds fired and the like, but until World War I all competitive army shooting had to be done in the field uniform—shooting was, after all, preparation for combat. In the early days soldiers wore the field cartridge belt or cartridge box during all firing for record. For a while officers even had to be equipped with field glasses as well as pistols, although sabers could be omitted. Pershing's 1919 competition in France for the victorious U.S. troops required the men to wear the field uniform, and for some competitions even the steel helmet was essential.[29]

As shown in the 1904 Infantry Drill Regulations, when firing, soldiers were to wear standard uniforms, complete with caps or hats and either cartridge belts or cartridge boxes.

Soldiers carried early bullets in pouches or special boxes, and at first they simply placed the newfangled and limited-issue special brass-cased rounds into these containers. However, the widespread introduction of metallic cartridges after the Civil War resulted in civilian frontiersmen's wearing homemade leather belts fixed with loops to hold their ammunition. Anson Mills, cavalry captain and brevet general, took this technique and eventually patented a series of woven, looped ammunition belts that the army ultimately adopted after considerable bureaucratic fussing. On campaign in the West many soldiers simply added bullets in their pockets, sometimes even when they had the looped belts. When Krag-Jorgensen rifles came into service during the 1890s, the army was able to buy double-row belts, increasing the capacity from the initial forty-five or fifty rounds (which depended upon the length of the belt) to nearly twice the number of rounds.[30]

Introduction of the M 1903 Springfield rifle, with its five-round loading clip, caused the looped belt to be replaced by one with nine woven pockets, each pocket designed to hold the five rounds that were joined at the base. Often modified, this concept of pocketed belts continued through the Korean War, with various versions created by pocket size, number of pockets, and other changes. It was these various belts that soldiers wore during early qualification firing, but after World War I such gear was discarded when they fired in the National Matches.[31]

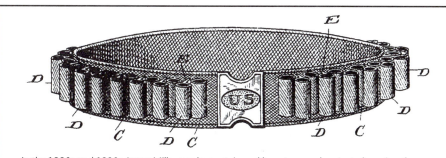

In the 1880s and 1890s Anson Mills, cavalry captain and brevet general, patented a series of woven, looped ammunition belts used by the U.S. Army. This particular version has two rows of cartridge loops and is from a patent of October 1893.

For the Springfield 1903 rifle, the U.S. Army brought out an olive drab nine-pocket web belt designed so that each pocket would hold five rounds joined at the base. This concept of pocketed belts continued through the Korean War, with the pocket sizes and number of pockets changing.

Nineteenth-century army clothing was the traditional dark blue that continued until khaki cotton coats and trousers came into use at the time of the Spanish-American War. High-velocity bolt-action rifles, smokeless powder, and machine guns caused the brightly colored uniforms and shiny insignia to be replaced by camouflage-inspired olive drab clothing and black-colored insignia beginning in 1902. In the U.S. Army the phrase "olive drab" came to represent over one hundred dark shades, which were soon distinguished by numbers—a practice that remained until after World War II.

On ranges that hosted competitive shooting, civilian jackets with padding on elbows and a shoulder appeared nearly simultaneously with the olive drab uniforms, and after World War I all firers adopted such garb when allowed. This effectively marked the end of standard uniforms as shooter's clothing in most high-level matches, although in the twentieth century some combat courses required normal uniforms, and the army prescribed combat clothing for standard range firings when soldiers were shooting for qualification.

The army ordered new prize designs for the general 1889 competitions, and as in the initial gestation period, the mint again could not supply the awards in time. Simultaneously, the War Department issued Blunt's new *Firing Regulations for Small-Arms*. While many changes were incorporated into the new regulations, the most significant was the inauguration of special cavalry competitions. Blunt changed cavalry firings to carbines rather than rifles, and for the first time introduced pistol contests. Until this time, cavalrymen could use rifles when competing for prizes and the Nevada Trophy. Blunt's alterations provided the obvious great advantage that cavalrymen used their actual weapons in practice as well as combat.

As a result, with the elimination of skirmishing and the addition of the cavalry competition, the set of prizes changed considerably.[32]

The army was always slow to recognize the time required to negotiate with the U.S. Mint in design of both the 1881 and 1889 prizes, but within the Treasury Department the engravers were even more sluggish. In some cases it took more than a year to procure the lavish prizes. Ordnance Department officers and Philadelphia artisans exchanged sketches and notes, changed concepts, were at times oblivious to their deadlines, professed immense interest, but carped when other organizations took their time. Hardly unique, the mint had many customers and made many medals, and

Fig. 6.6. The army department marksmanship gold prize, 1881–88. The full award was suspended from a brooch so it could be worn. The U.S. Mint made thirty-three bronze strikings as nonawarded samples (including this particular one) and fifty-nine gold badges for presentation. The design is similar to that of a later department award, but this first version is distinguished by the wording around the edge, **ARMY DEPARTMENT MARKSMAN-SHIP**, *while the later design is worded* **FIRST PRIZE DEPARTMENT MARKSMANSHIP**. *The first is designated Design-1 or D-1, while the later design is designated D-13.*

the army had to queue up along with everyone else.

Officers competed with enlisted men for all of the various prizes, but over time questions arose about the wisdom of this policy. In the view of some those prizes won by officers were taken away from enlisted men. In June 1897 the War Department announced a new policy of holding competitions for enlisted men only and, after the conclusion of those matches, holding officers' matches. Identical prizes were to be given in both contests: gold medals for first place, and for two second class prizes, smaller gold medals of lesser value. Despite the planning and publication of the implementing order and the issuance of *Firing Regulations for Small Arms* in 1898 that contained this provision, the restriction was not implemented until the twentieth century.[33]

Subsequent sections of this chapter list each prize and the quantities struck, except for seventy-eight replicas made in 1905–6, for which detailed figures are now imprecise. Rock Island Arsenal gold and silver plated these 1905 prizes to make various display boards, which are now disassembled, though some remain at the arsenal in their museum. Due to the dearth of information on the early 1880s prizes made in 1905, one can speculate that some were likely assembled with improper brooches. In April 1882 the secretary of war also ordered six sets of all of the various medals in bronze, without any brooch but in presentation boxes, for reasons now unknown.[34]

Before examining the designs of the various prizes, it is worth noting that the world quickly changed as the use of these prizes came to an end. The shooting contests ended in a twinkling with the explosion of the battleship Maine, the mobilization of the militia, and the movement of regular-army, volunteer, and militia units to the South and West coasts for transport to Cuba and other Spanish possessions. The U.S. Army reverted to the ancient scheme in place ever since the army had been founded—firearms training became the responsibility of the company and regimental commanders, with the central army authorities providing little direction. In the rush to war the 1898 staff tossed out Sheridan and Schofield's carefully

crafted training program, which the army had established with great zeal after Custer's death and improved upon during years of peace.

FIRST-PERIOD PRIZES, 1881–1888

The marksman having the best aggregate score in each of the department competitions received a gold medal. For ease of identification, the various prizes described in this chapter are numbered D-1 (design one) through D-26 (design 26), this initial award being assigned D-1.[35]

With the 1881 army having nine departments, it awarded nine D-1 gold medals in each of the first two years, then eight medals each year between 1883 and 1888 inclusively, although the army had one extra medal struck in 1886. This prize, which is a typical 1880s ornate vignette, includes a Federal shield, crossed rifles and flags, a target, intertwined letters **US**, a star, and a wreath, with the legend **ARMY DEPARTMENT MARKS-MANSHIP** around the edge as shown in figure 6.6. The D-1 award is similar to the prize that later replaced this award, but the later award (D-13) has different wording around the design. The reverse bears a wreath with small letters **U. S. MINT** below.

In September each of the three division commanders "assemble[d] the several department teams of twelve [soldiers]" for competition. The first prize, D-2, a gold medal 2 inches in diameter, shows a horse-mounted rifleman in dress uniform firing to the observer's right. Around the edge is the wording **FIRST**

Fig. 6.6

PRIZE ARMY DIVISION MARKS-MANSHIP. Six of these were first struck in 1882, with three prizes given to the 1881 division winners. Each succeeding year through 1888 the mint made three prizes, with one extra sample produced in 1884, for a total of twenty-five. The mint reused this same vignette for D-19, but with different wording.

Those men placing second, third and fourth in the division competitions each received a smaller second class prize gold medal. These 1 3/4–inch diameter prizes (D-3) show a dismounted soldier in dress uniform, standing with a rifle at the ready by his waist, with **SECOND CLASS PRIZE ARMY DIVISION MARKSMANSHIP** inscribed around the edge. The mint made nine of these medals in each of the seven years between 1882 and 1888, but the army did not retroactively award any for 1881, since those soldiers received special prize rifles. To fill the needs of the three divisions and three places in each division, the army provided nine of these prizes each year, for a total of sixty-three prizes. The mint prepared a number of unawarded sample bronze impressions of each prize, and D-3 had a great many, with a total of thirty-three, most being made in 1882. This design is similar to that of D-17, the wording around the edge being the easiest way to distinguish between the two.[36]

General Benét, chief of ordnance, made it clear that the second class prize "marksman rifles" given at the 1881 division contests were chambered for service ammunition, and further, that the rifles were not to be of such special design as to preclude their use in shooting contests. His premise was that if marksmen used something other than standard weapons, the other soldiers' confidence in issued weapons would be undermined. Benét did direct that the prize rifles "should be made a handsome and valuable weapon, with all of the modern appliances and plate for name, etc., no objection to the cost of being as much as $50 each." The Ordnance Department initially produced nine of these weapons, which were given to each of the three 1881 second class winners in the three U.S. military divisions—Division of the Atlantic, Division of the Pacific, and the Division of the Missouri. The soldiers preferred prize medals, and thus in 1882 gold prizes (D-3) replaced the rifles. The nine soldiers who received the special marksman rifles in division contests are listed in table 11.[37]

After the one first prize and the three second class prizes, the next eight top scores comprised the division team of twelve shooters. These soldiers received silver medals (D-4) two inches in diameter, displaying within a wreath the profiled head of Pallas Athena looking to the observer's left. Around the edge appear the words **ARMY DIVISION MARKSMANSHIP THIRD CLASS PRIZE**. The helmeted head of Pallas Athena later appeared on another prize, D-26, but it is worded **ARMY THIRD CLASS PRIZE** and has no wreath. The D-4 medal was awarded to 24 soldiers each year between 1881 and 1888,

Fig. 6.7. D-2, a gold first prize given for division marksmanship. Each of the three divisions awarded one prize annually from 1881 to 1888, and the U.S. Mint made one replacement, for a total of twenty-five.

Fig. 6.8. D-3, a gold second class prize for division marksmanship, 1882–88. Shooters who placed second, third, and fourth place received these. The original prize was suspended from a brooch so the winner could wear it. The design is similar to that of a later prize, D-17, but this version contains the word **ARMY** at the eleven o'clock position, while the later award does not.

Fig. 6.7

Fig. 6.8

Table 11. *1881 Winners of Marksman Rifles*

Winner	Rank	Unit	Division	Place	Score
R. C. Van Vliet	2d Lt.	10th Infantry	Atlantic	2	122
A. C. Taylor	1st Lt.	2d Artillery	Atlantic	3	121
J. H. Festus	Pvt.	5th Artillery	Atlantic	4	120
D. P. Nevins	1st Sgt.	Company G, 13th Infantry	Missouri	2	119
Charles H. Osborne	Sgt.	Troop H, 8th Cavalry	Missouri	3	118
William F. Shipp	Sgt.	Company K, 9th Infantry	Missouri	4	118
Charles Bernard	Pvt.	Company E, 8th Infantry	Pacific	2	128
Edward P. Wells	1st Sgt.	Company H, 2d Infantry	Pacific	3	124
E. C. Terry	Pvt.	Battery H, 4th Artillery	Pacific	4	124

Data extracted from National Archives, Record Group 108, Entry 56, "Register of Marksmanship of Military Personnel in Small Arms Firing Competitions, 1881–1903," 1–8.

Fig. 6.9. *D-4, a silver third class division prize, 1881–88. Soldiers who placed fifth through twelfth place in any of the three division matches received this prize. The brooch has been lost, although the claw that held the planchet remains.*

Fig. 6.10. *The reverse of the prize shown in figure 6.9. The beautifully crafted engraving, done in a variety of styles, tells the story:* **Won by Sgt. F. W. Weeks Co. 'E' 6th Infty at Div. of Missouri Rifle Competition Sept. 5th, 7th, 9th & 10th 1885**. *Weeks was one of the earliest men named a distinguished marksmen, in 1885.*

with one extra medal struck in 1886, for a total of 193. It is interesting to note that in at least one of the division competitions for 1881, the medal winners received their prize with their place engraved on the reverse, as was done for the award to First Sergeant J. Hackett of the 7th Infantry.[38]

In both 1885 and 1886 the Division of the Atlantic did not hold formal department competitions. Although the division awarded various prizes, soldiers received them for preliminary matches and for separate matches, and overall standing within the division could not be used to determine the top twelve shooters who would have ordinarily constituted the Division of the Atlantic's team. As a result the army commander later ruled that those who received a department prize within the Division of the Atlantic for these two years could not count it towards distinguished credit.[39]

Nineteenth-century engraving is artistically magnificent work. Today's machine engraving cannot begin to compare with the old hand script, which includes curved flowing lines of text and a full range of wording sizes. Engraving on the reverse was without a specific format, but generally showed the winner's name, rank, and unit, with the match name usually added. So elaborate was the engraving that the Ordnance Department allotted $1.50 per prize for local engraving, and in some cases the Department of the Missouri spent even twice that amount for theirs, at a time when a private's pay was a magnificent $13.00 a month and a silver prize cost $5.00.[40]

The top bar (brooch) for all the above department prizes is rectangular, with capital letters **DEPA MENT**. The center two letters are left to the reader's imagination, since this area is covered by a small concave square displaying a Federal eagle.

As in subsequent nineteenth-century army-level competitions, the first-place winner for the entire army received a 2-inch-diameter

Fig. 6.9

Fig. 6.10

Fig. 6.11

Fig. 6.12

gold prize (D-5) showing an eagle with out-stretched wings grasping a wreath and rifle, with thirteen stars above the eagle. The legend around the outside is **ARMY MARKS-MANSHIP ★ FIRST PRIZE ★**. The army only awarded four of these initial medals (D-5). The army gave prizes carrying the same design but with a slightly different reverse starting in 1890 (D-25). The wreath on the back of the D-5 prize has a large, open area for engraving, but unlike the later army first prize, this first version does not have a row of dots. Except for the last of these first-period awards, brooches for army-level competitions were rectangular bars with the upper portions capped by half of a stylized sun, normally with **ARMY** impressed on the bar. For the U.S. Army infantry championship match at the start of the twentieth century, however, the army changed the bar to a narrow one with a laurel wreath in the center, enclosing a square target.

Besides the 1882 prize awarded late to Engineer Sergeant Barrett, one each was given in 1884, 1886, and 1888. For each of these army matches, the headquarters of the army selected the number of marksmen from each division who would compete. In 1888 the selections allotted to the division commanders by the War Department were two from the Division of the Atlantic, six from the Division of the Missouri, and four from the Pacific. In that year the cavalry dominated, with five of

the first six places going to cavalrymen, the first three places all from the 2d Cavalry. Given the single first-place prize, the two second class prizes, and the third class prizes, any of the twelve soldiers selected for the army competition had a good chance of winning an impressive addition to his uniform.[41]

The army gave gold **SECOND CLASS PRIZE ARMY MARKSMANSHIP** awards to the 1882 second- and third-place finishers, both cavalrymen: Sergeant Cyrus Clark from B Troop, 1st Cavalry, and Sergeant Albert James, B Troop, 8th Cavalry. The helmeted head of Mars, looking to the left, is the central design of this 1 3/4 inch–diameter gold prize (D-6). Two were awarded in each of the first four army contests, in 1882, 1884, 1884, and 1888. This changed to six gold medals each year for 1890, 1891, 1892, 1893, and 1894. In 1897 the army changed the prize to silver and awarded six, and in 1902 it returned to gold but awarded only three for the infantry matches. The initial brooch consisted of the word **ARMY** below the top half of a sunburst design. Evidently in 1897 and certainly in 1902 the brooch was rectangular, with sprigs of laurel wreath on either side of a Federal shield.

The fourth- through sixth-place soldiers on the army team received silver prizes 2 inches in diameter (D-7), showing a soldier clad in a dismounted dress uniform, shooting from the kneeling position, with several contemporary army tents in the background. The wording around the edge is **THIRD CLASS PRIZE ARMY MARKSMANSHIP**. The general design is similar to that of the division skirmishers' medal discussed below, except that that award (D-9) has a background of

Fig. 6.11. Locally engraved by hand in flowing script, this gold prize shows the typical craftsmanship of the nineteenth century. Sergeant Richardson, after one enlistment in the 7th Cavalry that started in 1876, became an artilleryman and a distinguished marksman.

Fig. 6.12. D-5, a gold first-place army-level shooting prize. The army only had four of these made, for the overall champions in 1882, 1884, 1886, and 1888. These prizes are distinguished from the post-1888 versions by a star beneath each of the eagle's wing tips. The original brooch is of the same design as that of the brooch shown with the prize in figure 6.13.

Fig. 6.13. *D-6, the only prize totally unchanged from 1882 through 1902. Made in gold except for six prizes struck in silver for the 1897 contest, these were initially given by the army to second- and third-place finishers at the army contest and then, starting in 1890, to second-, third-, and fourth-place soldiers.*

Fig. 6.14. *D-7, the third class prize in silver for the semiannual army marksmanship contest, 1882–88. Similar to three other prizes (D-9 for skirmishing, D-18 for third class division, and D-20 for second class cavalry), this award has a background of tents but is most easily distinguished by the wording* **THIRD CLASS PRIZE ARMY MARKSMANSHIP**. *In this prize the US at the bottom is especially shifted in relationship to the platform holding the scene, versus the US in D-18.*

Fig. 6.15. *D-8, the only prize given in a division skirmish competition. Similar to a later cavalry prize, this silver award of a soldier firing from behind a tree can be distinguished from a similar motif (D-21) by the wording around the edge:* **DEPARTMENT SKIRMISH PRIZE**.

Fig. 6.13

Fig. 6.14

First Lieutenant William B. Homer of the 5th Artillery.[42]

SKIRMISH PRIZES, 1884–1888

These three prizes are a rare set of U.S. Army awards. The silver department skirmishing prize, 2 inches in diameter (D-8), shows a rifleman standing at the edge of a woods, behind a tree. Around the edge are the words **DEPARTMENT SKIRMISH PRIZE** encompassing the top three-fourths of the disk, with two crossed laurel sprigs filling the lower quarter. Each of the eight departments gave one of these, starting in 1884, with the last presented in 1888. One extra prize was struck in 1886 as a replacement award, for a total of twenty-two such awards in silver. Several bronze samples, some with accompanying bronze brooches, are in government type collections. Engravers at the mint later used this same vignette on a third class cavalry prize that was first presented in 1889, but with different wording.

Fig. 6.15

mountains behind the soldier. In 1889 the mint reused the vignette with tents behind the soldier on D-18.

In the initial 1882 army contest the infantry won not a single prize; artillerymen won the three third class prizes, including the only 1882 army-level medal that went to an officer. These winners were Sergeant Joseph Daly, Battery G, 1st Artillery; Private Alphonso Harrington, also of the 1st Artillery but from Battery C; and

Each of the three divisions provided large, 2-inch silver prizes (D-9) for the best skirmishing challenger, starting in 1884 and continuing through 1888. The scene on these prizes shows a cavalryman kneeling in his dress uniform and firing, with a background of mountains. This same scene was later used on the second class prize for cavalry competition. The wording on D-9 reads **DIVISION**

SKIRMISH PRIZE. Divisions gave a total of fifteen silver prizes, three each year for 1884 through 1888 inclusively, and the mint also made twenty-two bronze examples. Rock Island Arsenal gold plated at least two bronze strikings that are now in their collection.

Brooches are unique to skirmishing prizes. They bear the word **SKIRMISHING** prominently, with small laurel sprigs at each end and two rifles above, crossed over a sunburst.

The lone gold skirmishing prize awarded at the semiannual army competitions, D-10, is 2 inches in diameter and shows a prone rifleman in his service uniform. Around the upper portion of the vignette are the words **ARMY SKIRMISHING PRIZE**, and below the scene are two laurel sprigs. The reverse displays a wreath with the tiny words **U. S. MINT** below. This is the rarest of the nineteenth-century prizes; the army presented a frighteningly small number—one each in 1884, 1886, and 1888—although the mint also struck twenty-two samples in bronze for display.

DISTINGUISHED MARKSMEN COMPETITION, 1887–1894

Perhaps the most opulent and desirable prizes reflected the army's obsession with the best shots. Philip Sheridan's creation of distinguished marksmen was brilliant in its reach, since it kept competition alive for great shooters who had not yet earned the title "distinguished."

Fig. 6.16

Fig. 6.17

Those soldiers who earned the distinguished designation, however, still wanted to shoot. Starting in 1887 and continuing for seven short years, the U.S. Mint struck two beautifully designed disks that the army gave to the ultimate shooting titans in the competition among distinguished marksmen. These prizes had to be more magnificent than other awards, since every competitor had already won at least three prizes and a distinguished shield. As pieces of art, these two superb masterpieces deserve particular attention.

The first prize for distinguished marksmen, a radiant gold disk 2 inches in diameter, shows a mounted Indian with bow and arrow, pursuing a buffalo, with • **COMPETITION OF DISTINGUISHED MARKSMEN • FIRST CLASS PRIZE** around the edge. This prize is designated D-11.

Along with the second class prize, described below, the two awards for distinguished marksmen competition depict American Plains Indians and thus are some of the first outward, army-wide indications of wistful feelings towards the native ways of life that the army itself had changed and were already gone forever. In a few short years hunters decimated the free-roaming herds of great, shaggy American bison that dominated the plains. They roamed in the millions as late as the late 1870s, and even the hunters were aghast at the beasts' slaughter, which left less than 10,000 bison by 1885. Both the Indians and

Fig. 6.16. D-9, the division silver skirmish prize, awarded by the three divisions each year between 1884 and 1888. Nearly identical to D-20, this prize has the wording **DIVISION SKIRMISH PRIZE** around the outer edge.

Fig. 6.17. D-10, the rarest of all prizes. The army only awarded three of these gold 2-inch-diameter army-level skirmish prizes. A prize with a similar scene, also in gold, is D-16. The three winners of D-10 were Lieutenant Lewis Merriam, 4th Infantry (1884), Corporal Christian Michel, L Troop, 4th Cavalry (1886), and Corporal Adam Dell, F Troop, 2d Cavalry.

the buffalo were forever vanished from the Great Plains, due in great part to the army.

Along with seven bronze proofs or samples, the mint ultimately struck eleven of the D-11 gold prizes, the army awarding one for the 1887 rifle champion, followed by two each in 1889, 1891, 1892, 1893, and 1894. During this time in which the army awarded two prizes, one was given to the rifle champion and one to the cavalry carbine champion. A sunburst behind a crossed bow and quiver is at the center of the brooch, with a sprig of laurel leaves at each end. A list of the winners of these contests is shown in table 12.

The distinguished marksman competition did not draw soldiers equally from rifle-equipped and carbine-equipped units. In 1889 the rifle tournament for distinguished marksmen had two soldiers each from the Departments of the East and the Platte and one each from the Departments of Dakota, the Missouri, Texas, the Columbia, California, and Arizona. The carbine match had two cavalry troopers from each of the Departments of Dakota, the Columbia, and Arizona and one each from the Departments of the Platte, the Missouri, Texas, and California.[43]

Table 12. Winners of Distinguished Marksmen Contests

Year	Place*	Winner	Unit
1887	1	Sgt. E. H. Stevens	G, 7 Infantry
1887	2	Sgt. H. Griffith	D, 8 Cavalry
1887	3	Sgt. G. N. King	F, 20 Infantry
1889	1st Rifle	Sgt. J. J. Wolford	E, 20 Infantry
1889	2d Rifle	1st Sgt. L. Roper	F, 4 Infantry
1889	3d Rifle	Sgt. E. H. Stevens	G, 7 Infantry
1889	1st Carbine	1st Lt. A. C. Macomb	5 Cavalry
1889	2d Carbine	Sgt. F. Hayden	D, 6 Cavalry
1889	3d Carbine	Sgt. M. C. Gustin	B, 2 Cavalry
1891	1st Rifle	Sgt. Bynum Merwin	E, 15 Infantry
1891	2d Rifle	Sgt. J. W. Davis	B, 16 Infantry
1891	3d Rifle	Corp. V. H. Sweinhart	D, 22 Infantry
1891	1st Carbine	Blacksmith A. Keiser	H, 6 Cavalry
1891	2d Carbine	Corp. P. M. Hoke	B, 5 Cavalry
1891	3d Carbine	Corp. E. H. Steiner	B, 2 cavalry
1892	1st Rifle	Sgt. F. Rose	A, 18 Infantry
1892	2d Rifle	1st Sgt. N. Ray	A, 10 Infantry
1892	3d Rifle	Sgt. F. D. Powell	D, 14 Infantry
1892	1st Carbine	Sgt. H. Heuser**	G, 2 Cavalry
1892	2d Carbine	Corp. P. M. Hoke	B, 5 Cavalry
1892	3d Carbine	Capt. W. P. Hall	5 Cavalry
1893	1st Rifle	Sgt. R. N. Davidson	G, 16 Infantry
1893	2d Rifle	1st Sgt. N. Ray	A, 10 Infantry
1893	3d Rifle	1st Sgt. W. N. Puckett	F, 20 Infantry
1893	1st Carbine	Sgt. H. Heuser**	G, 2 Cavalry
1893	2d Carbine	1st Sgt. M. Rohrer	K, 1 Cavalry
1893	3d Carbine	Capt. J. Garrard	9 Cavalry
1894	1st Rifle	Sgt. F. D. Powell	D, 14 Infantry
1894	2d Rifle	Sgt. T. O'Rourke	G, 15 Infantry
1894	3d Rifle	1st Sgt. F. Rose	A, 18 Infantry
1894	1st Carbine	Sgt. H. Heuser**	G, 2 Cavalry
1894	2d Carbine	Sgt. H. Griffith	D, 8 Cavalry
1894	3d Carbine	Sgt. Michael H. Barry	G, 1 Cavalry

*First place received a gold medal, D-1; second and third places received silver medals, D-13.

**The only man to win more than one first-place medal in this competition.

Data taken from General Orders for respective years.

Fig. 6.18

Fig. 6.19

Fig. 6.18. *D-11, a gold first prize for the competition of distinguished marksmen. The engravers at the U.S. Mint sunk the design based upon photographs supplied by the Department of the Interior. The army awarded eleven of these prizes, and the mint struck seven additional copper proofs. The brooch is unique to this prize.*

Fig. 6.19. *D-12, the extravagant and beautifully struck second class prize for the competition of distinguished marksmen. The army gave two of these silver second class prizes for each D-11 prize awarded. Like D-11, these were given in 1887, 1889, and 1891 through 1894. The brooch is unique to the second class prize.*

Second class prizes for distinguished marksmen, made in silver, are also 2 inches in diameter. Artistically, they are the most perfect of the prizes. Mint engravers who created the beautiful vignette showing a Plains Indian encampment (D-12) depended upon Interior Department photographs as accurate guides. Wording around the edge is the same as for the first class prize, except for the substitution of the words **SECOND CLASS PRIZE** on the lower edge. The U.S. Mint struck seven bronze samples, along with twenty-two silver prizes.

The most improved shot to fire in the distinguished marksmen competition and the conqueror of this set of prizes was undoubtedly Henry Heuser, who, as a corporal in the 2d Cavalry, became a distinguished shot after winning a silver carbine prize and a bronze revolver prize in 1889, following his fifth place the previous year in the Department of the Columbia. He then proceeded to win the first place gold prize in the army carbine competition in 1891 and for three successive years won the first place gold in the competition of distinguished marksmen in 1892, 1893, and 1894. No one else was able to win even two first place prizes in the competition—the closest were Hoke of the 5th Cavalry and Ray of the 10th Infantry, who each won two second places, and Rose of the 18th Infantry and Powell of the 14th Infantry, who both won a first and a third.[44]

The reverse of these prizes is similar to that of other prizes, consisting of a full laurel wreath near the edge with a large central area for engraving. Brooches for the second class distinguished marksmen prizes fit the American Indian motif with the design consisting of two crossed bows and two decorated and arrow-filled quivers, superimposed over rays that emanated from the pendant suspension point.

SECOND-PERIOD PRIZES, 1889–1902

Beginning with the 1889 competitions and continuing until the start of the next century, the War Department prizes reflected a more balanced set of contests: rifles for infantry and carbines and pistols for the cavalry. All matches were divided into these two general divisions. The new cavalry competitions, really a combination of known distance and skirmish carbine firings plus a revolver match, recognized the basic differences in the weapons used by the two branches. The bi- and tri-departments that combined to form cavalry competitions varied over time. In 1889, for example, representatives from cavalry troops stationed in the Departments of Dakota, the Platte, and the Columbia met at Bellevue, Nebraska, near Omaha. Fort Leavenworth hosted troops from the Departments of the East, the Missouri, and Texas, while the Departments of California and Arizona met at Fort Wingate, New Mexico. The Departments of Dakota and the Platte held a bi-department carbine

124

and revolver meet in 1890, while the Departments of the East, the Missouri, and Texas had a tri-department competition, as did the Departments of the Columbia, California, and Arizona. In these competitions each cavalry troop generally sent one enlisted man and, in addition, each cavalry regiment selected two officers.[45]

The zenith of firing competitions occurred during this second period, when the soldiers' major time demand was not chasing Indians and the troops welcomed any diversion. Matches away from the local post afforded a welcome excuse for travel by officers' families, many wives looking upon shooting contests as significant social events. One contemporary writer noted that families accompanying these officers were excellent shots and that at the posts "where the competitions were held, [the women] graced

the ranges with their presence and transformed them into scenes of lively interest and animation. The spectators outnumbered the contestants, and the great interest in the subject was manifested by the earnest discussions of the relative merits of the competitors and the probable outcome of the contest." At the 1891 army matches held at Fort Sheridan, many local businesses offered small prizes to support the festivities. At this event the top enlisted skirmish score took $100 prize money and the best single enlisted skirmish run earned $50, while the purse for the greatest number of bull's-eyes came to $100. Officers received local gold medals for the highest single-skirmish run and the best overall-skirmish score, and Lieutenant Colonel Hotchkiss of the Illinois National Guard won a gold medal for the greatest number of bull's-eyes overall.[46]

CAVALRY CARBINES

A carbine is simply a shorter, lighter rifle. Cavalrymen used such a weapon since on horseback they could handle a shorter barrel more easily, while the accuracy of the rifle was not significantly compromised. The lesser weight also had an advantage because it could be held with a single hand, along with the reins, leaving the other hand free to load. The breech-loading Hall carbine carried by the dragoons in the 1840s was especially prone to inadvertent discharge. One recent author recounts a particular series of tales involving the dragoons and Hall carbines that were responsible for nearly a dozen accidents in 1843–44. Perhaps the root cause of these carbine accidents was the weapons adjustable trigger, which could be set very lightly.[47]

In the post–Civil War West the cavalry used modified Model 1873 Springfield carbines until they were replaced in 1879–80 by Model 1879 carbines. Model 1884 carbines in turn replaced these, until the Model 1884s were exchanged about the time of the Spanish-American War for Krag rifles and carbines. The first Krag carbine was a Model 1896 magazine version made in limited quantities. Three years later this was modified with a different sight and stock, becoming the Model 1899 carbine. As all regular cavalry regiments were armed with the Model 1896 Krag carbine in that year, cavalry units that saw service in the Spanish-American War took that model weapon to Cuba. The 1899 model saw service during the Philippines Insurrection.[48]

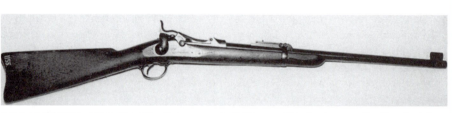

A U.S. Model 1884 carbine. The .45 caliber weapon is slightly over 41 inches long, making it easier to handle on horseback than a longer rifle.

As noted above, the grouping of departments to make up the matches continually changed. The Department of the Platte, headquartered in Omaha, hosted several of these

gladiatorial events. In 1894 teams from California and the Department of the East traveled to Bellevue (the county south of Omaha, along the Missouri River, and site of the current Offutt Air Force Base) in order to compete with the Platte soldiers. On September 13, 14, and 15 the Department of the Platte held preliminary firings for their rifle competition simultaneously with a preliminary match related to the 6th Annual Cavalry Competition for the three departments. Three distinguished marksmen also fired in this preliminary cavalry competition, placing second, third, and fifth. Following the weekend, rifle competition took place on September 18, 19, 20, and 21, coinciding with the formal cavalry match. In this latter contest three distinguished marksmen also participated but could not compete for medals. Second Lieutenant J. R. Lindsey of the local black 9th Cavalry won the carbine match, while First Sergeant J. C. Procter, I Troop, 9th Cavalry, took the revolver match.[49]

In this second period, starting in 1889, rifle competitions became reserved for soldiers not normally armed with carbines. This included artillerymen, engineers, and even post staff such as a post commissary sergeant who usually did not have a weapon. Even so, the matches were frequently called the infantry competition. Most departments held both cavalry and infantry competitions each year from 1889 through 1894 inclusively and again in 1897, although not all departments held matches in each of these years. In 1902, as a final encore, infantry competitions provided the last of the large prizes, a small bit of the nineteenth century leaking through to the twentieth.

Under the second-period scheme, cavalry troopers began to win prizes frequently. Cor-

poral (later Sergeant) Horace Bivins of the black 10th Cavalry is one such example. When the majority of the regiment transferred to Fort Custer, Montana, in 1892, Bivins started competitive firing and won a bronze prize for sixth place in the Department of Dakota revolver competition. The next year he won a second class silver prize in the same match, and then in 1894, the gold first prize in the revolver match and at the same time the Department of Dakota gold first-place carbine prize. Advancing to army-level competition, Bivins won the gold 1894 army carbine first prize and became a distinguished marksman. As will be seen in chapter 9, Bivins was the earliest qualifier for the Distinguished Pistol Shot badge, established in 1903.[50]

The army instituted second and third class prizes in department tournaments for the first time in 1889, while also slightly modifying the first prize. This second era, 1889–1902, influenced by the depression of 1887–88 and then the Panic of 1893, resulted in smaller prizes made from less valuable metals. The changes (described in detail below) can be summarized as follows. For the cavalry, the mint initially made carbine medals from gold and silver, copying two of them from the just-discarded skirmishers' medals. The first prize was a smaller copy of the division first prize for marksmanship, subsequently abolished in 1891. The Ordnance Department designed new revolver prizes. The gold first-place infantry prize was a smaller copy of the previous gold department prize. Both the silver second class and the bronze third class prizes were new designs. In addition the army planned to change the number of prizes to one first, three second, and six third class prizes in the various contests, except for the distinguished marksmen contests.[51]

Rock Island Arsenal initially prepared these awards for presentation in square, red leather boxes, each with a high, round top, while the boxes later became more rectangular. In all cases the

Fig. 6.20

boxes displayed the prizes on an elevated and tilted base. The 1902 prizes themselves were assembled slightly differently from other prizes. For that year only, the mint inserted a pin through the clasp that held the planchet. This pin prevented the disk from rotating within the grasp of the brooch's claw and thus always kept the scene properly oriented.

This second-period department gold first prize (D-13) shows an ornate assembly of crossed rifles, a pair of guidons, a Federal shield, and the letters **U** and **S** with a star above, the whole within a wreath. The design is very similar to that of the original department prize (D-1), but the legend around the edge has changed to **FIRST PRIZE DEPARTMENT MARKSMAN-**

Fig. 6.23a

Fig. 6.23b

SHIP from the original **ARMY DEPART-MENT MARKSMANSHIP**.

When the first contests ended in August 1889, the mint did not yet have prizes ready, so parades and recognition of the winners occurred without tangible rewards. The army later forwarded the D-13 prizes to the winners. The mint struck fifty-seven of these, one for an "extra" in 1889, with awards of eight each in 1889, 1890, and 1891; seven each in

Fig. 6.21. Only in 1902 were the clasps or claws pinned to prevent the prize from rotating. All previous prizes developed the problem that they rotated with a small amount of wear, the vignette then becoming disoriented. The head of the pin is the small circle on the claw that holds the planchet. This astonishingly well-preserved decoration, D-14, a silver second class prize for department competitions from 1889 through 1902, has very few surface scratches or edge knocks, suggesting that Private Johannes Smeets, Company K, 3d Infantry, Department of the Lakes, did not wear it often. Smeets, born in the Netherlands in January 1860, was a typical professional soldier, serving thirty years as a private in the 3d, 20th, and 28th Infantry Regiments as well as three years in the general service (recruiting duty). He never married and after discharge lived in St. Paul, Minnesota, with his sister. The mint struck 160 of these 1 1/2–inch-diameter prizes.

Fig. 6.22. Rock Island Arsenal issued nineteenth-century shooting prizes in various versions of red-leather high-topped boxes. This example, which has sharper edges than earlier boxes, is from the 1890s.

Fig. 6.23a and b. The inside of the presentation boxes displayed prizes on a raised and slightly angled platform that was recessed on top to fit the planchet and brooch.

Fig. 6.21

Fig. 6.22

1892 and 1893; six in 1894; three in 1897 for the cavalry (one for combined East and Missouri; one for Dakota, Platte, and the Columbia; and one for the Colorado, Texas, and California); one for the infantry in 1897 (combined tournament for the Columbia and California only); and eight in 1902 for the infantry-department competitions.[52]

First Sergeant Archie Deuberry, Company B, 22d Infantry, was the only man to earn a distinguished marksman shield in 1902. Previously, he had won only a silver second class prize for a third-place finish in the 1894 Department of the Platte infantry match while he was a private in F Company, 22d Infantry. Deuberry did poorly in the preliminary 1902 competition conducted during the last two days in July, placing fourteenth by scoring 100 points less than the first-place finisher, the regimental quartermaster sergeant from his own unit. Deuberry steeled his nerves and for the first three days of August shot the best of all entrants, finishing first with a score of 503 points. His first 1902 medal was the department gold first prize. Having started by earning a D-13 prize, Deuberry shortly went on to win a coveted second-place gold at the army level.[53]

The reverse of D-13 is like that of most other prizes of the period, with a closed wreath near the edge and the small wording **U. S. MINT** between the wreath and the rim. The brooch for this award is also identi-

cal to the brooch for other department prizes, with a rectangle carrying the capital letters **DEPA MENT** and a small square in the center bearing an eagle.

Developing an appropriate new design for the second and third class department prizes proved a challenge for a now-unknown engraver at the mint. The resulting device (D-14, fig. 6.21) is a superimposed monogram US forming a backdrop to three stacked arms, with a spiked infantry dress helmet resting on top. The wording • **DEPARTMENT MARKSMANSHIP** • goes around the upper

Fig. 6.24

Fig. 6.24. *D-13, the second-period (1888–1902) gold first prize for department competition. It is very similar to D-1, but its legend is different.*

Fig. 6.25. *These are nine of the ten soldiers in the competition of the army rifle team of distinguished marksmen of 1889. The contestants are: (front row, left to right) Sergeant J. P. Kelly, Company E, 6th Infantry; First Sergeant L. Roper, Company F, 4th Infantry, who placed first and won the gold prize; Sergeant J. J. Wolford, Company E, 19th Infantry, who placed second and won a silver prize; Sergeant G. H. Stevens, Company G, 7th Infantry, who won the gold prize at the first competition two years before but placed sixth in this contest; Private J. Gormley, Battery B, 5th Artillery, who placed third and won the last silver prize; and (back row, left to right) First Sergeant G. N. King, Company F, 20th Infantry; Sergeant W. Williams, Company E, 20th Infantry; First Lieutenant W. A. Mercer, 8th Infantry, who placed 4th; and Corporal W. D. Umphray, Battery I, 1st Artillery. The contestant missing from the photograph is First Lieutenant R. C. VanVliet, 10th Infantry.*

Fig. 6.25

Fig. 6.26. D-15, the most common of the nineteenth-century prizes, with 316 awarded. Though the prizes were made in bronze, at least one—awarded in 1894 by the Department of the Dakota to a sergeant in Company A, 20th Infantry— was gold plated by the winner.

half, and **SECOND CLASS PRIZE** completes the lower portion. Soldiers placing second, third, and fourth place usually received these prizes. The mint struck 160 of these in silver, and the army distributed 24 each in 1889, 1890, and 1891; 21 in 1892 and 1893 (the Departments of California and the Columbia combined competitions in these years); 18 in 1894; 12 in 1897; and 16 in 1902. For the last competition the army supplied the prizes only for second and third place. The prize carried the standard department brooch in silver.[54]

The bronze medals that the army initially awarded in the summer of 1889 for the third class department prizes are designated D-15. Their simple design consists of a Federal shield, over which are superimposed crossed sabers with a pistol above. The wording around the edge reads • **DEPARTMENT MARKSMANSHIP • THIRD CLASS PRIZE**. This is by far the most common of the nineteenth-century prizes, as the mint made 316 of these 1 1/2–inch-diameter awards between 1889 and 1902, including four replacements (two in 1890, one in 1891, and one in 1892). Soldiers placing fifth through tenth

usually received these prizes. In 1902 each of the eight departments gave the second- and third-place finishers silver prizes (D-14) and these bronze prizes for fourth through sixth place, for an army-wide total of twenty-four D-15s that year. The reverse of the D-15 contains a closed wreath, and the brooch is standard for the department prizes.

Fig. 6.26

AN INTERESTING GROUP OF SHOOTING PRIZES AND GEORGE CUSTER

Sergeant James A. Richardson was one of the outstanding army marksmen during the late nineteenth century. After serving five years with the 7th Cavalry he became an artilleryman, and he finally retired with thirty years service in the early twentieth century. During his competitive shooting time he won three large silver department prizes and a massive gold division prize, becoming a distinguished marksman in 1889. As an old soldier, Richardson romanticized his years as a soldier, and in 1909 he finally spoke to a newspaper reporter about the adventurous army life. No modern Western author could invent a life better than Richardson's. He described how he was a member of C Troop at the battle of the Little Big Horn and was left behind with the pack mules, becoming part of Captain Frederick W. Benteen's command that joined Reno's desperate group.

It is well known that George Armstrong Custer took personal command of C, E, F, I, and L Troops of the 7th Cavalry Regiment and attacked a large encampment of Indians on June 25, 1876, in "Custer's Last Stand." Indians completely wiped out this force of 210 men, while the balance of the 7th Cavalry, divided into three other commands shortly before the charge, desperately rejoined forces under the command of Major Marcus A. Reno and was soon besieged by Indians on June 25 and 26. Brigadier General Alfred H. Terry and Colonel John Gibbon and their troops lifted the siege on June 27, discovering the horrors inflicted by the Sioux, Cheyennes, and Arapahos.[55]

Richardson's gripping story, as finally relayed in 1909, included the statement that "I was with the pack train in the rear where B Troop, Captain McDougall was taking its turn as rear guard. I saw [the officers] gather about the general on a little knoll at the head of the column. It was a picturesque group . . . [and then the command split up with Richardson and others left behind with the pack mules]. At 11:30 we heard the firing up the valley and knew that Custer was engaged. He was then about three miles away."

As Major Reno joined the pack train in what Richardson describes as an understandable panic ("the major said, 'The river bottom was swarming with Sioux,'"), everyone began to dig in. Richardson continued:

We were told to dig ditches there and dig them quick, and we did. Tin cups, plates, and a few trowel bayonets, hands, everything were used to scoop out those ditches. . . . Things were getting desperate indeed when night came on the 26th of June. The carbines were Springfields. They were inaccurate and mighty poor tools. Many of the extractors got broken and the guns were useless. We did the best we could however, and when daylight came on the 27th [we] expected it to be our last day, for the odds against us were tremendous.

At dawn the beleaguered troopers found that most of the Indians had withdrawn, and during the morning the relief column under Terry and Gibbon arrived.

Richardson's Indian fighting continued the next year when, on September 30, 1877, three troops of the 7th Cavalry plus portions of the 3d Cavalry and the 5th Infantry cornered Chief Joseph and his band. Richardson was shot, being one of 53 wounded or killed that day out of the 115 7th Cavalrymen engaged. The bullet passed through his leg and killed his mount.

After being discharged from the 7th Cavalry, within a few days Richardson enlisted in Battery M, 3d Artillery, a unit with which he served for many years, rising in two years to corporal and then, after two more years, to sergeant. In 1896 James Richardson became the post ordnance sergeant at Fort Preble, Maine, located in the harbor at Portland, a position he held until he retired in 1905. During his shooting days Richardson won a Division of the Atlantic silver third class prize in 1885, then another Division of the Atlantic silver third class prize in 1888. These were followed in 1889 by a Department of the East second class silver prize and a substantial Division of the Atlantic gold second class prize, thus earning him a distinguished marksman badge that year.[56]

The shooting prizes and medals of Sergeant James A. Richardson, an 1876 member of the 7th Cavalry. Richardson won these army shooting awards between 1885 and 1889 while he was a member of the artillery. He became a distinguished marksman in 1889. The hand-chased second-prize gold medal is engraved on the reverse, showing that it was won at Creedmoor in September 1891. The two campaign medals in the lower row are for service in the Spanish-American War and the Indian Wars.

The army introduced campaign medals in 1905, expanded them to the Civil War and the Indian Wars in January 1907, and provided medals to current and former soldiers who had served in specified campaigns. In 1908 retired Ordnance Sergeant James A. Richardson wrote the adjutant general requesting his "Indian War Badge." In his letter of application Richardson wrote that he was entitled to his badge by virtue of his 7th Cavalry service with General Terry when the Sioux were disarmed at Standing Rock in late October 1876, when he helped chase the Nez Perce the next summer, and when he participated in the capture of the Northern Cheyenne Indians in October 1878 on Shattern Creek, Nebraska. What happened to any mention of his service at the Little Big Horn and the action against Chief Joseph?

When word of the stunning Custer disaster reached the East at the height of America's centennial celebration, many young men immediately signed up as "Custer avengers." One of these was a young Texan from Basque County, who in August 1876 joined Captain Tom Custer's old unit, C Troop, 7th Cavalry (Tom having been one of George's two brothers also to die at the Little Big Horn River). His name was James A. Richardson, and in his later life his time with the 7th Cavalry just had to be improved. Despite his stretching of the truth, he was a noted marksmen in the artillery.

Fig. 6.27. D-16, a division first prize, 1889–90. The army awarded only six of these gold prizes.

Fig. 6.28. D-17, 1 ⁵⁄₈ inches in diameter. The gold division second class prize, with the infantryman in his 1885-pattern dress uniform, rifle at the ready, was awarded exclusively in 1889 and 1890 by each of the three divisions to those soldiers placing second, third, and fourth, so only eighteen were ever struck. Sergeant James Richardson won this particular prize.

Fig. 6.29. D-18, an 1889–1890 division third class prize. The design of a kneeling infantryman first appeared on the army-level third class prize of 1882, D-7; changed to a cavalryman, the vignette was carried to D-9 and D-20. This version is distinguished from the other awards by the wording and the brooch.

The War Department discontinued the military divisions (Atlantic, Missouri, and Pacific) on July 2, 1891; thus the second-period prizes given at division rifle competitions are scarce, the army having only three in each year for 1889 and 1890. The gold first prize, D-16, is centered around a vignette showing a prone rifleman aiming to the left, with the legend **FIRST PRIZE DIVISION MARKSMANSHIP** surrounding the scene. The design is similar to that of D-10.

Fig. 6.27

Fig. 6.28

Fig. 6.29

Division competition second class prizes are of gold, showing an infantryman in his dress uniform with spiked helmet, holding a rifle, its muzzle slightly upward, at his waist. Around the edge for design D-17 is **SECOND CLASS PRIZE DIVISION MARKS-MANSHIP**. The brooch is rectangular, with crossed rifles and an eagle with wings out, ready for flight, at the center. Divisions gave three of these for second, third, and fourth places in 1889 and 1890, for a total of eighteen prizes. The scene is similar to that in another gold prize, D-3, which has a slightly larger diameter and different wording.

Silver third class division rifle prizes, D-18, reintroduced a common vignette, that of a soldier firing from the kneeling position. For this rifle prize the firer wields a rifle and wears an infantry uniform with a spiked helmet; the scene has tents in the background. A similar cavalry design shows a cavalry trooper in his plumed helmet against a background of hills,

firing a carbine. The scene is similar to that used on D-7 except for the wording. Men who placed fifth through tenth inclusively received these infantry-contest prizes in 1889 and 1890.

The first prize for department carbine competition shows a mounted cavalryman in dress uniform, with the horse facing left and the soldier firing a carbine to the right. The vignette is a copy of that from D-2, the initial army-division championship prize. Around the upper three-fourths of the scene for this prize are the words **FIRST PRIZE**

CAVALRY COMPETITION. The design, D-19, is executed on a 1 ³/₄–inch-diameter gold prize. The army had twenty-six of them made and in 1889 and 1890 awarded three each year. One tri-department competition consisted of cavalry from the Departments of Dakota, the Platte, and the Columbia; another included the Departments of the East, the Missouri, and Texas; and the bi-department competition comprised the Departments of California and Arizona. Effective December 1890, the army stipulated four cavalry contests each year. This action resulted in four first prizes awarded each year for 1891, 1892, 1893, and 1894.[57]

In 1897 new army firing regulations totally revised the cavalry competitions. Under these rules the cavalry matches, spread over four days, required troopers to fire forty rounds with a carbine at rectangular targets one day, then to fire an additional forty rounds in two skirmish runs (one in the morning and one in the afternoon) the second day. This was followed by a day of dismounted pistol firing, and the last day was devoted to mounted pistol shooting. The highest total scores received the cavalry prizes. The mint struck four prizes in 1897, since the new regulations called for four combined department competitions. However, when the headquarters of the army set up the 1897 matches, it called for only three combined department competitions. As a result the army only held three matches, leaving one first prize as excess. The reverse of the prize displays a closed wreath the same as that on most other prizes. The brooch is a thin bar bearing representations of a raised bullet on each end section, with a center circle holding a U.S. monogram.[58]

The second class prizes for department cavalry matches, D-20, are 1 ⁵/₈ inches in diameter, the obverse displaying a hilly background with a kneeling cavalryman in dress uniform in the foreground. The design of a kneeling soldier firing a weapon is similar to that on D-9, the division skirmish prize, and on D-18, the third class division competition prize. Nine of these D-20 cavalry gold prizes were awarded in 1889 and nine in 1890, then the army began to make them in silver, awarding twelve each in years 1891, 1892, 1893, and 1894. Only nine were awarded in 1897, due to the reduced number of matches. Appropriate wording, similar to that on the other two cavalry completion prizes, surrounds the vignette.

The last of the cavalry-department carbine prizes, D-21, shows a cavalryman firing to the right, standing behind a tree—a design nearly identical to that on the department skirmishing medal, D-9. Prize D-21 is 1 ⁵/₈ inches in diameter and is thus smaller than D-9. The mint made these prizes in silver for 1889 and 1890 and following that in bronze, bringing the metals used for all third class department prizes after 1890 into uniformity. Around the edge are the words **THIRD CLASS PRIZE CAVALRY COMPETITION**, and at the

Fig. 6.30. This 1 ³/₄–inch-diameter division gold first prize, D-19, has the word **CAVALRY** around the edge, distinguishing it from the earlier prize with a similar scene.

Fig. 6.31. D-20, a second class prize, 1 ⁵/₈ inches in diameter, for the 1889–97 cavalry carbine competitions. The design is nearly identical to that of D-9. In both 1889 and 1890 the mint made the prizes of gold, then switched to silver for subsequent awards.

Fig. 6.30

Fig. 6.31

Fig. 6.32. The reverse of D-20 is unique in that the design provided a raised ribbon for engraving the winner's name.

Fig. 6.33. D-21, similar to D-8 except for its wording, was given as a third class prize for carbine competition. The prize was made in silver in 1889 and 1890, then in bronze in 1891, 1892, 1893, 1894, and 1897. This particular award, which is bronze, was won in 1892 by Sergeant M. Finnegan, a member of Troop A of the black 10th Cavalry.

Fig. 6.34. D-22, the gold first prize for cavalry revolver matches, 1 ⁵/₈ inches in diameter, shows cavalry troopers so perfectly aligned that even the horses are in step. The army awarded a total of thirty of the prizes in bi- and tri-department matches from 1889 to 1894.

Fig. 6.32

Fig. 6.33

Fig. 6.34

bottom are two crossed laurel sprigs. Twenty-four bronze prizes were struck in each of the same years as the other cavalry prizes, 1891 through 1894 and 1897, with only eighteen awarded in the last match. The proper brooch has intertwined US letters in a circle, with a horizontal bullet on each side of this central design.

Revolver contests, the other cavalry competition added in 1889, lasted only until 1894. The first prizes are gold, second class prizes are silver, and third class prizes are bronze. Generally, these were awarded for bi-department and tri-department matches, the contests that replaced division matches.

In the first two years of the awards, 1889 and 1890, the army gave a total of six gold first prizes, with four given in each of the following four years. The design, D-22, consists of a line of four horsemen wearing dress uniforms and aiming pistols. The wording around the top of the scene is **REVOLVER MATCH** and below, **FIRST PRIZE**, with the two legends separated by a six-point star on each side. The planchet is 1 ⁵/₈ inches in diameter, suspended from a brooch decorated with two crossed revolvers. The reverse contains a nearly closed wreath and a large central space for engraving the contest, the winner's rank, his name, his unit, and the date.

Second class prizes for revolver matches, D-23, are 1 ¹/₂–inch silver medals depicting a cavalryman astride a rearing horse, aiming a revolver at an Indian who is drawing a bow and aiming an arrow at the soldier. The legend is **REVOLVER MATCH** and **SECOND CLASS PRIZE**. Like the other cavalry medals, these were awarded at bi- and tri-department contests. Lieutenant John J. Pershing, 6th Cavalry, won one of these prizes in August 1889 at the Department of the

Fig. 6.35

Fig. 6.36

Fig. 6.35. One and one-half inches in diameter, D-23 is in silver. Sergeant Elmore Welch, Troop B, 8th Cavalry, won this particular prize at a bi-department match between the Departments of the Columbia and Dakota at Fort Keogh, Montana, 17–22 August 1891. Other winners in this competition were from the 1st, 4th, and 8th Cavalry Regiments.

Fig. 6.36. D-24, the third class prize for revolver competitions, was always struck in bronze, 1889–94, for a total of 132 prizes.

Platte's annual cavalry competition, held at the Bellevue rifle range, and then won another in August 1891 in the third cavalry competition, also at Bellevue. When Pershing thought his marksmanship skills had "rusted," he requested and received a delay in reporting to his assignment as the head of the military department at the University of Nebraska just so he could participate in a match.[59]

The reverse and the brooch are similar to those of the revolver first prize. The army presented a combined total of eighteen D-23 prizes in 1889 and 1890 and then twelve each year in 1891, 1892, 1893, and 1894.

The army awarded a total of 132 third class revolver prizes, 1 1/2 inches in diameter and struck in bronze. The prominent image is a standing cavalryman aiming his pistol to the left and on the right holding a pawing horse by its reins, with **REVOLVER MATCH** and **THIRD CLASS PRIZE** around the vignette. The prize, D-24, was made and awarded only in bronze, with 24 given each year from 1891 through 1894 and 36 combined in the first two years, for a total of 132. The reverse wreath and the suspending brooch are the same as those on the other two revolver prizes.

INDIANS IN THE U.S. ARMY

Fast Dog was a tall Indian, at 5 feet, 11 3/4 inches. When the army published Fast Dog's name in orders, it was in italics, as though he was a ship or something other than a man. A Sioux, he was born during the Civil War in what became Montana, on the Powder River. Although many Sioux fought against the U.S. Army, when Fast Dog was twenty-eight he joined the 6th Cavalry, four months after the Battle of Wounded Knee. The 6th Cavalry had more Medal of Honor recipients in the West than any other unit and was one of the regiments that had fought at Wounded Knee. In mid-1890 Secretary of War Redfield Proctor had reduced the cavalry by inactivating two troops in each regiment. The following March he partly restored the reduction by activating L Troops of the 1st through 8th Cavalry regiments with Indian enlisted men. Soldiers considered the Indian troops of the 6th Cavalry at Fort Niobrara and the 3d Cavalry at Fort Meade to be the elite Indian units. Both were selected to represent all of the Indian troops at the World's Columbian Exposition in Chicago in October 1892.[60]

Fast Dog, Henry to his soldier friends, was one of these soldiers. He was such a good trooper and phenomenal pistol shot that his troop commander picked him as the troop's outstanding soldier, and then the regimental commander selected him to represent the entire 6th Cavalry Regiment at the annual firing competition of 1893, held at Bellevue, Nebraska.

General Brooke and his staff, who arrived by special train for the awards ceremony, initially pinned a shooting prize on the Indian's chest, to the cheers of the crowd and

melodies played by the 2d Infantry band, but then senior officers from Washington weighed in, creating problems after this firing competition. Lieutenant Colonel Daniel W. Benham, 7th Infantry and the inspector for small-arms practice in the Department of the Platte, noted that Fast Dog, although a sergeant, "was debarred from the decorative benefits of the competition by orders from the Headquarters of the Army. He was, however, permitted to shoot by the Department Commander. The results indicated that this Indian was quite equal to the average white or colored soldier with the carbine, and with the revolver he stood three amongst thirty competitors." In an attempt to serve justice Colonel Benham continued, "I can hardly see why the Indian soldier should longer be debarred from our competitions. His status in the Army is exactly that of any other soldier. . . . why should he not be given . . . the privileges pertaining to the enlisted man?"[61]

Fast Dog, of the Sioux tribe, in about 1912. As a sergeant of the 6th Cavalry's L Troop in 1893, Fast Dog placed third in the Department of the Platte's cavalry competition, but he was denied one of the prizes because of his race.

The next year, in October 1894, Fast Dog was discharged, two years before his enlistment ended, with his conduct noted as excellent and still without his second class revolver prize. A far cry from the fair reward due Native Americans. It has been reported that during World War II, if all Americans had volunteered at the same rate that American Indians had volunteered, the draft would have been unnecessary.[62]

Army-wide rifle contests provided the most exclusive shooting prizes, and these, besides the department rifle prizes, were the only nineteenth-century-designed prizes to be awarded in the twentieth century. The first prize, D-25, is a gold planchet very similar to the original army marksmanship prize. The front of this revised design simply eliminates the stars near the edge between **FIRST PRIZE** and **ARMY MARKSMANSHIP**. The reverse includes not only the usual wreath, but also an inner circle of dots just inside the wreath, a distinction used only on this award. The brooch is of the same design previously used on army prizes, the upper half of a sunburst outline above the word **ARMY**, except for a 1902 change to a brooch with a square target within a wreath, all on a horizontal bar.

Two army-level first prizes were awarded each year in 1890, 1891, 1892, 1893, 1894, and 1897, one to the rifle (infantry) champion and the other to the carbine (cavalry) champion. In the first year of the award, 1890, Captain J. B. Kerr of the 6th Cavalry had the highest score, but he was already a distinguished marksman and was not eligible to receive the prize. As a result Corporal J. C. Thornton, A Troop, 6th Cavalry, who had the second highest score, received the first prize medal, leaving the two second class prizes of 1890, D-6, to the 6th Cavalry's blacksmith, A. Keiser, and the 5th Cavalry's Captain W. P. Hall.[63]

The final use of the gold army first prize occurred in 1902, when matches resumed after the Spanish-American War. For this infantry-only contest, the army made the unlikely return to the 1889–94 scheme: gold for first and second class prizes. The change back to gold for second class prizes was evidently to compensate for the increased number of soldiers resulting from the army expansion of 1901. The sole first prize awarded in 1902, D-25, went to the 18th Infantry's artificer, P. Savage, who had a score of 629.

The second class prizes used between 1889 and 1902 were unchanged from the 1882–86 versions (D-6). Normally, the army gave six of these gold prizes each year in this second period, for second, third, and fourth place in the infantry and in the carbine contests. For 1897 only, the mint struck six prizes in silver in an attempt to save some of the army's money. For the 1902 match, however, the 1889–94 scheme returned, with D-6 in gold. In 1902 only three prizes were made, since the cavalry did not shoot. These last winners of the army gold second class prizes were First Sergeant A. Deuberry, 22d Infantry, with 611; Private F. Weik, 20th Infantry, also with a score of 611; and First Sergeant J. Rauhuff, of the Puerto Rico Regiment of Infantry, with a score of 568.[64]

Third class army-level prizes changed after the 1888 army matches. The new vignette, D-26, shows a helmeted Pallas Athena looking left and is generally similar to D-4, a

Fig. 6.38

Fig. 6.37

Fig. 6.37. D-25 is nearly identical to D-5 except for the exclusion of two stars, one just below each of the eagle's wing tips. The mint made only thirteen of these gold prizes.

Fig. 6.38. The reverse of D-25. The row of dots outside the wreath is unique to this prize.

division third class rifle prize. The most obvious change is the omission of the earlier wreath. The wording around the edge of this new Athena is **THIRD CLASS PRIZE ★ ARMY MARKSMANSHIP ★**. Between 1889 and 1902 soldiers placing fifth through tenth in the army-rifle and army-carbine contests received this award, which is 1 3/4 inches in diameter. Initially the army gave the top twelve shooters prizes, but it switched to awarding only the top ten places in 1889, while simultaneously dividing the contests into rifle and carbine matches, which actually resulted in twenty prizes rather than the earlier dozen. The army gave twelve third class silver prizes (six for rifle and six for carbine) each year in 1889, 1891, 1892, 1893, 1894, and 1897 and six in 1902 for the rifle contest.

The brooch changed over time. In the nineteenth century it was a half-halo of rays with **ARMY** below. For 1902 the brooch changed to a square target with a wreath on a narrow horizontal bar. Evidently this change was made because the cavalry did not compete, and it was not truly an army-wide event. One nineteenth-century sketch shows this brooch, so it may have appeared earlier.

The unequivocal pinnacle of U.S. Army shooting prizes occurred during 1880–97.

Once the toast of the American army, these gold, silver, and bronze prizes, which come in twenty-six different designs, now rest in obscurity mainly in army museums and in private collections. As a class they are unrivaled in beauty. Except for the Legion of Merit and the Purple Heart medals, some of these prizes are the only U.S. Army awards that can compete with many European orders and decorations in terms of composition and grace. It is unfortunate they are so little known.

Fig. 6.39. The third class army prize, D-26, as awarded in the nineteenth century. A modification of the earlier third class division prize (D-4) but without the wreath; this army-level prize was also distinguished by its brooch, a stylized half sun, usually with **ARMY** on the bar.

Fig. 6.40. D-26, as awarded in 1902. This brooch was used several times, including 1902, when the army hosted only infantry matches.

Fig. 6.40

Fig. 6.39

CHAPTER SEVEN

PRIZES, 1903–1922

THE TRANSITION TO SMALLER PRIZES

THE SINKING OF THE battleship *Maine*, the battle of San Juan Hill, the Philippine insurrection, and many other well-known happenings rudely interrupted the army's carefully crafted marksmanship program. Division and department contests just reinstituted in 1897 remained suspended for four years until August 1902, when the army again held department and division infantry competitions at Fort Sheridan, Illinois. This early twentieth-century resurgence of national-level tournaments was but one indication of a strong determination by staff officers in Washington to renew the soldiers' interest in being marksmen. The new Model 1903 Springfield rifle, the introduction in 1904 of the expert rifleman rating, and congressional action to create the National Trophy (discussed in chapter 10) are further examples of this revival nearly a quarter of a century after the rise of the army's first true interest in shooting.[1]

The 1902 infantry match was the last gasp of the large, rich nineteenth-century ornate prizes, since in 1903, the replacement awards took on a totally new look. The 1903 prizes became significantly smaller than the Brobdingnagian versions awarded since 1881, and these new twentieth-century prizes had as their dominate feature an enameled target— the hallmark of army prizes until after World War I. Near the end of 1902 the adjutant general convened a board and noted, "At present large, heavy and costly medals are given. Such medals are handsomer that medals given for distinguished conduct in action." Then he unveiled an ambitious plan by stating that the new prizes would "cost less than the [prizes] now given, be more appreciated by the recipients, and be in every way more suitable," although one must wonder how a smaller, stylized gold medal would be more appreciated than a large, artistic one.[2]

The army halted shooting tournaments and marksmanship training in general during the Spanish-American War, and the War Department did not revive matches until 1902. As Lieutenant Colonel James Parker, senior officer on the board that revised the army firing regulations in 1903, wrote, "From 1898 to 1901, inclusive, the demands of the service precluded the prosecution of systematic target practice, but in 1902 it was resumed, and soon developed the fact that the changed conditions demanded a revision of the existing regulations."[3]

In 1903 the U.S. Army, now intensely interested in marksmanship, fully restored competitive shooting by presenting the full offering of contests: infantry (rifle), cavalry (carbine), and pistol. For these the army provided new prize designs that lasted into the early 1920s, and in a few cases into the Great Depression. The War Department's revised prizes took on a totally new look. The prizes became significantly smaller than the earlier huge awards, and these new twentieth-century bangles were eminently sensible in that they were not ostentatious, while they were still made in three metals to distinguish the level of a shooter's placement.

From 1903 to 1910 the army lavished many rewards and much attention upon its soldiers solely for the skill of shooting. The 1880–94 and the 1920–30 periods vie for second place in their attention to shooting, but clearly the 1903 army staff attacked marksmanship training with enormous renewed energy. The military leadership achieved their goal in a multiplicity of ways, using increased ammunition and ranges, incentive pay, new badges, and—the topic of this chapter—new prizes.

The 1903 prizes have two physical parts— the brooch and the planchet. Brooches for

Fig. 7.1. Sergeant Jessie Baker, H Troop, 10th Cavalry, 1904. Baker wears a bronze prize he received for placing twelfth in the Northern Division cavalry match, held at Fort Riley, Kansas, that summer. It was not too unusual to be only a sharpshooter rather than an expert and still win a department prize, since in 1903 only one member of the entire 10th Cavalry qualified as expert, whereas twenty-four men reached the grade of sharpshooter.

long-arm prizes had special wording and, especially after 1907, this wording often changed for each shooting match, varying considerably by year. In many years after 1910, the army held no tournaments due to emergency deployments related to Mexico. Throughout the 1903–22 time frame some select departments or divisions held matches only for a specific year or two. In Cuba, for example, the army held matches only in 1908. To complicate identification of these prizes, the shape of the brooches for rifle and carbine prizes varied, with rounded arrowhead ends used initially and then swallowtail ends used later. Pistol prizes generally followed the same conventions for the frequently changing brooch inscription, even though the brooch always had swallowtail ends.[4]

The planchets vary with the type of competition and the date when the army gave prizes. Overall, planchets fall into four styles: cavalry team, infantry team, rifle, and pistol. Between 1903 and 1906 teams dominated the rifle and carbine competitions. In 1907 the emphasis returned to individual competition in the division and army matches, although in that year the army issued some of the older planchets, marking it as a transition year. Changes had occurred in the army's awards ever since the initial winning of prizes in 1880,

and the 1903 and 1906–7 awards were no exception.

BROOCHES AND YEARS OF USE

The top bar, the brooches for the 1903-style prizes, carried specific wording that frequently changed from year to year. When we examine brooches for these prizes, we encounter enormous complexity. The many brooch modifications were due to the constant refining of the administrative divisions and departments throughout the army. The War Department vacillated, sometimes dividing the United States into three or four geographic divisions and at other times doing without these intermediate headquarters, which were seen by some people as places that simply shuffled papers. Two or more geographic departments— the smallest administrative sections—comprised a geographic division until 1913, but these departments continually changed titles and boundaries. Frequently the annual round of matches started with department competitions, the winners advancing to the division level, but in 1903, rather than the intermediate division competition, the army held departmental competitions. Those shooters with sufficiently high scores went directly to the army match. The War Department usually awarded prizes at the department, division, and army levels, although at times when divisions did not exist the military created equivalent-level intermediate contests known as combined-department matches. The endless forming and reforming of these organizations during this time affected the rewards given to the skillful shooters.[5]

The 1903 brooch design had wording that at first blush would appear to indicate the level— **ARMY** or **DEPARTMENT**— with **DEPARTMENT** showing either bi-department or single department matches, as directed by Washington. In 1903 the army announced the reorganization of continental divisions that would take effect in 1904, and this pending reorganization evidently influenced the brooches for 1903. The new divisions were Atlantic, Northern, Pacific, and Southwestern. The army faced a dilemma for combined department competitions: any inscribed brooch would be used only in 1903.

Fig. 7.1

A few surviving prizes from the 1903 competitions and documents from the time paint a picture that is not yet clear, and it is certainly possible that the army used a range of brooches bearing various titles. For the one tri-department pistol competition, the army used a brooch bearing the front inscription **ARMY**, with **TRI-DEPARTMENT** engraved on the reverse. These 1903 and 1904 matches generally marked a return to annually held small-arms competitions, replacing the bi- or tri-department matches that had been instituted in 1889.

The transition from the nineteenth-century prize scheme to that of the twentieth-century continued in 1904, when the brooches changed further. At the division level the number of gold, silver, and bronze medals varied depending upon the number of participants, while at the army level the top four winners received gold medals and the next eight, silver. Regardless of the color of the medal, the brooch showed one of the two competitions. The highest level—the army—was always embossed **ARMY**, while the lower levels, division and/or department, had many other inscriptions.

Brooches for the new twentieth-century prizes came in two shapes. For rifle and carbine competitions army prizes are suspended on top bars bearing the word **ARMY** on a brooch with rounded arrowhead-shaped ends. The 1903 long-arms department prizes also had top bars with rounded ends, but they bore the word **DEPARTMENT**; while starting in 1904 the brooches for the lesser matches were inscribed **DIVISION**. This "army" and "division" scheme was fully in effect for the years 1904, 1905, and 1906. In 1907 most division prizes for rifle matches included ribbon-shaped brooches with swallowtail ends embossed with the division name, although in the Philippine Islands the brooch continued to carry **DIVISION** through 1911. Pistol-competition brooches throughout 1903–21 were of the swallowtail ribbon design.

In another vain attempt to save funds, the War Department abolished territorial divisions effective June 30, 1907, but for the

Fig. 7.2

Fig. 7.3

Fig. 7.4

Fig. 7.5

Fig. 7.2. *A typical long-arm shooting prize of the general style introduced in 1903. Prizes came in gold, silver, and bronze, with the central target enameled in black and white. Brooches for these early rifle and carbine prizes are distinguished by their rounded arrowhead ends, whether inscribed* **ARMY**, **DIVISION**, *or* **DEPARTMENT**.

Fig. 7.3. *Starting in 1907, brooches for long-arm prizes began to have swallowtail-end brooches of this design. Pistol prizes always had this style of brooch. The name of the division began to appear on the brooch in 1907, as in this example from the Western Division.*

Fig. 7.4. *In the Philippine Islands the older brooches, embossed* **DIVISION**, *continued to be used until 1911.*

Fig. 7.5. *Prizes for the 1903 tri-department pistol match had the front of the brooch impressed with* **ARMY** *while the reverse was engraved* **TRI-DEPARTMENT**, *presumably as a way to avoid making new brooches with the proper front markings, since an army reorganization had already been announced.*

purposes of small-arms competitions the United States continued to be divided into four combined departmental regions around which the War Department held shooting matches. The shuffling left the nine departments that had previously been grouped into four divisions to report directly to army headquarters. The 1907 shooting tournaments went on as they had previously, and the military awarded prizes with brooches impressed with **DIVISION**, but by the latter part of 1907 the army brass had decided to rename the competitions "combined department." Thus the army created brooches bearing the titles of the old divisions that represented the combined departments: Atlantic, Northern, Pacific, and Southwestern. Since the Philippine Division remained intact, for contests in the islands the brooches continued to bear the wording **DIVISION** as before. This remained in effect for 1908 and 1909.[6]

American forces ended their occupation of Cuba in 1902, but the new government could not keep peace. As a temporary measure, in October 1906 the army intervened to maintain law and order and thus established the Army of Cuban Pacification as an additional command. By 1908 army headquarters in Washington treated the force in Cuba as a division, and in that year allowed forces in Cuba to conduct their own shooting competition at the division or "combined department" level. As a result, for 1908 only, prizes included some with ribbon brooches bearing **CUBAN**. The lone Cuban match was held at Camaguey in May 1908 "with very satisfactory results." Some keen-eyed shooters from Cuba went on to the army rifle match, where one enlisted man won a gold prize and another a silver, while four officers won gold rifle prizes and then three officers won gold pistol prizes. As troops began to withdraw in early January 1909, the War Department terminated even routine small-arms practice in Cuba.[7]

New firing regulations took effect in 1909, and these vaguely called for matches in alternate years. Accordingly, the secretary of war decreed that the matches would occur in odd-numbered years, thus negating the need for competitions in 1910, 1912, and 1914. After 1910 the matches rapidly dwindled. In 1911 the secretary of war canceled the matches in the continental United States because of problems in Mexico. Many troops had temporarily moved to southern Texas and southern California because of the unrest, causing matches to be held only in the Philippine Division.[8]

Also in 1911, the army reinstituted geographical divisions and changed some of the subordinate departments that reported to the divisions. Later that year, for the first time, the War Department designated Hawaii as a department in still another adjustment. Complicating the situation was the initial mobilization of the U.S. Army for the first time since the Spanish-American War. Mexican instability caused President Taft to call for a "maneuver division" to be mobilized in south Texas in 1911, even though the army had no tables of organization for a division. Again, in 1913, the army activated the new 2d Infantry Division in Texas to protect the southern border. These actions caused the various matches hosted by geographic divisions to play second fiddle to real soldiering.[9]

By this time details of Rock Island Arsenal's prizes had changed, although the grand vision survived. Generally, the prizes employed a ribbon-shaped brooch with the title of the generic geographic section on the brooch, be it a "geographic division" or a "combined department." As the military held few competitions in 1911 and 1913, prizes that were common in the first decade of the century were now awarded less frequently. The names of the geographical partitions used by the army also became less important, so when the army set up the Western Division in 1911 and then dissolved it in 1913, it continued to provide brooches bearing **WESTERN** for the "Western combined department." Table 13 summarizes the inscriptions on division and combined-department ribbon-style brooches and their years of use.

After 1913 department competitions became even more irregular, in part because the President mobilized many troops due to continued unrest in Mexico. Over three thousand men went ashore at Vera Cruz. As a consequence geographic-division matches suffered during this immediate pre–World War I period, and the 1913 contests were the last until 1919. The 1913 army matches, held at Fort Niagara, New York, included fifty-seven enlisted and three commissioned competitors in the rifle contest and resulted in four gold and eight army silver prizes, as had been the practice since 1904. No commissioned officers won. The 1913 army revolver match provided a hefty four enlisted and three commissioned gold prizes and eight enlisted and three

Table 13. *Division or Combined Department Rifle Prizes (ribbon-shaped brooches)*

Brooch Inscription	Match Years	Notes
AUTO RIFLE	1919	Used only for AEF BAR match.
·A·E·F·	1919	Stands for American Expeditionary Forces.
·A·F·G·	1920–21	Stand for American Forces in Germany.
ATLANTIC	1907–9	
CUBAN	1908	
DIVISION	1906	Used in continental United States only.
	1907	Used in United States and in Philippines.
	1908–9 & 1911	Used in Philippines only.
EASTERN	1913	
HAWAIIAN	1920–27	
NORTHERN	1907–9	
PACIFIC	1907–9	
PHILIPPINES	1913, 1915–16, 1920–22	
SOUTHERN	1913	
SOUTHWESTERN	1907–9	
WESTERN	1913	
8TH CORPS AREA	1921	

commissioned silver prizes. As will be seen, officers did not directly compete with enlisted men; thus, the officers' medals were over and above those reserved for enlisted soldiers. The Central, Hawaiian, and Philippine Departments did not hold competitions in 1913, leaving only the Eastern, Western, and Southern Department soldiers as prizewinners.[10]

In an old story, the Mexican border troubles caused cancellation of all division matches for 1915. Deployment of troops along the Mexican border for this prolonged period naturally atrophied the army-wide competitive élan that had developed from 1902 through 1911. Despite the inability of the army to host matches, in 1915 the bureaucracy published changes that allowed Signal Corps Aero Squadrons and field and telegraph company members to compete, along with other enlisted men selected by battalion or regimental commanders. The world war interfered with the matches in 1917 and 1919, although after the war's conclusion the AEF held the army's largest shooting contest in 1919. It would be 1921 before

Table 14. *Infantry Competitions below Army Level, 1903–1906 (brooches with round arrowhead ends)*

Brooch Inscription	Match Years	Competitions
DEPARTMENT	1903	Lakes and Dakota★
		Colorado and Texas★
		East
		California
		Columbia
		Missouri
DEPARTMENT	1904	Visayas
		Mindanao
		Luzon
DIVISION	1904	Atlantic
		Northern
		Pacific
		Southwestern
DIVISION	1905	Atlantic
		Northern
		Pacific
		Southwestern
		Philippines
DIVISION	1906	Atlantic
		Northern
		Pacific
		Southwestern
		Philippines

★ Designated "combined departments" competitions by War Department.

Table 15. *Cavalry Competitions below Army Level, 1903–1906 (brooches with round arrowhead ends)*

Brooch Inscription	Match Years	Competitions
DEPARTMENT	1903	Lakes and Dakota★
		Missouri and Texas★
		East
		California, Columbia, and Colorado
DEPARTMENT	1904	Mindanao and Luzon★
DIVISION	1904	Atlantic
		Northern
		Pacific
		Southwestern
DIVISION	1905	Atlantic
		Northern
		Pacific
		Southwestern
		Philippines
DIVISION	1906	Philippines

★ Designated "combined departments" competitions by War Department.

Table 16. *Pistol Competitions below Army Level, 1903–1906 (ribbon-shaped brooches with swallowtail ends)*

Brooch Inscription	Match Years	Competitions
DEPARTMENT	1903	Missouri and Texas★
		East
ARMY (Has **TRI-DEPARTMENT** engraved on reverse.)	1903	California, Columbia, and Colorado★
DEPARTMENT	1904	Luzon, Mindanao, and Visayas★
DIVISION	1904	Atlantic
		Northern
		Pacific
		Southwestern
DIVISION	1905	Atlantic
		Northern
		Pacific
		Southwestern
		Philippines
DIVISION	1906	Atlantic
		Northern
		Pacific
		Southwestern
		Philippines

★ Designated "combined departments" competitions by War Department.

the War Department would really have department- or division-level matches back on track and 1923 before the next army competition.[11]

LONG-ARMS PRIZES, 1903–1922

In general a planchet for a 1903–5 long-arms prize displays the letters and central dots •U•S• immediately below the target and the curved words **INFANTRY** or **CAVALRY** near the top face in the wreath's opening. Weapons displayed on the front change to match the top inscription—rifles with bayonets on an infantry prize and plain carbines for the cavalry. Figures 7.6 and 7.7 show the two general types of long-arms planchets given at competitions between 1903 and 1907. The reverse has a nearly closed laurel wreath near the raised edge, with the center of the disk blank, so that the winner's name, unit, and year could be engraved. Made in gold, silver, and bronze, these prizes still carried on the concept of branch teams: cavalrymen fired only with carbines, while others, including artillery and engineers, showed "infantry" rifles.

For army contests the disks were 1 1/4 inches in diameter, while the department and division competition had 1-inch-diameter prizes. The brooches were sized accordingly and bore the words **ARMY**, **DEPARTMENT**, **DIVISION** or other appropriate impressions, as already discussed. All prizes were made in one of three metals—gold, silver, or bronze—and, as will be seen, design detailed varied. The War Department held competitions and awarded prizes at the army level in 1903 and at division and department levels as shown in tables 14–16. Division prize designs were similar to the army versions but were simply 1 inch in diameter. In 1907 the War Department replaced these awards, used in 1904–6, but during 1906, in at least one case, the army awarded the new design. The stocks of prizes already made played into this overlap.

The Philippines Division held a cavalry tournament between January 3 and January 11, 1906 and was the only division to do so that year. It presented one gold, three silver, and eight bronze medals for the cavalry competition, while top Philippine infantry contestants (in one of several infantry matches in 1906) received three gold, seven silver, and nineteen bronze prizes. The unusually large number of competitors resulted from the Philippine Division commander's hosting them one week before the division athletic military meet. The event was so well attended that a program containing all of the contestants was even printed, and the adjutant reported with some pride that during the skirmish firing, men threw themselves to the ground "as in actual combat or in hunting game."[12]

By 1907 matches that awarded prizes bearing **CAVALRY** or **INFANTRY** on the planchet came to an end, except for some use of surplus planchets in the 1920s that the army pressed into service when appropriations were sparse.

In February 1906 the Ordnance Department, anticipating the introduction of the M 1903 magazine rifle to both the infantry and the cavalry, began to design a single new prize that constituted the third long-arm design. Displaying the same overall concept as before, the March 1906 design changed in some of its details. Branch designations of cavalry or infantry disappeared, allowing the letters **U.S.**

Fig. 7.6

Fig. 7.7 *Fig. 7.8*

Fig. 7.6. Besides being marked **INFANTRY** in the upper quadrant, infantry planchets from 1903–6/7 show crossed M 1903 rifles with bayonets attached.

Fig. 7.7. Cavalry planchets for the 1903–6/7 period display crossed carbines, **CAVALRY** above the black-and-white enameled target, and the marking •U•S• below.

Fig. 7.8. Army-level long-arm prizes are 1 1/4 inches in diameter, while division and department prizes for both cavalry and infantry matches are 1 inch wide, 1903–6. Brooches are similarly scaled.

Fig. 7.9. In 1907 planchets for all long-arm matches changed to a universal design. The 1907 design (used in a few instances in 1906) is shown on the left, with the **U.S.** above the enameled target, while a typical earlier design is shown on the right. The 1907 planchet also displays rifles with slightly loosened slings, without bayonets. This general design lasted until after World War I.

Fig. 7.10. Prizes given in the 1903–15 period were handsomely engraved. This example awarded to Sergeant David Sulway, Company L, 10th Infantry, has the award year, 1907, hand engraved on the reverse, in addition to several artistic swirls and decorative lines.

Fig. 7.11. An all-bronze prize awarded to Captain R. E. Willis, 6th Illinois Infantry. Willis was a member of the regiment's rifle team from 1911 through 1915; the team placed in state competitions in 1913 and 1915, as shown by the bars.

to be enlarged (this time with periods) and placed squarely above the enameled target. The two weapons became bolt-action M 1903 rifles without bayonets and with slightly loosened slings. These prizes came in gold and in silver for army level, with the same reverse as before. Shown in figure 7.9 are two army-level prizes, pre- and post-1906, side-by-side for comparison. Both are 1 ¹/₄ inches in diameter. The style of the letters used on the brooches is also slightly different. Many of these 1906 designs (most were actually first issued in 1907) are slightly thicker overall than the 1903 prizes, allowing parts of the wreath and the front design to extend above the newer prizes' rims.[13]

The reverse of a 1907 prize, shown in figure 7.10, is characteristic of the 1903–22 prizes, with a raised, nearly full wreath. The open area was typically engraved in beautiful fashion with rank, name, unit, and year of award. The army awarded the silver prize shown to Sergeant David Sulway, Company L, 10th

Infantry, in 1907. The obverse of the award is in figure 7.9.

In contrast to army prizes, division prizes became significantly more diverse with the March 1906 change. Planchets, enlarged to 1 ¹/₈ inches in diameter, had the same design as the army prizes, but the top brooches varied widely, and it is this feature that further set these prizes apart. Beginning in 1906 some division brooches were made of a design previously used only on pistol prizes—that of a ribbon folded back under itself on either side of the appropriate inscription, with swallowtail ends. After 1907 the army always used this style brooch with the new planchet form.

The general Federal design with crossed rifles, bayonets attached and behind a target, became a popular motif with several National Guards. New Hampshire and Illinois, for example, adopted these 1 ¹/₄-inch-diameter planchets, suspended from arrowhead-ended brooches, for state prizes. Such state awards did not bear the letters U.S. and were often, but not always, without enamel. In the case of Illinois the top bar indicated the team member's regiment; for winning years, a bar was inserted between the brooch and the planchet.

Fig. 7.9

Fig. 7.10

Fig. 7.11

PISTOL PRIZES, 1903–1922

Sergeant Bent Howe of the 8th Cavalry Regiment was the army's best pistol shot in 1903. A member of E Troop for many years, Howe won the first-place revolver gold prize while representing the Department of the Missouri and immediately reenlisted as a sergeant in M Troop, then went to the army competition, where he won an army-level gold medal.[14]

Revolver prizes, 1 inch in diameter, came in gold, silver, and bronze for department, division, and combined departmental matches and in 1 $^1/_8$-inch-diameter gold and silver versions for army competitions and the 1903 tri-department, with the special engraving on the brooch reverse. After World War I all of the pistol prizes came in the larger diameter. For prizes given in the American Expeditionary Forces' 1919 contest and for the American Forces in Germany (the post–World War I occupation force) matches, the pistol prizes were also 1 $^1/_8$ inches in diameter. This meant that the surplus larger pistol planchets used in the 1920s in Hawaii and the Philippines were the same size as the rifle versions. In some revolver contests the winners of gold prizes received the option to select "a pistol of special design and superior workmanship, provided with the most improved sights," but it is not known how many men availed themselves of this opportunity, as apparently most soldiers selected the wearable prize.[15]

Central to the revolver-match prize design is a white-enameled rectangular target with circular black rings. The lower half of the planchet displays a partial laurel wreath that covers only the lower outside front of the disk. On the reverse is a full laurel wreath near the edge, leaving the center free for engraving. Ribbon-style brooches with swallowtail ends, the same design as that on the post-1906-style rifle prizes, suspends the planchet from two sets of chains. This brooch design was introduced with the 1903 revolver prizes. Brooch inscription used in the pistol competitions generally parallel the wording in the rifle competitions. These pistol prizes became so popular that the War Department spelled out the limits on those who could compete: In 1908 enlisted competitors were limited to two from each infantry regiment, including the regimental staff and band, one per dismounted engineer battalion, one for each four coast artillery companies, and only one from the various post noncommissioned staffs within a department. Officers had limits such as one from the three engineer battalions, three in total from the field artillery, ten from the coast artillery, and five from all of the staff departments and the General Staff Corps.[16]

Fig. 7.12. A gold 1 $^1/_8$–inch-diameter pistol prize awarded at the army-level match. All pistol prizes given from 1903 through 1922 have a rectangular, enameled target above a half wreath. The planchets are suspended from a swallowtail, double-folded brooch.

Fig. 7.13. For contests in the United States after 1907, the name of the division or combined department was applied to the brooches. This 1-inch-diameter 1903–22 pistol prize typically carries wording on the brooch that shows the geographic division.

Fig. 7.14. Of all the newly formed corps areas, only the 8th Corps Area held matches and provided prizes in 1921.

Fig. 7.13

Fig. 7.12

Fig. 7.14

The reason for the smaller diameter revolver prizes with the unique early ribbon-style brooch is not recorded. It is reasonable to assume smaller pistol prizes resulted from a desire to make the outline more distinguishable from that of the long-arm prizes. The swallowtail ribbon brooch and smaller diameter would make the handgun prize more distinct from the larger long-arms prizes, with their arrowhead brooches (at least early on, until the rifle prizes adopted this style brooch).

For the 1919 AEF pistol competition, planchets grew to the 1 1/8-inch diameter used previously in army matches, making them equal in size to those given for the rifle tournaments. Although the AEF contest was larger than any other pistol match, it was still considerably smaller than that for the rifle. Many officers carried pistols, and therefore a higher percentage won pistol prizes than rifle prizes. A dozen officers earned gold AEF pistol prizes, equaling the number of enlisted men who earned the highest pistol prize.[17]

THE .45 CALIBER M 1911 PISTOL

Originally designed by the well-known weapons expert John Browning, the .45 caliber automatic pistol held a seven-round clip. After extensive testing for several years the Ordnance Department finally adopted the M 1911 .45 caliber pistol and initially ordered over thirty thousand of the weapons. The increased stopping power provided by the new weapon was significantly superior to that of the lighter pistols that proved deficient in the Philippines, but during World War I soldiers encountered minor problems. As a result the army introduced the improved

The M 1911 automatic pistol, which replaced numerous army revolvers. The pistol was developed as a result of the Philippine insurrection, when soldiers needed increased short-range stopping power.

M 1911A1 version in 1922. Changes included a shortened trigger, a modified butt to better fit a person's hand, and other lesser modifications.

The M 1911A1 pistol, introduced in 1922, had a grip that was contoured to fit the hand better and a trigger with reduced pull. The U.S. Army issued these pistols into the 1980s.

The 9mm, M-9 pistol, which replaced the long-used M 1911 and M 1911A1 .45 caliber pistols.

The famous .45 caliber automatic pistol replaced a wide range of revolvers used during the Spanish-American War. During World War I the army again issued a great variety of handguns, but by World War II the M 1911A1 pistol was the common U.S. Army pistol. The army used it as the standard during World War II, the Korean War, and the war in Vietnam and ultimately purchased over 2 million of the weapons. The M 1911A1 lasted over seventy years, until it was replaced in the mid-1980s by the NATO standard 9 mm Beretta pistol, known as the U.S. M-9 Pistol.

Officers usually carried pistols, as did some NCOs and many horse-mounted soldiers. With mechanization in the 1930s, many vehicle crewmen carried M 1911A1 pistols.

Numerous versions of the M 1911 .45 pistol exist, including special models with a shorter barrel for general officers.

In national matches at Camp Perry between the world wars many shooters did not use the M 1911A1 except in the required military matches, preferring to use various revolvers, a practice that drew comments regarding its accuracy from some observers. The army's initial interest in national pistol matches rested primarily with the cavalry, but during the Great Depression other branches fielded teams, and overall interest in pistol competition grew. In 1937 the U.S. Infantry team edged out the U.S. Marines, although both were behind the cavalry team.[18]

Table 17. *Pistol Competitions, 1903–1920s: Awarding Organizations and Years (ribbon-shaped brooches with swallowtail ends)*

Brooch Inscription	Years Used	Notes
·A·E·F·	1919	Stands for American Expeditionary Forces.
·A·F·G·	1920–21	Stands for American Forces in Germany.
ARMY	1903–9	
ATLANTIC	1908–9	
CUBAN	1908	
DEPARTMENT	1903–4	1904, used in Philippines only.
DIVISION	1904–6	Used by all divisions through 1906.
DIVISION	1907–9, 1911	Used only in Philippines.
EASTERN	1913	
HAWAIIAN	1913, 1920–27	Perhaps used 1928 and later.
NORTHERN	1907–9	
PACIFIC	1907–9	
PHILIPPINES	1913, 1915–16, 1920–22	Also used in 1920s, until some stocks exhausted.
SOUTHERN	1913	
SOUTHWESTERN	1907–9	
WESTERN	1913	
8TH CORPS AREA	1921	

No Matches: 1910, 1912, 1914, 1916, 1917, 1918.
Only 1911 and 1915 competitions were in the Philippines.
Only 1919 competition was by AEF in France.

POST-1922 USE

Throughout the 1920s the army used some of the remaining early 1-inch bronze planchets with bayoneted rifles, along with appropriate leftover brooches, to make prizes for Hawaii and the Philippines. After initiation of the 1922-style prizes, the army continued to issue the 1903-style pistol prizes for the Philippines and Hawaii in both 1- and 1 ¹/₈-inch sizes, since brooches for the two organizations existed and remained in stock. Army price lists called for the use of these old badges through 1930.[19]

For most of 1920, 1921, and 1922 the army had no prizes with appropriate brooches, as Congress had just introduced the corps-area concept in June 1920. During these three years in the continental United States only the 8th Corps★ awarded prizes and then just in 1921. After initially making the 1922-designed prizes in 1923, the army retroactively issued them for the 1920–22 matches and for some other earlier contests.

SPECIAL AEF PRIZES

Starting in 1914 and 1915 the army's marksmanship training program was in truth a pawn to Mars. The methodical and structured effort developed between 1903 and 1912 could only

★Starting in World War I the U.S. Army expressed tactical corps in roman numerals, and this practice continues today. Between the world wars congress and the army divided the United States into nine geographic areas and assigned a corps to each of these areas. While the tactical corps itself was designated in roman numerals, the corps geographic area was designated with an arabic numeral. Thus the army assigned the VIII Corps to the 8th Corps area. The 1921 prize with **8th CORPS AREA** reflects this practice.

Fig. 7.15

Fig. 7.15. *The Hawaiian Department is
the one corps area or department that
awarded the 1903-style prizes annually
for several years after 1922, giving
them through 1927.*

be redeemed by a Herculean effort. John J. Pershing was the one officer who had the personal background (he had taken extra time in 1891 to train for matches) and who understood the need for rigorous individual and small unit training (he was promoted from captain to brigadier general in 1906).

Three months after the world war's end, in early February 1919, the American Expeditionary Forces' commanding general and old distinguished marksman, John J. Pershing, directed that the AEF hold rifle and pistol competitions the coming May. Pershing, a soldier with a shooter's enthusiasm for excellence, began not only a project to help keep the troops busy but a vigorous training program right out of the peacetime army's book. As a result the world's largest rifle matches were held near LeMans. Initially, the AEF's general headquarters listed three competitions—rifle, pistol, and revolver, and a special musketry match. By early April they added two other matches, an automatic rifle competition and a machine gun match. To support the competition, Pershing even had the AEF print its own two-volume version of a small-arms firing manual in April 1919, a most interesting development that shows Pershing's push for training. Instructional drawings in the manual show doughboys wearing the overseas cap or British-style trench helmets, usually firing the Enfield rifle. Even during wartime training and combat in France, the AEF did not print its own manual.[20]

The largest weapons competitions ever held by the U.S. Army took place at D'Auvours Rifle Range between May 5 and 20, 1919, under the control of Colonel A. J. Macnab, an infantryman who had seen service since the Spanish-American War. The AEF provided special prizes for automatic rifle, musketry, and machine gun contests. Platoons competed in the musketry and machine gun matches and each member of the winning unit received a prize similar to those given for rifle and pistol.[21]

AEF rifle and pistol prizes, engraved in France using simple block-style letters, (which, when compared to the prewar flowing script, appear rather crude), included elementary unit abbreviations and no award date. This made the rifle and pistol prizes noticeably different from those awarded before the war. The three special AEF prizes (musketry, automatic rifle, and machine gun), by contrast, had to be designed and two of them had to be struck. Presentation of these specially struck prizes actually occurred in the fall of 1920. As a consequence, the unique musketry and machine gun AEF prizes have the usually flowing-script engraving done in the United States.

The AEF headquarters scheduled the matches just prior to its major 1919 athletic competition—another activity to keep the troops busy. As units departed to return to the United States, those individuals selected for participation in the shooting and athletic meets were allowed to stay until the end of the events if the soldiers desired to do so. All winners in these feats of skill received a large, handsome medal, the front showing a soldier in an athletic T-shirt and shorts, at attention and saluting, a pack and helmet at his feet. The reverse displays the upper portion of the Statue of Liberty and stylized waves across the bottom, leaving room to engrave the name of the event won. Some men added a ring and suspended the medals from red, white, and blue neck ribbons but most left theirs in table-medal format, that is, without any suspending device.

The U.S. Army's first automatic rifle competition was lightly attended. U.S. Marine Corps Private F. Kramer of the U.S. Army's 2d Division, which included Kramer's 6th Marine Regiment, won the only gold medal. Two army men took silver prizes and five infantrymen won bronze. Prizes awarded for the match were simple modifications of the rifle versions. The planchets were of the standard rifle variety with the brooch engraved **AUTO RIFLE**.[22]

The significance of this match was not the thin participation but the fact that an automatic rifle contest even took place. After all, this was the introduction of a new individual weapon into competitive shooting. The initial automatic rifle contest consisted simply of

Fig. 7.16a

Fig. 7.16b

Fig. 7.17

Fig. 7.16a and b. The U.S. Army's American Expeditionary Forces in France held athletic and marksmanship contests in the late spring of 1919. Winners received table medals of this style.

Fig. 7.17. An example of the rare automatic rifle prize, given only in 1919. Corporal Guy Sparger won this particular award, one of five bronze, two silver, and one gold presented personally by General John Pershing in May at the end of the shooting match.

Department–approved prizes for the first two rifle and pistol matches.[24]

Musketry became a World War I term for "teamwork in the conduct of fire," coming from the army's School of Musketry at Fort Sill, Oklahoma. For 1919 musketry competitions, the platoons that were ready to enter knew precious few details of their match. Only one prior announcement provided a hint, and that was that the competition would to be in the form of an attack, with the platoon's advance to depend entirely upon its own fire in an assigned sector. The formation adopted, the estimate of the tactical situation as shown by the dispositions, the application of firepower, the orders, and the conduct and control of the platoon, all formed a basis for scoring. Platoon members carried the same arms and equipment prescribed in the Infantry Drill Regulations, except that packs were not worn. Pershing's exploratory musketry competition became the basis for the chief of infantry's competition between the world wars and for the National Infantry Trophy, but with the unit size reduced to a squad.[25]

Each division commander held local matches to select one platoon of fifty-eight men and a platoon leader, based on the men assigned to a standard platoon on the date of the AEF invitation order (February 10, 1919). Pershing forbad that any platoon for the competition be comprised of handpicked men from various companies and battalions, insisting that only regular replacements were allowed if vacancies existed on the February date. Eleven divisions sent platoons to compete.[26]

four one-minute firings, each curiously without any limits on ammunition; two firings at 300 yards; and two at 500 yards. At each range one firing was at a target in the open and one at a target concealed by brush, all without any rest for the weapon and with the shooter in the prone position. This simple yet crucial act set the stage for BAR competition at the corps level during the approximately twenty-year inter-world-war period and the decade that saw an automatic rifle distinguished badge.[23]

The U.S. occupation troops, the American Forces in Germany (AFG), held matches in 1920, 1921, and 1922 but awarded a silver cup for first place and a bronze shield for second for all events except rifle and pistol competition, thus not perpetuating the 1919 designs. The AFG did provide War

*Fig. 7.18. General Pershing directed that a platoon musketry contest be held at the 1919 matches. The contest really measured how well a platoon could fire in the attack. All members of the winning platoon received prizes of this kind. Besides the placement of the words **PLATOON** and **US**, the wreath was slightly different from similar wreaths on other 1903–22 prizes. Brooches for the platoon prizes, struck in the United States after the match, also vary from rifle and pistol brooches in some of their details.*

Fig. 7.19. Reverse of the platoon prize shown in figure 7.18. The edge wreath varies from the wreaths used on individual prizes. All engraving was done by hand in this modified block style.

Fig. 7.20. Each American Expeditionary Forces corps was eligible to provide a machine gun platoon for the 1919 marksmanship matches. Winning team members earned bronze prizes.

Awards were generally similar to rifle prizes, with the additions of the word **PLATOON** above the target near the planchet's edge and •U•S• immediately below the target. The ribbon-shaped brooch carried •A•E•F•, like other May 1919 prizes. The Second Platoon, Company L, 310th Infantry Regiment, 78th Division, lead by Second Lieutenant William H. Hitchcock, won the match.[27]

To the casual observer these prizes appear not to have changed other than the wording, but due to the shift in **PLATOON** and •U•S•, the army struck an entirely new prize. Front and back details of the wreaths clearly vary, as does the brooch. The musketry prizes were not available at the time of the competition, the army making these awards in the United States several months after the match. Engraving on the platoon prizes varies considerably from that on the rifle and pistol prizes actually given in France, and all of the platoon prizes have their unique style, as shown in figure 7.19. The adjutant general's office mailed the prizes to the nearly sixty winners in November 1920.[28]

Pershing's headquarters invited one machine gun platoon from each corps to take part in a special match following the platoon musketry contest. This competition consisted of two parts. For indirect fire the machine gun commander was given a map showing the position of his directed gun, the position of two hostile targets, and the position of the reference object. Speed and accuracy in the calculation of the firing data and the preparation of firing charts were measured. The problem was fired and the results examined. Direct fire was

the second task. Scoring consisted of occupation of a position, disposition of personnel and material, quick recognition and designation of targets, rapidity of opening fire, and accuracy of fire.

Five corps entered platoons, and the First Platoon, Company A, 8th Machine Gun Battalion, 3d Division, commanded by First Lieutenant William F. Nimmo, walked away with first place. Forty-six enlisted platoon members each received a prize with the planchet bearing an enameled target in the center, a wreath surrounding the lower $^3/_4$ of the planchet, •U•S• below the target, and **PLATOON** filling in the open wreath from the eleventh- to one-o'clock position. Rather than pairs of rifles or pistols, the prize appropriately bore a single water-cooled machine gun on a tripod.[29]

Fig. 7.19

Fig. 7.18

Fig. 7.20

Gold Team Prizes

Competition for the National Match cavalry and infantry teams started in 1906. The army directed the top fifteen shooters selected for the National Matches to train exclusively for that tournament. This precluded team members from shooting in division and army competitions and from winning prizes in these lower-level contests. Since some of the unsuccessful competitors went from the national team selection contest to division and army matches, won prizes, and thus earned a distinguished shield, the adjutant general ruled that prizewinners in the national team match could count the national prize as one of the three prizes necessary to earn the distinguished designation. This ruling was published in War Department General Orders Number 44 in March 1907, and as a result three officers earned the distinguished designation: Captain Paul Wolf, 4th Infantry, Captain Charles Romeyn, 2d Cavalry, and First Lieutenant George Shaw, 27th Infantry, who had brought this inequity to the attention of the War Department.[30]

In August 1919 the army introduced two new glistening golden prizes and issued them to officers and enlisted men who, since and including 1906, had won a place as a principal or alternate on the infantry or cavalry rifle teams selected to represent the U.S. Army in the National Matches. These 14-karat team medals are 1 1/4 inches in diameter, with a white-and-black enamel target centered over crossed rifles, an edge wreath, and the letters **U.S.** The suspension brooches are 1 1/2 inches long and 3/10 inch wide and are the first army badges with a roll catch. The planchet's reverse shows a full laurel wreath around the edge, with a large, plain center to allow for engraving. These gold prizes were created because by this time soldiers could not wear the bronze National Match medals described in chapter 10 on their uniforms.

The army had provided two teams for the national matches: infantry and cavalry. Accordingly, the brooches are worded **CAVALRY** or **INFANTRY**. In 1920 artillery teams also began to receive these gold team medals with the straight-edged top bars bearing appropriate wording, and in early 1923 a similar special top bar was created for the coast artillery. The known coast artillery prize is struck from a die slightly different from that used

for the infantry, cavalry, and artillery prizes. The army ceased giving these gold team prizes in 1923.[31]

Fig. 7.21

Fig. 7.22a

Fig. 7.22b

Fig. 7.21. In August 1919 the army began to issue gold team prizes, 1 1/4 inches in diameter, to men who had been members of the National Match U.S. Army team since 1906, the first year the army held competitions for membership on the team. Wording on the brooch identified the men as members of the infantry or cavalry teams.

Fig. 7.22a and b. The reverse sides of the gold team prizes display a wide range of engraving styles, since they were issued over several years. These were the first badges issued with a roll catch, which locked the pin to prevent loss of the award.

The army authorized a similar pistol badge in 1922, retroactively to 1920, and all participating National Guard teams received these gold badges in 1923. Gold team badges lasted until early 1923, when the army replaced them with the bronze army prizes of the 1922 design (enamel rings and rectangular brooches).[32]

Also in 1923, the army expanded the number of teams that could earn the bronze badges with enamel rings. Rifle teams came from the infantry, cavalry, coast artillery, engineers, and Philippine scouts. These branches plus those from the field artillery, Air Service, and Signal Corps could field pistol teams. These bronze three-piece army-level prizes with enamel rings replaced the gold team prizes.

Fig. 7.23. Members of the National Match cavalry teams were the only shooters besides the infantry to receive gold team badges for firing between 1906 and 1919. The planchet is identical to that of the infantry prizes, with a black-and-white enameled target. The War Department awarded these prizes until 1923.

Fig. 7.24. In 1920 members of the Artillery National Team began to receive gold team badges, and in early 1923 coast artillery team members started to earn similar prizes. The coast artillery planchets and brooches were struck from slightly different dies, as shown in this example. Similar badges, but with pistols, were authorized in 1923, retroactive to 1920.

Fig. 7.23

Fig. 7.24

CHAPTER EIGHT

PRIZES, 1922 TO THE PRESENT

FROM THE COMMON SOLDIER TO THE ELITE

THE PRIZES OFFERED BETWEEN the world wars promised noticeable recognition for what was then considered a primary soldierly skill. Enlisted men shot their weapons regularly, and the incentive pay, badges, and prizes prompted everyone to do his best. Near the top of the rewards pyramid was the bronze-colored team marksmanship prize, by then officially called a badge. This symbol became widely recognized within the small pre–World War II army. In the 1950s and later, especially after the Vietnam War, the army downplayed the importance of individual weapons and promoted the mechanized, armor-heavy forces that faced the Soviets in Europe. This resulted in individual marksmanship's becoming less critical, with the result that many troops were ignorant of the excellence in competition prizes. Very few soldiers knew of the prizes, and some senior officers could not even recognize the bronze and silver awards worn on the few uniforms of top shooters. The change in training philosophy was decisive. During and after the Vietnam War, except for a few light-infantry troops such as snipers, most ordinary soldiers did not consider prizes to be incentives—they did not even know about the prizes.

As the army resumed its peacetime vigil after the Great War, it boasted of skillful soldiers, some with great marksmanship ability. Following two and a half years of stalemate in Europe and no real progress towards victory, American soldiers joined the fight to make the world safe for democracy. Within 1 $^1/_2$ years American met the great challenge, and the war was over. At war's end the army's competitive-shooting program was in shambles. The army entered the 1920s and returned to peacetime marksmanship competition. The departmental and army contests that had been carefully nourished between 1902 and 1910 had been wracked by the dual problem of the alternative-year plan instituted in 1911 and what turned out to be biannual troop deployments on the Mexican border. Frequent troop movements to and from the American Southwest disrupted small-arms training. The last and largest deployment in 1916 devastated both the annual qualification and the biannual match programs. Although the National Matches continued during World War I, army participation was minimal.

General John J. Pershing provided a fortuitous life-saving event with the massive 1919 AEF contest that had the dual purposes of distracting soldiers who were waiting to go home and initiating a badly needed return to peacetime training. Several confounding factors changed the army rifle and pistol matches when soldiers returned to the United States. Besides the enlarged regular army, military men eligible for shooting contests now included not only the National Guard but also the new reserve forces. Also, as part of the 1920 National Defense Act, Congress directed that the domestic force be administratively divided into nine corps areas rather than the previous divisions and departments. In addition the army created three overseas departments: Hawaii, the Philippines, and the Panama Canal Zone. Further, the Quartermaster Corps took over design, production, and issue of prizes for the reinstituted annual shooting contests.[1]

The post-world war restart of division and department competitions under the new title of corps area competitions noticeably varied. In the Pacific area both the Philippine and Hawaiian Departments held contests in 1920 and 1921. The new 8th Corps area (Texas, Oklahoma, Colorado, New Mexico, and Arizona) also hosted a match in 1921, but most of the new corps areas did not follow suit until

*Fig. 8.1. First Sergeant William L. Bailey of the 21st Infantry Regiment (seated second from left) wears a 1903-style infantry prize (crossed rifles with bayonets and **INFANTRY** on the upper portion of the planchet), which was awarded in 1922 with a **HAWAIIAN** brooch the army first made in 1913. To save money the army mixed parts of older badges and used up remaining stocks during the 1920s.*

Fig. 8.2. In 1920 and 1921 the U.S. occupation forces along the Rhine presented prizes with •A•F•G• (American Forces in Germany) brooches.

Fig. 8.3. American Forces in Germany pistol prizes were 1 1/8 inches in diameter, the size given before World War I only in army-level matches. The Quartermaster Corps also used some of these obsolete, larger pistol planchets in the 1920s to deplete surplus stocks.

the next year or even later. For those U.S.-based 1921 matches, some headquarters gave nothing, while one awarded the 1903-style leg badges with **8TH CORPS AREA** impressed on its brooches. For most 1920–22 matches no prizes were available. In 1923 the army retroactively awarded 1922-style prizes for 1916, 1920, and other "prizeless" matches. Up to a certain point the introduction of new competition prizes after World War I can be dated, but confounding factors inhibit our establishing even a single global year of introduction, although 1922 (the design year) is generally accepted despite the army's back-dating some prizes to 1916.

There are many reasons for multiple introduction dates of the 1922-style prizes. A major consideration was economy. The quartermaster general continued to supply some 1903-style prizes "until exhausted" in 1931. Indeed, even after that year numerous surplus prizes existed that could have been issued, as witnessed by the several examples of unissued gold pre–World War I Philippine rifle prizes that survive in private collections today. Both the Philippine and Hawaiian Departments awarded the older prizes nearly until the depression. As an example, First Sergeant William L. Bailey of the 21st Infantry Regiment, stationed in Hawaii, received a bronze 1903-style rifle prize for a 1922 match, although the design had been replaced in 1906–7. The War Department awarded both large and small 1903-style gold pistol prizes after the creation of the 1922 design, if remaining plan-

Fig. 8.2

Fig. 8.3

chets and brooches with appropriate wording were available. An example is illustrated in figure 7.15 in the preceding chapter.[2]

U.S. forces remained in Germany until early 1923, but Washington, D.C., provided prizes for matches in 1920 and 1921 only, as the occupation force soon became too small to rate national-level recognition.

THE 1922 PRIZES

The so-called 1922 prizes came about as the result of a quartermaster-general-initiated study that attempted to find a badge design in which the "several parts of . . . [the new prizes] . . . are composed [to] lend themselves to a successful re-arrangement to indicate Army, Corps or Department team, rifle or pistol, or Artillery, Cavalry or Infantry team." The study, completed in July 1922, developed the concept for a set of badges that are still worn today, albeit with some modifications. As a result, in September 1922

Fig. 8.1

the army published the concept as if the badges were already available. These 1922-style prizes nicely connect the size and wearability of the previous leg badges with the new versatility desired by the War Department's General Staff.[3]

The resulting prize had three parts. One was a top bar that indicated either army-level or corps/department-level competition and served as a brooch to affix the assembled device to the uniform. The second portion consisted of an intermediate clasp of crossed arms to indicate the weapon used to earn the award (rifle or pistol or, soon thereafter, automatic rifle), while the third, lower piece was a planchet that, if enameled, told the arm or the service. The crossed-weapons clasp was also colored gold, silver, or bronze when it was used with the corps/department badge as a means of showing the shooter's grade. In these competitions the planchet was not enameled but was left a solid bronze.[4]

Top bars/brooches were of two kinds. The army bar—bronze, square ended, and ornamented with oak leaves—was always worn with a bronze clasp and an enameled planchet prior to World War II. The corps area or department brooch had rounded ends and a smooth surface and was worn with a gold, silver, or bronze clasp and a solid bronze planchet. At the center of the corps area bar was a circle bearing a roman numeral (I through IX) to show the area. With some freshness of thought,

the Department bar carried one of three devices. Hawaii had a dolphin, Panama a portcullis, and the Philippines a sea lion.[5]

The American Indian motif, which was popular on the large gold and silver prizes given in the competition of distinguished marksmen (1887–94), pervades the 1922-pattern badges. The central design is a bow and a pair of arrows. The pendant (planchet) consists of three concentric designs. The inner circle,

Fig. 8.5

Fig. 8.4

Fig. 8.6

Fig. 8.4. A 1922-style army-level prize. The three-piece badge, given for competition at the highest levels, is distinguished by an oak-leaf-decorated rectangular brooch. In addition the ring with thirteen stars was enameled in various colors. The crossed arms that comprise the clasp for the army-level prize, whether rifles, pistols, or Browning Automatic Rifles, were always bronze.

Fig. 8.5. The 1922-pattern prizes awarded in corps area competitions had a narrow brooch with a circle bearing the corps designation in roman numerals. Planchets for the corps area and department matches were solid bronze, without any enamel.

Fig. 8.6. Three departments had symbols to show their awards. These were a sea lion for the Philippines, a dolphin for the Hawaiian Department, and a portcullis (a gate used by medieval castles) for Panama (shown). The clasp (crossed arms) of gold pistols shows that the winner placed in the top sixth of all those receiving prizes. Silver clasps showed placement in the next third below those who won gold, while winners in the bottom half wore bronze clasps.

.0625 inch in diameter, displays a compound bow and two crossed arrows, a symbol of marksmanship. Outside of that is a center ring, .015 inch wide, bearing thirteen stars. An oak-leaf wreath executed in bronze surrounds the entire design, making the planchet 1 ½ inches wide.

The star-filled intermediate ring was an incomparable 1920s and 1930s feature of this prize. When worn with the square brooch indicative of army-level matches, this intermediate ring was enameled in the basic color of the branch, and for those branches with a secondary color, the otherwise bronze stars were of the second color. Seven enamel schemes existed, but the Air Corps and Signal Corps competed only in the pistol events, leaving a total of five colors for award in rifle competitions. Those prizes with two colors were: Air Corps, ultramarine-blue ring and orange stars; Philippine Scouts, blue and scarlet; Corps of Engineers, scarlet and white; and Signal Corps, orange and white. The combatant arms had bronze stars with the ring enameled in light blue for infantry, yellow for cavalry, and scarlet for both coast and field artillery, although the field artillery competed in the pistol competitions and the coast artillery in both pistol and rifle events. Table 18 shows a summary of the colors, branches, and weapons associated with the prizes, officially called Excellence-in-Competition Badges.[6]

One finds named prizes from the 1920s and 1930s for all of the branches and the Philippine Scouts, but by far the most common are the army-level, infantry-colored prizes. This is because the War Department decreed that for National Guard teams composed of men from different branches, all members would receive infantry-type prizes. These army-level prizes replaced, in part, the 1 ¼-inch-diameter gold cavalry-, infantry-, and later artillery-team badges established in 1919 and retroactively awarded back to 1906.[7]

In 1924 the army retroactively issued the 1922-style army-level badges to soldiers who since 1916 had been on national teams, including the AEF 1919 team. These last soldiers all received infantry prizes, while the former received appropriate colored rings, depending upon the branch team they represented. Those soldiers who had fired on selected teams at the Camp Perry National Matches in 1916, 1920, and other years, for example, were deemed to have earned "army level" badges even if they had already received the 1919-style gold team prizes described in chapter 7. This actually gave many soldiers two prizes for participation in the same match and resulted in many more men than usual proudly fingering new distinguished shields in 1924.[8]

As it had before, the War Department continued to engrave the reverse of prizes with the winner's data. Prizes awarded through 1929 were hand-engraved script, and as before the engravers often added a few decorative lines and swirls, although these were frequently omitted in the initial rush to make up the missed awards from 1916 through 1922. Starting in 1930, the engravers switched to a more mechanical block-letter form. Regardless of engraving styles, during the interwar period the format was normally consistent: the top line had the winner's rank, the second line his name, the next line the organization, and the final line the award year.

Corps- or department-level competitions of the 1930s were held "at such places and times as may be designated by the respective corps area or department commanders" in those years authorized by the secretary of war. Commanders of each infantry and engineer company, cavalry troop, and similar organizations armed with rifles selected one enlisted competitor. For automatic rifles, one enlisted man was selected from each infantry weapons company. (There were three weapons companies in an

Table 18. *1922–1940 Army Level Excellence-in-Competition Badges*

Branch	Ring Color	Stars Color	Authorized Weapon Clasps
Air Service	Blue	Orange	Pistol
Cavalry	Yellow	Bronze	Rifle, Pistol, BAR
Coast Artillery	Red	Bronze	Rifle, Pistol
Corps of Engineers	Red	White	Rifle, Pistol, BAR
Field Artillery	Red	Bronze	Pistol
Infantry	Light Blue	Bronze	Rifle, Pistol, BAR
Philippine Scouts	Dark Blue	Red	Rifle, Pistol, BAR
Signal Corps	Orange	White	Pistol

Fig. 8.7

ment of infantry, cavalry, engineers, field artillery, and coast artillery and one from each engineer squadron, signal battalion, and U.S. Air Corps group. In addition one other pistol competitor was allowed for each fifty officers, excluding medical officers and chaplains. Prior to this, starting in 1920, the allotment was one officer from each cavalry, infantry, engineer, and coast artillery regiment; one from each mounted engineer and Philippine Scouts battalion; and one signal officer per department or corps area.[11]

The strength of the corps or department team was in direct proportion to the number of enlisted competitors engaged in the competition. Those selected as "team members" received prizes. Match officials compiled a list of all enlisted men with the highest scores first, and for every five of these competitors, officials selected one team member. All of these team members received bronze badges. Within the team administrators provided gold (first class), silver (second class), and bronze (third class) clasps to further distinguish the scores. These clasps depended upon the total number of enlisted competitors. One gold clasp was authorized for each forty-five and one silver clasp for each fifteen enlisted competitors. All others on the prizewinners' list earned a bronze clasp.

Officers—both commissioned and warrant—also fired, but their scores were ranked on a second, separate list made up of all competitors, both officers and enlisted men. The same rules for the awarding of prizes and clasps were then applied, and those officers who had qualifying scores received appropriate badges. In this way enlisted men competed only against other enlisted personnel, but officers competed against both themselves and enlisted men.[12]

Even during the Great Depression, when funds severely limited ammunition availability, the War Department continued to support the corps area matches, rifle-team tryouts, and similar events with at least half a million rounds each year. Half of the allowance, by 1939, included national-match-grade bullets.[13]

War Department Circular 165, Section II, dated May 20, 1942, suspended matches "for the duration of the war and for six months thereafter." At the close of World War II the competitive shooting momentum of the 1920s and the 1930s was gone. The training and energy of rifle and pistol teams that had been developed through twenty years had been

Fig. 8.7. A V Corps prize, with gold automatic rifle clasp. The army introduced automatic rifle clasps just a few months after announcing the design of these 1922-type prizes.

infantry regiment.) For the Chemical Warfare Service and other organizations equipped with automatic rifles, a "similar ratio" (one man per company) prevailed.[9]

The army controlled pistol competitors more precisely. In 1934, for example, it allowed one enlisted man from each cavalry troop and each battalion of field artillery, four from each infantry regiment, two from each engineer regiment, one from each engineer squadron, two from each coast artillery regiment, one from each air squadron, and one from each signal company.[10]

The War Department designed officer selection so that enlisted men competed only against enlisted men, but officers had to compete against both the enlisted men and their fellow officers. Each infantry, cavalry, and engineer regiment and each engineer squadron could pick only one officer, and other "similar organizations" armed with rifles were allowed only a single officer. In addition to these officers, up to one officer from every fifty could be permitted to fire in rifle matches. For the automatic rifle the army permitted one officer from each infantry and engineer regiment, as well as one officer for nine other types of companies equipped with the Browning Automatic Rifle.

Officers in 1930s pistol competition were allowed at the ratio of one from each regi-

Fig. 8.8. *Shortly after World War II numbered army and theater commanders were authorized to hold competitions and award the 1922-style prizes, but evidently few did. This German-made medal was given by the U.S. Army Europe for the 1948 European championships.*

Fig. 8.9. *In 1948 the army regularly resumed matches. As a result the new Department of the Army retitled the prizes "excellence-in-competition badges" and simplified the awards in four ways. (1) For competitions below those for the entire army the brooches were of the type shown, with no design in the central circle. (2) All planchets were solid bronze (enameled planchets previously given at national and army matches were eliminated). (3) Only bronze rifle and pistol clasps were given. (4) The rectangular brooch with oak leaves was given not only at army-level matches but also at national, interservice, and similar high-level contests.*

diverted to the war and the training of millions of soldiers. After firing billions of rounds on ranges and in combat, skilled marksmen were exhausted. It took years for the army as a whole to return to national peacetime contests. In 1946 the army authorized theater and service command commanders to host matches at their level, but it is unlikely that any awarded the bronze prizes. By 1948 the U.S. Army of Occupation in Germany consisted of one division and the constabulary. The European matches, started as a diversion after World War II, provided locally made medals with red, white, and blue ribbons rather than the proper prizes as allowed by regulations.[14]

POST–WORLD WAR II

To the exasperation of shooters, the army did not resume awarding leg badges after World War II as rapidly as it had after World War I. Demobilization and returning soldiers to the bright prospects of civilian life took priority. Army-directed matches finally made a sputtering resumption in 1948, but with several whimsical changes in the prizes. The old corps area bars were made totally uninspiring by removing any central design, so that the brooch was simply a round end bar $^2/_{10}$ of an inch wide with an unadorned circle $^4/_{10}$ of an inch in the center. The new Department of the

Army awarded these prizes for "area matches." The army brooch remained unchanged in design but became awarded only at the National Matches, as the U.S. Army matches had not been restarted. Interestingly, some of the restarted National Matches were not held at Camp Perry but moved around. Camp Matthews (San Diego) and San Francisco, California, hosted the 1951 National Matches, and Fort Benning, Georgia, was the host for the 1952 National Matches.[15]

All automatic rifle clasps and the gold and silver clasps for both rifles and pistols disappeared, leaving awards with only bronze rifle and bronze pistol clasps. In addition, the army declared enameled planchets obsolete, decreeing that thereafter all pendants would only be bronze. Criteria for the 1948 prizes was such that a list by scores of nondistinguished shooters was created for enlisted competitors, and the top 10 percent received Excellence-in-Competition Badges (renamed from the original, awkward name, "Army, Department and Corps Area Rifle, Automatic Rifle and Pistol Team Marksmanship Badges"). All other competitors (commissioned and warrant officers) were placed on another list according to their scores, and those who scored higher than the lowest enlisted firer earning a badge also received badges.[16]

Fig. 8.8

Fig. 8.9

In 1955 the National Board for the Promotion of Rifle Practice recommended several changes to various high-level prizes and badges. An assistant chief of staff at the Department of the Army rejected many proposals but forwarded the papers to the Office of the Quartermaster General with a request that the Excellence-in-Competition Badges have "a modification of the bar to indicate that the award was won in an Army match." Out of this simple request grew an enormous and complicated design study with many badges and many options.[17]

Ultimately in March 1958, after three years of study, the army staff approved a series of modified prizes and had samples made. The top bar for proposed prizes given at the National Matches was to have a Federal shield and a ribbon bearing **U. S. ARMY**. For the all-army matches a top bar carried the block wording **U. S. ARMY**, while for area matches the bar was similar to that of the old corps area/department version but with the central design of the shoulder patch for the appropriate army or for the Military District of Washington (MDW). When they were actually made, the prototype badges were only struck for the continental U.S. forces. Thus area match bars were made for MDW and First Army through Sixth Army but not for the Seventh Army (in Europe) or the Eighth Army (in the Far East). The army made ten of each design in each color with each clasp, that is, ten bronze prizes for National Matches with rifle clasp, ten more with pistol clasp, ten army area prizes for each of the areas with rifle clasp, and so forth.[18]

These 1958 clasps and pendants were without enamel and of the same design as before, but with the bars, clasps, and pendants in matching colors: gold, silver, and bronze, to denote the top sixth, the next third, and the lower half, respectively.[19]

The army made these new badges in various colors and sealed the samples but before it could describe them in regulations and make the initial issues, new generals in the Pentagon disapproved the prizes as constituting too large a change. The commanding general of the Continental Army Command objected to the new concept due to the sheer number of prizes and countered by recommending the Excellence-in-Competition Badges be issued only in silver. Pentagon staff officers pointed out that one key missing ingredient was any wording to identify the numbered army level

badges as awards by the U.S. Army. Lyman L. Lemnintzer was vice chief of staff and a former coast artilleryman who had won several of the old leg badges as a lieutenant in the 1920s. After General Lemnintzer became chief of staff in July 1959, he approved revised designs. The U.S. Army's Institute of Heraldry made more samples and sealed some of them as official. In early 1960 the Continental Army Command suggested that all prizes be silver, with the top

Fig. 8.10

Fig. 8.11

159

PRIZES, 1922 TO THE PRESENT

Fig. 8.10. One of the many prototype prizes made in 1958, this brooch was to be awarded to winners of the national championships. All prizes in the set were made in three degrees: entirely in gold color, in silver, and in bronze.

Fig. 8.11. Another of the 1958 prototype prizes. This Fifth Army prize is typical of the awards made for army-level matches, which replaced the 1922–40 corps area matches. The device in the central circle displays the shoulder patch of the appropriate army area.

Fig. 8.12. This brooch, designed in 1958 and marked U. S. ARMY, was originally intended for award in the annual all-army match. Although the brooch was not used as originally envisioned, between 1960 and 1962 the army evolved a plan that is still in use today—the prize is given in bronze and in silver to show high placement in any of the major military shooting matches. The artistic use of multiple tasteful components and of common design elements developed in 1922 evolved into the composition of these current badges.

brooch inscribed **U. S. ARMY**, and said that silver would be attractive on the new army green uniform. This scheme would also allow the awarding of these prizes at the newly instituted interservice matches without creating still another brooch design. While this high-level squabbling was going on, the army continued to award the plain bronze versions.[20]

The deputy chief of staff for personnel then proposed a compromise by suggesting two badges—one in bronze for awarding at the numbered army level and one in silver for the all-army, the interservice, and the National Matches. By January 1961, six years after the suggested changes and nearly three years after starting on the badge redesign project, the new chief of staff, General George Decker, approved two badges, one bronze and one silver. The brooches for each badge simply carried the inscription **U. S. ARMY**. The Department of the Army announced the new awards in March 1962. The two new prizes replaced both the bronze prizes with the rectangular brooch bearing oak leaves and the bronze area-matches prizes. The army gave silver for national and all-army championships and bronze for major command championships and NRA regional championships. These two bronze and silver prizes with **U. S. ARMY** brooches still exist today, although the requirements for the awards have changed many times as the army has moved to a system involving points rather than matches.[21]

The manufacture of gold- and silver-colored prototype badges in the 1950s and the use of silver badges from 1961 into the twenty-first century have provided a source of rifle and pistol clasps in gold and silver that allows either unscrupulous dealers or unknowing collectors to assemble gold or silver clasps to bronze pendants and brooches, creating badges that might appear to have been awarded in the 1930s. The easiest way to distinguish these clasps is by the markings on the reverse. Original gold-colored clasps dating from between the world wars are marked **14K** on the reverse-side butt of the weapon, while the prototype 1955 badges either are not marked (which allows for the false markings at this time) or are marked **$^{1}/_{20}$KGF★** at the weapons intersection. In addition some, but certainly not all, of the 1955 gold-colored clasps have reverse edges that are roughly stamped and, as a con-

sequence, small amounts of metal that extend beyond the smooth back of the clasp.

Original silver clasps are marked **STERLING** on a weapon's butt. Post–World War II silver clasps have a range of markings. These include **E. & H. SIMONING STERLING**, **STERLING**, **KREW G-1**, and others, most being at the weapons' intersection. Some of the prototype silver clasps and badges were unmarked, as were most of the bronze badges and clasps. Starting in the 1950s the army's Institute of Heraldry required manufacturers to mark on the reverse of insignia a code showing the maker, such as **G-1**, **G-22**, **V-21**, **A-28**, and the like. Officially made badges, clasps, and brooches from the 1960s and later should have this type of marking.

Until about 1962 firers could earn enough Excellence-in-Competition Badge points so they could qualify for the distinguished marksman shield simply by firing in local and regional matches, provided that they also placed in the top 10 percent of a National Trophy match. In 1962 the army's standard for a distinguished badge changed. The distinguished designation then came to recognize "an eminent

Fig. 8.12

★GF stands for gold filled, a process by which a layer of at least 10-karat gold has been mechanically applied to a base metal. This layer is usually at least one-twentieth of the total weight of the metal of the piece.

degree of achievement in target practice firing with the standard military service rifle or pistol."[22]

In major championships and in selected command matches, those shooters who placed in the top 10 percent received points towards a distinguished designation—thirty points being required to earn the coveted shields. Of those receiving points the highest sixth earned ten points, the next third earned eight, and the balance earned six points. Starting in the early 1960s, anyone receiving points earned a bronze Excellence-in-Competition Badge, while twenty points resulted in a silver Excellence-in-Competition version. Furthermore, anyone who fired in division and National Guard championships received four points simply for participating. Marksmen were restricted to firing in four matches annually, at which these "leg badges" could be given. For awhile only one of these two prizes (bronze or silver) could be worn, even if one was for rifle and the other for pistol, although many winners ignored this fine point.[23]

By 1999 the army awarded points to the top 10 percent of the nondistinguished competitors firing in major command championships, the U.S. Army or other service championships, the National Guard championships, interservice championships, and the National Trophy match. Army personnel who missed

these events could compete only once a year in selected Civilian Marksmanship Program matches, and if they placed sufficiently high, could be awarded points towards their "leg."[24]

Another 1955 change was the introduction of excellence-in-competition badges for award to civilians who had previously earned the army's bronze prizes. The U.S. Army, through the National Board for the Promotion of Rifle Practice, gave these civilian bronze badges at matches after January 1, 1955. The two badges are of similar design, with rifles or pistols crossed over a shield on an eagle's breast. This pendant is suspended from a bar bearing **UNITED STATES OF AMERICA** and **NBPRP**. **FOR EXCELLENCE IN** and **COMPETITION** appear above and below the eagle. These two designs were also executed in silver, providing two levels depending upon points earned, like the army Excellence-in-Competition Badges, so four of the badges exist—rifle and pistol, bronze and silver. When the Civilian Marksmanship Program replaced the National Board for the Promotion of Rifle Practice, the **NBPRP** letters on the brooch changed to **CMP**. Later badges also have a more dramatic contrast between the crossed arms and the darkened area behind the weapons, although the metal itself was no longer silver.[25]

Fig. 8.13. Introduced in 1955, this prize was given by the National Board for the Promotion of Rifle Practice to civilians who earned a pistol "leg badge." Initially made in silver, it was later also made in bronze. Both rifle and pistol versions exist, distinguished by the crossed arms on the eagle's chest.

Fig. 8.14. The current civilian excellence-in-competition prize has the letters **CMP** (civilian marksmanship program) in place of the original **NBPRP** (National Board for the Promotion of Rifle Practice). Like the earlier versions, it exists for both rifle and pistol and is made in silver and bronze colors. The later NBPRP and the CMP prizes, like this example, had a very dark area behind the crossed arms to enhance the contrast between the background and the crossed weapons.

Fig. 8.13

Fig. 8.14

CHAPTER NINE

DISTINGUISHED BADGES

REWARDS IN GOLD

THE CREATION OF GOLD and silver shooting prizes resulted in a success greater than anything imagined by Phil Sheridan. By the end of the 1883 matches competition among soldiers was fierce, but the same men kept winning. Sergeant Cyrus Clark, B Troop, 1st Cavalry, stationed at Fort Walla Walla, Washington, won second place in the Pacific Division competition in 1882, taking home a gold prize, then won the second-place gold prize at the army's first match, held at Fort Leavenworth, Kansas, in October 1882. Next year Clark won the Department of the Columbia first prize and then carried off the Pacific Division first-place reward. Sheridan, believing that bottlenecks of this type might discourage other soldiers, noted it was possible that these "splendid riflemen . . . will continue indefinitely to represent their companies and take all prizes offered. This is very disheartening to others scarcely inferior in skill."[1]

War Department General Orders Number 12, dated February 20, 1884, neatly solved the problem by creating a new elite category—distinguished marksmen. The establishing order in part stated that, "Hereafter, . . . whenever any marksman has been three times member of a department team or has won any three of the authorized prize medals, he will be announced in general orders from these headquarters as belonging to a distinguished class no longer eligible to compete for these honors without special permission from the Commanding General of the Army." This chapter covers the various distinguished badges that the army has awarded since 1884.

RIFLE AND PISTOL

Fifteen extraordinarily good shooters, including Sergeant Clark, were accordingly announced as the army's first distinguished marksmen in March 1884. In the order Sheridan "takes this occasion to congratulate those who have so repeatedly won a distinction which could scarcely have been attained without possessing all those qualities which combine to make a perfect soldier." After the October 1884 army match at Fort Leavenworth, eight more men were transferred to the distinguished class, including two first lieutenants, four NCOs, and two privates. Nowhere did the ostentatious medals hang more heavily than on Lieutenant Lewis Merriam of the 4th Infantry, a former Civil War sergeant of the 20th Maine who rejoined the army in 1872. Merriam won a silver medal in 1882 and a gold medal in 1883 as part of the Division of the Missouri team, then really triumphed in 1884 with a first-place gold prize from the Department of the Platte, a silver prize from the Division of the Missouri, the first-place gold medal for the entire army, and the gold medal for army skirmishing. Certainly, the class of distinguished marksmen was created for a man like this.[2]

In 1885 fifteen more soldiers joined the ranks of distinguished marksmen, followed by the next sixteen the next year. By the end of 1886 the War Department had fifty-nine officers and men sitting on the sidelines at shooting contests and on the distinguished list. Any who fired were ineligible for prizes. These best shots in the army grumbled and agitated for relief from their dilemma. As a result of this problem (as noted in chapter 6), the army created a new match exclusively for those who comprised the unquestionably preeminent class of distinguished marksmen.[3]

Part of Sheridan's innovative 1887 solution was still another reward: the distinguished marksman badge that was cut in a distinctive shield form so as to be readily identifiable from a distance. The members of the vaunted distinguished marksmen class would subsequently hold their own private contest, with the first- and second-place winners awarded large 2-inch-diameter circular prizes. Initially, the army planned for these exclusive matches to be held on years that alternated between the army championships, but this scheme was soon lost.

General S. V. Benét, chief of ordnance, reported in mid-1887 that three awards had been made—the new distinguished marksman shield and both first- and second-class prizes. For the competition among the distinguished marksmen, the army established two new beautiful two-inch-wide, gold awards. Charles E. Barber, renowned chief engraver

for the U.S. mint, corresponded with Benét, and presumably Barber had a hand in creating these latter two new dies.[4]

While distinguished marksmen could compete in their own contest for these magnificent prizes, all of these soldiers received a new badge—that of a distinguished marksman. Someone, evidently Captain Stanhope Blunt, sketched out a proposed design, which General Benét sent out for comments, first to Rock Island and then to the U.S. Mint at Philadelphia. Barber responded on April 11, 1887, stating that he had no improvements to offer, but he went on to say it would be better if the distinguished badge were made by a jeweler rather than the mint, as "There is a mistake,

Fig. 9.1

Fig. 9.1. First Lieutenant and Mrs. Michael H. Barry, 1899. Barry served as an enlisted man in the 1st Cavalry from April 1887 until he was commissioned in the 44th Volunteer Infantry in August 1899. Barry's medals are (left to right, top row): the gold first prize for carbine, won in 1893 while he was first sergeant of G Troop, 1st Cavalry; the army gold prize for second place with carbine, won in 1893 (this is easily recognized by the half sunburst top on the brooch); the distinguished-marksman shield awarded in October 1893; and (left to right, bottom row): Barry's initial medal, a silver revolver second class prize won in 1890 while he was a sergeant; a silver second class prize for his placing third in the 1894 distinguished marksmen competition; and a combination marksman/ sharpshooter badge with a three-year requalification bar. In 1901 Barry was commissioned in the Artillery Corps, and he rose to temporary colonel during World War I. He took a disability retirement in 1922, advancing on the retired list to permanent colonel in 1930.

Fig. 9.2. *A sketch of the 1885 Department of Dakota prize. The shield with elongated target became the basis of the U.S. Army's distinguished badge.*

Fig. 9.3. *A photograph taken at Fort Leavenworth, Kansas, showing a group of unidentified soldiers about 1886–87. The soldier on the right in the front row wears the 1885 Department of Dakota prize (his second medal from the right).*

this is a badge, and not a medal, and requires entirely different kinds of treatment, which the Mint has no facilities for doing." The ordnance office sent the sketch to Tiffany & Company and then to Jens F. Pedersen, both New York City jewelers, requesting estimates for the manufacture of the badges.[5]

The enduring design of this shield-shaped badge was amazingly similar to one created by Jens Pedersen for the Department of Dakota marksmanship contest in 1885, and it is probable that the inspiration for the Ordnance Department sketch came from Pedersen's establishment. Captain Blunt, a central player in the creation of the distinguished badge, had been the inspector of rifle practice for the Department of Dakota. The center of the gold shield bore a white rectangular target with a black elliptical bull's-eye and scoring rings representative of the midrange (500- and 600-yard) target "B," adopted by the army in 1885 through Blunt's *Instructions in Rifle and Carbine Firing.*

This first multicolored eared shield (gold, white, and black) was suspended by two large chain links that attached to an ornate brooch dominated by a large central federal shield carrying the letters **US** in the center. On each side of the brooch's shield was a simple floral design. An overall badge was made from 14-karat gold and weighed 0.8 ounce. Pedersen won the bid, then delivered the first sixty at the end of June 1887 and the final ten in October at a cost of $20 each. The reverse of these early badges showed only the two brads that affixed the white-and-black target to the main shield and the small stamping **JENS PEDERSEN** in an arc above **NY**. The U.S. shield, superimposed upon the brooch, is also

Fig. 9.2

attached with two brads, a distinction not carried over to later distinguished badges.[6]

After the Ordnance Department issued the initial seventy badges, it made the additional distinguished badges at Rock Island Arsenal. These are very similar to those with the Pedersen design, but slight differences mark the

Fig. 9.3

Fig. 9.4

Fig. 9.5

Fig. 9.7

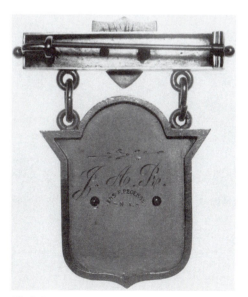

Fig. 9.6

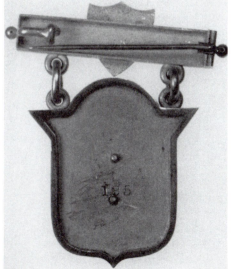

Fig. 9.8

Fig. 9.4. *On a Texas rifle range, 1888. Divisions and departments held competitions on ranges like this one. Most soldiers fired from a prone position, with feet pointed downrange.*

Fig. 9.5. *One of the original eighty distinguished badges issued by the U.S. Army starting in 1887. The original owner, Sergeant James A. Richardson, had his initials added at his own expense.*

Fig. 9.6. *The reverse of the badge shown in figure 9.5. These first eighty badges are marked **JENS PEDERSEN** in an arc above **NY**. (Pedersen was a jeweler in New York City.) The brooch has two brads that attach the shield to the front in addition to the two brads that attach the target to the shield.*

Fig. 9.7. *Rock Island Arsenal made the second group of distinguished marksman badges, which lasted until early 1906. The front shows only minor differences in the flower scrollwork on the brooch, the placement and details of the curved word **DISTINGUISHED**, and the target rings.*

Fig. 9.8. *The reverse of the badge shown in figure 9.7. The main differences between the first- and second-style distinguished badges are found on the back. The reverse of the brooch does not have the two brads to attach the shield to the bar. The pendant shield is marked **RIA**, followed by a serial number.*

second lot. Most noticeable are in the flower scrollwork detail on the brooch and the placement and details of the curved **DISTINGUISHED** above the oval target. Rock Island Arsenal stamped the reverse with **RIA** and, below that, a serial number. Besides the back markings, the reverse of the brooch has the front U.S. shield soldered and not attached with brads, although the unusual catch that covered the pin tip remained unchanged. By the spring of 1891 the owner of one of the distinguished badges had lost his, and the commanding general personally ruled that the duplicate shield had to be purchased, since the government would not bear the replacement cost.[7]

As the initial criterion for the distinguished marksman badge was winning three prizes at the division, department, or army level, some early distinguished marksmen received their designation by virtue of winning awards in rifle, carbine, and—after 1889—pistol contests. One example is John J. Pershing, who later rose to command the U.S. Army in France during the World War I and then became army chief of staff. While a second lieutenant and member of the 6th Cavalry Regiment, Pershing won two silver second class prizes in revolver matches and a silver carbine medal. He won his initial second class pistol prize in August 1889 and his second such prize in August 1891. The 1891 match was a big one

for Pershing, as he placed second in the pistol competition, just edging out Corporal M. L. Mitchell, also from the 6th Cavalry. At the same contest Pershing won a bronze prize— the highest bronze given—with a carbine, and as a result he became a distinguished marksman. Although most of Pershing's biographers discuss his shooting prizes, they fail to note that he became a distinguished marksman; interestingly, there are no known photos of "Black Jack" wearing his distinguished shield. The Smithsonian Institution now owns his prizes.[8]

Lieutenant Pershing, Sergeant Clark, and all of the other distinguished marksmen prior to 1906 received a badge that depicted the 1885 oval target. At the start of the twentieth century, however, the army abandoned elliptical targets and returned to circular versions. The Ordnance Department dutifully followed suit with the distinguished marksman shield in the spring of 1906 and modified the rifleman's prize to carry miniature targets "with circular divisions to correspond to the targets of recent model" when the existing stock of shields became exhausted. This 1906 general design, showing the 1904 "Target B," was not substantially modified until 1959. Between these dates, however, the construction techniques did change, minor badge differences appeared, and various styles of catches were used. Table 19 lists the early variations of the distinguished marksman badges.[9]

Table 19. *Early Distinguished Marksman Badge Types*

	Pendant			Brooch	
Target	Reverse	Notes	Catch	Notes
Oval	Marked **JENS PEDERSEN NY**. Has two brads. Not engraved when issued.	1887 design	Shields end of pin.	Two brads hold shield
Oval	Marked **RIA** and serial number. Has two brads. No engraving when issued.	Last issued 1906	Shields end of pin.	No brads to hold shield
Round, with glass cover	No markings on Reverse. No engraving when issued. No brads.	Third pattern	Shields end of pin.	Deep hollow reverse
Round, with narrow rings	No engraving when issued.	Known to have been issued 1919.	Open catch	Solid reverse

Fig. 9.9

Fig. 9.11

Fig. 9.10

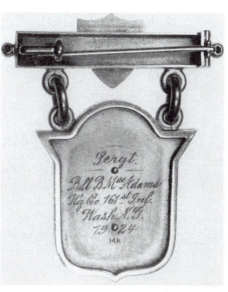

Fig. 9.12

Fig. 9.9. In the spring of 1906 the army made another batch of distinguished badges. At this time the artisans at Rock Island Arsenal adopted the representation of the round target recently created for army marksmanship. The domed glass cover used on the earlier badges continued with this third version.

Fig. 9.10. In the early 1920s the army switched to distinguished shields on which the enameled target rings had metal edges.

Fig. 9.11. The reverse of the badge shown in figure 9.10. The War Department began to engrave the owner's name, organization, and earning year on the reverse of the badges when it switched to circular targets. The back of the shield, which had been deeply recessed, became shallower with the purchase of new badges in the 1920s.

Fig. 9.12. Although the army switched to shields that had shallow backs, as shown in figure 5.11, some older badges continued to be awarded in the 1920s, showing that the army did not always issue the oldest badge first.

In the 1920s civilians began to fire for distinguished badges. Starting in 1923, regulations allowed those men who had earned some credits towards a distinguished shield while they were in the service to shoot in selected matches, so that if they were proficient enough, the men could complete the requirements for one of the elusive gold shields. Three years later, all civilians became eligible. In practice civilians began to earn the distinguished designation soon after the world war, and the regulations were simply reflecting actual occurrences. The army awarded identical badges to both military and civilian winners until 1959, when new designations and badges appeared.[10]

Distinguished pistol shot badges first materialized in 1903, the year the military introduced a separate pistol competition at the army level. Starting in 1889, departments and divisions held revolver competitions but no special pistol distinguished badge appeared then, since the revolver competition counted equally with rifle and carbine toward one's becoming a distinguished marksman.[11]

The army awarded the first two distinguished pistol shields in 1903, when Captain Farrand

Sayer of the 8th Cavalry and Sergeant Bent Howe of M Troop, 8th Cavalry, won prizes in the army pistol match. Sayer, as first lieutenant, had won a bronze pistol prize for the Department of Dakota in 1892 and then in 1903 won a silver prize for the Department of the Missouri and a bronze army prize (sixth place). Howe won his first revolver prize in 1891 from the Department of Dakota and then won two gold prizes for first place in 1903 in both the Department of the Missouri match and the army revolver match. Captain Arthur Thayer, 3d Cavalry, soon received his distinguished pistol shot shield, as he had won two bronze department prizes for revolver in 1889 and 1890 and then a silver revolver department prize in 1903.[12]

Both Captain Sayer and Captain Thayer were already distinguished, Thayer had won his long-arm badge in 1890 and Sayer his in 1903. Farrand Sayer, an active cavalryman all of his life, ultimately retired as a brigadier general after forty-one years of service, including a stint as vice president of the Cavalry Association while he was a major. Arthur Thayer, two years Sayer's junior, was a descendant of Sylvannus Thayer, "father of the U.S. Military Academy," and was on several shooting teams in the early twentieth century, ultimately rising to colonel in World War I.[13]

Some time later the War Department retroactively awarded a distinguished pistol shot badge to black Corporal Horace W. Bivins, who—as a member of the 10th Cavalry—had earned three pistol prizes (bronze in 1892, silver in 1893, and gold in 1894). While he was not recognized as such in 1903, Bivins was the earliest distinguished pistol shot. The War Department began to recognize the results of the increased revolver competitions, providing six distinguished pistol shot badges in 1904, eleven in 1905, and seventeen in 1906.[14]

These Distinguished Pistol Shot badges—gold, enameled, and ornate—are similar to the highly prized distinguished marksman's version, but the shield and brooch are slightly smaller (the shield is 1.075 inches wide rather than the 1.4 inches of the rifle and carbine badge) and different words surround the new target. The arched **DISTINGUISHED** still caps the black-and-white target, but **PISTOL SHOT** appears below it. The brooch is of the same design but $1/4$ inch shorter than the long-arm version. A new rectangular target with circular rings on the pistol badge differs from the enameled elliptical style on the

marksman badge, this white background being .45 inches wide and .55 inches high for the pistol targets, with narrow rings and a smaller bull's-eye. The white enamel center represents the 1904 target "A" used in the dismounted course, where the paper target itself was 4 feet wide and 6 feet high, with an outer ring of 46 inches, an inner ring of 26 inches, and an 8-inch-diameter bull's-eye. This overall badge design remained generally unchanged for over half a century.[15]

Pre–World War I distinguished pistol shot badges, made at Rock Island Arsenal, have reverses similar to those for distinguished marksman badges. The target is held in place by two brads and the catch covers the pin tip, as shown in figures 9.14 and 9.16. The badge front shows the two delicate rings and a bull's-eye in shiny transparent white enamel. After World War I, when shooting competitions started again in earnest, a great many soldiers qualified for the distinguished pistol shot shields, and at that time minor design changes appeared. On later pistol shields the white became opaque enamel, the rings were wider, and the catch changed. The first post–world war catch was simply a plain hook, while a few years later it was changed to a more modern ball catch with a locking device.[16]

In late 1956 the deputy chief of staff for personnel received comments from the Office of the Quartermaster General regarding recommended changes to the two distinguished shields. The major complaint was that the badges were not identifiable as awards given by the U.S. Army. The suggestion was to make

Fig. 9.13

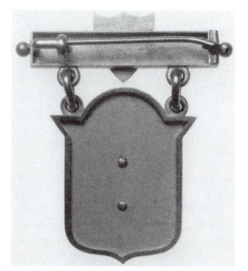

Fig. 9.14

the brooches simple rectangular bars bearing **U.S. ARMY**, with the brooches retaining the small knobs at each end. This would make the brooches similar to those used by the other services. The other change suggested was to make both the rifle and pistol shields the same size.[17]

General Lyman L. Lemnitzer, vice chief of staff from 1957 to 1959 and chief of staff from 1959 to 1960, became intimately involved in the final design revision of distinguished badges. As a coast artillery second lieutenant, Lemnitzer became a distinguished rifleman in 1924. Personnel of the quartermaster general's heraldic branch met with General Lemnitzer in April 1958, as the vice chief of staff had expressed a desire to be involved personally in design revisions of the historic distinguished shields. The

Fig. 9.15

Fig. 9.17

Fig. 9.16

Fig. 9.18

Fig. 9.14. The reverse of the early pistol shot badge shown in figure 9.13.

Fig. 9.15. A typical distinguished pistol shot badge, as awarded shortly after World War I. The edge of the shield is still thick, causing the background to be recessed significantly from the edge. In addition, the first and last parts of the word **DISTINGUISHED** are nearly horizontal and the target rings remain narrow. In 1920 the army purchased a new group of distinguished pistol shot badges that had brooches with flat backs, unlike earlier badges that had the edge bent over to give the appearance of greater thickness. These two styles were mixed, so the oldest badges were not always given out first.

Fig. 9.16. The reverse of the second-style pistol shot badge shown in figure 9.15. The target is held in place by two brads.

Fig. 9.17. A distinguished pistol shot badge, as awarded after World War II and into the 1950s. The edge of the badges is not as thick as were those made after World War I, and the word **DISTINGUISHED** is arched differently. The edge is thinner than the edge of the badge shown in figure 9.15, and the target does not have brads on the reverse.

Fig. 9.18. A distinguished pistol shot badge awarded in 1959. The target rings are wider than those used on any of the earlier badges.

Fig. 9.19

*Fig. 9.19. A badge typical of those given in the 1980s and 1990s. The word **DISTINGUISHED** is different from the word in the earlier styles, and the center bull's-eye is smaller.*

army's overall concept was to modify the distinguished badges and thus create a unique design exclusively for U.S. Army members. What really happened was that and more.[18]

For over two years artists dutifully created and modified an assortment of new designs, while staff officers circulated and commented on the changes. Generally the Quartermaster Corps artisans modified suspension bars (brooches) to show more clearly that the awards were given to U.S. Army members. Ultimately, the suspension brooch for both rifle and pistol badges became a bar inscribed **U.S. ARMY**, with a raised rim. Above and in front of the top edge was a shield composed of thirteen vertical stripes and a chief (the upper portion of the shield) containing thirteen stars. Two oak leaves on each side supported the shield. The designation of distinguished rifleman corresponded more directly with the parallel 1903 title, that of distinguished pistol shot. Accordingly, the wording underneath the target on the distinguished marksman pendant changed from **MARKSMAN** to **RIFLEMAN**. The smaller pistol-shot pendant remained unchanged.[19]

Civilian brooches retained the original shield and floral ornamented suspension bar design. From the beginning the brooch shield and two end knobs had been made separately and then brazed to the bar. General Lemnitzer clearly thought the reinterpretation of the historic designs went too far. For the revised U.S. Army awards, Lemnitzer personally sketched the two end knobs to the 1958 concept drawing and then specified that the knobs would be made separately and soldered to the brooch,

as had been done since the 1880s. Without this change the brooch would have simply been a rectangle bearing the wording **U.S. ARMY**, with a federal shield above.

Despite this high-level intervention, the caliber of the gold-colored distinguished badges rapidly deteriorated in the 1960s and 1970s. Shields and knobs soon became an integral part of the suspension brooch, so the 1960 style of distinguished badges, with the elevated shield and **U.S. ARMY** inscription, comes in two styles: the earlier style with applied shields and knobs, and the later ones with the components struck as part of the bar. In truth the manufacturers of the later style made badges with a great many different catches and back marks. For the new-style brooch with **U.S. ARMY** and oak leaves, the most noticeable variation is in the area between the shield and oak leaves. Initially the area was cut out or pierced, as shown in figure 9.22, but as the badges cheapened the manufacturing changed, so the later shield and oak leaves are only in relief, though the official specifications called for piercing.

In the late nineteenth century and even through World War II, distinguished badges cost between $12 and $34. As more shooters won distinguished shields their value decreased, not only because of the number awarded, but in real dollars as well. Curiously, by 1998 the price of a distinguished badge remained at approximately $30 despite a century of inflation.[20]

From the beginning, qualification requirements for a distinguished badge demanded three prizes, although they could be from division, department, or army matches. Soon after the start of the national matches in 1903, the army also counted these medals as one of the three awards for the distinguished award. In 1925 the War Department clarified that the three awards could be prizes from department, departmental, divisional, or army competitions; medals won in national individual matches; and medals awarded to the top sixteen rifle teams or the top ten pistol teams in the national team matches.[21]

This need for three awards continued into World War II. After the resumption of army matches in 1948, the qualification remained the winning of three prizes but with a few caveats. At least one prize had to have been won in a national match or, if won in an area match, the prize must have been awarded for placing in the top 50 percent of the winners receiving a prize. Besides the army "leg badges,"

Fig. 9.20

Fig. 9.21

With the resumption of post–World War II matches, women began to compete. In 1958 the first woman, Gertrude Backstrom, won a distinguished pistol designation, and three years later Alice H. Bull received a distinguished rifleman's badge. Sergeant Barbara J. Hile of the Army Marksmanship Unit was the first woman to earn both the distinguished rifle and distinguished pistol shields.[23]

After World War II the Department of the Army authorized lapel buttons "denoting awards of badges" for wear on civilian clothing. Diminutive badges, not exceeding $^{21}/_{32}$ inch in any dimension, came into existence. For the basic qualification badges these were made without any bars, and for the two distinguished badges and the Excellence-in-Competition Badge the lapel buttons were to be "a reproduction of the pendant only of the respective badge." The Civilian Marksmanship Program, successor to the National Board for the Promotion of Rifle Practice, has continued to issue the distinguished lapel pins into the twenty-first century.[24]

When Sheridan championed the distinguished designation in the nineteenth century, soldiers who won the badges simply shot as an adjunct to other army duties; they merely fired better than their peers. By the early twentieth century soldiers who earned a distinguished shield were usually excused from the regimental firing contests and could automatically attend division-level contests. Starting in the late 1930s and continuing until after the Korean War, coaches and the captain of winning national teams also received a credit towards their distinguished badge. After the Korean War the army created marksmanship training units, and the army's major shooting unit, the Army Marksmanship Unit, located at Fort Benning, Georgia, became the home for competitive shooters whose major duty was to shoot and to train regular soldiers in marksmanship. During the Vietnam War some members trained snipers and accomplished other soldierly duties, to be sure. A part of the U.S. Army Forces Command until March 1995, these special shooters also helped with general recruiting starting in 1999.[25]

certain badges won at the national rifle or pistol matches counted. Placing in the top sixteen rifle teams or top ten pistol teams at the National Matches became further refined. For awhile the National Board for the Promotion of Rifle Practice required not only that one win selected medals but also that one place in the top 15 percent of winning teams. Lastly, only one badge per year could be counted towards the distinguished designation. As many as 20 percent of the competitors received various medals at National Matches, but by 1963 only the top 10 percent of the nondistinguished firers received credit towards distinguished shields.[22]

Fig. 9.20. At the end of the Korean War the Department of the Army allowed commanders who were authorized to approve awards to "locally devise" a certificate that bore a reproduction of the badge. In the 1950s and 1960s the director of civilian marksmanship created various certificates. This distinguished pistol shot badge certificate is 8 x 10 inches. On some versions the badge was in yellow, white, and black, while on other certificates it was in gray, white, and black. The Department of Defense seal in the upper left corner is in blue.

Fig. 9.21. Major General William J. Sutton in 1967. Sutton was chief of the U.S. Army Reserves in the late 1960s. From the 1900s through the 1960s many senior officers wore distinguished badges that they had won as junior officers. Countless officers who joined the army during and after World War II did not consider marksmanship an essential personal skill, and consequently virtually none earned distinguished badges.

Fig. 9.22. In the spring of 1968 General Lyman L. Lemnitzer, while he was army vice chief of staff, intervened in the army's effort to modify its distinguished badge. As a result the army adopted this design. Rather than a rectangular brooch bearing U S ARMY, which was desired by the Quartermaster Corps designers, Lemnitzer retained the historic U.S. shield, although it became smaller and was supported by oak leaves. He also insisted that the historic small spheres at the brooch ends be kept. Early brooches of the new design have the area between the oak leaves and the shield pierced (cut out), while in later badges the area is solid. On the shield below the target, RIFLEMAN replaced MARKSMAN.

Fig. 9.23. Civilians continued to receive distinguished badges with the earlier-style brooch when the army switched to the badge shown in figure 9.22. This badge retains the older, original-style brooch but uses the new shield with RIFLEMAN below the target, marking it as a badge given to civilians after 1968.

Fig. 9.24. President John Kennedy (left) is using his hands to see the size of the ten-ring on the 300-meter rifle target so important to Gary Anderson (center), who in October 1962 won four world championships at the quadrennial World Shooting Championship. National Rifle Association Executive Vice President Franklin Orth is on the right. Kennedy awarded Anderson the first distinguished international shooter badge in 1963.

The army's philosophy towards top shooters runs counter to some training trends while dovetailing with others. Virtually no senior officers now qualify for leg badges, much less for a distinguished shield. Distinguished titles, while still hard to earn, have gone from being a reward earned as part of one's general military skill to being a prize that often results in a special assignment.

Fig. 9.22

Fig. 9.23

INTERNATIONAL SHOOTERS' BADGES

Every four years shooters from the various services entered the modern Olympics, initiated in 1896. Using the Model 1903 rifle, the U.S. Army team won America's first gold Olympic shooting medal in 1908. Individual winners soon followed.[26]

Second Lieutenant Sidney R. Hines, a 1920 West Point graduate and already a distinguished pistol shot (1922) and distinguished marksman (1923), represented the United States in the 1924 games in France. One of the best crack shots ever, Hines won two Olympic medals, including a gold in the free rifle team. These same Olympics also saw fellow second lieutenant and military-academy classmate George Rehm and two marines, Sergeant Henry M. Bailey and Sergeant Morris Fisher, as other members of the team.[27]

Participation in Olympic and other international competitions rated no special military recognition until army regulations changed in November 1963. In 1963 the National Board for the Promotion of Rifle Practice began to issue gold distinguished international shooter badges, the most recent of the distinguished awards. President John Kennedy presented the first distinguished international badge to Corporal Gary Anderson in April 1963, showing the lag time between the creation of the award and the initial authorization in print. Anderson won the first badge because he had won four world championships at the quadrennial World Shooting Championship the previous October.[28]

The suspending brooch is similar to that of the post-1958 rifle and pistol distinguished designs, but the bar carries the words **UNITED STATES** in plain, narrow capital letters, while

Fig. 9.24

the federal shield and some oak-leaf ornamentation is above. Suspended by two sets of rings is a disk 1 $^1/_2$ inches in diameter, with a relief map of the Western Hemisphere surrounded by two laurel branches. Around the outside are the words **DISTINGUISHED INTERNATIONAL SHOOTER** in capital letters 0.15 inch high.

All living people who had represented the United States in the Olympics, the Pan-American Games, and the International Shooting Union (UIT or Union Internationale de Tir, later the ISSF or International Sport Shooting Federation) World Championships and had won first, second, or third place (individual or team) retroactively received these badges. In 1956 the U.S. Army formed the Army Advanced Marksmanship Unit (later the U.S. Army Marksmanship Unit) at Fort Benning as the unit to select and train army personnel who would compete in the Olympics and other international shooting events. As a result most army winners of the U.S. distinguished international shooter badge since the late 1950s have been with this unit. Twenty-six distinguished international shooter badges were initially given to living personnel in 1963, including four women—Gail N. Liberty, Charlotte Bertkenkamp, Gertrude P. Schlernitzauer, and Marjorie Annan—but none were from the army. The first woman from the U.S. Army to receive the badge was Second Lieutenant Margaret L. Thompson, in 1966.[29]

The face of the original distinguished international shooter badge is a matte gold, but the reverse of this 14-karat, thin badge is highly polished. When issued, it was machine engraved with the winner's name and year of qualification. Anderson and others who earned the badge in 1962 and before had that year engraved on the reverse rather than the year of initial presentation, 1963. Those eligible personnel who were alive when the badge was created in 1963 received engraved badges, while relatives of those deceased were given certificates for the distinguished international badge. To the soldiers still on active duty or in the reserves, the National Board for the Promotion of Rifle Practice presented badges that carried **NBPRP** and a number—engraved in small, block font—at the reverse top of the badge. Sidney Hines and George A. Rehm were the first two army members to become triple distinguished with rifle, pistol, and international badges, although Morris Fisher, a U.S. Marine Corps sergeant for many years and chief warrant officer during World War II, achieved the feat first by winning his rifle distinguished badge in 1915 and a pistol shot badge in 1923, then representing the United States in the 1920 Olympics in Belgium. The army's next triple-distinguished winner was Frederick P. Dean, who won his pistol shield in 1962, a year after winning his distinguished rifle badge and the international badge in 1966.[30]

In the mid-1970s the badge material changed to a gold wash. Shortly afterward the engraving also changed, so that rather than the number and **NBPRP** being at the top in very small figures, the badge serial number, the military

Fig. 9.25. One of the 1 $^1/_2$–inch-diameter distinguished international shooter badges. The gold badge is mainly of a matte finish, with part of the design polished.

Fig. 9.26. The reverse of the early distinguished international shooter badges not only had the winner's year of qualification, name, and rank on the reverse center; it also had, in small font at the badge top, **NBPRP** and the serial number of the badge, in this case **13**.

Fig. 9.25

Fig. 9.26

rank (if applicable), and the recipient's name all went on the rear center of the badge, with no reference to the issuing board; that is, **NBPRP** did not appear. In some cases the reason for earning the badge also appeared. The badge given to Ray P. Carter, for example, has the number **202** at the top, **RAY CARTER** in the center, **CHAMPION-SHIP OF THE AMERICAS** under that, and **1977** at the bottom.[31]

When the Civilian Marksmanship Program replaced the NBPRP on October 1, 1996, the sequential number system continued uninterrupted. Between initiation in 1963 and the end of 1999, 438 badges were released, including 39 retroactively and a total of 30 for display and replacement of lost, missing, or otherwise misplaced badges. Recipients included personnel from all services as well as civilians who met the qualifications.[32]

Although the original criteria for the U.S. distinguished international shooter badge included placement in the Olympic games, Pan-American Games, and World Shooting Championships, other significant matches soon came on the scene. The first separate World Moving Target Championships, sometimes called the world trap and skeet championships, world shotgun championships, or similar names, were held in 1961. The first Championship of the Americas was held in 1973 in Mexico City.[33]

The criteria for the distinguished international shooter badge changed in 1977 to insure that a very high standard was retained, since in a few international shooting events only a small number of competitors entered, and in these cases one of the top three places was more easily attained than in other shooting contests. Issuing officials made minor adjustments in criteria until January 1, 1999, when a dauntingly complicated system of points was instituted—a system somewhat similar to that for the other two current distinguished badges, requiring a shooter to earn thirty points for the badge. Varying points, from five to thirty, are given for first through eighth individual

placement in Olympic games, world championships, and world clay-target championships; for being a member of first-, second-, and third-place teams in the Olympics, world championships, world clay-target championships, Pan American games, Championship of the Americas, and world junior championships; and for first-place team in the Championship of the Americans junior championship. Between five and twenty points can also be earned by first-, second-, or third-place individual placement in the World Cup matches, Championship of the Americas, world junior championship, and Championship of the Americas' junior championship. A new world record earns twenty points, and a tie of a world record earns ten points.[34]

Matches for air rifles and air pistols and for trap and skeet have allowed a soldier's badge to wander considerably from the standard used between the 1880s and the 1960s. A distinguished badge previously represented performance of an unusually high skill level, with "standard military service rifles [and/or] pistols."[35]

AERIAL GUNNER AND BOMBARDIER BADGES

As he stood at attention in the summer sun, Second Lieutenant Earle E. Partridge was quite proud of himself, ready to receive his three gold distinguished badges. This was the first time the new distinguished aerial gunner and distinguished aerial bomber badges were being awarded as a result of the U.S. Air Corps' annual bombing and gunnery matches, held at Langley Field, Virginia. Partridge had come a long way since he had enlisted at age eighteen

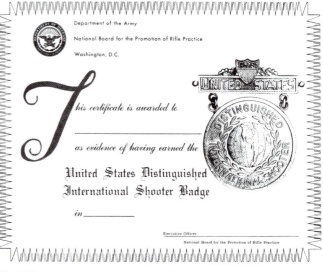

Fig. 9.27

during World War I and fought with the 79th Division in the Argonne offensive. A 1924 West Point graduate, he had won the observation and attack pilots' match in 1926 and in 1927 and now again in 1928.[36]

The War Department was recognizing Partridge, plus pursuit pilot Second Lieutenant J. J. Williams, observer First Lieutenant James E. Parker along with the championship bomber crew, pilot First Lieutenant J. F. Whitley, and bombardier First Lieutenant William M. Lanagan, and First Lieutenant A. I. Puryear, who won the lighter-than-air-category bombing competition. Special new gold badges had finally been approved in May 1928 for the competitions. Little did those present know that in just four short years, in 1932, similar gold badges would be awarded at Langley Field for the last time. After the 1928 matches, Assistant Secretary of War F. Trubee Davidson presented awards for that year and for the previous two matches, a total of ten distinguished aerial gunner's badges and nine distinguished aerial bomber's badges, although six of the previous winners were absent from the ceremony.[37]

As the awards ceremony began on June 9, someone noted that Partridge would only be able to wear one of the badges, as regulations did not provide for wearing more than one badge of the same design. A controversial decision then ensued on the spot, with unpleasant results. It was decided that Partridge would receive only one badge. Hastily given his choice, he selected the badge for 1926. He was so disgusted over not receiving the other two, however, that he never wore the badge again, although he had a very distinguished career, serving as Jimmy Doolittle's chief of staff and deputy commander in the 15th Air Force in World War II and as commander of the 5th U.S. Air Force at the outset of the Korean War. He received his third star in 1951, temporarily serving as Far East Air Force commander, and in 1955 he became head of the U.S. Continental Air Defense Command.[38]

After World War I the army started a formal peacetime aerial gunnery and bombing training. Initially the courses were considered "tentative" by the War Department, as the Air Service experimented with the best way to train. In 1924, for the first time, a national match was held at Langley Field, near Newport News, Virginia. These initial firing courses consisted of firing fixed and flexible (movable) guns at both ground and aerial targets and bombing from low altitudes, 5,000

Fig. 9.28

Fig. 9.28. This U.S. Army pilot wears one of the scarce 14-karat-gold distinguished aerial bomber badges awarded to the top aviators from 1926 through 1932.

and 8,000 feet. It took until January 1926 for the Air Service to publish its mission officially, which was to become the underpinning for its training prior to World War II. The mission included destroying enemy aviation, attacking enemy ground forces, and attacking other enemy objectives on land or sea. The fledgling air service established a set of standard courses in 1926 in conjunction with the three basic badges (expert, sharpshooter, and marksman) and began to issue qualification bars for aerial machine gun and aerial bombardment. These courses and accompanying qualification bars were primarily for officers. Once an officer had qualified as an expert aerial gunner or an expert in aerial bombardment, he was excused from further annual qualification. While the various aerial-gunnery courses allowed for qualification in all three grades, the only grade for a bombardier was that of expert.[39]

The logical climax to the regular practice season consisted of annual machine gun and bombing matches. The competition was open to "all components of the Army of the United States and the Bureau of Aeronautics of the Navy," although naval aviators never won the events. Three contests were held in aerial gunnery: pursuit pilot's match, observation and attack pilot's match, and observer's match. Aerial-bombardment matches were two—heavier than air and lighter than air. In all cases the winners of the matches were rated as "distinguished aerial gunner" or "distinguished

Fig. 9.29. *These aviators proudly wear their distinguished aerial gunner and distinguished aerial bomber badges immediately after the initial 1928 awards ceremony, at which the 1926 and 1927 badges were also awarded.*

aerial bomber." The lone winner for the lighter-than-air bomber's match was the initial recipient, Lieutenant A. I. Puryear, as the Air Corps did not hold this match again. In the airplane bombing competitions, planes were dispatched in flights of two.[40]

A general lack of military funds in the mid-1920s hurt training, and the Great Depression hampered training even further. During the time of the annual bombing and training matches held at Langley Field, scores went up and down contrary to expectations of the generals in Washington. In 1927 all scores rose compared to those of other years, but it was the only time of such improvements. In the late 1920s, at the height of the competition, teams flew from France Field, Panama, to participate.[41]

Funding was so short and training so scandalously inadequate that in 1929—when the War Department authorized all attack, bombardment, observation, and pursuit squadrons in the United States and the Canal Zone to send representatives to the annual matches—six squadrons did not do so. The next year some observations squadrons had no officer qualified for the matches. Chief of the Air Corps Major General James E. Fechet changed the matches from June to September in 1930, in the hopes that scores would improve, since most units held their annual practice and record firings in May, June, and July. Major General Benjamin D. Foulois became chief of the Air Corps in December 1931. A demanding trainer, like his predecessor he complained about the lack of ranges and of results by pilots. In June 1932 Foulois commented dryly that the results of the September 1 through 15, 1931, annual competition were "similar to last

year" and that "results were not up to standards." He blamed the stagnant scores on the lack of suitable ranges, although the root cause was the want of a modern bombsight, in addition to a funds shortage that prevented procurement of ranges. Scores did not improve the next year.[42]

The 1932 air maneuvers, the other major aerial-training event, could not even be conducted due shortages of money, equipment, and supplies, so continuation of the gunnery and bombing matches could not be justified. Some Army Air Corps units could not even conduct serious preliminary gunnery or bombing training due to an ammunition shortage, although on paper the army allocated plenty of bombs, including a special allowance specifically for the matches. These problems ultimately curtailed the matches and the associated distinguished badges. The requirements for officers to help manage the Civilian Conservation Corps also proved a great burden. The air corps was short of pilots throughout this time. Personnel issues, combined with the financial shortage and lack of rising scores, ended the matches. Military specifications continued to describe the badges into the 1950s, but they had been eliminated from official drawings immediately after World War II. The Air Corps last awarded these badges in 1932.[43]

There are two dies for each badge, one made by the War Department and the other by the Bailey, Banks, and Biddle Company (BB&B). Apparently the 1926, 1927, and 1928 awards were made using the War Department versions while the 1929 through 1932 awards came from the BB&B dies. The early War Department badges are 14-karat gold, with the back so marked (**14K**), while the commercial versions are marked **BB&B**. The

Fig. 9.29

War Department–struck badges are the thinner of the two styles, being approximately 0.12 inch thick, while the ones from the jewelry firm are about 0.16 inch thick. In addition the War Department style has a slight concave dish shape and an old-gold satin finish, while the Bailey, Banks, and Biddle badges have flat, shiny backs.[44]

DISTINGUISHED AUTOMATIC RIFLEMAN

When the army reorganized in 1920, it proved the new dominance of the machine gun. Each infantry regiment received three heavy weapons companies—one company in each battalion.

Within the remaining rifle companies, each squad contained a Browning Automatic Rifle (BAR). With its twenty-round magazine, one BAR equaled the firepower of several ordinary riflemen, providing a base of suppressive fire so others in the rifle squad could maneuver. In the cavalry the machine rifle, a variation of the BAR, was the equivalent weapon.

While the 1922-style leg badges and the training regulations took the BAR into account, award regulations only implied that after a soldier won three such leg badges he would be awarded a distinguished badge. Training Regulation 150-10 covered the automatic rifle during the 1920s and 1930s, and under that regulation various corps areas and overseas departments held the novel automatic rifle competitions. Firing consisted of rapid firing for one minute each from 200, 300, and 500 yards at man-sized silhouette targets, with no limit on the number of rounds. A point was allowed for each round that passed through a target. Then contestants fired for one

Fig. 9.30.

Fig. 9.31.

Fig. 9.32.

Fig. 9.33.

Fig. 9.30. One of the gold distinguished aerial gunner badges, displaying a winged bullet, which was made by Rock Island Arsenal and awarded for performance from 1926 through 1928.

Fig. 9.31. One of the gold-plated distinguished aerial gunner badges made by the jewelry company Bailey, Banks, and Biddle. These were awarded for performance from 1929 through 1932.

*Fig. 9.32. The reverse of the badges shown in figures 9.30 (right) and 9.31 (left). The **A.S.** stands for Air Service, the U.S. Army's aviation branch, which became the Air Corps later in 1926 and the Army Air Force in 1942. Merrick served as an enlisted man in the aero section of the New York naval militia in 1916 and as a private and private first class in the U.S. Army's enlisted reserve corps during 1917 and 1918. He was commissioned in the aviation section of the Signal Corps in February 1918. After being discharged in 1919 he joined the cavalry as a second lieutenant in 1921 and was transferred to the aviation service in February 1923.*

Fig. 9.33. An example of a gold-plated distinguished aerial bomber badge made by Bailey, Banks, and Biddle.

minute with a sandbag rest, again without a limit on the number of rounds, but the target was at a 6-foot-high and 10-foot-long screen divided into sixty, 1-foot squares, placed at anywhere between 200 and 600 yards. Shooters received five points for each different square hit, plus one additional point for each round that struck the screen.

In the Panama Canal Zone the army held more BAR competitions than other any department or corps area, and marksmanship competition was particularly keen in the 11th Engineer Regiment. In 1938 the 11th Engineers had one company that bragged 100 percent qualification with the rifle, while a second company had 99.6 percent, and two other companies of the 11th had above 99 percent. One such top marksman and BAR prizewinner in December 1925 was the first sergeant of Company E, 11th Engineers, Harold V. Goddard. With a score of 921 points, he won a badge with the bronze BAR clasp. The next year First Sergeant Goddard made a lower score of 907 and barely won his second automatic rifle prize; nevertheless, he won. Then he placed first in the Canal Zone December 1927 competition, with a score of 1,054, and received a gold-clasp prize. Harold Goddard had become the first man to win three prizes with an automatic rifle. In mid-January 1928 he applied through channels to the adjutant general of the army to be designated as a distinguished automatic rifleman. Little did Sergeant Goddard realize the saga that was to follow his simple application.[45]

BROWNING AUTOMATIC RIFLE

Weapons designer John M. Browning developed the Browning Automatic Rifle during World War I as the U.S. Army's counterpart to the Lewis machine gun, the Maxim gun, and the Hotchkiss gun. The Browning Automatic Rifle, or BAR, was first demonstrated early in 1917, before the United States declared war on Germany, and the United States made well over 50,000 of the weapons before the war's end, although only about 4,000 saw action in the trenches.

Thus supplied with "surplus" BARs, the army heavily used these sixteen-pound M 1918 weapons between the world wars. In 1937 and again in 1940 the army modified the weapon—primarily to add a bipod, a hinged butt plate, and a selector for automatic rates of fire—and then used the resulting twenty-pound, 47 3/4-inch-long, M 1918A2 BAR during World War II and the Korean War. These modifications allowed three rates of fire: single shot, 350 rounds a minute, or 550 rounds a minute. All versions of the BAR were supplied with twenty-round magazines. The M-14 rifle finally replaced the BAR during the early 1960s.

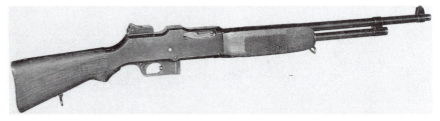

One of the original World War I sixteen-pound Browning Automatic Rifles (BARs).

An M 1918A2 BAR, as used in World War II and Korea. The bipod, a hinged-butt plate, and an internal mechanical addition that allowed various rates of fire resulted in a weapon weighing twenty pounds.

In mid-February 1928 Goddard's request found its way to Washington, D.C., after the adjutant of the Panama Canal Department noted that the regulations did not provide for a distinguished automatic rifleman's badge and that "in the absence of any specific information" the request was forwarded "for consideration." With a wariness bred from years in a small, tight-knit, rules-are-rules army, the chief of infantry rapidly concluded that distinguished awards should be confined to the rifle and pistol and provided a negative endorsement, but then within a week and a half the chief of staff's office ruled that a distinguished automatic rifle award would be made. This started the bureaucratic wheels in motion, and quickly the quartermaster general's office started to design a badge and to make changes in the training regulation and the regulation covering uniforms and insignia.[46]

Nonetheless, the real problems were just beginning. The quartermaster's office took over two months to draft a proposed design that was generally similar to the circular design, with laurel wreath used on the aerial gunner and aerial bombardier badges but with a detailed target in the center and a display of five bullets. The secretary of war also wanted the recommendations of the Fine Arts Commission, an organization that wielded considerable political clout in Washington. In response the quartermaster general pointed out the considerable difficulties the army was about to encounter. It had not been the "custom . . . to submit items of this nature to the Commission," and for good reason.

Commission approval always engendered considerable delays, and then the army was severely criticized when the proposed product was not ready within a short time. In addition the commission usually recommended a specific artist or sculpture, and then the army was in the position of not having the money to hire the person. While this was a seemingly minor problem, the challenge became more difficult because the recommended artists usually demanded about $1,500 for a design, while the existing law prohibited the Quartermaster Corps from paying more than $500 for anything without a competitive bid. After an anguished appeal from the quartermaster general, Major General William Hart, General Charles P. Summerall, the chief of staff, per-

Fig. 9.34

sonally concluded that it was not necessary to submit the design to the Fine Arts Commission. To Hart's chagrin, however, Summerall also directed that the badge needed a totally new design.

Despite the accusation that outside artists took too long to design a badge, it took a full additional year for the Quartermaster Corps to create the final version: an automatic rifle superimposed on a square turned on a corner, representing a target and laurel leaves. By now it was June 1929, one and one-half years since Sergeant Goddard had qualified for his distinguished award. It took another six months to refine the design and produce the prototype badge so the award could be officially approved. After that the final die had to be made and the initial badges produced. It was September 1930 before the secretary of war could state that Harold V. Goddard was to receive his engraved badge. Goddard had left the army, in the interim, in November 1929, but his legacy was established. Even the NRA established a national automatic rifle match in 1930.[47]

When the army revised national competition after World War II, it limited shooting matches to rifles and pistols and excluded automatic rifles. Accordingly, the Quartermaster Corps discontinued authority for the distinguished automatic rifle badge and eliminated the design from its official files, although the drawings did continue to show the aerial bomber and aerial gunner badges for awhile before they too were eliminated.[48]

Fig. 9.34. *A distinguished automatic rifleman's badge, first awarded in 1930 for competition in December 1927. The army withdrew authorization for the badge after World War II.*

CHAPTER TEN

TROPHIES AND ASSOCIATED AWARDS

OTHER REWARDS

THE START

Despite the immediate victory in the Spanish-American War, President Theodore Roosevelt and Secretary of War Elihu Root prodded Congress until they reorganized the army. With the help of Root's deft touch Congress created the General Staff Corps, expanded the army, and completely overhauled the artillery. Both the executive and the legislative branches tackled small-arms improvements in a twentieth-century way . . . by throwing some money at the problem.

Besides funding the new Springfield rifle, the Army Appropriations Act of March 3, 1903, created a national marksmanship trophy, medals, and other prizes, all to be open to regular-army soldiers and members of the National Guard and militias of the United States. Later amendments also allowed marines and sailors to be eligible for the prizes. Even before Congress acted to correct this oversight, the secretary of war directed that the U.S. Marines could participate in the first National Match, although the Treasury Department ruled the leathernecks ineligible for any of the prizes.[1]

The first National Matches were held at Sea Girt, New Jersey, in September 1903, under far from ideal conditions. The weather was overcast and cold for early September, and problems plagued the army team. It arrived late, and this allowed for just one day of practice at short ranges, although the team's weakness was at long ranges owing to its government ammunition, which did not perform consistently. Due to the army team's late arrival, it did not even have a camp established, but the New Jersey National Guard generously set up facilities for the regulars, using borrowed cots, blankets, and tents.[2]

The actual shooting was scheduled for two days, but that was not to be. Foggy weather prevented early starts, and the limited number of shooting points was totally inadequate. All of this kept the contestants firing until after 6:00 P.M. The event stretched into three days. Twelve-man teams fired first from the standing position at 200 yards and then from the prone position at 500, 600, 800, 900, and 1,000 yards. While in the nineteenth century "laying down" firing could have been in one of several ways, with the feet either towards or away from the target, in this first National Match all contestants had to fire with their heads pointed towards the target in the modern prone position, the army's only "legal" prone position after an 1897 regulation change.[3]

The inauspicious prematch start for the regular army team showed its lack of preparation. The National Guard and the marines out fired them, with the first five places going to the guard teams from New York, New Jersey, Massachusetts, the District of Columbia, and Ohio. The U.S. Marine Corps placed sixth and received only a certificate due to the legal limitations. The army infantry rifle team followed at seventh, and the army cavalry carbine team placed ninth, after the Connecticut National Guard.[4]

The following year the army hosted the fledgling National Matches at Fort Riley, Kansas, then returned to Sea Girt in 1905. Slowly the army edged up. The army infantry team placed third and the army cavalry team fourth in 1904, following New York and the U.S. Navy. In 1905 the infantry team edged out Ohio to place second, behind the most frequent winner, the New York National Guard, although the cavalry team slipped to eleventh.[5]

Up to this time army headquarters had simply appointed men to fire in the National

Matches. The training of the new but eager apprentice by the well-worn and skilled master takes place in all crafts, but when there is no true grand craftsman, the student is left to his own devices and his early works may be crude. So it was with the initial few competitions for the National Trophy. During 1906, for the first time, the army held tryouts for the national team, and the student was finally a master. All of the practice and persistence and the team tryout system finally paid off in 1906, when the U.S. Army took both first and second in the national rifle-team match, with the infantry team scoring 3,251 points and the cavalry 3,191. In the September 4–10, 1906, competition, held for the last time on the New Jersey coast, the New York team placed fourth among the forty-one teams with a score of 3,158, behind Massachusetts, which fired 3,176. The army never looked back at the militias.[6]

Trophies and unique prize medals were a prominent part of shooting rewards from the outset, and these beckoned irresistibly to many soldiers. A variety of wealthy late nineteenth-century philanthropists had provided several magnificent team trophies; however, each trophy was isolated from the others. A typical single match had its own unique first-place reward. When Congress established the National Matches in 1903, aside from providing a first-place trophy, it left the War Department to work out the details for other trophies and medals. As a result Washington officials, working with various militias and the NRA, were able to obtain some of the old, opulent trophies for award in the National Matches.

They collected the Hilton and the Soldier of Marathon trophies for presentation at the National Matches. One can imagine some of the delicate negotiations that must have taken place when the War Department solicited and then obtained these two heroic trophies, even if at the time they were only a quarter of a century old. Initially, the magnificent Hilton Trophy became the reward for second place in the National Match, and the older Soldier of Marathon Trophy became the third prize.

The first revision occurred in 1909, when competing teams were placed in classes. The regular military establishments had become so dominant in the annual National Matches that in each subsequent year the competing teams were divided into three classes (A, B, and C) based upon their relative standing the previous year. By this time the National Matches had captured the public imagination, and the contests began to receive a torrent of press coverage.[7]

As the military continued to dominate what became the premier annual match in the nation, the contest was again realigned. In 1916 rifle teams were classed to compete against each other in one of three groups: the various military-service teams; the

Fig. 10.1

Fig. 10.1. *Harry T. Cavanaugh, while he was a cavalry captain. Cavanaugh graduated from the military academy in 1891, was promoted to captain in May 1901, and became a temporary infantry colonel in World War I, where he won the Distinguished Service Cross. Cavanaugh was promoted to colonel of cavalry in the regular army in July 1920. He wears several shooting awards among his medals. Top row: Spanish-American War medal; Cuba pacification medal; gold medal for third place in the 1906 national individual-rifle match held at Sea Girt, New Jersey; and expert rifleman badge, earned in 1905. Center row: distinguished marksman badge, which was awarded in 1904; bronze medal for being on the cavalry team in 1906, which placed second and won the Hilton trophy; bronze medal for the cavalry team in 1904, which placed fourth at Fort Riley, Kansas, in the National Match. Bottom row: gold prize for fourth place in army-level match in 1903; gold prize for second place in army-level match in 1904; gold first prize for first place in the Department of the Missouri 1903 match; and gold first prize for first place in the 1904 Northern Division competition.*

Fig. 10.2. Major General Robert H. Allen, chief of infantry, examines the National Trophy in 1927, shortly after the infantry team won the trophy. Allen's bottom row of medals includes the distinguished rifleman badge (nearest the camera), won in 1910 while he was a captain in the 29th Infantry, and a pre-1919 National Trophy medal. The trophy and the associated medals display an ancient warrior with four hunting dogs on leashes.

Fig. 10.3. The Soldier of Marathon Trophy, a gift of General George W. Wingate, first inspector of rifle practice for the New York Militia (1874–79). The trophy was originally the first-prize award in the "State, Inter-State and First Division Matches." The oldest trophy awarded at the National Matches, it depicts a bronze figure of the Greek runner Pheidippides, who—although exhausted and fallen—still holds high the torch he is carrying to announce the Greek victory at Marathon.

militia and National Guard teams; and the colleges and universities, including the military and naval academies. Team groupings were again shuffled in 1921, and so were the three major trophies awarded for the best team in each class: (1) regular army and the recently established reserves; (2) National Guard; and (3) civilian. The first-place team overall received the National Trophy. The highest-scoring team from the remaining two classes received the Hilton Trophy, and the highest-scoring team from the last category, the Soldier of Marathon Trophy. ROTC and military-school competitors shot for lesser annual trophies until the introduction of the Minute Man Trophy in 1925. Accompanying these top trophies were prize medals depicting the prestigious awards.[8]

As these early changes took effect and the century approached the end of the first decade, the matches and prizes began to take on their own life with accustomed routines. After maneuvering from Sea Girt, New Jersey, to Fort Riley, Kansas, then back to Sea Girt, the matches settled into a comfortable new site at Camp Perry, Ohio. They are still held at Camp Perry to this day, although detours to other locations have occurred, as will be seen.

Fig. 10.3

Camp Perry, located in northern Ohio on Lake Erie, about forty miles east of Toledo, is an army post named for a sailor, Oliver Hazard Perry. The camp is not far from Perry's victory site during the War of 1812. The camp first hosted the National Matches starting on August 28, 1907. The National Board for the Promotion of Rifle Practice (NBPRP) set the detailed rules, the match sequence, and the prizes, as well as dividing the great event into several matches such as the National Individual Match and the National Pistol Match. In subsequent years the NRA also held its matches at Camp Perry, the two sponsoring organizations playing off of each other.[9]

Camp Perry got its start when General Ammon Critchfield★ of the Ohio National Guard was shooting ducks in the area and, as a marksman, realized that the space could be used as a target range after a bit of the marsh was filled in. The Ohio legislature responded by buying the first 300 acres, and the new spot was soon available. This roughshod taming of the wetlands that comprise the south shore of Lake Erie forever entrenched Perry firmly in the lore of American shooting. During World War I the army used Camp Perry to train a large number of army marksmen instructors. In World War II it served as a

Fig. 10.2

★A study of the officers of the National Matches between the world wars is revealing. One of the officers for several years was Ammon Critchfield's son, an infantry officer in the organized reserve corps who ultimately became a general and president of the NRA. Another officer was Major General (Ret.) Fred Ainsworth, the former adjutant general who fought the creation of the General Staff Corps, as it cost Ainsworth some of his considerable political clout shortly after the Spanish-American War. The 1925 NRA president was Senator F. E. Warren.

Fig. 10.4

Fig. 10.5

prisoner-of-war camp. Even today Perry is an incompletely finished and rambunctious military post a good many miles from much of what passes today for real civilization. The major national trophies reside in an innocent office building at Camp Perry, literally near the end of a pot-holed road. So obscure is the site that over ninety years after its founding, it still has the rude title of "Camp" rather than the solid permanence of "Fort." These rustic and familiar features make Camp Perry a favorite destination of experienced shooters, who enjoy the atmosphere more than any

Boy Scout at his summer camp. It continues to serve into the twenty-first century and the foreseeable future despite its rambling appearance, which makes it resemble an overgrown 1930s set of roadside cabins. The newcomer may experience some culture shock.[10]

As more and more non-military personnel participated in the NRA's combat at Camp Perry, profound changes occurred. Between the world wars the NRA allocated massive and impressive trophies and accompanying medals, so that military personnel and military teams could win only select matches, while civilian, police, and other special groups competed for another range of trophies. Arms and ammunition makers sponsored some of the latter. The army itself gave the NRA several trophies. Camp Perry matches—whether NRA contests or National Matches sponsored by the War Department or its subordinate office, the National Board for the Promotion of Rifle Practice (NBPRP)—came to be the premier annual shooting events. Indeed, the only difference between the two events was that the NBPRP controlled congressional funds that even provided for transportation of some civilian teams, while the NRA provided assistance such as publicity. A third agency was the Director of Civilian Marksmanship, an office that was originally part of the War Department, which handled the sales of government arms and ammunition to civilian shooters. In 1925, for example, the director was Lieutenant Colonel George Shaw, who was also the executive officer of the NRA. It was well after World War II before the strains between the NRA and the army offices supporting marksmanship came to a critical point of rupture.[11]

During the post–World War I era trophies previously given for other events became more heavily concentrated in the National Matches. The price paid for this convenient bureaucratic alignment was the loss of some of the most romantic and historic trophies ever created for the U.S. Army, the most notable being the Nevada Trophy (discussed below).

183

TROPHIES AND ASSOCIATED AWARDS

Fig. 10.4. The winning National Guard team for 1963 with the Hilton Trophy. Composed of soldiers from the Maryland National Guard, this is a typical state team with members from several units.

Fig. 10.5. A souvenir and advertisement of the first National Match held at Camp Perry, Ohio. The bronze planchet, 1 inch in diameter, is suspended by a red, white, and blue ribbon that has naturally folded vertically over time, and as a result the 1-inch-wide ribbon appears narrower than the medal. The reverse of the medal has the raised wording **COMPLIMENTS OF THE HAYES BROS. Co. NEWARK, N. J. MAKERS OF TROPHIES, MEDALS AND BADGES OF EVERY DESCRIPTION.**

The National Matches consist of several competitions that have grown up over time. Overall competitions fall into two general areas: National Trophy matches, which currently include seven contests, and the NRA national rifle and pistol championships, which now consist of four championships. Initially, the National Matches were the individual-rifle match, the individual-pistol match, and the rifle-team match. In 1920 the NBPRP added the national pistol-team match, and over time the National Matches have expanded to the current number. The trophies and medals listed in 1990s army regulations for the National Trophy matches are:

The President's Pistol Match
National Trophy Individual Pistol Match
National Trophy Pistol Match
The President's Rifle Match
National Trophy Individual Match
National Trophy Rifle Team Match
National Trophy Infantry Team Match.

Since the start of the National Matches, generous individuals and organizations have continued to contribute special trophies. In the second half of the twentieth century the absolute number of trophies has erupted. At the first National Match the War Department awarded only three trophies, although the NRA gave a few more. By 1925 shooters could receive sixteen military trophies, and this grew to thirty-three by the end of 1956. The NRA provided a great many other trophies, many of which were won by soldiers or were even reserved for the military. The 1990 armed forces regulation listed a numbing fifty-one national trophies provided by the National Board for the Promotion of Rifle Practice.

Police departments competed more heavily than the army in pistol matches during the 1920s and 1930s, and after World War II the men in blue sent teams in even greater numbers. The result was that some trophies became reserved for law-enforcement agencies.

As the number of various trophies expanded, several very old and historic trophies unfortunately became lost, damaged, or even downgraded due to a lack of historical perspective. Many of these old trophies and companion prize medals connected with the army are discussed in the second half of this chapter, where they are presented in order of seniority. Many of the trophies and medals awarded—especially in the nonarmy categories—have

been omitted from this book in the interest of space. Only limited information is given even for the contests that are discussed, as data on the medals and trophies presented at the National Matches could easily fill a large volume. Emphasis is placed on selected trophies and prize medals related to the military or to military arms.

Starting in 1930 and into the 1950s, the shooter or team winning a rotating trophy also received a miniature for personal retention. The actual trophy was sent in a special box to the winner's home via railway express once the engraving was complete. The winner returned the large trophy the next year and kept the small version. A few years after the Korean War this all changed. Wall plaques became the normal individual mementos. For a while some trophies given by the NBPRP were represented by handsome cast-metal replicas mounted to wooden shields or rectangles. Soon trophies were retained at Camp Perry, so the winner could not even bask in its reflected glory at home. The NRA settled for a less expensive memento solution, its plaques carrying an 8 x 10 black-and-white photograph of the trophy with a black-and-white plastic plate below. Figure 10.6 shows an example.[12]

Although things looked up for competitive marksmanship when the NRA and the Director of Civilian Marksmanship held matches at Camp Perry in the 1920s, this situation reversed during the depression. Paradoxically, unemployment allowed more shooters to participate, and prize money—no matter how

Fig. 10.6

small—was an encouragement to marksmen at a time when government support funds evaporated. Beginning in 1932 the budget ax fell on Camp Perry and the matches. To save funds the army sponsored a range of matches in each corps area and arbitrarily assigned various trophies to different matches. For the most part the NRA followed suit. Camp Perry only saw regional contests at this time. In 1932, for example, the Wimbledon Cup was presented as the trophy in the VI Corps Area for twenty shots at 1,000 yards rather than for a national championship, and the Cavalry Cup was awarded at an El Paso area match, the winner being Sergeant Roy A. McDaris of the 8th Cavalry.[13]

Congress, supported by Secretary of War Elihu Root,* created the National Board for the Promotion of Rifle Practice in 1903 at the urging of the NRA. The NBPRP's responsibility was to promote citizens' training in small arms so that nonmilitary citizens would be competent marksmen if they were called upon to serve in time of war. The secretary of war, and later the secretary of the army, appointed board members to the NBPRP. The Director of Civilian Marksmanship (DCM) was the implementing officer for the NBPRP, that person normally being a commissioned officer of the U.S. Army.[14]

Army officers appointed as the DCM and appointed to the National Board for the Promotion of Rifle Practice had the responsibility of supplying awards related to the national military matches, while the NRA provided awards for their various championships. The distinction between these organizations became more critical in the 1960s, as the NRA took a more political stance. Government support for the National Matches became a political football in the late 1960s, when the Vietnam War divided Americans. Vigorous protests against a wide range of causes became widely accepted in American culture, and that opened the door for strong divisions within the United States regarding many topics.

The NRA eagerly took up the standard for the right to bear arms, while opponents decried the use of government dollars to promote shooting or weapons support in general. The national competitive-shooting programs and the armed forces were caught in the middle. During the 1920s, 1930s, 1950s, and early 1960s the services supported various ranges at the National Matches, but in 1968 this personnel subsidization was withdrawn. National political divisions tore away at the NRA, army shooting, National Matches, and the NBPRP. An aggressively dismal confrontation between the military and the NRA continued to worsen until the time that the Civilian Marksmanship Program (CMP) was formed in 1996. While national government support waned in the 1960s and 1970s, the number of competitors at the Camp Perry matches dropped significantly as various sources of state organizational support also collapsed, reducing the number of competing military teams.

The metamorphosis was completed in the 1990s when Congress privatized the NBPRP, making it the Corporation for the Promotion of Rifle Practice and Firearms Safety. Under this arrangement, in 1996 the CMP became a nonprofit organization, run by a nine-person corporation board of directors. Controversy surrounded the transition, as many CMP employees initially believed the new board lined its own pockets at the expense of competitors, who paid entrance fees, and of the government, which continued to supply some weapons.[15]

MEDAL GIVEN WITH VARIOUS TROPHIES

The crack shots who won trophies also received medals to commemorate their victories; however, during the last forty years the design and construction of such medals evolved to cheaper and gaudier versions. During the first fifty years, both the NRA and the NBPRP awarded gold, silver, and bronze medals, using a set of clear historic designs. Team medals were primarily made in bronze, but in the 1930s some became gold colored. Select top medals continued to contain several dollars' worth of gold or at least were made of sterling silver until after World War II, but most medals decreased

---

*As secretary of war, Root also founded the U.S. Army War College and, with congressional support, developed the U.S. Army's General Staff Corps. A Republican, he also served as secretary of state, as a member of the Alaska Boundary Tribunal, and as honorary president of the Pan-American Congress in 1906. He was elected senator from New York in 1912, the same year he received the Nobel Peace Prize. He was made ambassador extraordinary and head of a special diplomatic mission to Russia in 1917. In 1929 he served as a member of the League of Nations committee to revise the World Court Statute. He died in Clinton, New York, in 1937.

in intrinsic value. For a short time after World War II "gold" individual medals continued to be made of 14-karat gold, as some had been before the war, but in the 1950s this designation was interpreted as referring to color only. Thus most post–World War II "gold" medals are gold in appearance only. Beginning in the 1950s even the historic designs fell prey to pressure from salesmen.

Awards made since the Vietnam War have been gold, silver, or bronze color with the number of each depending upon the number of entrants and upon whether the medals were for teams or individuals. These medals signified high placement in various matches. For team matches medals were awarded generally to include the top 15 percent of competitors, while in individual competition awards varied between the top ten and the top 20 percent. The top 10 percent of the nondistinguished individual competitors received medals that were further divided so that one-sixth received them in gold color (often with first, second, and third place designated by appropriate bars), one-third in silver, and one-half in bronze. Team medals for the 1960s included gold color to each member of the first team, with silver to those placing second and the rest in the top 15 percent receiving bronze. Ribbons, which suspended many NBPRP medals prior to World War II, had evenly divided red, white, and blue ribbons, although—as will be seen—the material varied.[16]

The absence of any widely published formal descriptions of the National Match medals has caused an astonishing dearth of information on these interesting awards. The NBPRP, the NRA, and even some companies who struck the awards cannot now fully describe their own medals. As these many awards generally have not been documented, few people are familiar with them.

When one examines a list of the National Matches, one sees that next to the year 1914 stands the first "no competition" note, a citation that is later repeated, especially during and immediately after World War II. Some of the most modern and interesting prizes came out of that first note.

In the years after 1903, the new, congressionally supported National Matches grew to dominate NRA competitions and finally, by 1914, totally engulfed them. To replace the 1914 Camp Perry matches the National Board for the Promotion of Rifle Practice created five regional contests called national divisional competitions. Although the army ultimately hosted only four of these regional matches rather than the planned five, each match consisted of the regional part of the national individual rifle match, the national team division match, and the national division pistol match.[17]

Fig. 10.7

Fig. 10.8

Fig. 10.9

The army's theory was that these divisional competitions would reduce travel time and expense, allowing more teams and national guardsmen to compete. A cardinal premise was that each state would spend nearly equal funds, so states from the South and the distant West would no longer be at a financial disadvantage. The four regional matches were: Division Competition A, held at Sea Girt, New Jersey, for those in New England and states immediately south and west, to and including Virginia, West Virginia, and Pennsylvania; Division Competition B, held at Jacksonville, Florida, for states south of Virginia and west, to include Mississippi and Kentucky; Division Competition D, held at Fort Riley, Kansas, including the area south and west of Arkansas to Arizona, Nebraska, and Colorado; and Division Competition E, held near Portland, Oregon, for western states extending east, including Montana and Utah. The match for Division Competition C, which was to comprise the upper Midwest was not held, so competitors in that area were allowed to compete in the "nearest adjoining division."[18]

At the War Department's request, the engravers in the Philadelphia mint created three 1 ½–inch–diameter prizes. The strikingly modern designs developed by the U.S. Mint's artists may have been influenced by New York City's great Armory Art Show of 1913, but whether the upheaval in the art world had a direct influence on them or not, the designers did scrap the old ornate look. One new vignette was based upon Daniel Chester French's 1875 first statue, the *Minute Man,* standing by his plow. The medal has **INDIVIDUAL RIFLE COMPETITION** engraved around the edge. The second, marked **RIFLE TEAM COMPETITION**, shows the ultimate marksman, William Tell, and his small son advancing to the front, with Tell's crossbow thrown over his right shoulder. The scene was taken from the monument sculpted by Richard Kissling and dedicated in Altdoft, Switzerland, in 1895. The third design has two M 1911 .45 caliber automatic pistols with barrels crossed, a U.S. shield between them and **PISTOL COMPETITION** across the bottom. Each of the three is suspended by two sets of chains from identical bars inscribed **DIVISION**; the bar's center also displays a laurel wreath. The reverse of each planchet shows an eagle with wings displayed, standing between two laurel branches; a tablet for the recipient's name; and **UNITED STATES OF AMERICA**. The back of each brooch carries **A**, **B**, **D**, or **E**, as appropriate for the division.[19]

The mint evidently struck the new prizes late in 1914, making four sets of gold, silver, and bronze prizes—one set for each division. Ultimately the National Board for the Promotion of Rifle Practice gave thirteen gold prizes to each winning team—one to each of the twelve team members and one to the alternate, the medals to the latter men actually being provided in March 1915. Army men won some gold, silver, and bronze prizes in both individual rifle and pistol competitions, and presumably these were in the same ratios as later, that is, one-sixth, one-third, and one-half.[20]

The matches were a flop—how did one determine an overall national champion, and how were the highest teams established, especially when different weather conditions influenced the results? The Militia Bureau attempted to have National Guard teams compete fully in these matches—indeed, that was the reason for the change in format—but as the disappointed chief of militia affairs reported, "Division C and E failed to hold any national guard competitions as contemplated. Only fourteen states participated in all the competitions." He concluded, "it [is] impossible to consider them successful." The Far Western teams had only

*Fig. 10.9. A medal given at the 1908 pistol matches. The brooch reads **THE NATIONAL MATCH** and **PISTOL 1908**. Outside the wreath is a ribbon inscribed **FOR EXCELLENCE IN PISTOL MARKSMANSHIP.***

Fig. 10.10. One of the distinctive team National Match medals given for the 1914 regional meets held at four locations across the United States. These strikingly modern medals, designed and made by the U.S. Mint, marked a radical artistic departure from the earlier awards.

Fig. 10.11. The 1914 rifle team medals designed by the mint show William Tell and his small son advancing to the front, with Tell's crossbow thrown over his right shoulder. The scene is based upon a statue in Altdoft, Switzerland. All of the regional medals in the 1914 set have **DIVISION** on the wreathed brooch.

Fig. 10.12. For the 1914 national pistol competitions, the mint design shows two crossed M 1911 automatic .45 caliber pistols and a national shield. This general design became the basis for later pistol medals used into the 1950s, although red, white, and blue ribbons suspended the subsequent awards.

Fig. 10.13. All of the three 1914 styles of medals had identical backs that display an eagle below an area left blank for engraving the winner's name and unit. For awarded medals the brooch carries a letter **A**, **B**, **D**, or **E** to show the competitor's division.

Fig. 10.14. Some 1914-style medals are found with a **NATIONAL** brooch. Evidently these were mailed to the division winners with the highest scores in the nation.

used finances as an excuse for previous failures to participate.[21]

The national division competition was held in 1914 only, but the army counted prizes won as any other "leg" towards a distinguished designation. These three 1914 designs are also found with a brooch carrying the inscription **NATIONAL**. Evidently such prizes were mailed to winners of the matches after evaluation of the various division scores.[22]

With troubles on the Mexican border in 1916, the army and navy entered no teams in the National Matches that were held unusually late, 20–25 October. The lateness resulted from hosting the contest in the heat at Jacksonville, Florida, where the marines entered a

Fig. 10.12

Fig. 10.10

Fig. 10.13

Fig. 10.11   *Fig. 10.14*

team and won first place. With the start of the war, for the first time the War Department heavily pushed marksmanship training onto the newly recruited soldiers. Many experienced marksmen, such as those who participated in prewar National Matches, either became instructors in the military services—where as part of their daily job they fired on ranges—or joined tactical units. This resulted in a cakewalk for the navy and a host of unusual teams' placing high in the 1918 National Team match, as shown in table 20.[23]

The National Matches, revived in August 1919 with full military participation, were hosted by the U.S. Navy at their ranges in Caldwell, New Jersey, twenty miles northwest of the narrows between Staten Island and Long Island. The matches opened on a windy, rainy, cold day, and fierce, swarming mosquitoes and frequent rains added to the dismal atmosphere. After three weeks some of the teams continued competitions at the twenty-sixth annual interstate competition held at Sea Girt, New Jersey. The U.S. Army entered five teams in the postwar National Match. The teams included a scrappy AEF group thrown together from troops just returned from France,

the cavalry team, the infantry team, and two new teams, one from the coast artillery and one from the Philippine scouts. Only one of the army teams placed in the national medals, but the high individual was Sergeant T. B. Crawley, a shooter from the AEF. Including the NRA matches, the marines placed first in thirteen contests and the cavalry in one, with civilians winning the last two.[24]

Individual and team National Match medals, for both rifle and pistol, varied over the years. Except for the 1914-style medals (mentioned above) and the early national rifle team match medals (described below in a section on the National Trophy), a medal consisted of a red, white, and blue ribbon hung from a brooch, suspending a planchet. Early top brooches with pointed ornate corners were engraved **THE National Match-INDIVIDUAL, THE National Match-TEAM, THE National Match**, or similar inscriptions, sometimes along with the year. The minute engraving covers two lines.

The early planchets, suspended by frail silken red, white, and blue ribbons, represent targets, with various engraving added near the edge.

Table 20. *National Team Match Competition Results, 1918, Dominated by the U.S. Navy*

Place	Team
1	U.S. Marine Corps Team 1
2	U.S. Navy Team 1
3	U.S. Navy Caldwell, N.J., Range Team
4	U.S. Navy Team 2
5	U.S. Marine Corps Team 2
6	U.S. Navy Mount Pleasant, S.C., Range Team
7	U.S. Army Cavalry
8	U.S. Navy Camp Logan, Ill., Range Team
9	District of Columbia Civilian
10	U.S. Navy Rumford, R.I., Range Team
11	California Civilian
12	U.S. Navy Great Lakes, Ill., Range Team
13	U.S. Navy Virginia Beach, Va., Range Team
14	New York Civilian
15	U.S. Navy Peekskill, N.Y., Range Team
16	Idaho Civilian
17	U.S. Army Infantry Team 1
18	U.S. Navy Wakefield, Mass., Range Team
19	Washington Civilian
20	U.S. Navy Annapolis, Md., Range Team

Note that the top ten teams comprised the Class A category (those that would compete for the National Trophy the following year) and the next ten teams comprised the Class B category (eligible the next year for the Hilton Trophy).
Data taken from War Department Bulletin 17, May 1919.

Fig. 10.15. *National pistol match medals given from 1915 through the early 1950s carry crossed automatic .45 pistols. In both rifle and pistol contests, if a soldier won the same match later, he received a bar showing the year of his subsequent win. The original medal was won in 1922, and the second twenty-four years later.*

Fig. 10.16. *This bronze 1929 individual pistol match medal has a second-win bar in silver. The design is unusual, since details on the bar are different from those on the brooch. In most cases the bar was identical to the brooch, as shown in figure 10.15.*

Over the target design just outside the engraving is a raised outer edge representing a wreath front and back (for rifle matches), or ornate streamers (for pistol matches), giving the planchet significant thickness. Even so, gold medals are less bulky than those of silver or bronze. Over the front of this general device is applied the motif of a single rifle (individual rifle competition), crossed rifles (rifle team competition), or crossed pistols, all of which are applied over the richly decorated target. Starting in 1907 and continuing until World War I, soldiers who won "authorized medals" in the national team match and who were members of a prize-winning team were allowed to count the medals as a "leg" towards their distinguished badge.[25]

Subsequent national pistol match medal designs, instituted just prior to World War I and generally continuing until after World War II, include crossed automatic pistols, a national insignia, and an appropriate inscription such as **INDIVIDUAL PISTOL MATCH**, **PISTOL COMPETITION**, or, after 1920, **PISTOL TEAM MATCH**. Occasionally, the medals made just before and during World War I either had no bar across the top as a brooch or had a brooch with a design unique to the year. The second pattern of standard brooches, introduced after World War I, with the year and the inevitable red, white, and blue ribbon, completes the medals. These brooches are the hallmark of most NBPRP prize medals awarded between the world wars. During the interwar period a bar that looks like a brooch indicates a subsequent win of the same medal. In addition the War Department gave other bars with inscriptions such as **COACH**. Some match medals or bars bear the notation **TYRO**. This is a term used to designate an American shooter who had never previously competed in any National Match or annual NRA competition held in conjunction with the National Matches.

Just before and during World War I and in the immediate postwar years, there were unique, short-lived individual rifle match medals. These consisted of a circular planchet with an eagle from the Great Seal of the United States dominating the center and near the edge, a ribbon that carried various inscriptions. This general design was evidently first made for medals presented at the 1913 international shooting tournament held at Camp Perry. One of them, obverse and reverse, is shown in figures 10.18 and 10.19. For team matches a similar design was used for a few more years (fig. 10.20).

Fig. 10.15

Fig. 10.16

Fig. 10.17

Fig. 10.19

Fig. 10.18

Fig. 10.20

Fig. 10.17. Even though new brooches appeared at the National Matches in 1954, for a few years the National Board for the Promotion of Rifle Practice continued to issue the older-style bars to recognize subsequent wins, as had been done since the World War I period.

Fig. 10.18. For the 1919 National Matches, held at Caldwell, New Jersey, the War Department supplied medals with a decidedly national flavor. For the individual rifle match (shown) a brooch was not used, but the year is impressed at the bottom of the medal at the five o'clock position. The National Rifle Association introduced planchets of this general design for some medals as early as 1913.

Fig. 10.19. Reverse of the medal shown in figure 10.18. This award, won by a marine, is inscribed on the raised, ribbon-like portion of the reverse: **Sgt. M. Fisher, Caldwell, New Jersey, 1919**. *The reverse, like the obverse, was intro-duced before the start of World War I for some National Rifle Association awards.*

Fig. 10.20. A 1924 National Match rifle team medal.

At the close of World War I rifle medals, very much like pistol medals, took on a design that lasted for over a third of a century. The design includes crossed rifles with a U.S. eagle above and a circular **US** monogram below. In the lower angle, between the rifle butts, appears the wording **INDIVIDUAL RIFLE MATCH**. It was during the early 1920s that this standard-style War Department brooch, used until 1954, came into being. At one end is a circular **US** logo of the type found on the rifle planchet, while at the other

*Fig. 10.21. National Match rifle medals evolved into a design of crossed rifles, eagle, circular **US**, and inscription shortly after World War I. The first made with this design was for the individual rifle match, as can be seen here in the medal for 1921.*

*Fig. 10.22. Many medals given at Camp Perry by the National Rifle Association from the 1920s through the 1950s are similar to those awarded during the National Matches, except that the ribbons usually carried narrow central red, white, and blue stripes on various colored backgrounds—green in this case, for rifle matches. The brooches had logos and wording in angular form, and the circular logo **NRA** replaced **US**. This particular award is for the Wimbledon Cup, as noted on the upper portion of the planchet.*

Fig. 10.21

Fig. 10.22

War Department–sponsored National Trophy matches. The easiest distinguishing feature of medals awarded before World War II is color—NRA ribbons usually were not red, white, and blue, although occasionally the NRA did use these. Most NRA medals in the 1920s and 1930s had very narrow center stripes of red, white and blue, with the main background green for high-powered rifles, violet for small-bore matches, and yellow for pistols. Over time the NRA wandered further and further from this scheme.

During the 1920s, 1930s, and 1940s most NRA brooches had diamond-shaped logos rather than the army's circular configuration. Planchets for some NRA matches were similar to those for the National Trophy matches, except that they carried circular **NRA** logos. A few medals were similar in design to National Trophy match medals, but with a change in words. One example in figure 10.22 has **WIMBLEDON CUP** above and **RIFLE MATCH** below, crossed rifles in the center with the national eagle above the rifles and the circular NRA logo below; another medal for the Leech Cup, which is generally similar, is shown in figure 10.23. A pre-1932 medal for the President's Match is shown in figure 10.24. However, for several NRA matches each had its own unique planchet, as will be seen. Over the years the number of medals presented with any given trophy varied greatly. During the 1930s, for example, in many trophy matches the high shooter from each state received a bronze medal in addition to a gold first, a silver second, and third through tenth bronze medals.[26]

From 1954 through 1966 national match medals carried a more impressive brooch: the head and upper wings of a stylized eagle above the letters **NBPRP** (National Board for the Promotion of Rifle Practice) and below that **NATIONAL TROPHY MATCHES**, with the year at the bottom. At first the red, white, and blue ribbons and the older planchets remained (fig. 10.25), but soon a new planchet appeared, so that by 1959 rifle medals had evolved even further from the older 1920s design. With these changes in the 1950s and later, the use of added bars affixed to the ribbons also increased.

The NBPRP made a rapid series of changes in brooch designs following the relatively short-lived 1954–66 standardized brooch. The history of earlier NBPRP medals was lost as members changed at the NBPRP. In

end of the brooch is the match year in circular form. The words National Match appear between the two.

Medals given in NRA-sponsored matches at Camp Perry differ from those given in

Fig. 10.23

Fig. 10.25

Fig. 10.24

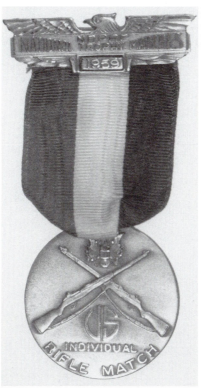

Fig. 10.26

Fig. 10.23. *A 1923 National Rifle Association 14-karat-gold medal for the Leech Cup. Between the world wars, medals given to the top winners were actually gold, while later awards were simply gold colored.*

Fig. 10.24. *A 1928 medal from the President's Match, held each year to determine the best individual rifle shot in the United States. In the twentieth century, the top one hundred winners were declared the "President's 100," and the ribbons to their medals carried a miniature of the president's flag.*

Fig. 10.25. *Starting in 1954, the brooches for National Match medals carried the head and upper, outstretched wings of an eagle. Under the head are the letters* **NBPRP** *(National Board for the Promotion of Rifle Practice), the arm of the Department of the Army that had responsibility for the National Matches. At the bottom of the brooch is the award year. The planchet design, instituted shortly after World War I, continued past the end of the Korean War.*

Fig. 10.26. *In the late 1950s this less-artistic planchet replaced that shown in figure 10.25. During this time "gold" medals were of a gold-colored medal rather than being real gold, but silver medals continued to be struck in sterling.*

Fig. 10.27. In 1967 National Match
medals began to have large brooches
bearing the seal of the National Board for
the Promotion of Rifle Practice. Early
brooches were of a solid color—gold,
silver, or bronze—and carried a small tab
below showing the award year. This
Marathon Trophy medal shows the brooch
as it evolved. It later became enameled,
and the year tab was eliminated
in favor of a year bar.

Fig. 10.28. This Daniel Boone Medal
from 1961 shows the trend, adopted in
the late 1950s, of eliminating the historic
standard, circular planchets in favor of
distinctive versions.

1967 a circular seal dominated the overall brooch design. Below the seal, in semicircular form, are the words **NATIONAL TROPHY MATCHES**, with a small tab showing the year. A star at each end of the swallowtail-shaped device finishes the brooch. Soon the year tab was dropped and a bar that was added to the ribbon indicated the year. Within a couple of years the seal became enameled.

During the late 1950s and the 1960s personnel at the NBPRP, ignorant of the historic medal designs and egged on by salesmen, constantly approved new medals in the name of improvements. In reality they only cheapened the awards. The heavy hand of commerce was actually responsible for the many and frequent changes of brooches. All changes sold by the suppliers of awards snuck in under the guise of "newer and better." Remaining faithful to this cheapening process, artificial and then cotton ribbons replaced the silk ones.

At the end of the 1950s the circular medal planchets continued to display crossed rifles, the eagle from the U.S. Great Seal, and a smaller circular **US** cipher, but the wording format below the weapons changed. Besides

the font's modification, word placement moved slightly: **INDIVIDUAL** was straightened, as the central design shifted upward to make room for the change. This general design, shown in figure 10.26, resulted in the fifth style of rifle planchet. (The first two were the 1903 style, with single and crossed rifles overhanging a wreath; the third style was the version with the Great Seal of the United States; and the fourth and most long-lasting one, which was used from World War I, is shown in figure 10.25.)

During the 1960s and 1970s the NBPRP created more medals and modified others given at the National Matches. Army regulations of the time simply cited that gold, silver, and bronze medals would be given without reference to any design. Records from the NBPRP have been lost, which limits the ability to locate demarcation of these changes. As will be seen, the Daniel Boone Trophy is awarded for the national individual rifle match. Medals given for this match show the typical trend toward new designs. Into the early 1950s the medals were like those shown in figures 10.21 and 10.25. The 1961 equivalent is shown in figure 10.28, displaying a miniature Daniel Boone statue. With this and similar changes the older circular planchets disappeared from the National Matches. Ultimately, the early

Fig. 10.27

Fig. 10.28

"universal" circular designs, further cluttered, became the standard awards for regional matches.

When the Civilian Marksmanship Program sponsored its initial National Matches after assuming responsibilities on October 1, 1996, many competitors complained about the cheap appearance of the medals. As a result, in subsequent years better finishes returned to the medals, although the coarse cotton ribbons remained in place of the nylon and rayon that had already supplanted the pre–World War II silk.

As previously noted, some historical matches had their own special medals to provide emphasis and prestige. Some of these awards, which accompanied the unique match trophies, are discussed in the appropriate sections on the various trophies.

Reserve Officers' Training Corps (ROTC) and Citizens' Military Training Camps (CMTC) students who fired at Camp Perry between the world wars in National Matches received special medals. In the 1950s those cadets in the top 20 percent of all cadets who did not receive any other medal received place medals. This practice remains, although the medals have changed. Beginning in 1985, all junior firers not receiving any other award received bronze medals. In the same 1985 change, service-academy and ROTC teams received special first-place gold, second-place silver, and third-place bronze medals and the number of medals was reduced to 10 percent, the same as for other firers.[27]

Pistol medals used from the 1920s through the 1950s retained the same general design: two crossed M 1911 .45 caliber pistols with the eagle from the Great Seal of the United States between the pistol butts. The only difference is the curved wording on the lower part of the planchet: **INDIVIDUAL PISTOL MATCH** or **PISTOL TEAM MATCH**. As the medal designs for both rifle and pistol eroded following the Korean War, the historic designs, more cluttered and distorted, ultimately migrated to regional matches. If the original parent was the beautiful 1914 pistol medal and the son was the close copy in the 1920s–50s pistol medals, then the disfigured grandson is shown in figure 10.32. In the only technical improvement, the pistols are finally updated from the M 1911 versions to the M 1911A1.

"President's Hundred" Designation

The current lore is that the President's Match was first fired in 1894, although records show that for many years prior to that the match existed. The President's Match evolved from the Military Championship of America match,

Fig. 10.29. *Medals of this special design came into use at the National Matches in the 1930s for award to reserve officers training corps students. CMTC (Citizens' Military Training Camps) students earned somewhat similar, specially designed medals.*

Fig. 10.30. *A 1936 medal given for placement in the individual national pistol match. Crossed automatic pistols first appeared on National Match medals in 1913, but with a Federal shield rather than the eagle. The original wording was* **PISTOL COMPETITION,** *but soon it changed to that shown here.*

Fig. 10.29   Fig. 10.30

Fig. 10.31. *A 1935 medal given for placement in the national pistol team match. The only difference between this planchet and that shown in figure 10.30 is the wording along the bottom face.*

Fig. 10.32. *The transformation of traditionally designed medals based upon crossed weapons and the U.S. eagle began to evolve in the 1950s. Ultimately, the descendant medals were issued only for regional matches during the last quarter of the twentieth century, as shown here. The artistic qualities inherent in the first designs continued to decline as more words appeared and the simplicity of the two weapons did not dominate the planchet.*

Fig. 10.31

Fig. 10.32

match was open to all members of the active military of the United States and to the National Guard of the various states, and in 1884 the title was changed to the President's Match for the Military Rifle Championship of the United States. In 1977 the NRA turned the match over to the National Board for the Promotion of Rifle Practice.[28]

Initially, the match had two stages. In 1886, for example, competitors fired seven shots each at distances of 200 and 500 yards, and those who placed in the top ranks then shot in the second stage, consisting of ten rounds from 600 yards. By 1894 the match was decided by seven shots each from 200, 300, 500, and 600 yards. This was increased to ten shots at these same distances in 1896. Starting in 1910 the match added skirmish runs, and a few years before it also began to require firing at 1,000 yards. By the time of the Caldwell, New Jersey, match in 1919, the contest was twenty shots each at 200, 500, and 1,000 yards.[29]

Recognition from the match varied over time. Starting in 1894 the annual winners received a gold medal and $50, although certainly before 1894 the winners received some sort of gold medal. Every year after 1904 the winner also received a congratulatory letter from the President of the United States, although this tradition ended under President Clinton. In 1913, for example, the first-place winner received a medal with a gold-and-enamel planchet bearing the seal of the NRA, the entire circular device suspended directly from a rectangular bar embossed **19•WINNER•13**. The second-place shooter received a similar medal in silver, and third place received one in bronze.[30]

Beginning in 1919 the top one hundred rifle competitors received a distinctive brassard, which has changed over the years. The 1919 historic two x five–inch brassard, peculiar to that year and made of olive drab cloth with gold-wire embroidery, is shown in figure 10.33. It was intended to be worn on the left sleeve between the elbow and the shoulder. After the 1919 National Match, the only one held at Caldwell, New Jersey, the NRA adopted a standard metal brassard.

These coveted insignia, $^{13}/_{16}$ inch high and 3 $^3/_8$ inches long, were awarded from 1920 until the suspension of matches for World War II. The light copper-colored rectangles of the 1920s were often painted with a gilt wash in the 1930s to provide a richer appearance. In

first fired in 1878 (Sergeant J. S. Barton of the 48th Regiment, National Guard of New York, won). This was the NRA contest that decided the national individual-rifle championship. The

the center of the metal brassard is an enameled version of the early twentieth-century presidential flag: a dark-blue field bearing a presidential eagle in the center, with a white star in each corner. Embossed in the metal strip itself are US and NRA in circular logo form, **PRESIDENT'S HUNDRED** in block letters, and the year. These peculiar devices were initially formed in a slight arc to better conform to the upper arm. They were usually fastened to the left coat sleeve by small screw posts on the insignia's reverse and held by small nuts, although some were made with a single long pin.[31]

Awarded between 1920 and 1940 inclusively, these metal brassards returned when the President's Matches resumed. Although awarding of the metal brassards continues, in 1958 the NRA and the Department of the Army collaborated in the authorization of a cloth shoulder tab that would be prescribed for wear on army uniforms. The result was a yellow cloth arc with the green letters **PRESIDENT'S HUNDRED**, an insignia that is still provided today.[32]

To avoid the expense of making a new die each year, about 1960 the year was added to a

Fig. 10.33

Fig. 10.34

Fig. 10.35

Fig. 10.36

Fig. 10.37

narrow metal strip below the old presidential flag rather than being embossed on the base metal brassard itself, as shown in figure 10.35. Still later, the date disappeared from the front altogether and was stamped on the back. The NBPRP pressured the NRA to turn over the President's matches to them, due to the falling out between the two organizations, and in 1977 the National Board for the Promotion of Rifle Practice assumed responsibility for the contest and awards. Starting that year, the metal brassards began to carry the seal for the NBPRP rather than the NRA logo on the right end. The left end carried a small Seal of the President of the United States.[33]

A few exceptions are noteworthy. From 1941 through 1956 the top shooters were not named. For the 1953 match, a change in score-keeping procedures made it impossible to determine later who comprised the top one hundred shooters. In 1957, when the top one hundred shooters were again listed, a decision was made that retroactive brassards would be given to all shooters who scored 130–0 for that year. Also, starting in 1954 and continuing for several years, two high scorers received presidential letters. One letter went to the high scorer with the M 1 service rifle, the other letter to the high scorer with the M 1903 rifle.[34]

Fig. 10.33. One of the original brassards given in 1919 to the highest scoring one hundred shooters in the President's Match. The 2 x 5–inch olive-drab cloth strip with gold embroidery was to be sewn on the left uniform sleeve.

Fig. 10.34. A typical metal sleeve brassard issued from 1920 to 1940 and again after 1957. Winners could attach the ${}^{13}/_{16}$ x 3 ${}^{3}/_{8}$–inch device to their shooting jacket, and military personnel sometimes wore it on their left uniform sleeve until 1957.

Fig. 10.35. Between the Korean and Vietnam Wars the design of the metal President's Hundred brassard changed to that shown here, with the flag raised and the year shown on a separate metal strip. This reduced the cost of making a totally new die each year.

Fig. 10.36. The present design for the President's Hundred brassard. The year is stamped on the reverse.

Fig. 10.37. In 1957–58 the U.S. Army and the National Rifle Association jointly developed a lemon-yellow cloth arc 4 ${}^{1}/_{4}$ inches wide with bottle-green letters for wear on the upper left sleeve of army uniforms. Army personnel who post scores in the top one hundred rifle or pistol shooters in the President's Match at the National Matches wear the arc.

198

Fig. 10.38. Prior to George Washington's two-hundredth birthday in 1932, the National Rifle Association adopted a special planchet for use in the President's Match. The National Rifle Association subsequently switched to a red, white, and blue ribbon, previously used at Camp Perry exclusively by the National Board for the Promotion of Rifle Practice. The ribbon's colors and this style of planchet continued to be used into the 1950s.

Fig. 10.39. Originally made to be put on the ribbon of medals (as shown in fig. 10.24), the small enameled pins, which looked like the presidential flag in use from the post–Spanish-American War period until shortly after World War II, had become simply lapel pins by the 1950s.

Fig. 10.40. The Army Ordnance Association announced in 1925 that it would award an "Ordnance Trophy" annually to the winner of the President's Match. The trophy was an M 1903 rifle with a special plaque let into the butt. Shown above is the original plaque design.

Until 1966 only rifle shooters received the President's Hundred designation. Starting that year, the NRA began the President's Hundred Pistol Match and provided the top one hundred pistol shooters a unique, oval-shaped brassard depicting three different handguns. This continued until the rectangular brassard became the award for both rifle and pistol.

The NRA provided place medals to the top 10 percent of the shooters in the President's Match. Figure 10.24 shows an example from 1928. Place medals of this general design continued until shortly before the bicentennial of Washington's birth in 1932. George Washington mania swept the nation, and many events celebrated his birth, including the establishment of the Purple Heart medal (bearing Washington's profile and given since World War II for wounds received in combat). In preparation for this event the NRA struck a specially designed planchet that continued for many years. Figure 10.38 is a 1953 example of one of these President's Match medals awarded by the NRA, but with the red, white, and blue ribbons that were previously reserved for NBPRP awards. The initial versions of this

Fig. 10.39

medal had the standard green NRA ribbon. By the late 1950s the awards were without any pin and were embedded inside a clear block of plastic for a desk memento.

Between the world wars those shooters designated as the President's Hundred also received miniature enameled presidential flags (fig. 10.39), and most of the winners attached them to their medal ribbons. In the latter half of the twentieth century, those designated as President's Hundred also received a pocket coin.

In addition to the above awards given in the President's Match, some top shooters received special M 1903 trophy rifles. Only five such rifles were apparently awarded. These pre–World War II presentation arms carried an engraved plaque or plate on the butt to commemorate the match. Starting in 1925 the Army Ordnance Association announced that it would award "an Ordnance Trophy" annually to the winner of the President's Match, the trophy to be "a rifle representative of the highest development of the art of rifle manufacture at Springfield Armory." Although the barrel was specially selected, the overall rifle varied from the standard M 1903 rifle only in that the stock was checkered and that a gold plate, engraved with the winner's name, was let into the right side of the butt.[35]

Fig. 10.38 *Fig. 10.40*

MATCH TROPHIES

Soldier of Marathon Trophy, 1875–Present

The army's friend in marksmanship, General George W. Wingate, first inspector of rifle practice for the New York Militia from 1874 to 1879, initially presented the Soldier of Marathon Trophy as first prize to the "State, Inter-State and First Division Matches" in 1875. The first year, the NRA presented the trophy to the New York team as the best team in interstate militia matches. This makes it the oldest military trophy used today at the National Matches. The following year, a California team won the trophy, a bronze figure of the Greek runner Pheidippides, who—although exhausted and fallen—still holds high the torch he is carrying to announce the Greek victory at Marathon. The trophy continued to be awarded to militia teams until the early twentieth century.[36]

Starting in 1903, the National Board for the Promotion of Rifle Practice awarded the trophy to the third-place team for rifle competition in the National Matches. The trophy has since been on an odyssey, becoming the first prize for the class C match in 1908 and in 1921 first place for the third class team (which that year happened to be the high-civilian team). Starting in 1938, it became the award to the high-civilian team in the National Trophy matches.[37] In the 1920s teams of ten competed for the trophy, reduced

Fig. 10.42

from the earlier twelve but more than the post–World War II six-person team. As for all major trophies, the requirements for this award have changed considerably over the years.[38]

Most medals for the Soldier of Marathon Trophy are based upon the design of the trophy and depict that award. Early versions of the medal had a raised rim and carried only the trophy, while post–World War I versions lost the rim and added an Arms of the United States. The top brooches changed by showing the year. A recent medal is shown in figure 10.27, with older medals shown in figures 10.41 and 10.42.

Wimbledon Cup, 1875–Present

The National Rifle Association of Great Britain presented the Wimbledon Cup to the U.S. NRA for annual competition to any U.S. citizen making the highest score with twenty shots at 1,000 yards. The trophy is an ornate tankard-style mug with hinged lid and figures depicting seated lions that comprise the cup's three feet. The first winner, in 1875, was U.S. Major Henry Fulton, who won with thirty shots at 1,000 yards. Fulton, a famous shooter in his day, had a special firing position, as shown in chapter 2, figure 2.3.[39]

Medals given with this trophy widely varied over time, with the early versions having planchets based heavily upon the Wimbledon

Fig. 10.41

*Fig. 10.41. This early circular medal, suspended from a red, white, and blue ribbon, shows the Soldier of Marathon Trophy. The wording **CLASS C** refers to the fact that the trophy was competed for by teams that had placed below thirtieth in the National Matches the previous year. Just prior to World War I brooches showing the year were added to the Soldier of Marathon medals.*

Fig. 10.42. In the 1920s medals given with the Soldier of Marathon Trophy added an eagle from the Great Seal of the United States. This planchet design continued for many years, as can be seen in this 1958 example with a 1954–66-style brooch.

Cup. The then–standard NRA green ribbon with narrow central red, white, and blue stripes suspends all of these pre–World War II medals. A conventionally shaped medal of the type used between the world wars is shown in figure 10.22, the upper portion of the plan-chet bearing the inscription **WIMBLEDON CUP**. This example includes a miniature cup pinned to the ribbon, a symbol that, according to oral tradition, was given only to the winner.

Fig. 10.43. The 1963 plaque given to Sergeant First Class Charles Davis, who won the Wimbledon Cup trophy.

Fig. 10.44. A 1914 Wimbledon Cup medal.

Fig. 10.43

Fig. 10.44

THE KRAG-JORGENSEN RIFLE

In many a town square stands a blackened bronze Spanish-American War statue with green rivulets, frozen in time, running down the soldier. His garb includes a creased campaign hat and an open-collared shirt, and he rests his bolt-action long arm against his thighs, held in his downward extended arms. The weapon is a .30 caliber, five-round, magazine Norwegian rifle commonly known as the Krag-Jorgensen rifle, co-invented by Captain Ole Krag of the Norwegian Royal Artillery and by the master armorer of the Kongsberg factory, Erik Jorgensen. The weapon evolved through several models, and the U.S. Army generally used this arm in the Spanish-American War, with over 40,000 Model-1896 versions provided by mid-1898. A new sight that allowed adjustment for wind-induced drift was introduced in 1901, and this version was used by the army to win the Wimbledon Cup at Creedmoor in 1901 and again in 1902. A total of over 400,000 of these rifles were made in the United States by the time manufacture of the weapon ceased at the end of 1904.

The Krag not only was used in Cuba, but served as the primary weapon in the Philippines and in China as well. Other major U.S. rifles in service during the Spanish-American War were the .45-70 Springfield and the Remington-Lee. The Krag was the first army weapon to use a short-blade, knife-type bayonet that fastened under the barrel. The army made several styles of bayonets for the Krag.

The army also made several different models of the Krag-Jorgensen, including various carbines for the cavalry and a gallery-practice rifle that fired a .22 rim fire cartridge. There were three long-arm models—1892, 1896, and 1898—and three carbine models—1896, 1898, and 1899.[40]

A Krag-Jorgenson rifle introduced to the U.S. Army in 1892. The army made several different versions of Krag-Jorgensen rifles and carbines.

Fig. 10.45

Fig. 10.46

Leech Cup, 1875–Present

British Captain Arthur B. Leech presented this cup for competition by any U.S. citizen. The majority of early winners were military men, with the first civilian winner in 1878. The orntate silver cup was earned by firing prone at various long ranges that became standard at 1,000 yards in 1940, although for

1951 and 1952 the match was at 600 yards. The cup itself was lost in 1913, just before the National Matches were held at four different locations, although the Leech Cup competition continued. The cup was recovered and was physically awarded again after 1927. A post–World War I NRA gold medal for the Leech Cup match, 1 3/4 inches in diameter with the standard NRA year bar, is shown in figure 10.23.[41]

Fig. 10.47

Fig. 10.48

Fig. 10.45. *A 1919 medal given for the Wimbledon Cup contest.*

Fig. 10.46. *A 1933 Wimbledon Cup match medal. The* **QUANTICO** *bar refers to the location at which the match was held during the Great Depression, when no central National Match was held at Camp Perry.*

Fig. 10.47. *A 1973 Wimbledon Cup match medal with a contemporary National Rifle Association brooch.*

Fig. 10.48. *The metal-and-walnut plaque given by the National Rifle Association to the 1968 winner of the Leech Cup.*

Palma Trophy, 1876–Present

The riflemen of the NRA presented the Palma Trophy in 1876 as emblematic of long-range team championship. Initially this was the Centennial Trophy, awarded on the United States' one-hundred-year anniversary. The trophy was a full-sized replica of a Roman legionary standard, created by Tiffany & Company in gold, silver, and bronze. It bore the word **PALMA**, signifying the ultimate in excellence. After it was awarded in 1924 it fell into disuse for many years. The original 7 1/2–foot trophy disappeared in 1954. When twenty-man teams were revived in 1966, the NRA created a miniature of the original, which is still used today. During the 1920s the NRA also hosted an individual Palma match, awarding the Wright, Scott, and Crowell Trophies.[42]

Fig. 10.49

Hilton Trophy, 1878–Present

"Judge" Henry Hilton (1824–99), previously judge of the New York Court of Common Pleas and an extremely wealthy New York merchant known for his philanthropy, presented the Military & Naval Challenge Trophy to the NRA in 1878. When it was first in the hands of the War Department, this enormous trophy was open to teams from the army, navy, marine corps, U.S. militia, and foreign volunteers. The central design, a bronze plaque in relief that is 45 inches high and over 56 inches wide, depicts North American Plains Indians engaged in a buffalo drive. Shortly after World War II the bronze casting was modified and placed on a large wood easel, where it is now surmounted by the figure of an eagle and numerous elaborate smaller plaques.[43]

Tiffany & Company cast the original trophy at a cost of $5,500, in 1878. The motif of Indians in a western setting was popular at this time, as in the East the romantic image of the Indians had grown. Their way of life was so far gone by the time of the trophy's creation that in five short years the herds of buffalo had disappeared from the American scene. It has been reported that even the buffalo hunters were appalled by the rapid slaughter and disappearance of the animals in 1882 and 1883.[44]

In 1903, when Congress instituted the National Matches, the NRA presented the gargantuan Hilton Trophy to the U.S. government for an award. The requirements for the competition are engraved on the back, dutifully recorded for later generations but not now generally known, as the trophy is encased in a large wood rectangle. Between 1903 and 1908 the trophy was given to the team making the second highest rifle score in the National Match, and subsequently it was awarded to the winner of the Class B match.[45]

In the 1920s teams were divided into four classes: U.S. services and reserves; National Guard or state troops; Citizens' Military Training Camps and Reserve Officers' Training Corps; and civilian teams. The highest team received the National Trophy and the highest team in the remaining three classes, the Hilton Trophy. Awarded in 1940, the Hilton Trophy was not given again until 1952. After the Korean War it was awarded to the high National Guard team in the National Trophy rifle-team match. In 1972 the Hilton Trophy became the award for the highest scoring reserve component team.[46]

Over the early years of the twentieth century Hilton Trophy medals generally showed the central trophy design of an Indian buffalo drive, while above the scene appeared a title that changed with different versions of the medals. One common inscription is **MILITARY & NAVAL CHALLENGE TROPHY**. The entire scene is on an irregular out-

Fig. 10.50

Fig. 10.50. The Georgia state team in 1897 with their many trophies. In the center is the Hilton Trophy as it was presented until World War II. The small shields suspended from the bottom of the trophy list the winning teams, although the Pennsylvania teams who won in 1882 and 1892 were commemorated by keystones at the top corners of the trophy. To the right is the Soldier of Marathon Trophy, and on the floor just to the left of center is the Leech Cup.

Fig. 10.51. A Class B prize medal associated with the Hilton Trophy. After 1908 the top fifteen teams formed the Class A teams that would compete for the National Trophy the next year. Those teams placing sixteenth through thirtieth were Class B teams for the next year, and members received these medals to show that placement.

line, designed to recall the trophy with its small circular Indian shields around the edge. The few surrounding shields that remain today list early trophy winners. Prior to World War II, however, before the trophy was mounted on an enormous wooden easel, shields showing each winning team and the year were attached to the overall trophy by small rods. When teams from Pennsylvania won the trophy twice in the late nineteenth century, small keystones rather than shields were added. New Jersey, also a two-time winner, used eared shields. Sadly, like most of the small, circular shields, these have been lost. The trophy in its recent configuration is shown in figure 10.4.

Fig. 10.52. A 1925 medal given to members of the teams that competed for the Hilton Trophy. During the 1920s teams were divided into four classes: (1) U.S. services and reserves; (2) National Guard; (3) Citizens' Military Training Camps and Reserve Officers' Training Corps; and (4) civilian teams. The highest scoring team overall received the National Trophy, while the highest team from any of the remaining three classes won the Hilton Trophy.

Fig. 10.51

Fig. 10.52

Before the War Department assumed control of the Hilton Trophy, medals given with it were of very different designs. For example, the **1888** prize medals were silver-dollar-sized disks with **THE HILTON TROPHY MATCH** around the outside and **1888** in the center, with the two inscriptions separated by a laurel wreath. This was suspended from a brooch marked **CREEDMOOR**, which also held a red, white, and blue ribbon that served as a backdrop to the silver disk. In 1892 the medal was of similar design but **Sea Girt, N. J.** was impressed in the center of the wreath, with **Sept. 9, 1892** on a second line. In the case of the 1892 medal, the reverse was engraved with the winner's rank and name and stamped with his individual score, the total team score, and other data.[47]

Nevada Trophy, 1881–Present

William C. Church, editor of the *Army and Navy Journal* and cofounder of the NRA, used his publication to lobby for improvements in army marksmanship. As a result of his personal involvement, in late April 1881 he could write with great pride to General William T. Sherman, explaining that the citizens of Nevada and the First Nevada State Militia were presenting "a very handsome trophy, made of Nevada gold and silver, and purchased at a cost of $500 . . . to be offered in competition as a yearly award for the best score made in target practice by any company or battery in the Army." The *Army and Navy Journal* even ran an engraving of the award on the front page.[48]

In a time when pinchpenny congressional appropriations were tight and a new private earned all of $12 a month, such an expensive and magnificent prize was a most noteworthy event within the army. Sherman immediately accepted the award and published the army rules for the contest on May 11. Since the army had only recently instituted firing standards and established national training policies, the Nevada Trophy became the centerpiece reward for unit training.

In October each department commander examined the monthly firing records of each company or battery under him. The unit having the highest score at 400 yards for any given month was to be identified to the adjutant general of the army. The headquarters of the army then published the winner in a general order. This trophy became so important that the possessor of the trophy was to be noted in the *Army Register* "opposite the letter of the company holding it." The initial winner was Battery K, 3d Artillery, stationed at Plattsburg Barracks, New York; accordingly, the commander, Captain Lewis Smith, "was summoned [to Washington] to receive, at the hands of the General of the Army, the trophy."[49] Table 21 shows subsequent winners of the Nevada Trophy.

Troop E, 2d Cavalry, was the last unit recipient of the Nevada Trophy. On January 4, 1898,

Table 21. *19th Century Nevada Trophy Winners*

Year	Winning Unit	Awarding authority
1881	Battery K, 3d Artillery	HQA AGO, GO 6, 1882
1882	Company B, 21st Infantry	HQA AGO, GO 8, 1883
1883	Company B, 21st Infantry	HQA AGO, GO 13, 1884
1884	Company K, 25th Infantry	HQA AGO, GO 15, 1885
1885	Company D, 3d Infantry	HQA AGO, GO 22, 1886
1886	Company D, 3d Infantry	Not applicable
1887	Company F, 21st Infantry	HQA AGO, GO 79, 1887
1888	Company H, 7th Infantry	HQA AGO, GO 111, 1888
1889	Company H, 7th Infantry	HQA AGO, GO 1, 1890
1890	Company H, 7th Infantry	HQA AGO, GO 1, 1891
1891	Company G, 7th Infantry	HQA AGO, GO 1, 1892
1892	Company G, 7th Infantry	HQA AGO, GO 1, 1893
1893	Troop K, 5th Cavalry	HQA AGO, GO 1, 1894
1894	Company G, 7th Infantry	HQA AGO, GO 1, 1895
1895–96	Not Awarded due to weapons change.	
1897	Troop E, 2d Cavalry	HQA AGO, GO 1, 1898

the trophy was "at Headquarters of the Army, [and] will be forwarded by express to the commanding officer of E Troop." The army went off to war in mid-1898 with the 2d Cavalry fighting in Cuba, and when it resumed regular target practice in 1902, the trophy had been misplaced. As a result, the Nevada Trophy never regained its premier place in the army. Ironically, the 1897 revised firing regulations listed the Nevada Trophy for the first time in standing regulations, the army having previously awarded it under the provisions of general orders.[50]

In 1909 Colonel Church (as he was commonly called due to his volunteer service in the New York Militia between October 1862 and June 1863) located the trophy he had instituted and revived competition for it. Thus the Nevada Trophy became an individual long-range match award. Sometime later the New Jersey Rifle Association somehow came into ownership of the trophy. During the mid-1920s the New Jersey group awarded the Nevada Trophy for a combination of 600 yards in the President's Match and an additional firing at 900 yards. The New Jersey Rifle Association turned it over to the NRA in 1954, where it became a team trophy. The NRA made it an individual trophy in 1962 and modified the award by placing it in a laminated plastic block that is mounted on a wooden base.[51]

Fig. 10.53

Fig. 10.54

National Trophy ("Dogs of War" Trophy), 1903–Present

When the 2d Session of the 57th Congress, on its last day, created the National Matches in 1903, the law simultaneously provided for the creation of this significant trophy. The resulting large bronze relief plaque, commonly called the "Dogs of War" Trophy, depicts a warrior of ancient times with four dogs on leashes. The wording on the trophy is **NATIONAL TROPHY PRESENTED BY THE CONGRESS OF THE UNITED STATES FOR EXCELLENCE IN TEAM MARKSMANSHIP**. First awarded in 1903, before World War II it was won by the New York National Guard, U.S. Marines, U.S. Navy, and various U.S. Army teams, including the infantry team, the cavalry team, and the engineer team. It is now awarded to the winning team in the National Trophy rifle-team match. (See fig. 10.2 for the trophy in 1927.)[52]

Medals given with the "Dogs of War" Trophy have always depicted the trophy—a narrow bronze shield with flat top and straight sides bearing the ancient warrior with the four dogs. Until World War I medals given to individuals were usually suspended directly from bronze rectangular brooches, as shown in figure 10.1, although the 1913 medal, for example, used a ribbon. In 1919 the practice became to suspend the shield from a red, white, and blue ribbon. Starting in 1920, the top brooch, which pinned the medal to the winner's clothing, carried the central legend

Fig. 10.53. *A sketch of the gold-and-silver Nevada Trophy as it originally appeared in the nineteenth century. Between 1881 and 1898 the Nevada Trophy was the most prestigious unit award given in the U.S. Army. The commander of the company-sized unit with the best average score for a given month personally received the award from the army commander. The trophy is currently encased in transparent plastic and given by the National Rifle Association at its annual matches.*

Fig. 10.54. *Colonel William C. Church, editor of the* Army and Navy Journal, *cofounder of the National Rifle Association, and captain (brevet lieutenant colonel) of volunteers during the Civil War. Church lobbied for improvements in army shooting and, through his office, helped provide the Nevada Trophy.*

Fig. 10.55. A typical bronze medal given before World War I to members of top-placing teams in the National Trophy match. **SECOND** is engraved under the four dogs, followed by the integral words **HIGHEST AGGREGATE SCORE 1908**.

Fig. 10.56. This bronze National Trophy medal, won by a U.S. Cavalry team member, has **CLASS A** on the top line at the bottom, then **PRIZE 1909**, made as part of the medal, with **FOURTH** engraved in front of **PRIZE**.

Fig. 10.57. Unlike previous National Trophy medals, this Class A second prize for 1913 has a brooch marked **NATIONAL TEAM MATCH 1913**. The brooch, unlike others of this period but similar to those used for several other medals in 1913, shows the award year.

National Matches, while the rounded letters **US** and the year were at each end—the general pattern of the second style of national-match brooches.

For the first seventeen years, design details of the medals changed annually. Some years the medals had a raised edge, while in others they were plain. The top left of the medal carried a circular medallion bearing the arms of the United States, with bars below. Initially, the first four bars were impressed with the words **ARMY**, **NAVY**, **MARINE CORPS**, and **NATIONAL GUARD**. Starting in 1920 a fifth bar was added bearing the word **CIVILIAN** (civilian teams first participated in 1916). To the top right of the shield is the legend **NATIONAL TROPHY, PRESENTED BY THE CONGRESS, OF THE UNITED STATES, FOR EXCELLENCE IN TEAM, MARKSMANSHIP**, with the founding year in roman numerals. Interestingly, the first medals had the founding year as 1904, while in the early 1920s the year was corrected to 1903.[53]

At the bottom of later medals is a scroll design, but initially a variety of wording appeared. Some medals had a blank and the word **PRIZE** on one line and below that the

Fig. 10.56

Fig. 10.57

Fig. 10.55

year in arabic numerals. The blank space could be engraved with **FIRST** or other placement. The area above the blank and **PRIZE** also had room for engraving, so **CLASS A, CLASS**

Fig. 10.58. Besides team prizes, high placement in the national team match could earn a keen-eyed marksman a "Dogs of War" medal like this, which is marked at the bottom, **SIXTH HIGHEST AGGREGATE SCORE 1907**. Color Sergeant Maurice Parker, of the 6th Massachusetts Infantry, won this particular medal.

Fig. 10.59. A never-engraved 1919 bronze National Trophy match medal, with its recently introduced red, white, and blue ribbon. In the lower portion of the shield there is a blank space for engraving, followed by the words **PRIZE 1919**.

Fig. 10.60

Fig. 10.60. In the 1920s the bronze National Trophy medals were replaced by ones of gold color, like this example. In some years the ribbon was suspended from a ring on the rear of the medal, as shown. At this same time the National Board for the Promotion of Rifle Practice adopted its standard brooch to the "Dogs of War" medals. Since the brooch showed the year, the lower portion of the shield was modified to show simply the scrolls below the dogs and specialized wording disappeared.

Fig. 10.58

Fig. 10.61. This 1940 example of the National Trophy match medal has the more normal suspension, with the ring on the top of the planchet. The wording on the upper right of the shield is **NATIONAL TROPHY, PRESENTED BY THE CONGRESS, OF THE UNITED STATES, FOR EXCELLENCE IN TEAM, MARKSMANSHIP**.

Fig. 10.59

Fig. 10.61

Fig. 10.62. *A National Trophy match medal with a 1954–66-style brooch. The top left of the medal planchet carries a circular medallion bearing the arms of the United States, with bars below. Initially, the first four bars were impressed with the words **ARMY**, **NAVY**, **MARINE CORPS**, and **NATIONAL GUARD**. In 1920 a fifth bar was added, bearing the word **CIVILIAN**.*

Fig. 10.63. *A typical recent NRA medal for the Rumbold Trophy, showing the dish-shaped silver trophy over crossed rifles.*

B, or **CLASS C** could also be engraved. In other examples the space at the bottom of the shield had a space for a first line in which **FIRST** or some other place could be listed, **HIGHEST AGGREGATE** on the second line, with **SCORE** and the year on the last line.[54]

Many competitors received these medals, usually including the top 15 percent of participating teams, although the exact number varied. In several different years members of the top ten teams in classes A, B, and C all received medals simply for participation in the National Trophy match. All of these pre–World War I medals were bronze. Immediately after the world war, medals for the event actually became gold colored, although it was 1958 before regulations recognized this practice.[55]

With the resumption of the National Matches after World War II the historic design for the National Match medals returned, still suspended from the red, white, and blue ribbons. Like similar "Camp Perry" medals, the brooch changed in 1954. Since the military dominated this match, in 1954 the NBPRP began to award the top ten civilian teams silver medals and the next ten civilian teams bronze medals. The medals given at the National Matches each year are surely the 57th Congress's most lasting contribution to American marksmanship.[56]

Rumbold Trophy, 1906–Present

The Rumbold Trophy is a rather shallow, hand-hammered, four-footed silver punch bowl with two crouching Indians on opposite sides of the rim. Presented in 1906 by Brigadier General Frank A. Rumbold, adjutant general for Missouri, it was originally awarded to the best six-man regimental military team. Initially each firer must have been a bona fide regimental or separate battalion member. By 1923 training units and schools could also compete, provided all members were from that unit. Typically, the NRA modified rule details for this trophy about every dozen years in an effort to improve competition. The 6th Massachusetts Infantry won the trophy in 1906, 1907, 1908, and 1910, while the 1st Colorado Infantry won in 1909. Post–Korean War medals show the trophy over crossed rifles.[57]

Fig. 10.63

Herrick Trophy, 1907–Present

This NRA trophy is a massive, ornate silver cup with two large handles. Originally, the Herrick Trophy was open to service teams of eight men from the infantry, cavalry, coast artillery, U.S. Navy, U.S. Marine Corps, military and naval academies, Philippine Scouts, Puerto Rico Regiment of Infantry, and National Guard from each state, plus one civilian team from each state. By 1940 the

Fig. 10.62

eight-man teams could be from the infantry, cavalry, marines, marine corps reserves, naval reserves, National Guard from each state, American Legion, and any foreign nation.[58]

Marine Corps Cup, 1909–Present

This silver cup bears the figures of two marines, one standing and one kneeling. Captain Douglas C. McDougal, U.S. Marine Corps, was the initial winner. Competition was open to anyone.[59]

The trophy was initially given for firing at 600 and 1,000 yards from the prone position. In 1951 it was awarded for the high score at 600 yards, then later in the 1950s it was given for firing from 300 yards. Now it can be won by anyone in the National Match.[60]

The Navy Trophy, 1910–Present

The navy match was instituted in 1910 and the trophy presented by the U.S. Naval Association in 1923 for award to the high competitor firing with a military rifle from the standing position. The winner also received a gold medal. In addition, in the 1920s up to twelve bronze medals were awarded, while in the 1930s second place received a silver medal, third through tenth bronze medals, and the high scorer from each state received a bronze medal.[61]

Enlisted Men's Team Trophy, 1911–Present

The 44-inch-high trophy is a bronze statue of a marine enlisted man in an end-of-the-nineteenth-century field uniform and cradling a rifle. The statue stands on an octagonal wooden base. The enlisted men in the U.S. Marine Corps presented it for award to the top six-man enlisted team from the various services, including the National Guard (and subsequently the reserves).

The U.S. Navy enlisted team won it initially, followed by the Massachusetts National Guard and then the army's cavalry team. It was not awarded in 1914 because of the four divisional-match concept. The Massachusetts National Guard won the trophy in 1915, then the marines then won it each year until the U.S. Infantry team earned the trophy in 1921. In 1940 it became the award for ten-man teams, whose members did not need to be enlisted. In 1952 the teams were reduced to four members. The trophy was still awarded in the 1990s but only to armed forces teams.[62]

Fig. 10.64

Fig. 10.65

Cavalry Cup, 1911–Present

During the firing of the skirmish run in the National Team match at Camp Perry in 1910, a marine officer standing in the rear of the U.S. Marine Corps team made some remark regarding the first shots fired, which was held to violate the rule prohibiting coaching. As a result the marine team was disqualified. The marine team score had put them in second place, just above the army's cavalry team. As an expression of goodwill, the cavalry team

Fig. 10.64. The Marine Cup, presented annually by the National Rifle Association. The legend is that the army's cavalry rifle team and cavalry officers purchased this silver cup after World War I and asked that it be given to the marine corps member making the highest score in the President's Match. The date of the cup's presentation is in dispute.

Fig. 10.65. A 1935 medal given with the enlisted men's trophy. First presented in 1911, the trophy was given by the National Rifle Association to the top six-man rifle team from the various services, the National Guard, and later, the reserves, composed solely of enlisted personnel. In 1940 it was awarded to teams composed of ten men, enlisted or not, and in 1952 teams were reduced to four members. The planchet continued well after World War II, with changes to newer National Rifle Association brooches and with red, white, and blue ribbons.

Fig. 10.66. The National Rifle Association's Cavalry Cup, which was initially awarded to the high cavalryman in the President's Match.

Fig. 10.67. Lieutenant Hinsley, stationed at Fort Riley, Kansas, in 1912, wearing a medal given to the winners of the United Services Trophy match. The U.S. Army won the match only in 1912 (when this photo was taken) and in 1920. While the navy won in 1911, the U.S. Marine Corps won most of the other team matches through 1929.

requested that the Marine Corps' score be counted, and after consideration, the National Board for the Promotion of Rifle Practice approved the request.

In appreciation of this action the Marine Corps presented a cup—the Cavalry Cup—asking that it be awarded annually to the cavalryman making the highest score in the President's Match. When matches resumed after World War II, the cup was awarded to the high-scoring army competitor in the President's Match. Between 1968 and 1977 the trophy was not awarded, and when it was returned to competition in 1978, the NRA set criteria allowing its award to anyone without regard to service. The Cavalry Cup is the oldest of the individual trophies awarded in the President's Match.[63]

Fig. 10.66

United Services Match Trophy, 1911–Present

Originally this match was composed of twenty men from each service, then later sixteen from each, firing from 200 to 600 yards. Actual firing as a team continued until 1928, when the "teams" changed to existing only on paper, with the members composed of the twenty high competitors from each service. The team competition lasted until 1930, when the trophy went into retirement. The physical trophy was returned to service in 1970, when the NRA began to award it to the high regular-service competitor in the service-rifle championship.[64]

Fig. 10.67

The Adjutant General's Cup, 1919–1925

The first adjutant general's match was fired in 1915, and in 1919 Brigadier General William W. Moore, the adjutant general of South Carolina and three-time match winner, donated a cup for 600-yard slow-fire competition, reserved for state adjutant generals. General Toombs, of the Louisiana National Guard, also won this match three times.[65]

Gold Cup Trophy, 1920–Present

The Chinese minister of war presented the elegant Gold Cup Trophy as the award for first place in the pistol match held among the allies at Le Mans, France, in 1919. The trophy is a helmet-shaped gold cup, engraved and mounted on an ebony base. The American Expeditionary Forces pistol team won the trophy on June 28, 1919, and subsequently presented it for annual competition in the National Trophy pistol team match. It has been awarded to the winning team in that match since 1920. The initial three winning teams were all from the U.S. Marine Corps. The U.S. Infantry then won the Gold Cup Trophy for three years (1923–25), and then the marines reclaimed it.[66]

Criteria for the match have varied. In 1990, for example, each team member fired thirty shots: ten rounds slow fire from 50 yards, two strings of five shots each in timed fire (twenty seconds per string) from 25 yards, and two strings of five shots each of rapid fire (ten seconds per string) from 25 yards. Awards have also changed over time. In the 1930s a medal went to each member of the top one-third of the teams; in 1949 a medal went to members of the top ten teams; and in 1990 the top team received gold-colored medals, the second team silver, and the third-place team bronze. This trophy was controlled by the NBPRP and is now owned by its successor, the CMP, not the NRA.[67]

presented by Queen Marie on behalf of the Rumanian government at the interallied rifle competition in 1919. It was won by the AEF team. The trophy is a wide, nearly 18-inch-high, silver-lidded urn with two handles, as shown in figure 10.6.

General Pershing presented the trophy to the NRA, and the U.S. Infantry team won it initially in 1921. Despite Pershing's request that the trophy be given to armed-forces teams, the NRA later opened the match to various nonarmy teams, and teams representing Vermont and Pennsylvania won the trophy in 1979 and 1980, respectively.[68]

Fig. 10.68

Fig. 10.69

AEF Roumanian [sic] Trophy, 1920–Present

Another trophy that grew out of the Great War, the AEF Roumanian Trophy was initially

Fig. 10.70

High Infantryman's Trophy, President's Match, 1922–1927

This was a typical award given in the President's Match. In 1927 it was replaced by the Farnsworth Medal, named after the first chief of infantry, 1920–25, and presented by the then-current chief of infantry.[69]

Infantry Trophy, 1922–Present

Officer and enlisted infantrymen raised money for this trophy (sometimes called the Infantry Match Trophy) by private subscription and then presented it to the NRA in time for the 1923 competition. In raising funds the chief of infantry "desired that [no] officer contribute

Fig. 10.68. A small copy trophy given to a winner of the Gold Cup competition, for his retention. The Chinese Minister of War presented the original Gold Cup as the award for first place in the pistol match held among the allies at Le Mans, France, in 1919. When the American Expeditionary Forces pistol team won the trophy, it became the award in the National Trophy pistol team match.

Fig. 10.69. A recent medal given to members whose teams placed in the top of the National Trophy pistol team match.

Fig. 10.70. A 1937 medal given with the Roumanian Trophy to the best six-man rifle team.

*Fig. 10.71. The Infantry Trophy and a
typical contributor who was selected at
random to represent his fellow soldiers in
1922. Designed by E. M. Viquesney of
Spencer, Indiana, the trophy was donated
by many individual infantrymen, who
contributed from five cents to a few dollars.*

more than $1 or any soldier more than 10 to 15 cents." This statuette by E. M. Viquesney, depicting World War I infantrymen in action, was initially given to the winning team competing as a combat squad. Like the Chemical Warfare Trophy match of 1924, it grew out of new World War I experiences and fit the 1903 congressional intent of preparing citizens already to have shooting skills when called upon to serve as soldiers.[70]

The match was created with the idea of putting riflemen in the attack on a competitive basis. A successful attack includes not only accurate fire, but also the distribution of fire by a squad and proper control and techniques of advance. Between the world wars the initial targets were three paper strips ten feet long and six feet high, each strip imprinted with two "F" silhouettes representing men. In the 1920s the eight-man unit (seven riflemen and one with a Browning Automatic Rifle) started at 500 yards, and squad sections could advance as much as 250 yards in 50-yard rushes. Soon this became a match in which the firers advanced at a walk. After 1936 units started at 600 yards and advanced in 100-yard increments to within 200 yards, firing at standard "D" silhouette targets. For the national team, the infantry typically directed about forty men to compete for the spots on the squad team. The match was not fired in 1926 or from 1932 to 1935.[71]

After being fired in 1940 the trophy fell into disuse until 1955, when the Department of the Army revised the match in a different form. Only service rifles were used, and six-man teams fired thirty-six rounds on eight silhouettes at 200, 300, 400 and 600 yards from the standing, sitting, kneeling, and prone positions at targets exposed for sixty seconds. Special formulas were used to encourage the hits to be distributed evenly among the many targets. The army's Blue Team won the first post–World War II revised match in 1955. Other trophies awarded in this match are the Leatherneck Trophy and the Celtic Chieftain Trophy.[72]

Early medals for the military winners of the infantry match have a top brooch similar to that of other National Trophy match medals of the 1920s and 1930s: the US and the year at each end, with **National Match** between the two. The lightweight planchet has a raised edge of small dots with a running figure of a World War I infantryman carrying a rifle in his right hand as the central scene. The planchet has an unusual rectangular slot rather than the common ring for the suspending ribbon. The entire affair, including a ribbon of light blue—the infantry color—was designed by A. H. Donderro, an insignia maker whose 1920s place of business was in downtown Washington, D.C., not far from the chief of infantry's office. Interestingly, Donderro used this same planchet for other shooting medals he supplied to states and other organizations that held shooting contests.[73]

Civilian teams could compete in this interesting and novel match, and indeed, that was the original intent. In 1928 and 1929 twenty-nine civilian teams entered, but with more free time due to the depression, the number of participants grew to thirty-eight teams in 1930 and fifty-two teams in 1931. The army discontinued this popular match in 1932, when National Matches were held at dispersed locations.[74]

Fig. 10.71

The Infantry Trophy team match was incorporated into the National Trophy matches in 1936, and then the NRA placed the trophy in the custody of the National Board for the Promotion of Rifle Practice for awarding to the winning team. At this time the brooch on the medals changed to a round US, and the ribbon became red, white, and blue. The medal planchet continued unchanged, with the brooch being updated after World War II.[75]

Fig. 10.74

Fig. 10.72

Fig. 10.73

Coast Artillery Trophy, 1923–Present

In 1923 the Coast Artillery Corps presented this sterling-silver cup to the commandant of the Marine Corps in appreciation of all the coaching and assistance given by the members of the marine teams to the coast artillery teams between 1910 and 1922. The Coast Artillery Trophy became an award in the National Matches, presented to the high coast artilleryman in the President's Match until World War II. The coast artillery, officially disbanded in 1950, had declined during World War II, when old-fashioned brick-and-mortar fortifications became obsolete and the remaining coast artillery units switched to air defense missions.

The Coast Artillery Trophy was awarded in 1952 to the high-scoring U.S. Air Force competitor in the President's Match. Not in competition between 1953 and 1958, in 1959 it became an award for anyone firing from the prone position.[76]

Between the world wars the winner of the cup received a distinctive silver medal that was generally rectangular in shape, depicting the cup and insignia of the U.S. Marine Corps and the U.S. Army's Coast Artillery Corps.[77]

Chemical Warfare Trophy, 1924–1931

The chemical warfare rifle matches were fired at 200 yards (ten rounds slow fire while standing and ten rounds rapid fire either sitting or kneeling from standing), with the

Fig. 10.72. A 1937 medal given to a military team in the Infantry Trophy match, in which a squad of riflemen and one automatic rifleman deployed in a line five paces apart and walked towards the targets. When targets appeared, the squad stopped and everyone fired under the direction of the leader.

Fig. 10.73. Eight-man civilian teams competed in the Infantry Trophy match in the 1920s and 1930s, complete with Browning Automatic Rifles. The high-placing teams received medals like this one given in 1925, with an National Rifle Association–style brooch and a light-blue ribbon.

Fig. 10.74. The planchet for the Infantry Trophy match was first used in 1922 and continued to be used for many years. When this 1959 medal was awarded, the match, revised in 1955, had six men distribute fire at eight targets, with thirty-six total rounds.

*Fig. 10.75. The National Rifle Associa-
tion's silver Coast Artillery Trophy,
instituted in 1923 for the high-scoring
coast artilleryman in the national rifle
match. Revived in 1959, it became an
award for high score in the prone position.*

*Fig. 10.76. A medal given to the marine
with the highest prone score, 1961.
The pendant and bars are of a
gold-colored metal.*

*Fig. 10.77. Between 1924 and 1931
the National Rifle Association sponsored
the Chemical Warfare Service Trophy, in
which competitors fired at 200 yards
wearing gas masks. The awards' number
and color (gold, silver, and bronze) varied
by the year, but generally between nine
and twelve competitors received
medals of this style.*

Fig. 10.75

Fig. 10.76

Service insignia. The first-place shooter received
a gold version of the medal, and initially a handful of other high scorers won bronze medals
of the same design (twelve in 1924, nine in
1927). In the last years second-place finishers
earned a silver medal with third through
tenth receiving bronze.[78]

Fig. 10.77

Daniel Boone Trophy, 1925–Present

In March 1925 the National Board for the
Promotion of Rifle Practice purchased this
major trophy, which depicts the marksman
Daniel Boone, American pioneer from Kentucky and Missouri, offering it as the rotating
award to the winner of the National Trophy
individual rifle match. Ordered from Dieges
and Clust of New York City in March 1925
at a cost of $800, the 22-inch-high solid-
bronze figure is mounted on a wood base.[79]

The individual winning the Daniel Boone
Trophy initially received a miniature of the
trophy. In 1959 Sergeant First Class Charles
Davis of the Army Marksmanship Unit was
the first winner to receive a large walnut
plaque with a brass relief depicting the trophy.
Prior to the trophy, only medals recognized
individual achievement in the individual rifle
match. Examples of these awards for the
period before World War I is shown in figure
10.7, for 1919 in figure 10.18, and for the
period between the world wars in figure
10.21 (1921 example). During the late 1930s,
when matches resumed at Camp Perry, the
top fifteen nondistinguished competitors usually received gold medals, the next twenty-
five silver medals, and the next one hundred
bronze medals.[80]

Following World War II the top 10 percent
of the individual competitors received medals.
These fell into three classes: the top one-sixth
took home gold medals, with the first, second,
and third places designated by appropriate

contestants wearing gas masks. In the first
years of the match's existence it was popular
as a novelty, but the concept of precision firing under simulated combat conditions never
really became a staple. After the newness wore
off, participation dropped and the match was
eliminated.

Chemical Warfare Trophy medals are not
suspended from a ribbon. The entire award
simply consists of a brooch and pendant, the
latter displaying a kneeling soldier firing in a
mask, superimposed on a Chemical Warfare

bars; the next one-third earned silver medals; and the last one-half, bronze. A medal awarded in the Daniel Boone Trophy competition in 1962 is shown in figure 10.28.[81]

Fig. 10.78

Minuteman Trophy, 1925–Present

Dwight F. Davis, acting secretary of war in 1925, approved the purchase of this artistic trophy for award in the national rifle team match. At that time teams were divided into classes: U.S. armed services, the National Guard, the reserves and military-training organizations, and the civilian teams. The highest ranked team in the lowest of the four classes received this trophy. Later the composition of the classes changed, and consequently the teams eligible for the trophy changed. Starting in 1937 the National Board for the Promotion of Rifle Practice awarded it to the highest ROTC or service-academy team in the National Trophy rifle team match. The trophy most recently has been awarded to the highest scoring junior team in the National Trophy rifle team match.[82]

This bronze statuette is a replica of the first statue ever made by Daniel Chester French, who created the original statue of the minuteman of Concord and sculpted the Abraham Lincoln statue in the Lincoln Memorial in Washington, D.C. Much of the history of the trophy has become lost, as the plaques used prior to 1959 were removed and are not now with the trophy.[83]

The pre–World War II medals awarded with the trophy are circular, 1 3/4 inches in diameter, and display the minuteman statue, with the arms of the United States on the left, the circular monogram US on the right, and the wording **CITIZENS MILITARY CHAMPIONSHIP** around the edge. The top brooch and red, white, and blue ribbon were standard, as with most others of the period. The highest ten competitors received gold medals and the next fifteen, silver medals prior to World War II.[84]

Fig. 10.79

General Custer Trophy, 1927–Present

The dramatic General Custer Trophy was purchased by the National Board for the Promotion of Rifle Practice in the fall of 1926 and was first awarded in 1927 to the winner of the National Trophy individual pistol match. Unchanged since its inception, it is still awarded to the winner of the National Trophy individual pistol match.[85]

The 50-inch-high trophy consists of a figure depicting Major General (Lieutenant Colonel) George Custer in a buckskin jacket firing a pistol. The cast bronze figure, which is on a marble base, cost $750 when it was purchased in 1926 from the Gorham Company of Providence, Rhode Island. At the time of the trophy's introduction pistol shooting was considered a small-time affair, with as few as fifty competitors entering the match and many of them police, but just before World War II, pistol shooting had increased in popularity and hundreds competed.[86]

Fig. 10.78. The plaque given to U.S. Army Sergeant First Class Charles Davis, the 1959 winner of the Daniel Boone Trophy. Prior to this year winners received small trophies, and later winners received only mounted photographs of the actual award.

Fig. 10.79. This large medal was given from 1925 until World War II to the highest twenty-five ROTC and service-academy competitors in the national rifle team match. The first ten shooters received gold medals, the remaining fifteen, silver.

Fig. 10.80. A medal given in the National Trophy individual pistol match. It shows the General Custer Trophy, symbol of individual pistol excellence. After World War II the top 10 percent of firers received medals, with one-sixth earning gold, one-third, silver, and the last one-half, bronze.

Fig. 10.81. The Pershing Trophy, which was awarded to Sergeant William F. Bissenden of the 8th Infantry, Fort Moultrie, South Carolina, for the score of 294 out of a possible 300 points in the 1927 national team match held at Camp Perry, Ohio. Sergeant Bissenden set a world record in match shooting.

Figure 10.9 depicts a typical medal provided for matches held before World War I and prior to the trophy. Medals struck between the world wars were based on the 1914 medal design (see fig. 10.12). These awards—one of which, for 1936, is shown in figure 10.30—came in gold, silver, and bronze. The top twelve nondistinguished competitors received gold, the next twenty-four, silver, and the next thirty-six, bronze. After World War II the top 10 percent of all firers received medals, with one-sixth earning gold, one-third silver, and one-half bronze.[87]

Fig. 10.80

Fig. 10.81

attaining the highest figure of merit for shooting within an army area.)[88]

The special gold, circular medal that accompanied the trophy between the world wars bears as its central design the head and shoulders of John J. Pershing in uniform and wearing a cap, with the wording around the edge, **THE PERSHING TROPHY**. The planchet is suspended from a standard red, white, and blue ribbon but with a gold brooch bar having a circular US at the left end, the year at the right, and **National Match** in the center. This rich, impressive medal was given only to the highest individual competitor in the national rifle team match. The initial winner, Sergeant W. E. Bissenden of the 8th Infantry, was also a member of the first-place team.[89]

Edwin Howard Clarke Machine Gun Trophy, 1927–1940

The trophy is named for Captain Edwin Howard Clarke, who graduated from the U.S. Military Academy in 1917. In World War I he served with the 18th Infantry Regiment and the 1st Machine Gun Battalion, both in the 1st Division, and with the 2d Division. He was shell shocked in 1918, retired for disability in 1920, and died in July 1923. His estate established the trophy in 1927.

The actual trophy varied, consisting over time of a silver cup, a plaque with a cast three-dimensional view of a machine-gun crew in

Pershing Trophy, 1927–Present

While John J. Pershing commanded the American Expeditionary Forces, he presented a statuette of an American serviceman firing a pistol for team competition at the 1919 Inter-Allied Games in Paris. The AEF team won it, and at the request of the National Board for the Promotion of Rifle Practice the trophy was placed in the custody of the board. In 1927 it was placed in competition for award to the person making the highest individual score in the National Trophy rifle team match. (This award should not be confused with the Pershing Trophy given by the National Guard Bureau after World War II to the state team action, and an actual sculpture showing a crew of three World War I soldiers manning a Browning water-cooled machine gun on an octagonal base. Each machine gun or heavy weapons company could compete for the trophy, but every man in the unit had to fire the course, and the highest average score determined the winning unit. Later requirements included section and platoon problems in indirect lay and a fifteen-mile road march in full field equipment.

Company D, 28th Infantry at Madison Barracks was the initial winner. In 1929 and 1930 Company H, 18th Infantry (the 18th Infantry was one of Clark's combat units) won the trophy. In the mid-1930s the 9th Infantry was a major top competitor, as in 1934, when M Company won the trophy and the other two regimental heavy weapons companies placed fourth and sixth out of seventy-five competing companies. Company H, 31st Infantry, stationed at Manila, Philippine Islands, was the first overseas unit to win the trophy when it beat the second place unit, Company H, 45th Infantry (Philippine Scout), in 1937.[90]

Edwin Howard Clarke Memorial Trophies, 1927–1940

Various trophies were established by Edwin Clarke's estate under circumstances similar to those for the machine gun trophy above. One was given in the President's Match to the high civilian, including CMTC student, and one was presented to the winner of a special pistol match.[91]

Fig. 10.82

Warrior Trophy of the Pacific, 1928–1984

The University of Hawaii ROTC rifle team fired in competition at summer camp in 1925 at Camp Lewis, Washington, and defeated all other teams. In a myopic view the War Department declared Hawaii ineligible for prizes, since the rifle competition was officially for the IX Corps Area and Hawaii was outside that region. When the cadets returned from summer camp, many prominent citizens of Honolulu shared the great disappointment suffered by the sixteen members of the team in losing the trophy on a technicality.

Sparked by Colonel Adna G. Clarke, then Professor of Military Science and Tactics at the University of Hawaii, a campaign led by the *Honolulu Advertiser* started funds for the establishment of a trophy for which the Hawaii team would be eligible. A total of $329.96 was collected, and the 22-inch-high bronze statuette, the Warrior of the Pacific Trophy, came into being.[92]

In May 1927 D. L. Crawford, president of the University of Hawaii, offered the trophy so it could be awarded annually to the ROTC infantry unit whose cadets made the highest average score in record firing at the Fort Lewis summer camp. The trophy remained the property of the university, although the War Department administered the proceedings each summer. The University of Hawaii promptly won it. To widen the competition, the university offered it to all colleges and universities in 1928.[93]

The bronze sculpture represents a Hawaiian soldier of about the period when Kahemaheha I conquered the islands and established the Hawaiian dynasty. Gordon Usborne, Hawaii's best sculptor at the time, designed it and had William Wise, captain of the University of Hawaii's football team, pose for the trophy. It was cast at Providence, Rhode Island, in 1925.[94]

This competition was unlike most ROTC rifle matches, which were ordinarily fired with .22 caliber weapons and with the teams composed of a small number of selected members. For this trophy cadets used the standard service rifle, and the "team" consisted of all cadets attending summer camp from an institution, providing at least twenty cadets attended. In any year the University of Hawaii had less than twenty cadets, all eligible teams included those with at least a corresponding

Fig. 10.82. The Edwin Howard Clarke Machine Gun Trophy, given to the best weapons company between the world wars.

Fig. 10.83. The Warrior Trophy of the
Pacific, awarded between 1928 and 1984
to the highest team at ROTC
summer camp.

Fig. 10.84. A bronze Rattlesnake
Trophy medal awarded in 1963. The
planchet shows the trophy—a Frederic
Remington statue of a cowboy on his
horse, surprised by a rattlesnake. The
trophy was first given in 1938. This
medal was awarded to the high-scoring
reserve team in the national rifle
team match.

number of men. Firers had to wear normal field uniforms, although shoulder and elbow pads were an authorized exception. This became a major trophy and was announced in War Department/Department of the Army General Orders each year.[95]

Between the world wars members of the winning team received bronze medals suspended from green-and-white ribbons. The circular planchet depicts the trophy. Around the edge are the words **WARRIOR PACIFIC TROPHY**, while behind the trophy are crossed rifles and the enameled letters **U** and **H**.

University of Hawaii teams won the trophy each year through 1939, then again in 1941 and 1961. In 1984 fire destroyed the records, and the trophy fell into disuse. It was lost until the early 1990s, when an alumnus of the University of Hawaii visited the school and inquired as to the trophy's whereabouts. A search resulted in a return of the trophy to the University of Hawaii, where it resides today, retired.

Fig. 10.83

Automatic Rifle Match, 1928–1931

In 1928 the NRA instituted a special, unique match that initially allowed unlimited rounds for the Browning Automatic Rifle. The 1931 match consisted of two ten-round magazines fired from kneeling or sitting at 200 yards and two ten-round magazines fired prone at 300 yards. While the 1928 match had 17 entries and interest had grown to 46 entries in 1930, the match attracted few of the 2,612 Camp Perry shooters, and the next year was no more popular with 47 entries of the 2,749 at the camp. A contemporary writer stated that the match simply refused to become popular due to some question as to the orthodoxy of the weapon. The NRA never supplied a trophy, providing only medals. When the matches were dispersed and held at various locations in 1932, the lack of shooters eliminated the contest.[96]

Hearst Rifle Trophy, 1937–Present

William Randolph Hearst donated a cup as the original Hearst Rifle Trophy for the National Trophy matches of 1937 for individual recognition of the high-scoring cadet or midshipman. J. W. Scannel, VIII Corps Area ROTC, won the original cup. Hearst intended that the cup be a rotating award, presented annually, but it lapsed since the War Department mistakenly believed the cup was to be a permanent award. Once the army gave the cup away, Hearst did not replace it.[97]

Fig. 10.84

Hearst revised the award in early 1940, when he donated a magnificent firearm from his collection, clearly indicating that the antique weapon was to become a rotating trophy. Insufficient ROTC students participated in the 1940 and 1941 matches, which kept the weapon from being awarded. Due to World War II and a lack of students, the new trophy, a seventeenth-century Spanish flintlock carbine in blunderbuss style, was not awarded until 1954, when it was presented to Midshipman First Class Thomas J. Ebner of Oregon State University.[98]

The ROTC or service-academy competitor making the highest score in the National Trophy individual rifle match presently receives the trophy. A lack of maintenance in the 1970s and 1980s resulted in the flintlock's deterioration.[99]

Rattlesnake Trophy, 1938–Present

A statuette by Frederick Remington, the famous western artist, forms the basis of this trophy, which the National Board for the Promotion of Rifle Practice purchased in 1938. It is given to the high reserve team from any service in the National Trophy rifle team match. The trophy depicts a cowboy on a rearing horse, with a rattlesnake at the horse's front.[100]

Teams from the U.S. Marine Corps Reserves initially won the trophy. Starting in 1956, it was awarded to the high reserve or veteran team. In 1973 the trophy changed to an individual award, being presented to the highest-scoring army competitor—active, reserve, or National Guard—in the National Trophy rifle team match. Distinctive bronze medals were given starting in 1958.[101]

THE M-1 RIFLE

John C. Garand started designing the primary U.S. rifle of World War II in 1920. Significant modifications took place during further development, and in 1936 the army standardized his design, the result becoming the M-1 rifle. The weapon operates by bleeding off a small amount of the gas that propels the bullet down the barrel. This gas drives back a piston that opens the bolt, extracts and ejects the spent cartridge case, cocks the hammer, and compresses a spring that then returns the weapon to its ready-to-fire position, loading the next round automatically. The rifle holds an eight-round clip, and when the last round is fired, the bolt automatically stays open and ejects the empty clip, making it ready to receive another.

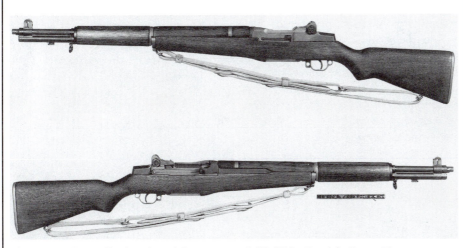

The U.S. Army's M-1 rifle, the primary infantry weapon in World War II and the Korean War.

The nine-pound, eight-ounce weapon, which is forty-three inches long, was made at the Springfield Arsenal and at the Winchester Repeating Arms Company of Connecticut. The M-1 Garand rifle started production in 1937, and by the day Hitler invaded Poland in September 1939, the United States was producing one hundred M-1 rifles a month. This superior weapon, well liked by both the troops and generals, served marksmen well after World War II.[102]

25th Infantry Division Trophy, 1955–Present

The 25th Infantry Division Trophy lists the campaigns and illustrates the World War II area in which the division saw combat. The National Board for the Promotion of Rifle Practice accepted the trophy in 1955 from the 25th Infantry Division Association. It is awarded to the high-scoring infantryman, regular army, army National Guard, or army reserve in the National Trophy individual rifle match.[103]

General Mellon Trophy, 1957–Present

Major General Richard K. Mellon, deputy adjutant general for the state of Pennsylvania, presented this trophy, which shows a giant, erect Kodiak bear on a multitiered circular base. It is symbolic of the great outdoors and wilderness that is a part of the tradition and dreams of the American rifleman. The trophy, first awarded in 1957, was initially given annually to the high National Guard team in the National Trophy pistol team match. Since 1973 the highest-scoring army competitor (active or reserve) in the National Trophy pistol team match receives the General Mellon Trophy.[104]

Leatherneck Trophy, 1957–Present

This trophy is a small replica of the life-sized "Iron Mike" statue at Quantico, Virginia, dedicated by Major General John Lejeune in 1921. In 1957 General R. McP. Pate, commandant of the Marine Corps, presented this trophy to the National Board for the Promotion of Rifle Practice in the name of the officers and men of the Marine Corps. It is awarded each year to the high civilian team in the National Trophy Infantry Match. As is the case with some other trophies, team members received special bronze medals.[105]

U.S. Coast Guard Memorial Trophy, 1957–Present

Vice Admiral A. C. Richmond, commandant of the coast guard in 1957, presented this trophy to the National Board for the Promotion of Rifle Practice. It shows a replica of the Coast Guard Memorial located in Arlington Cemetery, with statuettes of coast guardsmen holding pistols. It is awarded to the high reserve team from any service firing in the National Trophy pistol team match. There was an earlier Coast Guard Trophy presented in 1930, a bronze statuette that was a reproduction of the Alexander Hamilton statue located by the Department of the Treasury Building in Washington, D.C.[106]

Intercollegiate Trophy, 1959–Present

The National Board for the Promotion of Rifle Practice purchased this trophy in 1958, and it was placed in competition the next year for award to the high ROTC or service-academy competitor in the National Trophy individual pistol match. The trophy is a sterling silver urn that depicts a battle scene in a war between the Romans and Celts in 43–44 A.D.[107]

Celtic Chieftain Trophy, 1959–Present

John Henry Foley of the Union of London executed the original statue of Caractacus, British chieftain of the tribe Catevellauni. Caractacus led the native resistance against the Roman Aulus Plautus (43–47 A.D.). This trophy, a miniature of the statue by J. A. Hatfield, was purchased by the National Board for the Promotion of Rifle Practice in 1958. The following year it was placed in competition and awarded to the highest-scoring reserve team, regardless of service, in the National Trophy Infantry Match.[108]

ASSOCIATION OF THE UNITED STATES ARMY TROPHY, 1962–PRESENT

The Association of the United States Army established this 16-inch-high statuette of a World War II–Korean War–period soldier, mounted on a wood base. Presented to the National Board for the Promotion of Rifle Practice in 1962, it is awarded each year to the highest-scoring army competitor, regular, reserve, or army National Guard, in the National Trophy individual rifle match.[109]

Army Cup, 1963–Present

The Army Cup is a sterling silver, lidded cup, the lid surmounted by an eagle with its wings reversed. The cup is mounted on a three-tiered wooden base. The trophy, presented by the U.S. Army to the NRA, is awarded annually to the person winning the service-rifle competition.[110]

Golden Eagle Trophy, 1963–Present

The trophy shows a golden eagle with wings uplifted, mounted on a walnut base. Originally, this award was presented to the highest-scoring junior competitor other than service-academy and ROTC entrants, in the

Fig. 10.85

National Trophy individual rifle match. In the 1980s the awardee became the highest-scoring junior competitor in that match. The National Board for the Promotion of Rifle Practice and then the CMP provided special medals to ROTC and academy cadets in this match. Initially, the top ten scorers received bronze medals showing the Golden Eagle Trophy, while the balance of the top 20 percent of shooters received lesser medals.[111]

Citizen Soldier Trophy, 1964–Present

Presented by the Reserve Officers Association of the United States in 1964, the trophy is awarded to the high reserve member competing in the National Trophy individual rifle match. The trophy design shows the five insignia of the armed services, encompassing a large Reserve Officers' Association seal.[112]

U.S. Army Reserve Memorial Trophy, 1969–Present

The U.S. Army Reserve donated this trophy in 1969. It depicts the citizen soldier leaving his civilian occupation to take up arms in defense of his country, and is in memory of those who have given their lives in this duty. The highest-scoring reserve competitor in the National Trophy individual pistol match receives this trophy.[113]

Alden Partridge Trophy, 1971–Present

The president of Norwich University, in Northfield, Vermont, presented this trophy to the National Board for the Promotion of Rifle Practice in 1971. The trophy is a bronze bust of General Alden Partridge, founder and first president of Norwich, the first institution of higher learning to include military training as a part of the curriculum. This trophy is awarded to the highest-scoring service academy or ROTC team in the National Trophy pistol match.[114]

National Guard Association Trophy (Pistol), 1978–Present

The National Guard Association presented a trophy to the National Board for the Promotion of Rifle Practice in 1978. The current trophy, given in 1983, depicts a helmeted guardsman in bronze, mounted on a two-tiered base. This is awarded to the highest-scoring National Guard competitor in the National Trophy individual pistol match.[115]

National Guard Association Trophy (Rifle), 1978–Present

This trophy is similar in all respects to the National Guard Association Trophy (pistol), except that it is awarded to the highest-scoring National Guard competitor in the National Trophy individual rifle match.[116]

Junior Infantry Team Trophy, 1984–Present

The National Board for the Promotion of Rifle Practice authorized this trophy in 1983 and first presented it the following year to the highest-scoring junior team in the National

Trophy Infantry Match. This trophy consists of three M 1903 Springfield rifles.[117]

U.S. Army Forces Command Pistol Trophy, 1978–Present

The artisans of the Rock Island Arsenal designed and constructed this trophy, which consists of a mounted brace of Colt Army Special caliber .38 revolvers from about 1900. It is awarded to the active army competitor making the highest aggregate score in the National Trophy individual pistol match and the National Trophy pistol match.[118]

U.S. Army Forces Command Rifle Trophy, 1978–Present

The artisans of Rock Island Arsenal also designed and constructed this trophy, depicting mounted Winchester rifles from 1900. The weapons, with consecutive serial numbers, were the last chambered for the caliber .22 short cartridges. The trophy is awarded to the active-army competitor making the highest aggregate score in the National Trophy individual rifle match and the National Trophy rifle team match.[119]

CHAPTER ELEVEN

FROM BEGINNING TO MODERN DAY

TUCKED AWAY IN THE second paragraph of chapter 1, I noted the three legs of the stool upon which weapons training is built: technology, tactics, and finances. These three inter-related factors dictated in great part the U.S. Army's training programs and the rewards given. While officers create and massage tactics, they have always had lesser control over the other two factors. Technology had to be adapted to army purposes and money successfully begged from Congress and the White House before it was carefully allocated.

The least mentioned of these three factors has been technology. Certainly the modern technical miracle is hardened steels, which has led to the ability to accurately and easily mass-produce firearms, the machinery to create millions of bullets and bombs, and the capability to design and assemble ever larger weapons, from cannons to airplanes. That is not to say technology is less important that the other factors, but it has not been my purpose to dwell upon metallurgy and mechanical engineering. Manufacturers and other captains of industry always did their job, and the army took advantage of their work.

Captain C. Etienne Minie brought forward a new invention. The Ordnance Department studied barrel movement during the instant when bullets pass down barrels. Inventors such

Fig. 11.1

as John Browning built upon the work of others. Today lasers and fiber optics allow soldiers to aim and fire unseen by foes and yet consistently hit their targets. The grim reaper owes the efficiency of his scythe to scientists, engineers, inventors, and others who stretch technology.

Improvements have always affected armies since the founding of the American republic. In the early years engineers and inventors did precious little to help improve marksmanship, but by the Civil War riflemen had the ability to deliver fire with great accuracy. Firepower was not always in small arms. Artillery—and, in the twentieth century, airpower—added to the carnage. As any combat veteran can testify, increased technology equates with increased killing. Those who better apply technology tend to win.

As the U.S. Army has done before and is trying to do again today, it used inventions to transform itself while allocating some of its limited cash to training. Changes in battle-field tactics result, however painfully slow. With a historical perspective we can now see that some nineteenth- and twentieth-century changes in tactics over the last 150 years were steps forwards and others were steps backwards. Implementing these tactical changes came down to training. A soldier's expertise with his weapons is essential.

As combat leaders know, mission, enemy, terrain, troops available, and time—METT-T in army shorthand—are the factors that influence battlefield leaders. The mission, the enemy, the terrain, and the time available are thrust upon soldiers at all levels. Commanders can have some affect on the time and, through training that has usually occurred off of the battlefield, the effectiveness of the troops available.

From the Revolution through the Civil War the army did not recognize the need for

Fig. 11.1. On the firing line at Camp Perry, Ohio, in the 1920s.

Fig. 11.2.

Fig. 11.2. In 1935 William Randolph Hearst offered a special trophy to the National Guard rifle team that finished first in the Hearst match. This team from Williston, North Dakota, was the winner.

Fig. 11.3. Even the advertisements of the day bragged about the new marksmanship sport.

marksmanship training. All a soldier had to know was how to load and fire, and firing was done simply by pointing towards the target and pulling the trigger. While armies are certainly tied to firearms, the United States historically has had a stronger, more long-time attachment to guns than any other country. It is ironic that the U.S. Army was late in initiating firearms training and shooting awards.

By comparison, when the United Kingdom was threatened with invasion by Napoleon III in 1859, some of the newly formed units practiced marksmanship; indeed, the books George Wingate ordered for training his company during the American Civil War came from England. The National Rifle Association of Great Britain was formed in 1860 with the purpose of promoting and encouraging marksmanship throughout the various military forces.

In 1800 the British organized the 95th Regiment of Foot (the Rifle Brigade), a special rifle unit, and the British instituted the Queen's Medal in April 1869 for the best shot. By the time this award lapsed in 1883, the U.S. Army was just starting its award program.

Much to General Philip Sheridan's credit, he was able to direct effective training and to wring funds out of Washington. Like Tommy Atkins in Rudyard Kipling's poem, though, the American peacetime army, especially before the Korean War, has been habitually unappreciated, and that usually translates to chronic underfunding. Shortages of bombs, bullets, and cannons have predominated peacetime and hindered training. My parents tell of seeing soldiers in the Philippines drill with wooden rifles in 1941, a repeat of American experience during World War I. The U.S. maneuvers of 1940 with trucks carrying signs reading "tank" have entered our folklore.

When the U.S. Army instituted qualification awards, starting with the marksman button of 1879, it greatly motivated soldiers to become rifle experts. Steadily building upon this with the marksman bar and sharpshooter cross and then the expert rifleman badge, coupled with extra pay, training bcame a way of life. Troops truly did become experts, thus giving commanders a more effective force when applying tactics. Thanks to the National Guard Association, the army soon adopted pistol qualification badges. All the while, starting in 1891, the artillery gave badges and then sleeve insignia to encourage proficiency. While not nearly as tangible as the weapons themselves, badges—especially when associated with high standards—have worked wonders.

Pershing and the new weapons developed for

Fig. 11.3

Fig. 11.4

World War I resulted in the present style of qualification badges showing levels of proficiency, and until the Vietnam War even senior officers proudly displayed these silver badges with their qualification ladder. The plans for using firepower to defeat the Soviets and the resulting tactics with emphasis on crew-served mechanized vehicles, coupled with massive artillery and airpower, shifted training emphasis exclusively to helicopters, tanks, armored personnel carriers, and similar vehicles. As a result, individual marksmanship skills deteriorated and qualification badges became less prized. In their place mechanized-force soldiers added field jacket qualification patches. The ultimate awards for U.S. forces in Germany from the 1960s through the 1980s were these pieces of embroidered cloth. Rather than recognize these incentives—as had Ord, Sherman, Wingate, Pope, and other senior nineteenth-century officers—commanders in Europe and the Pentagon finally took away this training carrot. They did so for the sake of uniformity, rather than recognizing human nature's desire for recognition and amending the army's uniform regulations. Since World War II the army has frequently not capitalized on these sorts of intangibles in the way their predecessors did.

Well before the cold war, commanders gave unofficial awards for training proficiency.

Fig. 11.5. This wall plaque displays a colorful pocket patch, typical of local recognition given to tank crews during the last half of the cold war.

Fig. 11.6. Obverse and reverse of a local shooting medal, minus its ribbon, given in Germany after World War I.

Fig. 11.5

Fig. 11.6

Whether the chief of infantry or the chief of artillery between the world wars, company commanders from the Civil War to the present, or even commanders who sanctioned semiofficial medals, they all dangled incentives to encourage soldiers. We will never know the full history of all these trinkets.

Some key U.S. Army trainers—William Tecumseh Sherman and John J. Pershing—are well known to even casual students of American history. Others are very obscure today, although they were well known in their own time. Captain Henry Heth of the 10th Infantry developed the first true U.S. Army marksmanship program, and Major General Charles Farnsworth, the first chief of infantry, pushed the squad fire-and-maneuver concept to the point that even the National Rifle Association instituted the Infantry Trophy Match at Camp Perry to emulate this army tactic.

Many soldiers became expert shooters and were known only in the small fraternity of their regiment, except when their names were read at a parade or printed in a newspaper after a contest. Sergeant Heuser, for example, was champion among distinguished marksmen and a member of G Troop, 2d Cavalry, and Lieutenant Lewis Merriam was one of the first fifteen distinguished marksmen. Soldiers from the twentieth century are renowned to those who study shooting, their names including Corporal Gary Anderson, the first international distinguished shooter, and Lieutenant

Sydney Hines, who won gold in the 1924 Olympics and ultimately became a general.

To recognize the acme in training, the War Department introduced annual contests with magnificent gold, silver, and bronze prizes in the 1880s. True extensions of training, the distinguished designation grew to include even aerial proficiency and combatlike how-much-can-you-fire-accurately courses for the Browning Automatic Rifle.

Almost immediately after establishing training and qualification courses, there is a movement toward an ultimate contest. While there are a few exceptions, this natural tendency appears in armies worldwide. In Sherman's and Sheridan's army, contests started in 1880 with the 2-inch and 1 1/2–inch gold prizes and 2-inch silver prizes, which lead directly to the category of distinguished marksmen. The attempt to climb to the small pyramid top, with its very limited number of prizes, attracts many competitors. In the case of nineteenth-century rifle shooting, the NRA and other groups conducted international competitions, and these grew to the Olympics and other great matches, resulting in the Distinguished International Shooter badges. Even in tank gunnery conducted in the 1970s and 1980s there was the Canadian Army Trophy match, conducted in Germany for the top NATO crews, and the United States was inevitably a top contender, using the latest version of the medium battle tank (the best technology), manned by thoroughly trained crews. Military training events became international contests.

Within the U.S. Army, shooting prizes evolved with the smaller 1903 series, followed by the 1922-style prizes that are still given, even with significant modifications. In the artillery, a cerebral branch that studies mathematics, the top awards were for tests and schools: the pre–World War I master gunner badge and the pre–World War II Knox medals and plaques. Swordsmanship was so far gone as a combat skill that when the army finally gave a badge, it was not highly sought after and a prize never developed.

Unofficial awards—such as the designation of Master Gunner for armor sergeants, resulting from a special course at Fort Knox, Kentucky, several years after the Vietnam War—might have been recognized by the entire army through a change in army regulations in previous days. Certainly, from the early shooting days such local recognition was handed out, and even the strict spit-and-polish American Forces In Germany from 1920 to 1923 acknowledged illustrious training results with their machine gun badge and with special medals.

The rise of the National Rifle Association in 1871 forced the U.S. Army to confront its lack of marksmanship training. For over 125

Fig. 11.8

years the army and the NRA have had a love-hate relationship, usually to the benefit of neither. At the zenith of the positive relationship during the first half of the twentieth century, the NRA helped train thousands of citizen-soldiers, and the army encouraged this by underwriting weapons and ammunition and providing support personnel.

The strongest firearms support developed after the American victory in the Spanish-American War, when Congress established the National Matches. As the matches grew in popularity, the army and the NRA scratched each others' backs at Camp Perry between the world wars. After the assassination of President Kennedy and the protests against and public disillusion with the military and the Vietnam War, the army and the NRA fell out. Even so, the National Matches persist, currently under the direction of the Civilian Marksmanship Program, and the NRA continues to award their historic trophies. Like other weapons skill events, these will not end but will simply adapt to the changing world, in part by creating still more awards. An impressive and varied cast of characters, large and small, determined the badges, prizes, and trophies the army gave for weapons training for over 150 years. In the future new personalities and awards will certainly have a motivating influence.

Fig. 11.7. A Browning .38 caliber automatic pistol, made by Colt.

Fig. 11.8. An olive drab and black master-gunner patch for the M60A3 tank. In the 1980s and 1990s the U.S. Army Armor School at Fort Knox also recognized master gunners for other M60 and M1 series of tanks.

Fig. 11.7

NOTES

1. THE EARLY YEARS: SETTING THE STAGE

1. Coffman, "The Duality of the American Military Tradition," 968.

2. Higginbotham, *The War of American Independence,* 4.

3. McChristian, *An Army of Marksmen,* 39.

4. Heitman, *Historical Register* 1:141.

5. Stubbs and Connor, *Armor-Cavalry, Part I,* 9–10.

6. Crist and Dixon, *The Papers of Jefferson Davis* 6:188–95.

7. Headquarters of the Army, Office of the Adjutant General, General Orders No. (hereafter HQA AGO, GO) 8, 1854; Heitman, *Historical Register* 1:526–27.

8. Grant, *Personal Memories of U. S. Grant,* 60.

9. War Department (hereafter WD), *Annual Report, Chief of Ordnance, 1883,* 108.

10. McChristian, *An Army of Marksmen,* 10.

11. Heth, *A System of Target Practice,* front pages.

12. Ibid., 37–42.

13. WD, *Annual Report, Secretary of War, December 1859,* 1126.

14. WD, *Annual Report, Secretary of War, 1860,* 984.

15. Parker, *The Old Army,* 22.

16. Eicher, *Robert E. Lee,* 87.

17. Bourke, *On the Border with Crook,* 11.

18. McChristian, *The U.S. Army in the West,* 105–15.

19. HQA AGO, GO 50, 1869.

20. Dorothy Johnson, *The Bloody Bozeman,* 273.

21. HQA AGO, GO 50, 1869; Department of the Platte, GO 9, 1869.

22. Department of the Platte, GO 26, 1872; *Annual Report, Chief of Ordnance, 1883,* 95–96; Platte, Unnumbered circular, 27 February 1877.

23. Department of Texas, GO 7, 1877; Department of the Platte, GOs 9 and 26, 1872; Department of the Platte, GO 8, 1873.

24. Department of Texas, GO 7; Department of the Platte, GOs 11 and 15, 1879; AGO, GO 95, 1877.

25. Zimmer, *Frontier Soldier,* 23, 58, 60, 65, 159.

26. Department of the Platte, GOs 3 and 8, 1873; Coffman, *The Old Army,* 279.

27. Department of the Platte, GO 16, 1875; Department of the Platte, GOs 17, 21, 29, 1881; Department of the Platte, Circulars 10 and 48, 1881.

28. Thomas and Son, *Sporting Good Illustrated Catalogue.*

29. Gilmore, "The New Courage," 97.

30. Gilmore, "Crack Shots and Patriots," 54–56; Bigelow, *William Conant Church,* 184; NRA web site, January 2001; Gilmore, "The New Courage," 97.

31. "Military Rifles and Rifle Firing" 1: 289–91.

32. WD AGO, GO 103, 1874; WD AGO, GO 105, 1875; WD AGO, GO 14, 1876; WD, *Annual Report, Secretary of War, 1882* 1:103.

33. HQA, GO 54, 1883.

34. WD, *Annual Report, Secretary of War, 1882* 1:7, 103.

35. Heitman, *Historical Register* 1:611; Gilmore, "The New Courage," 97; WD, *Firing Regulations for Small Arms for the United States Army and the Organized Militia,* 5.

36. "Military Rifles and Rifle Firing," 293.

2. SHOOTING BADGES, 1881–1921: THE SOLDIER'S INSPIRATION

1. WD, *Annual Report, Chief of Ordnance, 1879,* 17–18; HQA AGO, GO 76, 1879; T. T. S. Laidley, *Colonel Laidley's Reply to the Charges of Infringement of Colonel Wingate's Copyright.*

2. Gilmore, "The New Courage," 98.

3. WD, *Annual Report, Chief of Ordnance, 1884,* 84.

4. Wingate, *Manual for Rifle Practice* (6th ed.), ii; Wingate, *Manual for Rifle Practice* (5th ed.), 144;

Till, *Military Awards; Army and Navy Journal,* March 18, 1881, 689, and April 16, 1881, 777.

5. Till, *Military Awards,* 40; Several examples exist. One is in Wingate, *Manual for Rifle Practice* (5th ed.), 132–33; Department of the Platte, Circular 1, 1890.

6. *Report of the Adjutant-General of the State of New Hampshire for . . . 1882,* 10, 18.

7. Wingate, *Manual for Rifle Practice* (5th ed.), 165–66; Laidley, *A Course of Instruction,* 122–24; Department of the Platte, GO 15, 1879.

8. Department of the Platte, GO 11, 1879; WD, *Annual Report, General of the Army, 1882,* 96–97.

9. "Military Rifles and Rifle Firing," 306–7.

10. Heitman, *Historical Register* 2:434–41, 447.

11. HQA AGO, GO 86, 1879; HQA AGO, GO 43, 1881; Department of the Platte, GO 11, 1879.

12. WD AGO, GO 36, 1897.

13. Laidley, *A Course of Instruction,* 170; HQA AGO, GO 86, 1879.

14. WD, *Annual Report, Chief of Ordnance, 1881,* 31; WD, *Annual Report, Chief of Ordnance, 1883,* 97, 100; summary of letters sent on shooting awards for 1884 between Rock Island Arsenal and Chief of Ordnance compiled by Leonard Ball, noting summary of letter 131, dated April 11, and letter 211, dated May 27; HQA AGO, GO 12, 1884; HQA AGO, Circulars 6, 7, and 9, 1883; Department of the East, Circular of September 15, 1881; WD, "Report of Major General John Pope," contained in *Annual Report, Secretary of War, 1883* 1:136.

15. WD, *Annual Report, Chief of Ordnance, 1884,* 51; HQA AGO, Circular 4, 1884; Department of the Platte, GO 6, 1883; Richard Upton, *Fort Custer,* 87.

16. National Archives (hereafter NA) enclosure to Office, Chief of Ordnance #22697, February 1906; McChristian, *An Army of Marksmen,* 62.

17. *Ordnance Notes Number 118,* 186; Blunt, *Instructions in Rifle and Carbine Firing,* 246–51.

18. HQA AGO, GO 37, 1888.

19. Blunt, *Instructions in Rifle and Carbine Firing,* 139, 143; Letter from Leonard Ball to author, August 11, 1997.

20. Kelton, *Information for Riflemen.*

21. WD AGO, GO 36, 1897, 108.

22. HQA AGO, GO 53, 1882, sect. IX.

23. WD, *Annual Report, Secretary of War, 1885* 1:725, 775–77.

24. Potter, "Firearms Accidents," 183–84.

25. WD AGO, GO 36, 1897, paras. 510–14.

26. HQA AGO, Circular 5, 1883; Kelton, *Information for Riflemen,* 85-6.

27. Photocopy of March 1, 1884 letter with enclosure from Benét, simply noted as letter 42, 1884; WD, *Annual Report, Chief of Ordnance, 1885,* 626–29.

28. Braudel, *Civilization and Capitalism* 1: 392–95.

29. Department of the Platte, GO 7, 1873.

30. WD, *Description and Rules for the Management of the Springfield Rifle, Carbine, and Army Revolvers, 1898,* 3–5, 30–31.

31. Schrader, *Reference Guide to United States Military History 1865–1919,* 20.

32. HQA AGO, GO 12, 1884; HQA, Circular 4, 1888.

33. WD AGO, GO 36, 1897, para. 500c.

34. Department of the Platte, GO 22, 1883, with attachment, "Report of the Instructor in Rifle Practice, Department of the Platte."

35. HQA AGO, GO 12, 1884; WD, *Annual Report, Secretary of War, 1883* 1:64; Kelton, *Information for Riflemen,* 100–101.

36. HQA AGO, GO 97, 1886.

37. WD, *Annual Report, Chief of Ordnance, 1888,* 36, 54; HQA AGO, GO 111, 1888; HQA AGO, GO 1, 1890, 16–17; HQA AGO, GO 1, 1894.

38. Armes, *Ups and Downs,* 192, 507; *Army and Navy Journal,* 16 June 1888, 936; Gilmore, "The New Courage," 99; HQA AGO, GO 53, 1882, para. I.

39. HQA AGO, WD, Circular 6, 1884; HQA AGO, GO 12, 1884; WD AGO, GO 36, 1897, para 500h; Examination of various samples.

40. WD AGO, GO 36, 1897; NA, Record Group (hereafter RG) 92, box 3244, "Memo to Secretary of the General Staff," October 24, 1905, found as enclosure 21 to letter of January 4, 1906.

41. WD, *Annual Report, Chief of Ordnance, 1885,* 628–29; WD, *Annual Report, War Department, 1919* 4:3919; Navy Department, Special Order 49, 1898.

42. HQA AGO, Circular 5, 1889.

43. Rice, *Small Arms Practice.*

44. Letter from the Adjutant General, dated September 5, 1889, per Department of the Platte, Circular 1, 1890; WD AGO, GO 36, 1897, paras. 500h and 510; Bell, *Commanding Generals,* 86.

45. Wingate, *Manual for Rifle Practice* (5th ed.), 99–118; Brophy, *The Springfield Rifle,* 254.

46. Department of the Platte, GO 16, 1883; Wingate, *Manual for Rifle Practice* (5th ed.), 62–63. In 1883, for example, in each month a Department of the Platte circular provided practice results. Circular 10 (January), 14 (February), and 19 (March) list gallery practice results, while circulars 24, 25, 31, 38, 42, and 48 list results from April through September. WD, *Annual Report, Secretary of War, 1894* 3:21; *Small Arms Firing Regulations for the Georgia State Troops,* 16.

47. Potter, "Firearms Accidents," 83.

48. WD, *Firing Regulations for Small Arms, 1904,* 65–68; WD, *Small Arms Firing Manual, 1913 (War Department Document 442),* 51–52; Atlantic Division, GO 24, 1906; WD AGO, GO 36, 1897, para. 163; Central Department, Bulletin 2, 1916.

49. Brophy, *The Springfield Rifle,* 254–308.

50. NA, RG 92, box 3243, letter 462420, Report of Department of California, June 30, 1903, "Report of Target Practice"; Philippine Constabulary, *Manual for Target Practice.*

51. Dickman, *Modern Improvements in Fire Arms,* 1–2.

52. Ibid., 12; Jones, "Marksmanship in America," 674.

53. Hale, "The New Firing Regulations," 14–20.

54. WD, *Small Arms Firing Regulations for the United States Army and for the Organized Militia of the United States, Amended to April 20, 1908,* para. 142; WD, *Provisional Small Arms Firing Manual, 1909 (War Department Document 338),* 97; WD, *Annual Report, Secretary of War, 1911,* 236.

55. WD, *Firing Regulations, 1904,* 6.

56. Parker, *The Old Army,* 388.

57. WD, *Annual Report, Chief of Ordnance, 1904,* 48; Memo from Chief of Ordnance to Commanding Officers, January 21, 1916; *Army and Navy Register,* September 25, 1915, 406; Department of the Missouri, GO 6, 19, and 46, 1905; WD, *Annual Report, Chief of Ordnance, 1909,* 46; WD, GO 52, 1904; HQ, Western Division, Special Order 227, 1912.

58. WD, *Small Arms Firing Regulations, 1906,* 122; WD, *Small Arms Firing Regulations, 1908,* 128.

59. WD, *Annual Report, Adjutant General, 1911,* 54; WD, *Annual Report, Secretary of War, 1910,* 201.

60. Blunt, *Instructions in Rifle and Carbine Firing,* para 510; Department of the Platte, Circular 3, 1891, 10; WD, *Small Arms Firing Regulations, 1904,* para 122.

61. WD, Changes 14, December 30, 1916, to *Small Arms Firing Regulations, 1913.*

62. Ordnance Department drawing 1728554, January 1911.

63. Ordnance Drawing 2, class 20, division 12, September 1904, revisions 17 through 21.

64. WD, GO 106, 1919.

65. WD, *Small Arms Firing Manual, 1913,* 70–73, 76, 207.

66. Ibid., 76–77; RG 92, letter #1725236, with 4 endorsements.

67. WD, *Small Arms Firing Regulations, 1904,* 122; NA, Military Secretary Officer #1188032, filed in RG 94, with #462420, dated December 29, 1906.

68. Division of the Atlantic, Circulars 7 and 50, 1906; WD, GO 106, 1906; Division of the Atlantic, Circular 11, 1907; WD, *Small Army Firing Regulations, 1906,* 66; WD, *Small Arms Firing Manual, 1913,* 163.

69. WD, *Small Arms Firing Manual, 1913,* 201–2.

70. HQA AGO, GO 50, 1903; Parker, *The Old Army,* 374–77.

71. WD, *Changes 6 to Small Arms Firing Manual, 1913;* NA AGO letter 2244449; NA, letter from First Cavalry brigade commander to AGO, dated December 30, 1914; WD, various editions to Army Regulations (hereafter AR) 30-30000.

72. Mead, *The Doughboys,* 170–76; Smythe, *Pershing,* 235–36.

73. HQA AGO, GO 57, 1882; Department of the Platte, GO 3, 1873.

74. Blunt, *Instructions in Rifle and Carbine Firing,* 301–5.

75. Armes, *Ups and Downs,* 179; Potter, "Firearms Accidents," 180; Norma Johnson, "Notes on the History of Fort Sisseton," 36.

76. HQA AGO, Circular 5, 1889; HQA AGO, GO 1, 1890, 19; NA, AGO #19249, "Annual Report of Instruction for Period Ending September 30, 1891."

77. Wells, *Shots That Hit,* 31.

78. WD AGO, GO 36, 1897, 74.

79. Scheips, "Darkness and Light."

80. WD, Circular 85, 1907; Series of unnumbered letters from the ordnance office, WD, to various commanding officers of ordnance facilities, Subject: Changes in drawing 20-12-2, badges, sent in February 1914, photostat copy on file at The Institute of Heraldry (hereafter TIOH) letter of February 1914; Series of unnumbered letters from the office of the chief of ordnance, WD, to various commanding officers of ordnance facilities, Subject: Changes in drawing 20-12-2, badges, January 21, 1916, photostat copy on file at TIOH.

81. WD, Circular 85, 1907.

82. WD, *Provisional Small Arms Firing Manual, 1909,* 213; WD, *Annual Report, Adjutant General, 1911,* 54; Department of the Missouri, GO 11, 1911, is one such example.

83. WD, *Small Arms Firing Manual, 1913,* 163–64; Director of the Mint, *Annual Report for Fiscal Year 1914,* 30; Series of unnumbered letters, to various commanding officers of ordnance facilities, sent in February 1914, and January 21, 1916, photostat copies on file at TIOH.

84. Chief of Ordnance letter, January 21, 1916; Visconage, "U.S. Marine Corps Marksmanship Badges," 8.

85. Unnumbered letter to various commanding officers of ordnance facilities, sent in October 1913, photostat copy on file at TIOH.

86. Eastern Division, GO 9, 1912; WD, *Annual Reports, 1914* 1:466–67; WD, *Annual Reports, 1915* 1:695.

87. HQA AGO, GO 18, 1897; WD, GO 62, 1902.

88. WD, GO 113, 1906; Hitt, "A Brief History of School of Musketry," 86–90; Webster, "Machine Gun Testing," 32–34.

89. WD, *Annual Reports, 1910* 3:139.

90. "Transition and Change, 1902–1917," from the Center of Military History web site, 17 January 2000.

91. WD, *Provisional Machine-Gun Firing Manual,* 226–55.

92. Ibid., 253–54.

93. WD, *Order of Battle* 1:173–91.

94. Mead, *The Doughboys,* 401; Wheatley, "The Expert Machine Gun Badge," 6.

95. Wheatley, "The Expert Machine Gun Badge," 5, 10; Mead, *The Doughboys,* 401; Cornebise, *The AMAROC News,* 201.

96. WD, GO 106, 1919.

97. 1st Endorsement, RIA 421.7/302, October 27, 1919, on file at TIOH; WD, *Rifle Marksmanship,* 81–82.

98. WD, *Automatic Rifle Marksmanship,* 18.

99. WD, GO 41, 1918; WD, GO 106, 1919; WD, Changes No. 4, Special Regulations No. 41, May 1918, para. 96(h).

100. HQ Philippine Department, GO 68, 1918.

101. HQA AGO, GO 24, 1903; WD, GO 112, 1904; WD, GO 1905; Thomas, *Woodfill of the Regulars,* 25.

102. NA, RG 94, No. 462420 and the attachment MSO No. 1089743 and Enclosure 1 dated October 31, 1905; WD, GO 153, 1908, 10.

103. WD, *Regulations for the Army of the United States, 1913,* paras. 1345, 1345 ½.

104. WD, GO 48, 1918; WD, Bulletin 4, 1919.

3. THE CURRENT BADGES:
SETTING THE STAGE

1. Vandiver, *Black Jack,* 2, 1012–14; American Expeditionary Forces, *(Provisional) Small Arms Firing Manual.*

2. WD, Circular 182, 1921; Memorandum for Executive Officer, War Planning Standardization, Subject: Badges, etc., April 27, 1922, on file TIOH.

3. Hallahan, *Misfire,* 267–72; Brophy, *The Springfield Rifle,* 2–20, 28, 37.

4. WD, Training Regulation (hereafter TR) 1–10, January 1939; WD, Training Circular 9, November 8, 1940.

5. Letter, Headquarters U.S. Army Engineer Center, 8 August 1994, to author.

6. WD, Office Quartermaster General, drawing CE-4-4-8, dated February 8, 1922.

7. WD, AR 30-3000, April 1923.

8. N. S. Meyer Catalog, "Military Insignia and Equipment," 71.

9. DOD Military Specification MIL-B-3628/14G.

10. WD, *Annual Reports, 1920* 1:396.

11. WD, Circular 50, 1923; WD, Circular 182, 1921.

12. WD, AR 775-10, 23 April 1931, para. 19; WD, AR 775-10, May 28, 1934, para. 92; WD, *Annual Report, Secretary of War, 1924,* 21.

13. WD, *Report of the Secretary of War, 1893* 3:529–30; WD, Circular 69, 1910; WD, Circulars 60, 159, and 253, 1921.

14. WD, Circulars 137 and 183, 1922; WD, AR 35-2380, editions of August 1925 and April 1934.

15. WD, Bulletin 1, 1931, section VII.

16. WD, AR 35-2380, various editions and changes; WD, AR 35-2380, Changes 1, 1937; WD, Circular 123, 1940; WD, AR 775-10, 1939, para. 9b.

17. WD, AR 35-2380, June 1940, paras. 2c and 4; WD, Circular 123, 1940; WD, Circular 219, 1942; WD, AR 775-10, 1939, para. 9b; WD, Training Circular 63, 1941; WD, TR 415-5, para. 11.

18. WD, AR 35-2380, various editions, 1920s and 1930s; WD, TR 150-25, January 2, 1928, para. 31b.

19. WD, AR 775-10, May 28, 1934, paras. 31 and 37.

20. HQA AGO, GO 76, 1879, 1.

21. WD, TR 50-25, December 20, 1923; Wood and Michaelson, "Close Quarters Combat and Modern Warfare."

22. WD, TR 440-40, editions of 1926, 1929, and 1935.

23. Letter from Armor Center and School, ATSAR-DMP, Subject: Recommendation for Aeroweapons Bar for Basic Marksmanship Qualification Badge, May 12, 1972; Purchase order, copy on file, TIOH, August 7, 1972.

24. WD, TR 150-10, 1923, 1–13; WD, TR 150-10, 1926, 9–13; WD, Training Circulars 7 and 11, 1940; WD, Training Circular 30, 1943; WD, AR 775-10, Changes 1, February 1944, Changes 2, August 1944, and Changes 3, June 1945.

25. Kamp, "Trainfire," 17–20.

26. Flynn, "Wanted: Realism in Weapons Marksmanship Training," 96–100; Groom, "Marksmanship," 44–52; Moore, "The New Rifle Marksmanship Course," 5–12; Taylor, "Wanted: Better Marksmen," 18–19; DA Pamphlet 355-14.

27. Letter from Albert Garland to author, 28 August 1999; DA, Field Manual (hereafter FM) 23-9, June 1974, 125, 134–35, and 138; WD, *Annual Report, Secretary of War, 1910* 3:257.

28. Letter, DAPE-HRP, Subject: WAC Weapons Training, June 13, 1975.

29. WD, TR 150-20, 1927, para. 1a; TR 150-25, 1928; TR 150-25, 1924, para. 25.

30. WD, *Pistol Marksmanship (Document 1050),* 1920, 48, 71; WD, TR 150-26, 1927, paras. 61–63, 85–86; WD, Training Circular 33, 1941.

31. DA, FM 23-35, July 1960, chapter 4.

32. DA, FM 23-35, September 1971, chapter 5.

33. WD, Training Circulars 87 and 119, 1943; *Army Times,* May 15, 2000, 12.

34. WD, TR 150-40, 1923 and 1930; WD, TR 415-5, 1932.

35. WD, Training Circular 14, 1941.

36. WD, TR 150-35, 1926.

37. WD, TR 435-211, 1926; WD, Changes 1 to TR 435-211, 1929.

38. WD, Circular 53, 1923.

39. "New Machine Rifle Marksmanship Course," *The Cavalry Journal,* April 1928, 295.

40. WD, TR 150-34, 1929, paras. 36, 37.

41. WD, *Automatic Rifle Marksmanship, Document 1011;* WD, AR 150-30, 1923, para. 6.

42. WD, Changes 1, AR 600-75, November 1931; WD, AR 600-75, December 1936; WD, Changes 1, AR 600-75, December 1942; Changes 2, AR 600-75, February 1946.

43. N. S. Meyer Catalog, 71–72.

44. Philippine Constabulary, *Philippine Constabulary Regulations: 1930,* front color plate; Philippine Constabulary, *Philippine Constabulary Small Arms Firing Regulations,* 1915, 56–57.

45. *Army Life and Recruiting News,* April 1948, 8.

46. Memorandum, TAPC-PDA, Subject: Revision of Marksmanship Qualification Badges, December 5, 1988.

47. Ibid.

48. DA, AR 672-5-1, August 31, 1989; DA, AR 670-1, September 1992, para. 28-16.

49. Poppel, Paganiai, and Rynbrandt, "Close Quarters Marksmanship," 39–42.

50. Chapman, *The Army's Training Revolution.*

51. Ibid.

52. *Army Times,* May 15, 2000, 12.

53. Gilmore, "The New Courage," 101.

54. *Army Times,* October 20, 2003, 14.

4. ARTILLERY AND SWORDSMAN'S BADGES:
MORE THAN JUST SMALL ARMS

1. WD, *Annual Report, Chief of Ordnance, 1884,* 113–40, appendix 13.

2. Heitman, *Historical Register* 1:961; Tidball, *Manual of Heavy Artillery Service,* 1880; Tidball, *Manual of Heavy Artillery Service,* 1881; Tidball, *Manual of Heavy Artillery Service,* 1891; Tidball, *Manual of Heavy Artillery Service,* 1898; Birkhimer, *Historical Sketch,* 310–11.

3. Tidball, *Manual of Heavy Artillery Service,* 1891, 190.

4. HQA AGO, GO 49, 1889.

5. HQA AGO, GO 96, 1882; Dorrance, "Campaigns of the U.S. Heavy Artillery," 3–19.

6. HQA AGO, GO 132, 1890.

7. Bell, *Commanding Generals,* 86; NA, RG 156, Letter 2426, with attached memorandum from M. G. Schofield to Chief of Ordnance, April 15, 1891.

8. Ibid., first endorsement.

9. Ibid., third endorsement; NA, RG 156, Letter 18251 from Capt. M. W. Lyon, to Chief of Ordnance, August 20, 1891.

10. NA, RG 156, Letter 7139 from Capt. M. W. Lyon, to Chief of Ordnance, October 20, 1891.

11. NA, RG 156, Memorandum, HQA to The Adjutant General (hereafter TAG) with letter of instruction to Chief of Ordnance, October 26, 1891, #7209.

12. Ibid.; WD AGO, Circular 41, 1896.

13. WD AGO, Circular 41, 1896.

14. Dorrance, "Campaigns of the Heavy Artillery," 15–16; WD, GO 141, 1904, para. 106.

15. WD, Circular 41, 1896.

16. Emerson, *Chevrons,* 219–26.

17. NA, RG 94, Decision, Secretary of War, June 22, 1897, File #55719/B.

18. NA, RG 156, Letter 22482, from Capt. William F. Steward, Commanding Battery E, 4th Artillery, to Chief of Ordnance, August 7, 1897, second Endorsement; HQA AGO, GO 41, 1896.

19. HQA AGO, GO 4, 1898, para. II; HQA AGO, GO 70, 1898, para. I.

20. WD, *Annual Report, Secretary of War, 1889,* 67; HQA AGO, GO 152, 1901; HQA AGO, GO 126, 1902; HQA AGO, GO 36, 1901; WD, GO 108, 1904.

21. HQA AGO, GO 152, 1901.

22. HQA AGO, GO 126, 1902.

23. WD, GO 108, 1904; HQA AGO, GO 98, 1903.

24. WD, *Annual Report, Secretary of War, 1903,* 431.

25. WD, *Annual Report, Secretary of War, 1909,* 43.

26. *Field Artillery Journal,* November–December 1938, 453–63; fact sheet from Casemate Museum; WD, GO 178, 1907.

27. WD, GO 30, 1907, para. III; HQA AGO, GO 60, 1903, para. II; WD, GO 197, 1904, 38.

28. WD, GO 24, 1907; WD, GO 176, 1907; WD, GO 25, 1909.

29. HQA AGO, Circular 15, 1901; HQA AGO, GO 9, 1901, sec. 7; WD, GO 80, 1908; *United States Army Recruiting News,* August 1937, 6–7.

30. NA, RG 156, Letter #22697-482, from Commander, Rock Island Arsenal, to Chief of Ordnance, second endorsement, with inventory of March 22, 1906; HQ Artillery District of San Francisco, GO 14, 1908.

31. Letter from Todd Wheatley to author, 24 November 1999.

32. NA, Chief of Artillery, Decision o.o. 26340-75; WD, *Annual Report, Chief of Ordnance, 1905,* 56; NA, RG 156, Letter #22697-482, from Commander, Rock Island Arsenal, to Chief of Ordnance, with second endorsement with inventory, March 22, 1906.

33. HQA AGO, GO 60, 1903.

34. WD, *Annual Report, Secretary of War, 1909,* 45; WD, *Provisional Drill and Service Regulations,* 1916; WD, *Special Regulations No. 53,* "Examination and Classification of Gunners of Field Artillery."

35. WD, *Field Service Regulation, 1914, Corrected to 1916,* 205; Mead, *The Doughboys,* 174.

36. NA, RG 156, AGO #2048103, Letter #22697-1965 from Rock Island Arsenal Commander to Chief of Ordnance, June 2, 1913.

37. Emerson, *Chevrons,* 161, 222.

38. WD, *Annual Report, Secretary of War, 1882,* 68; NA, MSO record cards #1215257, February 1907.

39. Bell, *Commanding Generals,* 100; WD, GO 16, 1914.

40. Blumenson, *The Patton Papers* 1:292–93, 297.

41. Patton, *The Pattons,* 163; Blumenson, *Patton,* 75; Blumenson, *The Patton Papers* 1:280.

42. WD, *Annual Report, Secretary of War, 1913,* 157; WD, GO 88, 1914.

43. WD, *Annual Report, Secretary of War, 1914,* 1, 7; Blumenson, *The Patton Papers* 1:329–42.

44. HQA AGO, Circular 8, 1883; HQA AGO, GO 29, 1898; WD, GO 53, 1904; WD, GO 50, 1916. Many examples of "companies" and "troops" exist, especially in various general orders. One example is Department of the Missouri General Orders 15, October 22, 1867. The 1867 series of GOs for the Department of the Missouri is unusual in that when General Sherman assumed command during 1867, GOs were started again with number 1, thus two GO 15, Department of the Missouri, exist for 1867. HQA AGO, Circular 8, 1883.

45. WD, Changes 3 and 5, AR 600-35, 1922; WD, AR 30-3000, various editions. One sample of a post–World War I swordsman badge is in the First Cavalry Division Museum, Fort Hood, Texas.

46. WD, Changes 5, AR 600-35, 1922; WD, Training Regulation 50-70, February 1922; Ball, "The U.S. Army Swordsman Badge," 27–30.

47. Ball, "The U.S. Army Swordsman Badge."

48. Peterson, *The American Sword,* 4–5, 16; WD AGO, Circular 44, 1864.

49. Armes, *Ups and Downs,* 462.

50. Richard Upton, *The Indian as a Soldier,* 29–30, 67, 128.

51. Ball, "The U.S. Cavalry Practice Saber and Single Stick."

52. NA, MSO letter 1215257, endorsement dated October 30, 1909.

53. Blumenson, *The Patton Papers* 1:264, 272; Blumenson, *Patton,* 74–75.

54. Peterson, *The American Sword,* 37; Blumenson, *Patton,* 74; Blumenson, *The Patton Papers* 1:269, 272, 312–13.

55. WD, TR 50–70, 1922 and 1927 editions; WD, Changes 2, TR 50-70, 1929.

56. WD, TR 50-70, 1922 and 1927 editions.

57. Peterson, *The American Sword,* 16; Ed Ramsey, "The Last Cavalry Charge," 3–4.

5. Unofficial Awards:
What Some Soldiers Wore

1. *Field Artillery Journal,* March–April 1928, 100; and January–February 1936, 42; *Army Life and Recruiting News,* August 1937, 4; and March 1940, 8–9; Gleim, *Medal Auction No. 35,* February 1997, Lot 9; *National Geographic Magazine,* October 1943, 440–41; WD, AR 775-10, 1931, para. 13o(2); WD, AR 775-10, 1934, para. 4b; WD, AR 775-10, 1939, para. 56b.

2. Gleim, *Medal Auction No 35; Field Artillery Journal,* 1926, 108; 1928, 107; 1931, 52; *National Geographic Magazine,* October 1943, 440–41.

3. *Field Artillery Journal,* 1931, 50–53.

4. *Field Artillery Journal,* 1926, 107–8; *Army Life and Recruiting News,* March 1940, 8–9; Letter from Fort Sill Museum to author, March 8, 1994.

5. Smith and Pelz, *Shoulder Sleeve Insignia,* 143.

6. U.S. Army Missile Command web site.

7. Letter from James A. Sawicki to author, December 8, 1996; letter from Center of Military History to author, undated (circa September 1996).

8. DA, HQ, 56th Artillery Group, Regulation Number 672-3, 6 December 1968, paras, 3, 5.

9. *The Giant,* vol 2, no. 20, November 29, 1968, 1.

10. U.S. Army Missile Command web site; U.S. Army Europe, *Unit Telephone Book,* 1982; Letter from James A. Sawicki to author, December 8, 1996.

11. DA message DAPE-HRL, Subject: Wearing of Unauthorized Items with the Uniform, 082355Z Dec 78.

12. Enclosures to letters from Fort Sill Museum to author, the enclosures taken from undated newspaper clippings extracted from the *Cannonier,* the Fort Sill newspaper.

13. Certificate from HQ Field Artillery Missile Group 9 to BG Grayson D. Tate, 1978; Letter, ATZR-CCO, Subject: Policy for the Award of the Field Artillery Missileman's Badge and Certificate, December 8, 1976; Letter AFFS-CBNCO to Tom Dinackus, December 10, 1975; Letter from Sgt. Maj. (Ret.) Daniel P. Gillotti to author, February 25, 2000.

14. Letter, ATZR-CCO, 1976.

15. *Infantry Journal,* May 1927, 527; WD, TR 420-270, June 1929.

16. WD, TR 420-270, 1929, sections II and X.

17. WD, TR 425-90, September 1931; WD, Changes 1 to AR 600-75, November 1931.

18. WD, TR 150-50, July 1935, paras. 9–13.

19. WD, Circular 23, 1940.

20. Certificate of Proficiency awarded May 11, 1943; Stanton, *Order of Battle, World War II,* 61–62; Letter from U.S. Army Center of Military History, to author, Subject: 10th Armored Division, Locations 43–44, dated September 25, 1997.

21. *Armor* magazine, November–December 1951, 43.

22. *The Trading Post,* October–December 1990 through January–March 1992 issues.

23. Conversation between Gen. (Ret.) Donn Starry, and author, May 4, 1997.

24. Several examples exist. One is in DA, *FM 17-12-8,* February 1999, which lists these three levels for cavalry gunnery. Another set of awards is described in *The Trading Post,* January–March 2001, 14.

25. *Infantry Journal*, May 1922, 569.

26. WD, TR, 145-5, 1923, Section VII; WD, Changes 1 to TR 145-5, 1928, Section VII; WD, TR 420-50, 1925, para. 4b.

27. WD, Office Chief of Militia Bureau, Training Circular No. 3, July 15, 1931; *Army Life and Recruiting News,* June 1937, 12; December 1937, 12; February 1938, 13; *Infantry Journal,* November–December 1931, 546.

28. *Infantry Journal,* August 1931, unnumbered page; November–December 1931, 546.

29. *Infantry Journal,* July 1924, 64; WD, *Small Arms Firing Manual,* 1913, plate, VI.

30. WD, Militia Bureau Circular 3, 1931; *National Matches Program,* 1923, 40–42; *Infantry Journal,* November–December 1931, 547–48.

31. Undated press release (circa 1935) from DCM files, Camp Perry, Ohio.

32. Hewes, *From Root to McNamara,* 400; WD, *Order of Battle* 3:284.

33. WD, *Annual Report, National Guard Bureau,* 1936, 17; 1937, 11; 1938, 17; 1939, 24; *Infantry Journal,* 1931, 386–87.

34. National Guard Regulation No. 44, May 1949 and September 1951.

6. NINETEENTH-CENTURY PRIZES:
THE HIGH POINT OF MAGNIFICENCE

1. Department of the Platte, GO 3, 1879; Division of Missouri, GO 2, 1879; WD, *Annual Report, Secretary of War, 1880* 3:X.

2. Frasca, *The .45-70 Springfield Book II,* 221–22.

3. WD, *Annual Report, Secretary of War, 1880* 3:X; Gilmore, "Crack Shots and Patriots," 114.

4. WD, *Annual Report, Secretary of War, 1881* 1:44; *New York Times,* September 17, 1881, 8.

5. Rickey, *Forty Miles a Day,* 104.

6. WD, GO 12, 1884; *Army and Navy Journal,* October 29, 1881, 271; HQA AGO, GO 53, 1882, para. III.

7. NA, enclosure to office of Chief of Ordnance, letter #22697, 12.

8. WD, *Annual Report, Secretary of War, 1894* 3:18–19; WD, *Firing Regulations for Small Arms,* 1898, 162; NA, RG 156, Letter 22697/448, box 1371, entry 28; HQA AGO, GOs 2 and 12, 1903.

9. WD, GO 53, 1882; Scheips, "Darkness and Light," 286.

10. Letter from Thomas N. Trevor to author, dated September 14, 2000.

11. HQA AGO, GO 44, 1881.

12. HQA AGO, GO 53, 1882.

13. HQA AGO, GO 54, 1882.

14. HQA AGO, GO 53, 1882, 4; WD, *Annual Report, Secretary of War, 1882,* "Report of General Pope," 102–3.

15. Fitzpatrick, "Emory Upton and the Citizen Soldier," 365–66.

16. Emory Upton, *Infantry Tactics,* 117.

17. Wingate, *Manual for Rifle Practice* (5th ed.), 128; WD, A *nnual Report, Secretary of War, 1886,* 75; NA, AGO #19249, "Semi Annual Report of Instruction for Period Ending September 30, 1891," from Col. J. F. Wade, Commander, 5th Cavalry, to Maj. Gen. Nelson Miles, Department of the Missouri.

18. WD, *Annual Report, Secretary of War, 1882,* 64; WD, *Annual Report, Secretary of War, 1885,* 65; Blunt, *Instructions in Carbine and Rifle Firing,* 1888, 122–23.

19. HQA AGO, GO 53, 1882, 4–5.

20. HQA AGO, GO 53, 1882; Rickey, *Forty Miles a Day,* 104; Richard Upton, *Fort Custer,* 88–89.

21. HQA AGO, GO 53, 1882; Wingate, *Manual for Rifle Practice* (5th ed.), 224–25.

22. WD, *Annual Report, Chief of Ordnance, 1885,* Appendix C.

23. WD, *Annual Report, Secretary of War, 1888* 1:68.

24. WD AGO, GO 36, 1897, 29–31, 33–34, 46.

25. WD AGO, GO 36, 1897; WD, *Firing Regulations for Small Arms,* 1898, 102–3; WD, *Firing Regulations for Small Arms,* 1904, 88–94; Coffman, *The Old Army,* 280.

26. WD, *Firing Regulations for Small Arms,* 1898, 103–4.

27. Blunt, *Instructions in Carbine and Rifle Firing,* 1885, para. 605; HQA AGO, GO 88, 1887.

28. HQA AGO, GO 53, 1882; HQ, Department of the Platte, GO 8, 1891.

29. WD, *Small Arms Firing Manual, 1913,* 62; 1919 AEF bulletins 7 and 29, 1919.

30. Olsen, "Development of the Looped Cartridge Belt," 9–11; Phillips, "The Woven Cartridge Belt, 1897–1903," Parts I and II, *Military Collector & Historian,* vol. 44, nos. 2 and 3: 64–72, 110–15; Zimmer, Frontier Soldier, 45, 121.

31. Phillips, "The Evolution of the Pocket-Type Rifle Cartridge Belt in the United States Services," *Military Collector & Historian,* vol. 22, no. 1: 1–10.

32. WD, *Annual Report, Secretary of War, 1889,* 66–67; *Army and Navy Journal,* June 18, 1881, 965.

33. WD AGO, GO 36, 1897; WD, *Firing Regulations for Small Arms,* 1898, 162.

34. Letter from Chief of Ordnance to Commander Rock Island Arsenal, December 8, 1905, #22697-448. The 1882 medals are cited in DF (October 5, 1962), comment 2, dated November 15, 1962, Subject: Identification of Medal, to PSSD, PAB, D & S Sec, from TIOH, to AGAH-A.

35. HQA AGO, GO 53, 1882.

36. Carlson, "U.S. Army Marksmanship Medals 1882–1897," 4–10.

37. Frasca, *The .45-70 Springfield,* 225.

38. Quantities of prizes struck were developed by using data contained in Julian's *Medals of*

the United States Mint, Carlson's "U.S. Army Marksmanship Medals," examination of various general orders, 1880–1902, and analysis of NA, RG 108, Entry 56, "Registry of Marksmanship," a ledger listing winners in various shooting contests, their scores, and prizes awarded. In addition 1905–6 correspondence between the Office of the Chief of Ordnance (letters #22697) and Rock Island Arsenal shows that additional bronze samples were struck. Some of these latter samples were gold or silver plated. These post-1902 quantities are not included in the sample numbers.

39. HQA AGO, Circular 2, 1889.

40. NA, AGO #19243, dated November 6, 1891.

41. HQA AGO, GOs 38 and 73, 1888.

42. HQA AGO, GO 127, 1882.

43. HQA AGO, GO 47, 1889.

44. HQA AGO, GO 78, 1889; NA, RG 108, Entry 56, "Register of Marksmanship," 74.

45. HQA AGO, GO 78, 1889; Department of the Platte, GO 11, 1890, 9; HQA AGO, GO 112, 1890.

46. Hale, "The New Firing Regulations," 14; *Army and Navy Register,* 1891, 621.

47. Potter, "Firearms Accidents," 176.

48. Steffen, *The Horse Soldiers* 3:29–30, 82; McAulay, *Carbines of the U.S. Cavalry, 1861–1905.*

49. Department of the Platte, Circulars 8, 9, 10, 11, 1894.

50. NA, RG 108, Entry 56, "Register of Marksmanship," 86; Richard Upton, *Fort Custer,* 205–9, 291.

51. White, *It's Your Misfortune,* 225; Foner, *The United States Soldiers Between Two Wars,* 119.

52. Department of the Platte, GO 10, 1889; WD AGO, GO 47, 1897.

53. NA, RG 108, Entry 56, "Register of Marksmanship," 65; Department of the Missouri, Circulars, 7, 8, 1902; HQA AGO, GO 116, 1902.

54. Director of the Mint, *Annual Report, 1903.*

55. Heitman, *Historical Register* 2:442; Hutton, *Soldiers West,* 108–10.

56. NA, RG 108, Entry 56, "Register of Marksmanship"; NA, Enlistment record of James A. Richardson.

57. HQA AGO, GO 46, 1889; HQA AGO, GO 143, 1890.

58. WD AGO, GO 36, 1897, 59–64; WD AGO, GO 47, 1897; HQA AGO, GO 64, 1897.

59. Vandiver, *Black Jack,* 102–3.

60. WD, GO 28, 1891; Letter from Bob Lee to author, January 6, 2000.

61. Department of the Platte, GO 19, 1893; *Omaha World Herald,* August 20, 1893, 3.

62. *Bishinik,* November 1999, 1.

63. HQA AGO, GO 112, 1890; HQA AGO, GO 81, 1891.

64. HQA AGO, GO 116, 1902; WD, GO 52, 1904; WD, GO 11, 1905.

7. PRIZES, 1903–1922:
THE TRANSITION TO SMALLER PRIZES

1. HQA AGO, GO 77, 1902.

2. NA, RG 94, Letter #462420.

3. WD, *Firing Regulations for Small Arms,* 1904, 6.

4. HQA AGO, 77, 1903.

5. HQA AGO, 65, 1903; WD, GO 207, 1908; WD, GO 64, 74, 127, and 129, 1911; WD, GO 19, 1912; WD GO 9, 1913; WD, *Annual Reports* as follows: *Secretary of War, 1904,* 5; *Secretary of War, 1906,* 17; *Chief of Staff, 1907,* 173–74; *Adjutant General, 1907,* 205; *Adjutant General, 1911,* 9–10; *Adjutant General, 1913,* 8–9.

6. WD, GO 95 and 129, 1907; NA, enclosure to Chief of Ordnance letter #22697, section entitled "4, Competitive, Medals and Prizes,"; WD, *Provisional Small Arms Firing Manual, 1909,* para. 264.

7. WD, *Annual Reports, 1908* 3:304; WD, *Annual Reports, 1909* 3:244.

8. TIOH files, AGO Memo, Subject: Small Arms Competition, May 22, 1920, cites AGO #1607363; WD, *Annual Report, Secretary of War, 1911,* 236; TIOH files, Letter from Chief of Ordnance to Commanding Officer, Rock Island Arsenal (Drawing change), dated April 1, 1908.

9. Huebner, "1911 and 1913 Mobilizations," 14–17.

10. WD, GO 175, 1906; WD, *Annual Report, Chief of Staff, 1906,* 175; King, Biggs, and Criner, *Spearhead of Logistics,* 90; WD, Bulletin 37, 1913.

11. WD, *Small Arms Firing Manual, 1913,* Changes 5 and 8, 1915.

12. WD, GO 198, 1906; NA, RG 94, #1362351.

13. NA, Office of the Chief of Ordnance, first endorsement to letter 22697-448, dated February 8, 1906.

14. WD, GO 52, 1904.

15. AEF, GO 82, 1919.

16. WD, *Small Arms Firing Regulations, 1908,* 144–45.

17. Ibid.

18. *Infantry Journal,* September–October 1931, 418–19, and November–December 1937, 553–54.

19. WD, AR 30-3000, various editions.

20. Gilmore, "Crack Shots and Patriots," 212; GHQ AEF, Bulletin 7, 1919; GHQ AEF, Bulletin 29, 1919; AEF, *(Provisional) Small Arms Firing Manual.*

21. NRA, *The National Matches, 1925,* 3; GHQ AEF, Bulletin 30, 1919, II; GHQ AEF, GO 81, 1919; Various AEF Bulletins issued daily at D'Auvours Rifle Range.

22. GHQ AEF, GO 81, 1919.

23. GHQ AEF, Bulletin 29, 1919.

24. *AMAROC News:* August 28, 1920, 3; August 10, 1921, 4; August 12, 1921, 4; August 13, 1921, 4; August 1, 1922, 4; August 3, 1922, 4; August 10, 1922, 4.

25. WD, *Musketry,* 5, 6; GHQ AEF, Bulletin 7, 1919.

26. GHQ AEF, GO 82, 1919.

27. Ibid.

28. NA, AGO file S-CE 421.37.

29. GHQ AEF, GO 82, 1919.

30. NA, RG 94, #1632150; NA, RG 94, MSO #1204992 (box 3244); WD, GO 44, 1907.

31. Ordnance drawing, Class 20, Division 12, Drawing 5, dated 1919; QMC drawing 4-4-16, dated April 1923; WD, Bulletin 2, 1923; WD, Bulletins 29 and 39, 1919.

32. WD, Bulletin 5, 1922; WD, Bulletins 1 and 2, 1923.

8. Prizes, 1922 to the Present: From the Common Soldier to the Elite

1. WD, GO, 50, 63, and 71, 1920; WD, Bulletin 25, 1920, 2.

2. WD, AR 30-3000, May 1930 and previous editions list the older prizes with note "until exhausted," but the June 1931 edition does not list the prizes.

3. WD, Changes 5 to AR 600-35, September 1922, para. 39d.

4. WD, Changes 8 and 9 to AR 600-35, 1923; TIOH files, letter QM 421 E-P, Subject: Samples, Clasps for Department and Corps Area Automatic Rifle Team Badges, March 25, 1924.

5. WD, Office Quartermaster General drawing 4-4-16, April 18, 1923.

6. Ibid.

7. WD, Bulletin 3, 1924, para. 3e; TIOH files, WD memo, dated April 16, 1923.

8. WD, Bulletins 1 and 23, 1924.

9. WD, AR 740-10, 1931 and 1934 editions, Section XII.

10. Ibid.; WD, *Pistol Marksmanship (Document 1050),* 1920, para. 130(b).

11. WD, AR 740-10, 1934; WD, *Pistol Marksmanship (Document 1050),* para. 139.

12. WD, AR 740-10, 1931 and 1934 editions, Section XII.

13. WD, AR 775-10, 1939, para 41d.

14. WD, Changes 2, AR 600-75, 1946.

15. DA, Bulletin 15, 28 August 1951.

16. DA, AR 370-10, 1948.

17. TIOH files, DF, G1 200.6 Badges, Subject: Award for Proficiency in the Use of Individual Arms, with comments 1 through 9, dated starting March 29, 1955, and continuing through 1956.

18. Fifth Endorsement to DF, QMGRE-H 421.4 (July 21, 1958), Subject: Badges, Qualification, Distinguished Rifleman and Distinguished Pistol Shot, dated November 5, 1958.

19. DA, TIOH drawings B-5-11 and B-5-12, both dated July 10, 1958.

20. TIOH files, Memo, OPS-OT-TR2, dated December 15, 1959; TIOH files, DF, ATTNG-TNG 200-6, with first endorsement, Subject: New Badges Qualification, EIC, National, All Army, and Area Matches, February 18, 1960.

21. TIOH files, Letter AMIH-Q 421.4, Subject: Qualification Badges, Excellence in Competition, National, All Army, and Army Area Matches, February 8, 1961; DA, Changes 1, AR 672-5-1, March 1962.

22. DA, AR 920-30, March 1962, 20; DA, Changes 1, AR 672-5-1, March 1962.

23. DA, AR 622-10, June 1963, para. 5; DA, AR 350-6, May 1985, table 2; DA, Changes 5 to AR 672-5-1, November 1963; DA, AR 350-6, 1971, para. 9.

24. "EIC Fact Sheet," January 1999.

25. *Army Information Digest,* August 1995, 23; DA, AR 622-10, 1955, para. 8b, and 1963, para. 10b.

9. Distinguished Badges: Rewards in Gold

1. NA, RG 108, Entry 56, "Registry of Marksmanship," 11.

2. HQA AGO, GOs 24 and 126, 1884; Heitman, *Historical Register,* 1:704.

3. HQA AGO, GO 103, 1885; HQA AGO, GO 78, 1886.

4. WD, *Annual Report, Chief of Ordnance, 1887,* 5; Julian, *Medals of the Mint,* 340; Memo for Record, Springfield Armory, July 22, 1982.

5. Memo for Record, Springfield Armory, July 22, 1982.

6. Sandusky, "America's Distinguished Marksmen," 92.

7. HQA AGO, Circular 3, 1891.

8. HQA AGO, GO 78, 1889; Department of the Platte, GO 11, 1891; HQA AGO, GO 81, 1891.

9. NA, MSO #1119649, April 5, 1906, and fourth endorsement, dated April 13, 1906, filed with RG 94, #462420; WD, *Firing Regulations,* 1904, 24.

10. WD, Circular 25, 1926.

11. WD, *Annual Report, Chief of Ordnance, 1904,* 48.

12. WD, GO 52, 1904, 26; WD, GO 124, 1904.

13. WD, *Army Register, 1928,* 808; *The Cavalry Journal,* 1913, front pieces; WD, *Army Register, 1918,* 189; Letter from U.S. MA Library to author, May 25, 1999.

14. HQA AGO, GO 62, 1894, 62; Analysis of WD, *Distinguished Marksmen and Distinguished Pistol Shots.*

15. NA, MSO #1119649, April 5, 1906, and fourth endorsement, dated April 13, 1906, filed with RG 94, #462420.

16. WD, *Annual Report, Chief of Ordnance, 1904,* 48.

17. TIOH files, DF, QMGRD-H 421.4, Subject: Awards for Proficiency in the Use of Individual Arms, November 8, 1956.

18. Bell, *Commanding Generals,* 132; *Armor* magazine, January–February 1960, 55.

19. TIOH files, DF, QMACH 421.4, Subject: Badges, Qualification, Distinguished Rifleman and Distinguished Pistol Shot, July 21, 1958, with endorsements.

20. *Army and Navy Register,* July 9, 1887, 443; WD, *Annual Reports, 1911* 1:702; WD, AR 30-3000, various editions; MIL-DTL-3628/1F, November 15, 1996; MIL-DTL-3628/2F, November 15, 1996.

21. WD, Circulars 24 and 34, 1925.

22. DA, AR 370-10, 1948; DA AR 920-30, Changes 2, March 1959; DA, AR 920-30, para. 70, 1962; AR 920-30, Changes 2, 1963.

23. Army Marksmanship Unit, *Profile of a Champion,* 26.

24. DA, AR 600-70, 1954, 18–19; CMP web page, November 17, 2000.

25. NA, RG 94, MSO letter #1204992, January 1907, box 3244; DA, GO 15, 1995.

26. WD, *Annual Reports, 1909,* 48; Wallechinsky, *Book of the Olympics,* 408, 415.

27. Wallechinsky, *Book of the Olympics,* 406, 410, 412.

28. DA, AR 672-5-1, Changes 5, 1963, para. 113.1.

29. Ibid.; Letter from Ray Carter to author, June 23, 1999; *Army Information Digest,* July 1956, 46; "List of Distinguished International Shooters," compiled by Ray P. Carter, provided by Gary Anderson to author, September 1999.

30. Schuon, *U.S. Marine Corps Biographical Dictionary,* 73–77; Sandusky, "America's Distinguished Marksmen," 38.

31. Correspondence from Ray Carter to author, March 21, 2000.

32. Letter from Ray Carter to author, June 23, 1999; "List of Distinguished International Shooters," compiled by Ray P. Carter, provided by Gary Anderson to author, September 1999.

33. Letter from Ray Carter to author, June 23, 1999.

34. Letter from Gary Anderson to author, June 14, 1999.

35. DA, AR 672-5-1, Changes 1, 1962.

36. WD, *Annual Report, Secretary of War, 1928,* 244.

37. Ibid.; *Annual Report, Chief Air Corps, 1928,* 31–32; *New York Times,* June 17, 1928.

38. Matray, *Historical Dictionary of the Korean War,* 374–75.

39. WD, TR 440-40, 1926; *Air Corps News Letter,* 1932, 406–8; WD, TR 440-15, 1926, para. 3.

40. WD, TR 440-40, para. 31e(1) and 32; *Air Corps News Letter,* 1932, 408.

41. WD, *Annual Report, Chief of Air Corps, 1928,* 31–32; WD, *Annual Report, Chief of Air Corps, 1929,* 28.

42. WD, *Annual Report, Chief of Air Corps, 1930,* 29; WD, *Annual Report, Chief of Air Corps, 1931,* 41; Maurer, *Aviation in the U.S. Army,* 480; WD, *Annual Report, Chief of Air Corps, 1932,* 44; WD, AR 775-10, 1931, para. 13p.

43. Maurer, *Aviation in the U.S. Army,* 224; Letters from Clifford Presley to author, July 28 and August 14, 1993; *Air Corps News Letter,* 1932, 406–8.

44. Letter from Clifford Presley to author, June 1, 1995; Emerson, "A Few Notes on the Distinguished Aerial Gunner and Bombardier Badges."

45. *Army Life and Recruiting News,* March 1939, 16.

46. WD, *Annual Report, Secretary of War, 1928,* 244.

47. *American Rifleman,* October 1930, 32.

48. OQMG Drawing 4-4-22, dated February 28, 1930, with Change 2, dated May 26, 1948; DOD Specification MIL-B-3628, November 1951.

10. TROPHIES AND ASSOCIATED AWARDS: OTHER REWARDS

1. WD, *Annual Report, Secretary of War, 1903,* 423.

2. Ibid., 422–23.

3. Ibid., 422.

4. Ibid., 423.

5. WD, GO 172, 1904; WD, GOs 195, 20, 1905; WD, *Annual Report, Secretary of War, 1905,* 33.

6. NA, RG 94, #1632150; WD, GOs 56, 147, 190, 1906.

7. WD, *Annual Report, Secretary of War, 1909,* 47; WD, GO 69, 1909, 4–5.

8. WD, Bulletin 6, 1916, 3; WD, Bulletin 4, 1921, 3.

9. WD, GO 47, 1907; WD, *Annual Reports, 1917,* 1:195.

10. Mitchell, "God, Guns, and Guts," 15; WD, *Annual Reports, 1918,* 1:212.

11. NRA, *The National Matches, 1925,* 5–7.

12. NRA, *The National Matches, 1931,* 114; NRA, *The National Matches, 1936,* 17.

13. *The Cavalry Journal,* November–December 1932, 39–41, and May–June 1933, 39.

14. Arthur D. Little, Inc., *A Study of the Activities and Missions of the NBPRP,* 1–12.

15. Letter from employees, CMP, undated but mailed January 2, 1999.

16. Many examples of medals being awarded from between 10 and 20 percent. Some are DA, NBPRP, *Official Bulletins: National Trophy Matches,* 1954 and 1965; DA, AR 920-30, 1954 and 1962 editions.

17. WD, Bulletins 11, 30, and 36, 1914.

18. WD, Bulletins 11 and 36, 1914.

19. *American Journal of Numismatics and Proceedings of The American Numismatic Society,* 1914. vol. XLVIII, 217–18.

20. NA, RG 94, Letter #2257254, dated March 1, 1914; WD, Bulletin 20, 1920, Table I entry for Weeks, and Table II, entry for Laughborough; WD, Bulletin 1, 1921, Table I, entry for Thomas.

21. WD, *Annual Report, Chief, Division of Militia Affairs, 1915,* 42–43.

22. WD, Bulletin 7, 1922; WD, Bulletin 6, 1923.

23. WD, *Annual Reports, 1916,* 1:194–95.

24. WD, *Annual Reports, 1920,* 1:192, 314–15; Ferris and Beard, "The Rock Island 1919 National Match Rifles," 37–38; McClellan, *The United States Marine Corps in the World War,* 70.

25. WD, GO 44, 1907.

26. Floyd, Johnson, and Paine, Auction Catalog 116, dated May 21, 1999, 38; NRA, *The National Matches, 1936.*

27. DA, AR 920-30, 1954, para. 52b; DA, AR 920-30, 1962, para. 68b; DA, AR 920-30, 1985, paras, 6-12b and 6-5c.

28. Letter from Edward Andrus, Director, NRA Competition Division, to Leon Laframboise, January 14, 1993; Frasca, *The .45-70 Springfield,* 246; NRA, *NRA Trophies,* 124; undated fact sheet, "NRA President's Match" sent to the author by TIOH, May 3, 1995.

29. Ibid.; undated NRA fact sheet (circa 1998), "The President's Match."

30. NRA, "Report of Rifle Shooting in the U.S. 1913"; U.S. Navy Shooting Team web site, January 8, 2001.

31. Laframboise, "A Brief History."

32. NRA files, DA Message AGPS-AD 421.4, dated March 3, 1958; TIOH drawing A-1-798, dated December 2, 1991.

33. Laframboise, "A Brief History"; NRA files, letter to DCSPER, from NRA Assistant Executive Officer, National Matches, dated May 27, 1958; NRA, *NRA Trophies,* 123–24; Letter from Edward Andrus, Director, NRA Competition Division, to Leon Laframboise, January 14, 1993.

34. Letter from Assistant Executive Officer, National Matches, to V. H. Blackington, March 6, 1959; Letter from Frank Orth, to Aide to the President, March 9, 1961.

35. Brophy, *The Springfield Rifle,* 213–14; Wilhelm, "The Army Ordnance Trophy."

36. Letter from Reference Department, The New York Historical Society to author, August 12, 1997.

37. WD, *Annual Report, Secretary of War, 1903,* 422.

38. NRA, *National Matches and International Matches, 1923,* 72–73.

39. NRA, *NRA Trophies,* 117.

40. Shockley, *The Krag-Jorgensen Rifle in the Service.*

41. NRA, *National Matches and International Matches, 1923;* NRA, *NRA Trophies,* 85; *The American Rifleman,* October 1925, 19, and October 1927, 34; Floyd, Johnson, and Paine, Auction Catalog 116, dated May 21, 1999, 38.

42. NRA, *National Matches and International Matches, 1923,* 53; NRA, *NRA Trophies,* 98–101; NRA web site, January 2001; NRA, *The National Matches, 1925,* 24.

43. *New York Times,* August 25, 1899, 1, 8.

44. Undated fact sheet from NBPRP, "The Hilton Trophy," sent to author, December 1996; White, *It's Your Misfortune,* 218–19.

45. WD, *Annual Report, Secretary of War, 1903,* 422; WD, GO 69, 1909, 4.

46. *The American Rifleman,* October 1928, 46; *The American Rifleman,* October 1929, 41; DA, NBPRP, *Official Bulletins: National Trophy Matches,* 1954; DA, AR 920-30, 1957; DA, AR 920-30, Changes 2, 1973.

47. Frasca, *The .45-70 Springfield,* 244; Floyd, Johnson, and Paine, Auction Catalog, dated November 16, 2000, 46.

48. HQA AGO, GO 45, 1881; *Army and Navy Journal,* May 14, 1881, 847.

49. WD, *Annual Report, Commanding General of the Army, 1882,* 29; HQA, AGO, GO 45, 1881.

50. HQA AGO, GO 1, 1898; HQA, AGO, GO 36, 1897, para. 515a.

51. Heitman, *Historical Register,* 1:301; *The American Rifleman,* October 1926, 8; NRA, *NRA Trophies,* 94–95.

52. Letter from Library of Congress to author, March 8, 2000; HQA, AGO GO 24, 1903, 24; DA, AR 920-30, various editions.

53. NRA, *The National Matches, 1931,* 126.

54. Emerson, "Medals of the National Trophy," 9–15.

55. WD, Bulletin 12, 1922; WD, Bulletin 8, 1939; DA, AR 920-30, Change 1, 1958, 3.

56. DA, AR 920-30, 1954, para. 52.

57. NRA, *NRA Trophies,* 106; NRA, *National Matches and International Matches, 1923,* 49; *The American Rifleman,* October 1931, 41; *National Matches 1922,* 40–41.

58. *The American Rifleman,* October 1924, 8, and November 1940, 48; NRA, *NRA Trophies,* 82.

59. DA, NBPRP, *Official Bulletins: National Trophy Matches,* 1954; NRA, *National Matches 1922,* 39–40; NRA, *The National Matches, 1936,* 26.

60. NRA, *NRA Trophies,* 87–88; NRA undated fact sheet, "Marine Corps Cup."

61. NRA, *National Matches and International Matches, 1923,* 38–39; *The American Rifleman,* October 1939, 41; NRA, *The National Matches, 1936,* 25.

62. NRA, *National Matches and International Matches, 1923,* 46; undated NRA fact sheet, "Enlisted Men's Trophy"; NRA, *NRA Trophies,* 77.

63. *The Cavalry Journal,* January 1923, 73; NRA, *NRA Trophies,* 61–62. NRA; *The National Matches, 1925,* 29.

64. NRA, *NRA Trophies,* 111–12; NRA, *National Matches 1922,* 51.

65. NRA file "NBPRP, 1904-52," *National Matches Program, 1919,* 28; NRA, *The National Matches, 1925,* 30–31.

66. DA, NBPRP, *Official Bulletins: National Trophy Matches,* 1954; DA, AR 920–30, various editions; *National Matches Program, 1931,* 119; *National Matches Program, 1937,* 68.

67. DA, AR 920-30, 1990, para. 5-3; WD, Bulletin 5, 1935; WD, Bulletin, 3, 1938; DA, Bulletin 21, 1949; DA, AR 920-30, 1990, para. 6-5.

68. NRA, *National Matches and International Matches*, 1923, 104; NRA, *NRA Trophies*, 104–5; undated NRA fact sheet, "Roumanina Trophy"; *Arms and The Man*, October 1921.

69. *The Cavalry Journal*, January 1923, 74; NRA, *National Matches and International Matches, 1927*; NRA, *National Matches and International Matches, 1928*; NRA, *National Matches and International Matches, 1922*, 45; NRA, *The National Matches, 1931*, 48.

70. *Infantry Journal*, May 1922, 569; DA, AR 920–30, 1955, para. 54k.

71. NRA, *National Matches and International Matches, 1923*, 39–44; NRA, *The National Matches, 1931*, 54; WD, Bulletin 8, 1939.

72. *Army Information Digest*, August 1955, 22–23, and July 1956, 46; discussions between author and various past Army Marksmanship Unit members, 1998–99; DA, AR 920-30, 1990, 18.

73. *Infantry Journal*, October 1922, 436; sample offered on eBay, item 246040407, ending February 1, 2000.

74. *Infantry Journal*, September–October 1931, 419.

75. WD, Bulletin 8, 1936; DA, Changes 1 to AR 920-30, 1956.

76. DA, NBPRP, *Official Bulletins: National Trophy Matches*, 1954; NRA undated fact sheet, "Coast Artillery Trophy."

77. National Geographic Society, *Insignia and Decorations*, 31.

78. *American Rifleman*, October 1924, 11; October 1927, 32; October 1930, 11, 24; NRA, *National Matches and International Matches, 1924*, 36; NRA file "NBPRP, 1904–52," *National Matches Program, 1931*, 36.

79. CMP files, invoice, dated July 31, 1925; CMP files, Letter from Executive Officer, NBPRP, to Assistant Secretary of War, March 7, 1925.

80. WD, Bulletin 3, 1938; WD, Bulletin 5, 1935.

81. DA, AR 920-30, 1967; DA, Bulletin 15, 1951.

82. WD, Bulletin 13, 1928, para. 16; WD, Bulletin 40, 1931, para. 21; *American Rifleman*, October 1937, 45.

83. DA, NBPRP, *Official Bulletins: National Trophy Matches*, 1954; DA, AR 920-30, 1957, para. 54d.

84. National Geographic Society, *Insignia and Decorations*, 31; WD, Bulletin 5, 1935; WD, Bulletin 3, 1938.

85. DA, NBPRP, *Official Bulletins: National Trophy Matches*, 1954; DA, AR 920-30, 1957.

86. CMP files, invoice, dated October 27, 1926.

87. WD, Bulletin 5, 1935; WD, Bulletin 3, 1938; DA, Bulletin 21, 1949.

88. DA, NBPRP, *Official Bulletins: National Trophy Matches*, 1954 and 1965; DA, AR 920-30, 1990, 17.

89. National Geographic Society, *Insignia and Decorations*, 31; *American Rifleman*, October 1927, 467.

90. *Infantry Journal*, March 1927, 297; June 1927, 648; July 1928, 68; August 1930, 187; May–June 1935, 266; *Army Life and Recruiting News*, July 1937, 10.

91. NRA, *The National Matches, 1931*, 49.

92. Letter, ATOD-AHI-UH, Subject: Warrior of the Pacific Trophy, to author, May 1, 1997.

93. Letter from D. L. Crawford, to Major General Lewis, May 12, 1927; WD, GO 5, 1926, III.

94. Letter from D. L. Crawford to Major General Lewis, May 12, 1927; Letter ATOD-AHI-UH, 1997.

95. DA, AR 145-395, 1955; DA, GO 65, 1954; DA, GO 41, 1956.

96. *Infantry Journal*, September–October 1931, 416, 418; *American Rifleman*, October 1928, 44; 1930, 32; NRA, *The National Matches, 1931*, 52.

97. NBPRP files on William Randolph Hearst Trophy, including a copy of the receipt signed by Scannel and various correspondence between 1936 and 1954.

98. Ibid., including Memorandum for the Secretary of the Navy from Assistant Secretary of the Army, Subject; Awarding of National Trophies, dated October 5, 1954.

99. DA, NBPRP, *Official Bulletins: National Trophy Matches*, 1954, "Official Bulletin Number 1"; DA, AR 920-30, 1962, 22.

100. DA, NBPRP, *Official Bulletins: National Trophy Matches*, 1954, cover; DA, AR 920-30, 1962, 23.

101. Ibid.; DA, AR 920-30, Changes 2, 1973; DA, AR 920-30, Changes 1, 1958, 3.

102. Hallahan, *Misfire*, 338.

103. DA, AR 920-30, 1962, 22.

104. DA, AR 920-30, Changes 1, May 1958; DA, AR 920-30, Changes 2, March 1973, 4.

105. DA, AR 920-30, 1962, 24; DA, AR 920-30, Changes 1, 1958.

106. DA, AR 920-30, 1962, 21; NRA, *The National Matches*, 1936, 25.

107. DA, AR 920-30, 1990, 15; DA, AR 920-30, Changes 2, 1959.

108. DA, AR 920-30, Changes 2, 1959; DA, AR 920-30, 1962, 24.

109. DA, AR 920-30, 1990, 17.

110. Undated NRA fact sheet (circa 1998), "Army Cup."

111. DA, AR 920-30, 1985, 3-3; DA, AR 920-30 1967, 44; DA, AR 920-30, 1963, 1; DA, AR 920-30, 1967, 24; DA, AR 920-30, 1962, 20.

112. DA, AR 920-30, 1990, 17.

113. DA, AR 920-30, Changes 2, 1973.

114. Ibid.

115. Although various versions of AR 920-30 give the initial date of the trophy as 1979, the trophy itself has 1978 as the initial award date.

116. Ibid.

117. DA, AR 920-30, 1990, 18.

118. DA, AR 920-30, 1990, 16.

119. DA, AR 920-30, 1990, 18.

BIBLIOGRAPHY

Air Corps News Letter [*sic*]. Issued monthly or twice monthly, by the Office of the Chief of the Air Corps in mimeograph form.

AMAROC News. Newspaper published for U.S. Army Forces in Germany, 1919–23.

American Expeditionary Forces. *(Provisional) Small Arms Firing Manual: American Expeditionary Forces, Part I, Individual Instruction, 1919.* Adjutant General Printing Division, General Headquarters, AEF, 1919.

American Journal of Numismatics and Proceedings of The American Numismatic Society, 1914. Vol. XLVIII.

The American Rifleman. Magazine for the National Rifle Association from 1927 to the present. Successor to *Arms and The Man.*

Armes, Col. George C. *Ups and Downs of an Army Officer.* Washington: n.p., 1900.

Armor magazine.

Arms and The Man. Magazine of the National Rifle Association through 1926.

Army and Navy Journal. Weekly newspaper.

Army and Navy Register. Weekly newspaper.

Army Information Digest. Official U.S. Army magazine.

Army Life and Recruiting News. Official U.S. Army magazine.

Army Marksmanship Unit. "EIC Fact Sheet," dated 15 January 1999.

———. *Profile of a Champion.* N.p., n.d.

Army Ordnance. Magazine of the Army Ordnance Association.

Army Times. 15 May 2000, 12. Weekly newspaper.

Arthur D. Little, Inc., *A Study of the Activities and Missions of the NBPRP.* Arthur Little, January 1966.

Ball, Leonard F. "The U.S. Army Swordsman Badge." *The Medal Collector* 18, no. 7 (1967): 27–30.

———. "The U.S. Cavalry Practice Saber and Single Stick," *Military Collector & Historian* 22, no. 4 (1970): 119–22.

Bell, William Gardner. *Commanding Generals and Chiefs of Staff, 1775–1987.* Washington, D.C.: Center of Military History, 1987.

Bigelow, Donald N. *William Conant Church and the Army and Navy Journal.* New York: Columbia University Press, 1952.

Birkhimer, William E. *Historical Sketch of the Organization, Administration, Material, and Tactics of The Artillery, United States Army.* James J. Chapman, 1884. Reprint, New York: Greenwood Press, 1968.

Bishinik: The Official Publication of the Choctaw Nation of Oklahoma.

Blitzer, Charles. *Age of Kings.* New York: Time-Life Books, 1967.

Blumenson, Martin. *Patton: The Man Behind the Legend, 1885–1945.* New York: William Morrow and Co., 1985.

———. *The Patton Papers, 1885–1940.* Boston: Houghton Mifflin Co., 1972.

Blunt, Capt. Stanhope E. *Instructions in Rifle and Carbine Firing for the United States Army.* New York: Charles Scribner's Sons, 1885.

———. *Instructions in Rifle and Carbine Firing for the United States Army.* New York: Charles Scribner's Sons, 1886. Reprint, Williston, N. Dak.: Little Munday Trading Company, 1995.

Bourke, John G. *On The Border with Crook.* New York: Charles Scribner's Sons, 1891.

Bovia, Anne L. *Camp Perry Revisited, 1905–1966.* Defiance, Ohio: Hubbard Co., 1997.

Braudel, Fernand. *The Structure of Everyday Life: The Limits of the Possible.* Vol. 1 of *Civilization and Capitalism, 15th–18th Century.* New York: Harper and Row, 1981.

Brophy, William S. *The Springfield Rifle.* Mechanicsburg, Pa.: Stackpole Books, 1985.

Burr, F. A., and R. J. Hinton. *The Life of Gen. Philip H. Sheridan.* Providence, R.I.: J. A. and R. D. Reid, Publishers, 1888.

Carlson, Carl W. A. "U.S. Army Marksmanship Medals 1882–1897: A Critical Reexamination." *Tokens and Medals Journal* (February 1983): 4–10.

The Cavalry Journal.

Chapman, Anne W. *The Army's Training Revolution, 1973–1990: An Overview.* Fort Monroe, Va.:

United States Army Training and Doctrine Command, 1990.

Coffman, Edward M. "The Duality of the American Military Tradition: A Commentary." *The Journal of Military History* 64 (October 2000): 967–80.

——. *The Old Army: A Portrait of the American Army in Peacetime, 1784–1898.* New York: Oxford University Press, 1986.

Cornebise, Alfred E. *The AMAROC News: The Daily Newspaper of the American Forces in Germany, 1919, 1923.* Carbondale: Southern Illinois University Press, 1981.

Crist, Lynda L., ed., and Mary S. Dix, coed. *The Papers of Jefferson Davis: 1856–1860.* Vol. 6. Baton Rouge: Louisiana State University Press, 1989.

Crowell, Benedict. *America's Munitions, 1917–1918.* Washington, D.C.: Government Printing Office, 1919.

Department of the Army. *Field Manual 17-12-8.* Washington, D.C.: Government Printing Office, February 1999.

——. *Field Manual 23-9: M16A1 Rifle and Rifle Marksmanship.* Washington, D.C., 14 June 1974.

——. *Field Manual 23-35: Pistols and Revolvers.* Washington, D.C.: Government Printing Office, 1960.

——. *Field Manual 23-35: Pistols and Revolvers.* Washington, D.C.: Government Printing Office, 1971.

——. *Pamphlet Number 355-14: Trainfire.* Washington, D.C.: Government Printing Office, 1958.

——. *United States Army in the World War: 1917–1919: Bulletins, G. H. Q., A. E. F.* Vol. 17. Washington, D.C.: Historical Division, 1948.

——. *United States Army in the World War: 1917–1919: General Orders, G. H. Q., A. E. F.* Vol. 16. Washington, D.C.: Historical Division, 1948.

Department of the Army, Headquarters, 56th Artillery Group. *Regulation Number 672-3,* 6 December 1968.

Dickman, Capt. T. C. *Modern Improvements in Fire Arms and Their Tactical Effects.* Fort Leavenworth, Kans.: General Service & Staff College Lectures, 3 September 1902.

Director of the Mint. *Annual Report, Fiscal Year 1914.* Washington, D.C.: Government Printing Office, 1914.

Dorrance, William H. "Campaigns of the U.S. Heavy Artillery, 1821–1901," *Journal of America's Military Past* 24, no. 2: 3–19.

Eicher, David J. *Robert E Lee: A Life Portrait.* Dallas: Taylor Publishing Co., 1997.

"EIC Fact Sheet." January 1999.

Elting, John R. *American Army Life.* New York: Charles Scribner's Sons, 1982.

Emerson, William K. "A Few Notes on the Distinguished Aerial Gunner and Bombardier Badges." *The Medal Collector* 49 (May–June 1998): 7–8.

——. *Chevrons: Illustrated History and Catalog of U.S. Army Insignia.* Washington. D.C.: Smithsonian Institution Press, 1983.

——. "Medals of the National Trophy." *The Medal Collector* 48 (November 1997): 9–15.

Farrow, W. Milton. *How I Became a Crack Shot, with Hints to Beginners.* 1882. Reprint, Prescott, Ariz.: Wolfe Publishing Co., 1980.

Ferris, C. S., and John Beard. "The Rock Island 1919 National Match Rifles." *Man at Arms* 23 (April 2001): 32–42.

Field Artillery Journal.

Field Artillery Missile Group Number 9 printed letter, ATZR-CCO. Subject: Policy for the Award of the Field Artillery Missileman's Badge and Certificate, 6 December 1976.

Fitzpatrick, David J. "Emory Upton and the Citizen Soldier." *The Journal of Military History* 65 (April 2001): 355–89.

Floyd, Johnson and Paine, Inc. *Auction of Orders, Medals and Decorations of the World.* Chicago: various dates.

Flynn, Capt. John R. "Wanted: Realism in Weapons Marksmanship Training." *Infantry School Quarterly* 37, no. 2 (1950): 96–100.

Foley, Vernard. "Leonardo and the Invention of the Wheellock." *Scientific American* 283 (January 1998): 86–100.

Foner, Jack D. *The United States Soldiers Between Two Wars: Army Life and Reforms, 1865–1898.* New York: Humanities Press, 1970.

Frasca, Albert J. *The .45-70 Springfield Book II.* Springfield, Ohio: Mack Printing Group, 1997.

The Giant 2, no. 20 (29 November 1968): 1.

Gilmore, Russell. "Crack Shots and Patriots: The National Rifle Association and America's Military-Sporting Tradition, 1871–1929." Ph.D. diss., University of Wisconsin, 1974.

——. "'The New Courage': Rifles and Soldier Individualism, 1876–1918." *Military Affairs* 40 (October 1976): 97–102.

Gleim, Albert F., *Medal Auction No. 35.*

Gluckman, Arcadi. *United States Martial Pistols and Revolvers.* New York: Bonanza Books, n.d.

Grant, Ulysses Simpson. *Personal Memoirs of U. S. Grant.* New York: Charles L. Webster and Co., 1894.

Groom, Maj. Kenneth G. "Marksmanship." *Infantry School Quarterly* 43, no. 1 (1953): 44–52.

Hale, H. C. "The New Firing Regulations for Small Arms." United States Infantry Association *Journal* 1, no. 1: 14–20.

Hallahan, William H. *Misfire.* New York: Charles Scribner's Sons, 1994.

Heitman, Francis B. *Historical Register and Dictionary of the United States Army, from Its Organization, September 29, 1789, to March 2, 1903.* 2 Vols. 1903. Reprint, Urbana: University of Illinois Press, 1965.

Heth, Henry. *A System of Target Practice for the Use of Troops When Armed with the Musket, Rifle-Musket,*

Rifle, or Carbine. Philadelphia: Henry Carey Baird, 1858.

Hewes, James E., Jr. *From Root to McNamara: Army Organization and Administration, 1900–1963.* Washington, D.C.: Center of Military History, 1975.

Higginbotham, Don. *The War of American Independence: Military Attitudes, Policies, and Practice, 1763–1789.* New York: The Macmillan Co., 1971.

Hitt, Parker. "A Brief History of School of Musketry." *Military Review* 41 (July 1961): 86–90.

Hogg, Ian V. *The Encyclopedia of Infantry Weapons of World War II.* New York: Thomas Crowell Co., 1977.

Huebner, Michael F. "1911 and 1913 Mobilizations Marked a Turning Point for the Army." *Army* 48, no. 8 (1998): 14–17.

Hutton, Paul A., ed. *Soldiers West: Biographies from the Military Frontier.* Lincoln: University of Nebraska Press, 1987.

Infantry Journal.

Johnson, Dorothy M. *The Bloody Bozeman.* New York: McGraw-Hill Book Co., 1971.

Johnson, Norma. "Notes on the History of Fort Sisseton." *The Journal of America's Military Past* 28, no. 1 (2002): 29–45.

Jones, Albert S. "Marksmanship in America." *Outing* 40 (1902): 673–77.

Julian, R. W. *Medals of the United States Mint: The First Century, 1792–1892.* El Cajon, Calif.: The Token and Medal Society, 1977.

Kamp, Lt. Col. A. M., Jr. "Trainfire." *The American Rifleman* (March 1956): 17–20.

Keegan, John. *A History of Warfare.* New York: Alfred A. Knopf, 1993.

Kelton, J. C. *Information for Riflemen on the Range and Battle-field.* San Francisco: n.p., 1884.

King, Benjamin, Richard C. Biggs, and Eric R. Criner. *Spearhead of Logistics.* Fort Eustis, Va.: n.p., 1994.

Laframboise, Leon. "A Brief History of the President's Hundred." *The Trading Post* 52, no. 4 (July–September): 17–18.

Laidley, Col. T. T. S. *Colonel Laidley's Reply to the Charges of Infringement of Colonel Wingate's Copyright.*

———. *A Course of Instruction in Rifle Firing.* Philadelphia: J. B. Lippincott and Co., 1879.

Matray, James I. *Historical Dictionary of the Korean War.* New York: Greenwood Press, 1991.

Maurer, Maurer. *Aviation in the U.S. Army, 1919–1939.* Washington, D.C.: Office of Air Force History, 1987.

McAulay, John D. *Carbines of the U.S. Cavalry, 1861–1905.* Lincoln, R.I.: Andrew Mowbray Publishers, 1996.

McChristian, Douglas C. *An Army of Marksmen.* Fort Collins, Colo.: The Old Army Press, n.d.

———. *The U.S. Army in the West, 1870–1880.* Norman: University of Oklahoma Press, 1995.

McClellan, Edwin N. *The United States Marine Corps in the World War.* Washington. D.C.: Government Printing Office, 1920.

McDougall, Thomas D., and Jeffrey B. Floyd. *Marksmanship Awards of the Massachusetts Volunteer Militia (MVM), Part II: A Concise Medallic History.* N.p., 1988.

Mead, Gary. *The Doughboys: America and the First World War.* London: Penguin Press, 2000.

"Military Rifles and Rifle Firing." *Journal of the Military Service Institute* 1 (1880).

Mitchell, John C. "God, Guns, and Guts Made America Free." *American Heritage* 29 (February/March 1978): 4–17.

Moore, Maj. Louis R. "The New Rifle Marksmanship Course." *Infantry School Quarterly* 32, no. 2 (1949): 5–21.

National Archives. Various record groups.

National Geographic Magazine (October 1943): 440–41.

National Geographic Society. *Insignia and Decorations of the U.S. Armed Forces.*

National Rifle Association. *National Matches and International Matches 1923: September 1 to September 27.* Official Program of the National Matches.

———. *National Matches, 1922.* Program of the matches.

———. *The National Matches, 1925.* Official Program of the National Matches.

———. *The National Matches, 1931.* Official Program of the National Matches.

———. *The National Matches, 1936.* Official Program of the National Matches.

———. *NRA Trophies.* NRA Competitions Division. circa 1982.

"New Machine Rifle Marksmanship Course." *The Cavalry Journal* (April 1928): 295.

"New Marksmanship Badges," *Armor* 64 (January–February 1960): 55.

New York Times.

N. S. Meyer Catalog, 1930.

Office of the Chief of Military History. Web site as of 17 January 2000, containing article "Transition and Change, 1902–1917."

Olsen, Stanley J. "Development of the Looped Cartridge Belt." *Military Collector and Historian* 6, no. 1 (1954): 9–11.

Omaha World Herald, 20 August 1893.

Ordnance Notes Number 118. Washington, D.C., 31 October 1879.

Ordnance Notes Number 141. Washington, D.C., 22 November 1880.

Parker, James. *The Old Army: Memories: 1872–1918.* Philadelphia: Dorrance and Co., 1929.

Patton, Robert H. *The Pattons: A Personal History of an American Family.* New York: Crown Publishers, 1994.

Peterson, Harold L. *The American Sword: 1775–1945.* New Hope, Pa.: Robert Halter, 1954.

Philippine Constabulary. *Manual for Target Practice: General Orders No. 84.* Manila: Bureau of Public Printing, 1904.

————. *Philippine Constabulary Regulations: 1930.* Manila: Bureau of Printing, 1929.

————. *Philippine Constabulary Small Arms Firing Regulations, Philippine Constabulary.* Manila: Bureau of Printing, 1915.

Phillips, William G. "The Woven Cartridge Belt, 1879–1903, Part I." *Military Collector and Historian* 44, no. 2 (1992): 64–72.

————. "The Woven Cartridge Belt, 1879–1903, Part II." *Military Collector and Historian* 44, no. 3 (1992): 110–15.

Poppel, Bret V., John Paganiai, and Jeffrey A. Rynbrandt. "Close Quarters Marksmanship: Training for Conventional Infantry Units." *Infantry* 89 (January–February 1999): 39–42.

Potter, James E. "Firearms Accidents in the Frontier Army, 1806–1891." *Nebraska History* 78 (Winter 1997): 175–85.

Prucha, Francis Paul. *A Guide to the Military Posts of the United States, 1789–1895.* Madison: The State Historical Society of Wisconsin, 1964.

Ramsey, Ed. "The Last Cavalry Charge." *The Cavalry Journal* 23 (September 1999): 3–4.

Reference Guide to United States Military History, 1865–1919. General Editor, Charles R. Schrader. New York: Facts on File, 1993.

Report of the Adjutant General of the State of New Hampshire for the Year Ending May 31, 1882. Concord: Parsons B. Cogswell, State Printer, 1882.

Rice, Col. James M. *Small Arms Practice for the National Guard, A Modification of Blunt's Small Arms Firing Regulations.* Springfield, Mass.: The H. W. Rokker Printing House, 1892.

Rickey, Don, Jr. *Forty Miles a Day on Beans and Hay: The Enlisted Soldier Fighting the Indian Wars.* Norman: University of Oklahoma Press, 1963.

Sandusky, Sue Ann. "America's Distinguished Marksmen." *American Rifleman* (May 1991): 36–39, 92.

Scheips, Paul T. "Darkness and Light: The Interwar Years, 1865–1898." On the Center of Military History web site, 17 January 2000.

Schuon, Karl. *U.S. Marine Corps Biographical Dictionary.* New York: Franklin Watts, 1963.

Shockley, Philip M. *The Krag-Jorgensen Rifle in the Service.* Aledo, Ill.: World-Wide Gun Report, 1960.

Shrader, Charles R. *Reference Guide to United States Military History 1865–1919.* New York: Sachem Publishing Associates, 1993.

Small Arms Firing Regulations for the Georgia State Troops. George Harrison, State Printer, 1900.

Smith, Richard W., and Pelz. *Shoulder Sleeve Insignia of the U.S. Armed Forces, 1941–1945.* Privately published, 1981.

Smythe, Donald. *Pershing: General of the Armies.* Bloomington: Indiana University Press, 1986.

Stanton, Shelby L. *Order of Battle of World War II.* Novato, Calif.: Presidio Press, 1984.

Steffen, Randy. *The Horse Soldiers.* Vol. 3. Norman: University of Oklahoma Press, 1978.

Stubbs, Mary Lee, and Stanley R. Connor. *Armor-Cavalry, Part I: Regular Army and Army Reserve.* Army Lineage Series. Washington, D.C.: Office of the Chief of Military History, 1969.

Taylor, Lt. Col. M. C. "Wanted: Better Marksmen." *Infantry School Quarterly* 37, no. 2 (1950): 18–19.

The Daily Graphic, New York.

The Giant. Newspaper of the 56th Field Artillery Brigade in Europe.

The Trading Post. Publication of the American Society of Military Insignia Collectors.

Thomas and Son. *Sporting Good Illustrated Catalogue.* New York, 1887.

Thomas, Lowell. *Woodfill of the Regulars.* Garden City, N.Y.: Doubleday, Doran and Co., 1929.

Tidball, John C. *Manual of Heavy Artillery Service for the Use of the Army and Militia of the United States.* Washington, D.C.: James J. Chapman, 1880.

————. *Manual of Heavy Artillery Service for the Use of the Army and Militia of the United States.* 2d ed. Washington, D.C.: James J. Chapman, 1881.

————. *Manual of Heavy Artillery Service for the Use of the Army and Militia of the United States.* 4th ed. Washington, D.C.: James J. Chapman, 1891.

————. *Manual of Heavy Artillery Service for the Use of the Army and Militia of the United States.* 5th ed. Washington, D.C.: James J. Chapman, 1898.

Till, Paul H. *The Military Awards of the Empire State.* Fort Myer, Va.: Planchet Press, 1989.

United States Army Europe. *Units Telephone Book.* 1982.

United States Army Marksmanship Unit. *Profile of a Champion.* n.p., circa 1973.

Upton, Emory. *Infantry Tactics, Double and Single Rank.* New York: D. Appleton and Co., 1874.

Upton, Richard. *Fort Custer on the Big Horn.* Glendale, Calif.: The Arthur H. Clark Co., 1973.

————, ed. *The Indian as a Soldier at Fort Custer, Montana.* El Segundo, Calif.: Upton and Sons, 1983.

Utley, Robert M. *Frontier Regulars: The United States Army and the Indian, 1866–1890.* New York: Macmillan Publishing Co., 1973.

Vandiver, Frank E. *Black Jack: The Life and Times of John J. Pershing.* College Station: Texas A&M Press, 1997.

Visconage, Michael D. "U.S. Marine Corps Marksmanship Badges from 1912 to the Present." Marine Corps Museum and Historical Division internship paper, 5 May 1982.

Wallechinsky, David. *The Complete Book of the Olympics.* New York: Penguin Books, 1988.

War Department. *Annual Reports.* Published each year in Washington, D.C., and printed by the Government Printing Office, these multivolume reports contain reports by the secretary of war, the commanding general of the U.S. Army, and various staff officers, including the chief of ordnance, the chief of the Militia Bureau, and various department and division commanders. The reports contain details of work accomplished during the fiscal year, especially from 1870 through World War I. The number of volumes and contents vary by year. Appendices contained in reports by department chiefs were often omitted in secretary of war reports that were also published by the Congress.

———. *Army Register*. Various years. Lists the names and a short history of U.S. Army officers. These were published annually as part of the congressional documents and also published by the War Department for sale to individuals.

———. *Army Regulations, 1913, Corrected to 1917*. Washington, D.C.: Government Printing Office, 1917.

———. *A System of Target Practice. For the Use of Troops When Armed with the Musket, Rifle-Musket, Rifle, or Carbine*. Washington, D.C.: Government Printing Office, 1862.

———. *Automatic Rifle Marksmanship, Document 1011*. Washington, D.C.: Government Printing Office, 1920.

———. *Description and Rules for the Management of the Springfield Rifle, Carbine, and Army Revolvers, Calibre .45*. Springfield, Mass.: National Armory, 1874.

———. *Description and Rules for the Management of the Springfield Rifle, Carbine, and Army Revolvers, Caliber .45*. Washington, D.C.: Government Printing Office, 1898.

———. *Description of the Automatic Pistol, Caliber .45, Model of 1911. Revised edition of February 14, 1914 (Ordnance form 1866)*. Washington, D.C.: Government Printing Office, 1917.

———. *Distinguished Marksmen and Distinguished Pistol Shots Designated by the War Department (Document No. 9a)*. 1926. Reprint, Arlington, Va.: Planchet Press, 1983.

———. *Examination and Classification of Gunners of Field Artillery (Special Regulations No. 53)*. Washington, D.C.: Government Printing Office, 1917.

———. *Field Service Regulations, United States Army, 1914, Text Corrections to February 4, 1916, Changes No. 4*. New York: Army and Navy Journal, 1914.

———. *Firing Regulations for Small Arms for the United States Army*. Washington, D.C.: Government Printing Office, 1898.

———. *Firing Regulations for Small Arms for the United States Army and the Organized Militia of the United States, 1904*. Washington, D.C.: Government Printing Office, 1904.

———. *Infantry Drill Regulations (War Department Document No. 229)*. Washington, D.C.: Government Printing Office, 1904.

———. *Musketry (War Department Document No. 631)*. Washington, D.C.: Government Printing Office, 1917.

———. *Official Army Register*. Washington, D.C.: Government Printing Office, various dates.

———. *Order of Battle of the United States Land Forces in the World War: American Expeditionary Forces*. 3 vols. Washington, D.C.: Government Printing Office, 1931–49.

———. *Pistol Marksmanship (Document 1050)*. Washington, D.C.: Government Printing Office, 1920.

———. *Pistol Marksmanship, November 1920*. Washington, D.C.: Government Printing Office, 1921.

———. *Provisional Drill and Service Regulations for Field Artillery (Horse and Light) 1916 (War Department Document No. 538)*. New York: Military Publishing Co., 1917.

———. *Provisional Machine-Gun Firing Manual, 1917, War Department (Document No. 615)*. Washington, D.C.: Government Printing Office, 1917.

———. *Provisional Small Arms Firing Manual, 1909 (War Department Document 338)*. Washington, D.C.: Government Printing Office, 1909.

———. *Regulations for the Army of the United States, 1913, corrected to April 15, 1917 (Changes Nos. 1 to 55)*. Washington. D.C.: Government Printing Office, 1917.

———. *Rifle Marksmanship, June 1920 (War Department Document Number 1021)*. Washington, D.C.: Government Printing Office, 1921.

———. *Rules for the Management and Cleaning of the Rifle Musket, Model 1863, for the Use of Soldiers*. Washington, D.C.: Government Printing Office, 1863.

———. *Small Arms Firing Manual, 1913 (War Department Document 442)*. Washington, D.C.: Government Printing Office, 1914.

———. *Small Arms Firing Manual, 1913 (War Department Document 442), with text correction to February 21, 1917, Changes No. 18*. New York: Military Publishing Co., n.d.

———. *Small Arms Firing Regulations, 1906*. Washington, D.C.: Government Printing Office, 1906.

———. *Small Arms Firing Regulations for the United States Army and for the Organized Militia of the United States, Amended to April 20, 1908*. Washington, D.C.: Government Printing Office, 1908.

———. *Small Arms Targets and Equipment of Target Ranges (Form Number 1992)*. Washington, D.C.: Goverment Printing Office, Office of the Chief of Ordnance, 1914.

Ward, Geoffrey C. *The West: An Illustrated History*. Boston: Little, Brown and Co., 1996.

Webster, Donald Blake. "Machine Gun Testing at Springfield Armory, 1917." *Military Collector & Historian* 49, no. 1 (1997): 31–34.

Wells, William R., II. *Shots That Hit: A Study of U.S. Coast Guard Marksmanship, 1790–1985*. Washington, D.C.: U.S. Coast Guard Historian's Office, 1993.

Wheatley, Todd. "The Expert Machine Gun Badge-American Forces in Germany (1918–1923)."

The Journal of the Orders and Medals Society of America 43, no. 5 (1992): 5–11.

White, Richard. *It's Your Misfortune and None of My Own: A New History of the American West.* Norman: University of Oklahoma Press, 1991.

Wilhelm, Glenn P. "The Ordnance Trophy." *Army Ordnance* (September–October, 1925): 109–10.

Wingate, George W. *Manual for Rifle Practice.* 5th rev. ed. New York: Army and Navy Journal, 1875.

———. *Manual for Rifle Practice.* 6th rev. ed. New York: Army and Navy Journal, 1878.

Wood, Ray O., III, and Matthew T. Michaelson, "Close Quarters Combat and Modern Warfare." *Military Review,* May–June 2000, from the Military Review web site.

Zabecki, David T. "Der Durchbruchmuller." *Field Artillery* (August 1990): 12–19.

Zimmer, William F. *Frontier Soldier.* Helena: Montana Historical Society Press, 1998.

Zogbaum, Rufus Fairchild. *Horse, Foot, and Dragoons.* New York: Harper and Brothers, 1888.

ILLUSTRATION CREDITS

ILLUSTRATION CREDITS

Box fig.	M1903A1 rifle. Rock Island Arsenal.
Fig. 3.6.	National Archives, RG 111-SC-108884.
Fig. 3.8.	War Department drawing CE-4-4-8, February 1922.
Fig. 3.9.	Author's Collection.
Fig. 3.10.	From *Army Life and Recruiting News,* January 1939, 11.
Fig. 3.11.	Joseph Suarez Collection.
Fig. 3.13.	Patton Museum of Armor and Cavalry.
Fig. 3.14.	Department of the Army.
Fig. 3.15.	Department of the Army.
Fig. 3.16.	Department of the Army.
Fig. 3.17.	Author's Collection.
Fig. 4.1.	From *Manual of Heavy Artillery Service,* plate 15.
Fig. 4.2.	Robert Borrell Collection, photo by the author.
Fig. 4.3.	Smithsonian Institution.
Fig. 4.4.	Smithsonian Institution.
Fig. 4.5.	National Archives.
Fig. 4.7.	Author's Collection (computer generated).
Fig. 4.9.	From Robert Borrell Collection, photo by the author.
Fig. 4.10.	John Cook Collections.
Fig. 4.11.	Author's Collection.
Box fig.	Fort Monroe. U.S. Army Casemate Museum, Fort Monroe, Virginia.
Fig. 4.13.	Douglass Scott Collection.
Fig. 4.16.	U.S. Army Military History Institute.
Fig. 4.17.	Todd Wheatley Collection, photo by the author.
Fig. 4.21.	Joseph J. Pennell Collection, Kansas Collection, Spencer Research Library, University of Kansas, 2596.1.
Fig. 4.24.	Smithsonian Institution.
Fig. 4.25.	Smithsonian Institution.
Fig. 4.26.	Smithsonian Institution.
Fig. 4.29.	WD, GO 88, 1914.
Fig. 4.30.	Rock Island Arsenal.
Fig. 4.32.	WD, TR 50-70, 1922.
Fig. 5.3.	From *Recruiting News Magazine,* March 1940.
Fig. 5.6.	Ron Fischer Collection, photo by the author.
Fig. 5.7.	Robert Borrell Collection, photo by the author.
Fig. 5.8.	Ron Fischer Collection, photo by the author.
Fig. 5.9.	Robert Borrell Collection, photo by the author.
Fig. 5.14.	Courtesy Ralph Hartley.
Fig. 5.20.	Peter Bonner Collection.
Fig. 5.21.	Peter Bonner Collection.
Box fig.	Army Air Force technician's badge. Author's Collection.
Box fig.	U.S. Army driver and mechanic badge. Author's Collection.
Fig. 5.28.	David Johnson Collection.
Fig. 5.33.	Courtesy S. G. Yasinitsky, redrawn by the author.
Fig. 5.34.	Courtesy S. G. Yasinitsky, redrawn by the author.
Fig. 6.1.	From Burr and Hinton, *The Life of Gen. Philip H. Sheridan,* 1888.
Fig. 6.2.	Donald W. Harpold Collection.
Fig. 6.3.	Thomas N. Trevor Collection.
Fig. 6.4.	Library of Congress, #223928.
Fig. 6.5.	U.S. Army Military History Institute, Guy V. Henry Collection.
Box fig.	U.S. Army soldiers' uniforms. WD, *Infantry Drill Regulations, 1904,* 54.
Box fig.	Ammunition belt. U.S. Patent 507,836.
Box fig.	Pocketed belt. Courtesy Hayes Otoupalik, photo by the author.
Fig. 6.6.	Thomas Trevor Collection, photo by Don Harpold.
Fig. 6.7.	Leonard Ball Collection, photo by the author.
Fig. 6.8.	Smithsonian Institution.
Fig. 6.12.	Smithsonian Institution.
Fig. 6.13.	Leonard Ball Collection, photo by the author.
Fig. 6.14.	Smithsonian Institution.
Fig. 6.15.	Leonard Ball Collection, photo by the author.
Fig. 6.16.	Thomas Trevor Collection, photo by Don Harpold.
Fig. 6.17.	Smithsonian Institution.
Fig. 6.18.	Smithsonian Institution.
Fig. 6.19.	Smithsonian Institution.
Box fig.	U.S. Model 1884 carbine. Rock Island Arsenal.
Fig. 6.20.	U.S. Army Military History Institute, Guy V. Henry Collection.
Fig. 6.22.	Richard Williams Collection, photo by the author.
Fig. 6.23.	Richard Williams Collection, photo by the author.
Fig. 6.24.	Leonard Ball Collection, photo by the author.
Fig. 6.25.	National Archives, #82424.
Box fig.	Shooting prizes and medals. Author's Collection.
Fig. 6.27.	The U.S. Army Infantry Museum.
Fig. 6.29.	U.S. Army, Rock Island Arsenal Museum, Rock Island, Illinois.
Fig. 6.30.	U.S. Army, Rock Island Arsenal Museum, Rock Island, Illinois.
Fig. 6.34.	Leonard Ball Collection, photo by the author.
Fig. 6.36.	Smithsonian Institution.
Box fig.	Fast Dog. Library of Congress.
Fig. 6.37.	The U.S. Army Infantry Museum.
Fig. 6.38.	The U.S. Army Infantry Museum.
Fig. 6.39.	Leonard Ball Collection, photo by the author.
Fig. 6.40.	Leonard Ball Collection, photo by the author.
Fig. 7.1.	Joseph J. Pennell Collection, Kansas Collection, Spencer Research Library, University of Kansas, 1242.
Fig. 7.5.	Cook Collections, photo by the author.

Fig. 7.12. Leonard Ball Collection, photo by the author.

Fig. 7.14. Cook Collections, photo by the author.

Box fig. M 1911 automatic pistol. Rock Island Arsenal.

Box fig. M 1911A1 pistol. Rock Island Arsenal.

Box fig. 9 mm, M-9 pistol. U.S. Army.

Fig. 7.15. Leonard Ball Collection, photo by the author.

Fig. 7.24. Ron Fischer Collection, photo by the author.

Fig. 8.1. David A. Parham Collection.

Fig. 8.6. Ron Fischer Collection, photo by the author.

Fig. 9.1. Joseph J. Pennell Collection, Kansas Collection, Spencer Research Library, University of Kansas, 440.

Fig. 9.2. Dr. Charles H. Cureton Collection.

Fig. 9.3. National Archives, 165-PF-159.

Fig. 9.4. Fort Sam Houston, Texas, Army Museum.

Fig. 9.7. Leonard Ball Collection, photo by the author.

Fig. 9.8. Leonard Ball Collection, photo by the author.

Fig. 9.10. Collection of Ron Fischer, photo by the author.

Fig. 9.11. Collection of Ron Fischer, photo by the author.

Fig. 9.12. John Cook Collections, photo by the author.

Fig. 9.13. Leonard Ball Collection, photo by the author.

Fig. 9.14. Leonard Ball Collection, photo by the author.

Fig. 9.15. Collection of Ron Fischer, photo by the author.

Fig. 9.16. Collection of Ron Fischer, photo by the author.

Fig. 9.21. Department of the Army.

Fig. 9.24. Gary Anderson Collection.

Fig. 9.25. Courtesy Army Marksmanship Unit, photo by the author.

Fig. 9.26. Courtesy Army Marksmanship Unit, photo by the author.

Fig. 9.28. Clifford A. Presley Collection.

Fig. 9.29. Clifford A. Presley Collection.

Box fig. Browning Automatic Rifle. Rock Island Arsenal.

Box fig. M 1918A2 BAR. Rock Island Arsenal.

Fig. 9.34. Leonard Ball Collection, photo by the author.

Fig. 10.1. Joseph J. Pennell Collection, Kansas Collection, Spencer Research Library, University of Kansas.

Fig. 10.2. National Archives, RG 111SC 99305.

Fig. 10.3. Civilian Marksmanship Program.

Fig. 10.4. U.S. Army.

Fig. 10.6. Trophy owned by SFC Charles Davis, photo by the author.

Fig. 10.7. Collection of the Kentucky Military Museum, photo by the author.

Fig. 10.9. Collection of the Kentucky Military Museum, photo by the author.

Fig. 10.10. Collection of the Kentucky Military Museum, photo by the author.

Fig. 10.11. Collection of Leonard Ball, photo by the author.

Fig. 10.12. Collection of Leonard Ball, photo by the author.

Fig. 10.13. Collection of Leonard Ball, photo by the author.

Fig. 10.14. Ron Fischer Collection, photo by the author.

Fig. 10.15. The National Infantry Museum, photo by the author.

Fig. 10.16. The National Infantry Museum, photo by the author.

Fig. 10.17. The National Infantry Museum, photo by the author.

Fig. 10.18. The U.S. Marine Corps Museum, Quantico, Virginia, photo by the author.

Fig. 10.19. The U.S. Marine Corps Museum, Quantico, Virginia, photo by the author.

Fig. 10.20. The U.S. Marine Corps Museum, Quantico, Virginia, photo by the author.

Fig. 10.22. The U.S. Marine Corps Museum, Quantico, Virginia, photo by the author.

Fig. 10.24. The U.S. Marine Corps Museum, Quantico, Virginia, photo by the author.

Fig. 10.33. Cook Collections, photo by the author.

Fig. 10.37. Courtesy U.S. Army Marksmanship Unit.

Fig. 10.38. Courtesy U.S. Army Marksmanship Unit, photo by the author.

Fig. 10.39. The U.S. Marine Corps Museum, Quantico, Virginia, photo by the author.

Fig. 10.40. From *Army Ordnance* magazine, September–October 1925.

Fig. 10.43. Trophy owned by SFC Charles Davis, photo by the author.

Fig. 10.44. Ron Fischer Collection, photo by the author.

Fig. 10.45. Ron Fischer Collection, photo by the author.

Fig. 10.46. The U.S. Marine Corps Museum, Quantico, Virginia, photo by the author.

Box fig. Krag-Jorgenson rifle. West Point Museum.

Fig. 10.48. Trophy owned by SFC Charles Davis, photo by the author.

Fig. 10.49. Ron Fischer Collection, photo by the author.

Fig. 10.50. Lindsey Henderson Collection.

ILLUSTRATION CREDITS

Fig. 10.53. Author's sketch, after an *Army and Navy Journal* drawing of May 14, 1881.
Fig. 10.54. *Armed Forces Journal International.*
Fig. 10.55. Leonard Ball Collection, photo by the author.
Fig. 10.56. Kentucky Military Museum, photo by the author.
Fig. 10.57. Kentucky Military Museum, photo by the author.
Fig. 10.58. Leonard Ball Collection, photo by the author.
Fig. 10.59. Leonard Ball Collection, photo by the author.
Fig. 10.61. The U.S. Marine Corps Museum, Quantico, Virginia, photo by the author.
Fig. 10.63. National Rifle Association.
Fig. 10.64. National Rifle Association.
Fig. 10.65. The U.S. Marine Corps Museum, Quantico, Virginia, photo by the author.
Fig. 10.66. National Rifle Association.
Fig. 10.67. Joseph J. Pennell Collection, Kansas Collection, Spencer Research Library, University of Kansas, 2471.
Fig. 10.68. Courtesy U.S. Army Marksmanship Unit, photo by the author.
Fig. 10.70. The U.S. Marine Corps Museum, Quantico, Virginia, photo by the author.

Fig. 10.71. Author's Collection.
Fig. 10.72. The U.S. Marine Corps Museum, Quantico, Virginia, photo by the author.
Fig. 10.75. National Rifle Association.
Fig. 10.77. The U.S. Marine Corps Museum, Quantico, Virginia, photo by the author.
Fig. 10.78. Trophy owned by SFC Charles Davis, photo by the author.
Fig. 10.81. © Henry Miller, News Picture Service.
Fig. 10.82. From *Recruiting News,* July 1937, 10.
Fig. 10.83. U.S. Army ROTC Department, University of Hawaii.
Box fig., U.S. Army's M-1 rifle. Rock Island Arsenal.
Fig. 10.85. Courtesy U.S. Army Marksmanship Unit.
Fig. 11.2. North Dakota National Guard.
Fig. 11.3. *Armed Forces Journal International.*
Fig. 11.4. Joseph J. Pennell Collection, Kansas Collection, Spencer Research Library, University of Kansas, 2791.1.
Fig. 11.6. Author's collection.
Fig. 11.7. Rock Island Arsenal.

INDEX